D1615798

Toward a More Perfect Union

TOWARD A MORE PERFECT UNION

The Civil War Letters of
Frederic and Elizabeth Lockley

CHARLES E. RANKIN

University of Nebraska Press
Lincoln

The University of Nebraska Press is part of a land-grant institution with
campuses and programs on the past, present, and future homelands
of the Pawnee, Ponca, Otoe-Missouria, Omaha, Dakota, Lakota, Kaw,
Cheyenne, and Arapaho Peoples, as well as those of the relocated
Ho-Chunk, Sac and Fox, and Iowa Peoples.

Names: Lockley, Frederic E., 1824–1905 | Rankin, Charles E., editor.
Title: Toward a more perfect Union: the Civil War letters of Frederic and
Elizabeth Lockley / Charles E. Rankin.
Other titles: Civil War letters of Frederic and Elizabeth Lockley
Description: Lincoln: University of Nebraska Press, 2023. | Includes
bibliographical references and index.
Identifiers: LCCN 2022049680
ISBN 9781496232984 (hardcover)
ISBN 9781496234919 (epub)
ISBN 9781496234926 (pdf)
Subjects: LCSH: Lockley, Frederic E., 1824–1905—Correspondence. |
Lockley, Elizabeth, 1843–1929—Correspondence. | United States. Army.
New York Heavy Artillery Regiment, 7th (1862–1865) | Soldiers—New York
(State)—Correspondence. | New York—History—Civil War, 1861–1865—
Personal narratives. | United States. Army. New York Infantry Regiment,
7th (1862–1865) | United States—History—Civil War, 1861–1865—Personal
narratives. | Married people—New York (State)—Correspondence. |
Wives—New York (State)—Albany—Correspondence. |
BISAC: HISTORY / United States / Civil War Period (1850–1877) |
LITERARY COLLECTIONS / Letters
Classification: LCC E601 .L84 2023 | DDC 973.7/80922—dc23/
eng/20230103
LC record available at https://lccn.loc.gov/2022049680

Set in New Baskerville ITC Pro by Mikala R. Kolander.

For Diane

Contents

Illustrations

Maps

Preface

The Huntington Library has in its collections 405 Civil War letters from the Frederic E. Lockley family, including 287 from Frederic Lockley and 118 from Elizabeth Lockley. Frederic was a Union soldier for almost three years. At thirty-seven years old, he enlisted in a newly formed volunteer regiment in Albany, New York, in August 1862. Unlike most of the men who enlisted with him, he would serve almost his entire term—and survive. Elizabeth, meanwhile, except for an occasional trip north to Schuylerville, New York, to visit her grandmother and aunt, plus one visit to New York City with her father, would remain in Albany the whole time he was away. Occupying the downstairs rooms of a two-story rented house, she maintained housekeeping and struggled to make ends meet with the help of Frederic's older sister, Emma, who came to live with her shortly after Fred's departure with his regiment.

When Frederic Lockley elected to enlist, Elizabeth was not pleased. *Horrified* might not be too strong a description. She was insecure. Just turned nineteen, she had married Fred a year and a half earlier. Half Frederic's age, she had little experience running a household herself. Having lost her mother at age eight, she had boarded subsequently among relatives for ten years, most recently with her grandmother and aunt in Schuylerville, before marrying. Equally worrisome for Lizzie, as her family called her, she was to lead a household that included Frederic's three young girls, ages five, seven, and nine, the offspring of his first marriage to a woman who had died from a spinal tumor in 1860.

For assurance, Fred promised to write to Lizzie twice a week while he was away, and she agreed to do the same. They wrote most often, or tried to, on Wednesdays and Sundays. He was an accomplished letter writer, she less so, but three years of writing letters improved her style and self-confidence.

Full of particulars and incisive personal observations, Fred's letters, like those of most Civil War soldiers, frequently addressed health, the weather, and financial concerns, both at home and in camp. He wrote profusely of military affairs as well. He was a common soldier, and few aspects of military life escaped his description. While serving in the defense of Washington DC, he wrote of living in muddy, crowded tents with too little heat and space and too much smoke and stink. He told Lizzie of having to deal with drunkenness, theft, and sickness; of how he and other noncommissioned officers protested the tyranny of insensitive officers; and of gaining the respect and warm camaraderie of fellow soldiers. When he took walks through the war-ravaged countryside surrounding his camp, he described the scenes he encountered, including the escaped formerly enslaved people and contraband workers who he thought deserved sympathy. When his regiment was called up in late spring 1864 to join Ulysses S. Grant in Virginia, he wrote to Elizabeth of long, hard marches that killed or so weakened others they could not go on, of terrible thirst while marching under an unrelenting Virginia sun with no water, and of the incomprehensible carnage of numerous battles. To not worry Lizzie too much, he wrote, almost cavalierly, of coming under enemy fire close enough several times to have killed him and of watching his regiment tragically reduced by bloody assaults, capture, and disease. When eventually reassigned from the siege trenches of Petersburg to guard duty at Camp Parole near Annapolis, Maryland, and then to Fort McHenry, he told Elizabeth of the pitiable condition of Union soldiers returned from Confederate prisons and of what seemed the comparably hardy condition of Confederate prisoners about to be returned home.

In return, he received from Lizzie constant assurances from home and an intimate view of home life and the struggles to maintain it. She told of trying to keep an even keel, especially with the children, and of endeavoring to tolerate, mostly in silence but not always, the pique of her sister-in-law, an unsubtle woman more than twice her age. Sometimes, Lizzie withdrew to the solitude of an empty room as the rest of the family slept, there to pour out her heart to Fred. Other times, she attempted to write at the dining room table with inquiring children at her side. She told of financial fears and then, maintaining fortitude, would urge Fred not to worry. As time went by, she grew interested in politics, intensely so heading into Lincoln's 1864 re-election, and she monitored the military news closely. She wrote much about neighbors—whom she liked and why, and whom she did not care for. She attended church regularly and often returned home with her optimism restored and at other times feeling the gloom of guilt as someone undeserving of Christian grace. She apologized for her inadequacies in writing letters, but she kept at it and in time grew notably confident and self-possessed. Throughout, she assured Fred of everyone's interest and concern for him, but she was most consistent in communicating to him her own hopes, concerns, and fears. By the end of the war, they were not only husband and wife and lovers but also best friends.

Many couples, both North and South, promised to write often. Largely unique among Civil War soldier families, however, Fred and Lizzie generally upheld their commitment. Rarer still, most of their correspondence has survived.[1] Elizabeth treasured and safeguarded all but one of Frederic's letters, or at least all those we know of.[2] And years later, she transferred them safely to her son, Fred, who eventually donated them to reputable libraries and archives.[3] Frederic, by contrast, was not, or could not be, as faithful in saving missives from home, but he did far better than most soldiers.[4] Part of the reason was his good fortune to spend his first twenty months of enlistment in a heavy-artillery regiment in defense of Washington DC, which meant he remained in camp. Moreover, during those twenty months, he increasingly assumed the duties of regimental clerk, which provided secure storage for official documents—and not-so-official papers, such as his wife's letters. When his regiment was called to Virginia in 1864 and then fought in the Petersburg siege, he served primarily as regimental clerk and adjutant. Held back from most of the fighting, he took advantage of being able to preserve many of her letters.

Not all of Fred and Lizzie's correspondence survives. For whatever reason, we have none of Elizabeth's letters from 1862, and there are gaps in her subsequent Civil War correspondence as well, most often explained by Frederic's being on active campaign. Internal evidence in his letters shows that Elizabeth was writing during these times, and often twice a week or nearly so. What happened to these letters we do not know, but enough of Lizzie's letters do survive, along with the diary she kept in 1863, for us to get to know her, to recognize how she changed and matured over their three-year separation, and to see how much she and Fred meant to each other. When matched with Fred's letters, they create an integrated story.

Also included are two items from Fred's older sister, Emma, then living with Lizzie and the three girls, as do two letters Fred wrote to his middle daughter, Emma Louise (Dollie). Evidence in surviving letters shows that Emma and Fred exchanged additional letters—"I am much obliged to Emma for her frequent communications," he said—and that he and his daughters also exchanged more letters than exist today, but what happened to them is unknown.[5] Nevertheless, the two surviving letters Fred wrote to his older daughters are especially notable, for they attest to a father's loving relationship with his girls. Neither condescending nor patronizing, his letters are warm, unabashed, candid, and detailed, as if written to an equal.[6]

Frederic wrote most of his letters knowing Lizzie would share them with others in the family and perhaps with neighbors and friends. But sometimes he intended them for her alone. With no dread of censorship, he could write anything he wanted—and often did—without fear of discovery, reprisal, or disapproval.[7] Elizabeth did similarly. Letters to her husband were often the sole means she had to give voice not only to frustration, loneliness, and despair but also to joy, family life, and requests for advice. Occasionally, they both ventured into intimacies. Mostly, they wished they could just be together. Whether they breached stereotypes of Victorian reserve is difficult to say; assumptions about Victorian behavior can still be priggish. Fred and Lizzie's references to physical love, needs, and attractions are real, for example, but in letters intended for each other's eyes only, they are generally suggestive and almost never explicit.

I first encountered the Civil War letters of Fred and Elizabeth

Lockley while working on my dissertation at the Huntington Library in the early 1990s. At the time, I was surprised at how little use had been made of them. When, after a career of aiding other authors in getting their books published, I decided to take up the Lockleys again three years ago, I was not a little relieved to find the collection had still been largely overlooked.[8] The reasons for that are probably numerous, but one may be that the Lockley story is a challenging one. As one author and friend of mine commented, the historian's task, paradoxically, can be made much harder when the source material is abundant. And with the Lockleys, it is abundant. Then again, after a researcher and would-be author has sifted, organized, and digested all that he or she has at hand, it is, inevitably, not enough. One invariably wishes he could, even for just a few moments, sit down with his historical characters and ask questions. As well, he would want to know, did I get this right? With people who lived more than 150 years ago, that, of course, is impossible. So, the author does the best he can.

With more than four hundred letters, most of them lengthy, I had to make a choice: either include them all or be selective for those I did include. Other compilers of such material have sometimes elected simply to include everything they have and let the reader sort it out. Such an approach is commendable for allowing the reader access to everything, but it tends to slow the forward momentum of the story and often bogs it down entirely. In few cases are such works read for pleasure. Instead, such a compilation becomes more of a reference work, used for consultation. Often also, the publisher of the unabridged volume—or someone else—ultimately issues a more succinct version later for a wider audience.[9]

Instead, I chose to be selective, hoping to produce a book that could be as faithful to the story as possible, read enjoyably as an evolving narrative, and contain most of the essential material.[10] But what to include, and what to leave out? I knew I wanted to establish a husband-and-wife conversation by including letters from both Frederic and Elizabeth, but otherwise I had to set some goals for what I hoped the book could be and establish some distinct criteria for what to select.

As simplistic as it sounds, I chose letters I thought were good;

that is, letters that were interesting or poignant, well written, and rewarding to read. I also tried to select letters that revealed character; that illustrated well who Fred and Lizzie were, both as individuals and as a couple; and that revealed their disarming honesty and lack of pretense. It was also important to select letters that connected with other letters, whether they were immediately adjacent chronologically, introduced or carried forward themes crucial to the story, or came at pivotal times. As noted, themes invariably included children and family life, health, financial concerns, the nature of letter writing, and the need to receive and to give love and assurance. Also important were letters that addressed themes important to the era, especially (and unavoidably) related to the Civil War. Such themes include desertion, treatment of and attitudes toward African Americans, wartime politics, religion, masculinity, intimacy, and the quirks and demands of military life, including physical hardship and fear of death. Also important were letters that illustrated the nature and effects of boredom, fear, resilience, despair, optimism, crises, and sad, heart-warming, or comical incidents in camp and field and at home. I looked for letters that offered some or all these elements and that I thought were well done and rewarding.

These criteria helped support my several goals for the book. First, I wished to produce a book of reasonable size yet deservedly comprehensive. If Fred and Lizzie were committed to sending a constant stream of correspondence, they were even more conscientious about "filling their sheets" when writing, even sometimes, as with other Civil War writers, writing perpendicularly across what they had already written. Rarely short of paper, Fred, in fact, sometimes even got carried away and wrote half again or twice as much as the normal folio allowed—and apologized for the additional postage Lizzie would have to pay when she received it. All that is to say they wrote a lot. Of their surviving letters, I selected 162 for inclusion. Together, with prologue and epilogue, substantive headings for some letters, and summaries for letters not used in whole but containing in one proportion or another information essential to sustaining their story, I had a compilation that pushed the boundaries of a sizable book.

A second goal was to eliminate duplication, repetition, and

extraneous tangents that diverted attention from the main storyline. Examples include Fred's sometimes lengthy disquisitions on religion, the bible, and literature or his flights of fantasy (such as when he would liken the rising sun to the nature of man), what he and Elizabeth called "nonsense." It answered his poetic impulse and satisfied his literary aspirations but, with a few notable exceptions, provided little genuine narrative substance. In that view, more did not seem better. Nevertheless, I have included or summarized everything that seemed essential, making selections as prudently as possible with that goal in mind.

A third goal was to recapture the nature and motivations, the flow and context of Fred and Lizzie's lives as lived during wartime. This is a Civil War story. It is also a love story set in the context of the Civil War, and it reveals inner lives in unexpected ways. A narrative approach seemed most fitting to do it justice. Historians sometimes recoil at narrative construction; they fear fabrication. But as Jason Phillips has argued, narratives need not preclude accuracy or argument. Stories have arguments, too, but unlike monographs, their primary purpose is not to assimilate disparate evidence to argue a thesis, but to relate a coherent story. As Phillips also has said, narratives need not be grand in scale, nationalistic in sentiment, or elitist in choice of characters.[11] In fact, the Lockley correspondence is none of these things, but this narrative does, as he suggests, closely follow how Fred and Elizabeth experienced the war. Taken together, their letters offer insights into "the private, internal, and introspective" that Stephen W. Berry II found was so often eclipsed by "public, external, and projected aspects" of Civil War soldiers' lives.[12] Peter Carmichael believes that much of the existing Civil War correspondence "can be catalogued as terse tales that never pierce the inner world of the writer." With a few exceptions, that may be true, but not here. These letters allow the reader to enter the inner worlds of Fred and Lizzie through an evolving narrative. Carmichael said his purpose in studying the common soldier was to "recapture the spontaneity of the historical moment," to get a ground-level view of the war from the ranks. So it is here—in the ranks of soldiers and among the ranks of family and friends at home.[13]

Thus, my goals were to be sympathetically selective, to assure representativeness as it related to Fred and Elizabeth, to let the power and pace of the story unfold naturally, to leave out nothing essential, and to realize the best readability possible. Others may find value in letters not included. If they do, all to the good. Others in pursuit of different interests may plumb this collection rewardingly, and I hope they do.

In editing these letters, I have left most spellings as they appeared in the original, except when meaning is otherwise uncertain, which is extremely rare. Punctuation is provided only when meaning is unclear or obscured without it. Paragraphing is introduced when a new line of thought was obviously being presented. An ellipsis is provided when a portion of a paragraph has been excluded. When an ellipsis appears between paragraphs, an entire paragraph has been omitted for lack of relevance or continuity. Frederic and Elizabeth rarely repeated words in their letters—most often when they seem to have been interrupted or distracted and then tried to pick up a thought again. Such repetitions are edited out. Similarly, words are added ([in brackets]) when they were obviously dropped by mistake, or if what they abbreviated is unclear without being spelled out. Rarely are words unreadable in the original letters—in fact, their handwriting, especially Frederic's, is remarkably legible, and few letters have cross-outs—but when something is undecipherable, I have sought to note it. I have used *sic* not to denigrate Fred and Lizzie's efforts but rather to show the reader how the spelling appeared in the original and that it is not a typographical error.

As with most writers in the nineteenth century, spelling conventions were less settled than they are today. Frederic was a stickler for good spelling and sometimes admonished Elizabeth for errors, although he himself could be guilty of mistakes or unconventional usages. *Haversac, Shakspere, Fort De Russey, Coal Harbor,* and *inditing* are examples. Lizzie, for whatever reason, often used double consonants unnecessarily, such as when she wrote *immagine* for *imagine* or *Jossie* for *Josie.* Frederic, so cable of drawing parallel examples from literature, peppered his letters with French expressions and quotable allusions to Charles Dickens, Homer, Lord Byron, Shakespeare, the Bible, and other literary works. I have tried to translate, explain, or cite these references and quotations when they occur.

Otherwise, every effort has been made to not only retain the way these letters were written originally but also preserve as much as possible the sound of Fred and Lizzie's voices as they come off the page—their despair, their begging and longing, their enthusiasms, their hopes and fears, their strengths and foibles, their optimism and occasional bravado, their practicality, their humor, their humanity. I hope I have done them justice.

Acknowledgments

It is a cliché to say that many people helped make a project like this happen. Clichéd or not, it is always true and no less so here. Many people and institutions made this book possible, and I am genuinely thankful to each and every one. Not least has been Peter Blodgett, H. Russell Smith Foundation curator of Western Historical Manuscripts at the Huntington Library in San Marino, California. From the first day I met and talked with Peter about this project more than thirty years ago, no one has been more steadfast in his or her encouragement and readiness to assist with my research into the Frederic E. Lockley Collection than Peter. Close to Peter in unfaltering interest and encouragement has been Richard W. "Dick" Etulain, one of my chief professors at the University of New Mexico. Dick read some of this work in dissertation long, long ago and for thirty years since has unfailingly urged me on. An author is lost without such encouragement.

Similarly, Paul Andrew Hutton has been instrumental in crucial ways. It's not too much to say I would never have known of Frederic Lockley or done this book without Paul, for Paul, my mentor in many ways, secured my first visit to the Huntington, a wonderous research facility, and introduced me to his mentor, Martin Ridge. Then director of research at the Huntington in the late 1980s when all this began and when the history of the American West occupied an esteemed place at the scholarly table, Martin secured for me the fellowships and encouragement that enabled me to haunt the Huntington's incomparable stacks and sit in the Ahmunson Reading Room to read Lockley letters.

If these wonderful people were instrumental at the outset, others have contributed no less indispensably along the way. They include Tom Ferris, Jeff Malcomson, Martha Kohl, Zoe Ann Stolz, Dolores Morrow, and Rebecca Kohl of the Montana Historical Society. I am especially thankful to Tom Ferris for making the digitized scans of Lockley family photographs, some of which are reproduced in this book. Jessica Watson of the Albany Medical College scanned and provided essential manuscript materials, as did a variety of people at the New York Historical Society, the New York State Library, and the Oregon Historical Society.

No manuscript fails to be made better by the suggestions and critiques of outside readers. I am in genuine debt to Robert Senkewicz, Durwood Ball, and Gregory J. W. Urwin, who read the manuscript in early versions and made vital suggestions. Sincere thanks also go to outside readers Peter S. Carmichael and longtime friend and colleague Edward G. Longacre. Lockley descendants were also crucial and generous. Jerry Shepard and John "Jack" Frewing, both descendants of Frederic Lockley's daughter Josephine, provided family material and photographs unavailable anywhere else, and Phil Sherburne, a descendant of Lockley's daughter Gertrude, likewise provided helpful information. Special thanks are due also to Ellen Stevens, whose husband, Errol Stevens, now passed away, was an author of mine at Oklahoma. A wonderful woman, Ellen put me up in her Whittier home and gave me French press coffee in the mornings and great dinners in the evenings during my most recent research trip to the Huntington.

Welcome institutional help has been forthcoming all along the way. As noted, the Huntington Library provided essential research fellowships in the early going and, of course, access to the Frederic E. Lockley collection itself. The Montana Historical Society's resources were abundant and available, especially while I worked at the Society in the 1990s, as have been the Sherburne and Fred Lockley collections at the University of Montana.

The always professional Bill Nelson has provided his excellent maps, and friends Paul Hedren, Eli Paul, Jerome Greene, Will Bagley, Bill MacKinnon, Gary Anderson, Rose Marie Beebe, and Janie Botkin, all of whom I have had the pleasure to work with as authors over the years, have never flagged in their assistance and encouragement. Thanks also to Bethany Mowry, former assistant of mine at the University of Oklahoma Press. Bethany provided similar encouragement and critique, as did my current University of Nebraska Press editor, Clark Whitehorn.

I am, of course, forgetting to mention others who have helped and encouraged me along the way, but three people I cannot forget are my wife, Diane, who read every word and suffered through many a detailed one-sided discussion of Lockley and the Civil War; my younger son, Andrew, who has suffered similarly and contributed greatly; and my older son, Nathan, always ready with a smile and a six-pack.

Toward a More Perfect Union

Prologue

In 1884 Frederic Lockley, by then a veteran newspaper journalist and proud former Union soldier, recalled writing letters home while on campaign with Ulysses S. Grant in Virginia twenty years earlier. Civil War soldiers on both sides wrote perhaps a half billion such missives under all types of circumstances—in the rain, in muddy trenches, even during lulls in battle. Desiring to reassure family, friends, and loved ones they were still alive—and often to encourage return letters from home—they took advantage of almost any opportunity to pen a few lines. Frederic's depiction, published in the *Albany Evening Journal*, one of three papers in his regiment's hometown, conjures up a field of soldiers in blue sprawled on green grass, propped against trees, or hunched over haversacks to pen quickly and eagerly something for home:

> While resting here, through the heated hours of the afternoon, our chaplain sent word to the different company commanders that he had made arrangements to despatch a mail, and he would take charge of any letters the men might want to send home. With what eagerness they availed themselves of the opportunity! To tell our anxious friends that, so far, we were yet safe; to narrate our experiences and impressions of the dread ordeal of battle; to speculate on the nature of our present inexplicable movement, and predict an early occupation of Richmond; could the several hundred letters that were hastily written at our chaplain's invitation have been all compared there is no doubt that these topics would have formed the staple of nine-tenths of them.[1]

The letters the chaplain collected that day filled two large haversacks, but they went undelivered. The haversacks had been tied together and thrown across a mule's back for transport, but the chaplain never got them posted. After two days, means of transport were so scarce on the march that the mule was needed for other duty. So, those letters containing money were returned to their owners and the rest destroyed.[2]

At the time, Lockley's regiment—the Seventh New York Volunteer Heavy Artillery Regiment, recently converted to infantry—had seen minor action on the Fredericksburg Road but was on its way to Spotsylvania and beyond. In the ensuing Overland Campaign and siege of Petersburg, the Seventh New York was all but destroyed. Lockley was one of the fortunate few to survive the war unscathed, returning home to his family in early summer 1865. He would be a citizen again and forever a former soldier. His own letter, written at the chaplain's behest that day in May 1864, was probably lost with the others, but most of the letters he sent home to his wife, Elizabeth—and many of the letters she wrote to him—did survive. This is the story of that correspondence.

1

The Setting

By the time of the South's secession and the war's early hostilities, Frederic had lost one wife and just married another. She was eighteen-year-old Elizabeth Metcalf Campbell, who the family called Lizzie. Lizzie was American born, but her father, a Scotsman's son, had shifted the family more than once from Perth, Canada, to the Northumberland area north of Schuylerville in upstate New York. Her parents, John Campbell and Margaret Metcalf, had married in 1836. Their first child came five years later in 1841, then Elizabeth in 1843, and three more children every twenty-four months or so like clockwork over the next six years.[1] Lizzie's mother, by then thirty-eight and weakened by previous childbirths, was ill-prepared for her sixth child, and when it did come in spring 1851, she could not sustain it. The infant perished within a few days, and Lizzie's mother died soon after. John Campbell moved his family back to Perth, Ontario, but when his house and tinware manufactory burned, he lost everything. Campbell was close to his children, but now destitute and deeply in debt, he had to consign them separately to the care of relatives, some of whom were glad to have them and others less so. Lizzie had thus boarded with relatives for most of the 1850s, and by 1860, she was recently arrived in Schuylerville, New York. There, living with her grandmother, Margaret Metcalf, and her aunt, Maria Mair, her grandmother's widowed daughter, Lizzie attracted the attentions of Fred Lockley, a door-to-door book salesman.[2]

Fred and Lizzie were wed in her Aunt Maria's home in Schuylerville five months later on the last day of February 1861. At the time, Frederic lived in Troy, New York, with his three young daughters, Josephine, Emma Louise "Dollie," and Gertrude, and sold books for Johnson, Fry & Company of New York. He spent much of his time on the road to serve his sales area, which extended from Albany north through upstate New York and as far east as Burlington, Vermont. He traveled most of each week and could be gone almost a month.[3] After two years of such work, judging from his subsequent correspondence, he was disliking it more each day, and it vexed him all the more to be away from his new wife. "Upon my word," he confessed at one point, "my disinclination to leave home seems to grow upon me."[4] Also nagging him was guilt for not supporting the Union cause in the Civil War, and when Abraham Lincoln called for three hundred thousand more volunteers in summer 1862, Lockley signed on with the 113th New York Infantry Regiment in late July. Formal enlistment would come two weeks later. Called the "Albany County Regiment" after where it was organized, the 113th would be reconstituted five months later as the Seventh New York Volunteer Heavy Artillery Regiment.[5]

Frederic's decision to enlist was not without ambivalence—his own and especially Elizabeth's. "His patriotism overcame his scruples," Lizzie recalled years later. "He says I was brave. I wonder. To think I would be left with three children not knowing whether he would ever come home."[6] Her memory jibes with his. When he told her of his intention to enlist, the news, he said years later, "almost broke her." For three days and nights, "she gave way to despair. But in the end she rose to the occasion, and with tearful kisses gave me leave to depart."[7]

Frederic would rationalize his duty to country as his first priority, but like many soldiers, his paternal ties were strong. Throughout the first year of the war, he believed his family needed him more and that he could support the war effort just as well at home. "For myself with a girl wife and three helpless children there was no excuse for my rushing into danger as long as the country did not actually need my services," he wrote later. "It was a saying that one man was wanted at home to sustain each armed man in the field, and I felt that I was but performing my duty by remaining with my family among the stay-at-homes."[8]

So, he had held aloof after the firing on Fort Sumter in April 1861. But as Union failures and lost opportunities multiplied during the first year of the war, he felt the tug of national duty. As he said, when Lincoln called for three hundred thousand more volunteers, "I felt the call came home directly to myself." Fidelity to home and loved ones notwithstanding, "if the country's liberties are imperiled, where is the security of family ties?" Moreover, the government had promised to impose a draft at the state and county levels if too few soldiers failed to answer the president's call to enlistment. As it turned out, more than a half million more men enlisted by the end of the year, but in July, new enlistments were slow and Frederic shrank from the idea of being forced to do through the draft what he wanted to do willingly.[9] "To put on the uniform of a soldier in compulsion," he said, "would rob the patriotic sacrifice" and remove "all tinge of heroism." It would also disqualify him from receiving bounty money.[10]

Fred Lockley had voted for Lincoln enthusiastically in November 1860, and he would do so again as a uniformed soldier in November 1864.[11] Like almost all soldiers, he grew discouraged at times, but paramount among his motivations was his loyalty to preserving the Union.[12] An immigrant from England, he had been in the United States almost fourteen years and had become a naturalized American citizen three years earlier in 1859.[13] Home was central to a proper life for him, but so was loyalty to defending his adopted country. "What is a cheerful, quiet home when your country is torn with treason," he would argue in a letter home in December. "I feel my sacrifice severely—but I do not complain—the cause sustains me."[14]

Fred Lockley felt his justifications intensely, but he joined the Union Army for other reasons as well.[15] For one, he was sick of the book business. Selling books door-to-door during the war, he said, was "like peddling figs in a hurricane."[16] Like others, he also embraced the bounties being paid volunteers. For Lockley, they would amount to what he estimated to be $200 (about $6,500 today), including $100 from the federal government, $50 from the state of New York, and $50 from Albany County, plus the local community's promise to help support the wives and children of volunteer soldiers.[17] Previously, he had made approximately $600 a year with Johnson, Fry & Company, the equivalent of just less than $20,000 in today's dollars, so his bounty, while generous enough early on, went only so far in helping support Elizabeth and his young children. In candid moments, he also said he welcomed the adventure. Like others, he felt the call of a historic moment in national life, and he did not want to miss it.

Moreover, the risk did not seem all that great. He and Lizzie, like most other people both North and South, believed the war would be short, and he thought his military service would position him for better employment after the war.[18] Thus, when he signed on in August 1862, Frederic believed he would never have to serve out his full enlistment term. In fact, he did not wish to. When the call for volunteers was first announced, two Albany regiments were planned, one, under Captain Lewis O. Morris, soon to be made a colonel, and another by a militia colonel. Morris's regiment would serve a three-year term; the militia regiment supposedly just ninety days. Frederic preferred to join the latter "as the lesser of two evils," but when there was no progress on its recruitment, he lost patience and joined Morris's regiment, thus committing himself to three years' service.[19] Still, he and Lizzie never dreamed he would serve almost the entire term. As his letters show, he thought he would be home by the first Christmas and then, in 1863, by the second Christmas. Even after the bloody spring and summer of 1864 and the seemingly endless siege of Petersburg, Lockley never imagined he would have to serve until summer 1865. As it turned out, he was honorably discharged only two months short of his full three-year term.

In the buoyant, hopeful summer of 1862, however, enlistment looked to be a wise choice, especially for a man seeking adventure, sick of his current employment, and hoping his term of service would be short. But he was aware of having created a precarious situation at home. In the best light, leaving three young children ages five to nine in the care of an inexperienced wife, by then just turned nineteen, was a bold decision. In the worst light, it was foolhardy. But he had resources, the best of which was his sister Emma. Frederic now called on Emma, and she came to live with Lizzie and the girls until it was clear by late spring 1865 that he would come home for good and in one piece.

If Lizzie came from a broken home, Frederic and his siblings came from a humble one. Frederic Edward Lockley was born on the last day of 1824 in a working-class London neighborhood seemingly straight out of a Charles Dickens novel. A place of factories, small shopkeepers, tradesmen, and meat markets, it was, he said, always crowded "like a fair." And his life as a youth was also not unlike that of a Dickens character. The son of a butcher and a mother whose family had made nails for a living, he struggled to break free of a tradesman's life, but his upbringing weighed heavily against his true interest in learning and literary refinement. "In my father's home our means were narrow," he recalled years later. Refinements "were out of our reach, and were not sought after." At home, he said, there was no taste for books, no one played a musical instrument, and "we had no garden, no dog or horse or cow to bring us in touch with nature." It was, he said, a "contracted existence."[20]

Formal education was meager as well. As a youth, he attended an "academy" for three years. He was "head boy," but the instruction was by rote, and he learned little. Six more months in a "post graduate" course afforded him the ability to "write legibly, read a plain narrative with spelling the hard words, and work a sum in vulgar fractions. This was learning enough my parents tho't."[21]

His life, therefore, was on a "humdrum" track. When he turned eleven, his father insisted he quit school and work as a delivery boy for the family butcher's business. Having little choice, he did so. That consumed his days, and nights were little different. When the family "gathered round the candles at evening, my father would propose a game of whist or Pope Joan, and two or three of the family would readily acquiesce simply as an escape from ennui."[22] Frederic never did care for card games and generally avoided the ones his Civil War comrades played in camp. He even insisted they not play cards on Sunday, at least not in his tent.[23] He also recoiled at drunkenness, although his comrades' enthusiasms persuaded him to imbibe on a few occasions.[24] When a boy, he had seen the degrading effects of drink on his London neighbors and even in his own family, especially the economic costs to people barely making ends meet. Ale was served to all in his family three times a day, for example, despite its cost. "My mother was frugal," but she never gave thought to economizing on ale. "Beer was an indispensable, the same as bread and meat." After the war, largely under Lizzie's influence, he grew abstemious and championed temperance avowedly later in life.[25]

As a boy, Fred was curious, too much so for his mother, and he chafed at intellectual limitations. As his awareness expanded, he grew to detest class distinctions, which stratified the population with "lines drawn distinctly between people even within the neighborhood." Caste was therefore a barrier. Schools were available, but entry to them "required influence to gain admission." His mother, caring enough toward her children but devout in her Old Testament views and devoid of ambition herself, discouraged intellectual pursuits. "Yes, you're mighty knowing, you are!" he recalled her telling him after he proudly announced to her some small revelation. "Can do more than wiser heads ever thought of! But wait till you get older, then you'll find lots of people that know more than you can think of." There were books in the house, "kept in a bureau drawer," but as children, he said, he and Emma and his other sister, Mary, were only allowed access to them on Sundays and special occasions.[26]

Refusing to surrender to intellectual languor, however, Fred became a struggling autodidact, although he did not call it that. In time, he read penny magazines, low-priced reprints, and the early works of Charles Dickens. "If the author's syntax was not to my liking, I would re-write a sentence, which rendered my reading laborious," he recalled. "Big words that I could not understand, I would copy on a scrap of paper, and when I had accumulated a score or more, I would repair to a second-hand shop, near the Victoria theatre—half a mile away—to hunt the definitions in a stray copy of Walker's Dictionary. Learning gained at this cost of labor was not readily forgotten."

He learned grammar by copying from a series of letters compiled into a book, titled *Advice to Young Men* and written by the British reformist William Cobbett.[27] He and Emma thus learned grammar together, studying Cobbett's *Advice* each morning one summer from 5:00 to 7:00 a.m., before he was called to handle early morning customers at the meat shop while his father surveyed the market for fresh meat on the hoof. His mother could not understand "the foolish notions my sister Emma and myself had got into our heads," but together, they continued their studies just the same.[28]

In time, Frederic joined a literary institute, which provided him with access to books. "My sister was an insatiable reader, and having access to books now, I kept her well supplied." He read voraciously himself, and in night classes, he exchanged his own guidance in English for lessons in reading French with a veteran of Waterloo. "One lesson a week is a slow way to learn a language, but I kept at it." His mother frowned on his efforts; basic English should be good enough for someone in the butcher's trade. Still, he absorbed enough, as he said, "to read a French author with facility." Later, he would sprinkle his Civil War letters to Lizzie with French expressions and almost always address her, "*Ma chére Femme.*"[29] He also dabbled in Latin, leaving scrawled experiments around the butcher's shop. His mother thought such things "stuff an' nonsense," but her discouragement, he said, "was the pope's bull against the comet on a small scale."[30]

Frederic's favorite author was the British historian and essayist Thomas Carlyle, whose work undoubtedly shaped his view of great men in history and informed him about the French Revolution. He said he even visited the historian once to seek guidance, but Carlyle, himself still early in his career, warned him away from becoming an author. It was a will-o-the-wisp endeavor, the learned man advised. Carlyle even wrote a letter to Frederic to that effect, which Frederic said was later lost when he entrusted it and other items to the care of Lancelot Davenport, the younger brother of the man his sister Mary would later marry. But his reading made him yearn for adventure. He even thought of running away to sea, but his parents, especially his mother, held him back, reminding him that he owed them useful service for their kindness in raising him.[31] Frederic might have benefited from going to sea, but the fact he did not underscores his faithfulness and deference, traits that would mark his service during the Civil War.

At eighteen he apprenticed to a butcher named William Rowe, a "a sordid, ungenerous soul" whom Fred also described as "grossly illiterate." Rowe had made deliveries with a horse and cart, but with his new apprentice, he sold the outfit and relied on Fred to make them on foot. Rowe would buy animals on Monday and slaughter one or two as needed, leaving the rest to survive for several days without feed. They lost weight, but Rowe figured the loss was less than the cost of feed. "Any humanitarian consideration of the suffering of the poor brutes never entered his pulseless breast," Lockley wrote contemptuously years later. "Ignorance," he observed, "narrows the sympathies." To illustrate the point, he told of how his work for Rowe "called me into the back premises many times a day, and as I passed the patient brutes[,] they would follow me with their moony eyes, and utter a plaintive moan that pierced me to the quick." Frederic grew to detest the butcher's trade—"that ungentle craft," as he called it—but he returned to it again and again once immigrated to the United States, when all other efforts to find work failed. During the Civil War, he put his butcher's skills to use as commissary sergeant—and, more than once, on runaway animals or while on forage—for the benefit of fellow his soldiers.[32]

After two years with Rowe, Fred struggled to find a calling, but he stuck with his dream of becoming a writer. Although almost four years his elder, Emma worshipped her brother, and after conspiring together as teenagers to study grammar, she now championed his idea of taking six months off to pursue his literary interests. When his parents reluctantly acquiesced, he read heavily in literature and toyed with creating poetry, turning some five hundred lines of the ancient poet Ossian's work into heroic verse. Intent on preparing eight thousand lines, he sought advice on its publication but was told poetry was "a drug on the market" and that rhymes of unknown writers such as himself rarely paid the cost of printing.[33] He abandoned his plan to publish, but he remained fascinated with Ossian throughout his life, sometimes identifying with the poet's gloominess in his Civil War letters to Elizabeth. Pages and pages of his Ossian work can still be found among his papers. A sensitivity to the sound of words on paper also remained with him. In later years as a newspaperman, he had on many occasions needed to correct the grammar of preachers and lawyers who he believed should have known better. Yet, he confessed, he could not master the artillery tables he was supposed to learn during the Civil War, tables he said an unlettered Irishman memorized easily. "I concluded to let faulty authors have their way with grammar."[34]

When his six-month sabbatical came to nothing, Fred went back to work for his father as per parental arrangement. Nonetheless, he was now thoroughly familiar with Carlyle, Macaulay, Shakespeare, Gibbon, Dickens, Mill, the Bible, Lord Byron, and a host of other English and French writers and historians, poets and novelists, many of whom he would quote with precision in his letters home during the Civil War. Reveling in histories of Oliver Cromwell and the English Civil Wars and the more recent Napoleonic Wars, he was attracted to heroic military life, at least as it was reflected in the literature he read. But his class status all but prevented his rising very far in a military career even if he had possessed genuine inclination, which he did not. Military discipline, battle tactics, and iron resolve were not of his nature. He was too much a thinker, too ambivalent toward absolutes, too independent in his own conclusions. Instead, he was drawn to editing and the book trade, and to writing. He even published a book himself, a novel titled *Arthur Frankland*, a story of a lost love. The book was issued in February 1848 by Sanders and Otley in what Frederic considered an overly expensive edition. At least one of his Civil War comrades—Stephen Treadwell—insisted on reading it in early 1864, and Frederic accommodated his wish by having it sent from home. The book's appearance in 1848 was ill-timed, however, coinciding with the revolutions in Paris and elsewhere that year in continental Europe. Although it received some critical attention, its sales faltered and died.[35]

That same year, Frederic signed on as a temporary policeman in England's Chartist movement. When perversely made to feel disloyal in defense of the Crown by a copoliceman who snubbed him, he had had enough of class pretense and seized on the suggestion of his brother-in-law, Lancclot, that they immigrate together to Australia. The cost of passage down under was too steep, so they opted for New York City instead.[36]

Having arrived in the United States as steerage passengers aboard the *Delta* in August 1848, Fred and Lancelot traveled extensively across the eastern half of the country, from New York to Chicago, Saint Louis to New Orleans, and back to Pittsburgh. Whether a copy of *Arthur Frankland* accompanied Frederic when he first arrived in America is unrecorded, but he clearly brought along his interest in writing. As in England, however, the work he secured hardly encouraged literary pursuits. Knocking about for almost two years with Lancelot and others, he worked in the butcher's trade in several cities, dug post holes for a farmer, did some clerking, wrote promotions briefly for a hat salesman, and journeyed down the Mississippi River from Saint Louis three times as a flat-boat operator taking cattle and sheep to New Orleans, perhaps passing Samuel Clemens, then a riverboat pilot, along the way.[37]

When news of his father's death reached him in summer 1850,[38] however, Frederic returned to England. He tried to carry on his father's business on behalf of the family, but he soon found London as stifling as ever. Placing his mother in a home for merchants' widows and leaving his second-oldest sister, Mary, and her family behind, he sailed again for America in 1851. This time, Emma accompanied him. They arrived on what Fred described as a tramp sailing vessel called the *Ocean Queen* and settled in New York City, where they would live and work together. Emma found the city terrifying at first. In the face of its unfamiliarity, rowdiness, and cacophony of languages, she thought of returning to England, but Frederic soon partnered with an Irish ward boss with interests in a foundry, a boarding house, and a bar in what is today west Manhattan. The ward boss liked Fred's idea of opening a meat shop, and once it was established, Emma helped by day, and they lived in a partitioned area in the rear by night.[39]

The arrangement lasted less than a year, and in its way, led to Fred's first marriage. In summer 1852, he opened a meat shop of his own in a new location, again with a dwelling in the rear and Emma in charge of the household. Next door, Robert Hill, a former seaman, operated a bakery with the help of a negligent wife and three of his four daughters.[40] The daughters were all attractive, Fred remembered, and only by close acquaintance could a person tell them apart. So, he found "oft occasion to run in there." Showing his proclivity for younger women, he soon focused on the youngest, Agnes Jeannette Hill.[41] He was twenty-seven when they married that August. Agnes, widowed with a two-year-old son, was about nineteen. Her child, John, nicknamed Jack, would surface from time to time as a troublemaker in Lizzie and Fred's Civil War correspondence.[42] Agnes's family had opposed the match and, fearing her father would reject Fred's bid for her hand, the couple all but eloped. Emma, who did not favor the marriage either but was ever loyal to her brother, stood in as the ceremony's only witness.[43]

In search of a better opportunity, Fred soon sold his meat shop, and he, Agnes, and Jack moved to Chicago. He met with success as a clerk and bookkeeper for an up-and-coming merchant younger than himself, and Emma soon joined them, then found millinery work in Peru, Illinois, southwest of Chicago. The couple was happy enough in the relationship, and Lockley seemed to have found the opportunity he was looking for, but, pregnant with a new child, Agnes was unhappy in the Windy City. She was lonely, so, within a year, they moved back to New York City, where she could be closer to family and friends and where Fred seemed to shift from one sort of job to another, though clearly gravitating to proofreading, copyediting, and publishing. In one instance, he wrote editorials for Horace Greeley's *New-York Tribune* after seeking out the eccentric publisher in Greeley's boarding-house room. Greeley seemed to like what Frederic produced and paid him $5 for each item, but the connection only lasted a few weeks. Upon Greeley's departure on one of his many speaking tours, Fred's contributions fell to Greeley's chief editor, Charles A. Dana, who rejected them so frequently, he gave up.[44]

Lockley then secured an assistant's position with Col. Thomas B. Thorpe, the antebellum humorist, painter, and author of the famed "Big Bear of Arkansas" tale.[45] Harper & Brothers had given Thorpe a manuscript to rewrite for publication, but he was too busy to handle it himself, so he passed it along to Lockley to rewrite for him. Harper & Brothers eventually published the manuscript, "Memoirs of Jim Beckwourth, a Crow Chief," as *The Life and Adventures of James Beckwourth: Mountaineer, Scout, and Pioneer, and Chief of the Crow Nation of Indians* in 1856. Fredcric said he spent six weeks on the "blood curdling narrative," but the 1856 edition, still available in reprint today, provides no indication of who may have polished it editorially, and Frederic offered no hint of whether the book encouraged his western travels after the war. Whatever the case, Frank Leslie afterward engaged Thorpe as editor for *Frank Leslie's Illustrated Newspaper*, and Lockley went along as subeditor and proofreader.[46] After a while, *Leslie's* underwent one of its periodic financial convulsions, and although the paper weathered the crisis, Fred dropped out. Tired of big cities and hoping to see more of the country, he became a traveling book salesman for Johnson, Fry & Company.

If Frederic's working life progressed erratically, his home life proceeded agreeably enough. Josephine, his oldest, was born in June 1853, and two more daughters—Emma Louise (whom the family would call "Dollie") and Gertrude—followed in succession two years apart. Thus, as the nation convulsed from one sectional crisis to another during the 1850s, and as Fred shuttled from one job to another, he and Agnes lived happily, to read from Frederic's memoirs, in "connubial devotion."[47]

The happiness faltered in late 1859 when Agnes developed numbness, first in her arms and then in her legs. An autopsy would later reveal an intensifying tumor adjacent to her spine. Agnes lingered in escalating agony until passing away in March 1860. Her death was a crushing blow to the family but especially to Fred, judging from his later descriptions. Devastated and desperate both to make a living and maintain his household, he called on Amelia, one of Agnes's sisters, to come help keep house. As he and Amelia maintained a stiff respectfulness, he pursued his bookselling. From his home now in Troy, Fred crisscrossed his sizable sales area, visiting numerous small towns day by day. When Schuylerville, New York, was added to his rounds, he encountered there a Mrs. Mair and her mother, Margaret Metcalf, Lizzie's Aunt Maria and Grandma. Recently come to live with them was Lizzie, their seventeen-year-old niece. Fred was dazzled from the first time he saw Lizzie, but she was slow to realize his intentions. Amelia, meanwhile, had precipitated a crisis at home by declaring she wanted to move to San Francisco to join her father, where he had gone to operate a new bakery business. Lizzie's inattention changed quickly after Fred visited the Schuylerville household a second time and asked if he might accompany her to church on Sunday. A four-month courtship ensued in fall 1860, conducted largely through correspondence.[48] The couple grew enamored, and Lizzie, while on visit to Troy to meet Fred's family, was won over entirely when Dollie, then five, asked her, "Won't you come and be my Mama?"[49] They were married in Mrs. Mair's Schuyler home on February 28, 1861.

For the rest of that year and well into the next, Frederic continued his bookselling—history and biography by subscription series—but as the early, heady days of the Civil War lengthened into bloody deadlock, his delivery business grew dull and unrewarding. When stranded off Lake Champlain by storms in September 1861, he chafed at the tedium. "I have been casting about for employment," he wrote Lizzie. Having no cigars and nothing to read, he told of watching the waves on the lake "till I have grown tired of it" and whittling sticks "till my fingers are sore." Next day, in professing his love for her, he noted that Dr. Samuel Johnson had thought if people would exclude love and news from their letters, their compositions might be more tolerable. "Exclude love from letters to my wife! Rather would I eschew mustard to my roast beef!"[50] Even his watch contributed to the dullness. "I have met with another annoyance," he wrote from Fairhaven, Vermont, in November. The mainspring on his watch had broken, "and I have the pleasant prospect of traveling for the next ten days in these backwoods regions in entire ignorance of the time. It is like losing an intelligent companion."[51] It would not be the last time Fred had trouble with a watch. He had bad luck with them.

The lack of intelligent companions notwithstanding, Fred could no more keep the momentous affairs of the war from his letters than he could from his mind. In November he noted, innocently enough, that the government was asking for a large increase in infantry. Having consumed all his stationery, he composed his letter on the back of a company flier. Mirroring his divided mind almost perfectly, he composed words of love and reassurance to Lizzie on one side, while, on the reverse, his makeshift writing paper shouted in bold type, "Revolutionary, Indian, 1812, and Mexican Wars!! The Battles of the United States by Sea and Land! With official documents and biographies of the most Distinguished Military and Naval Commanders!" The nation's past, the flyer proclaimed, was full of heroic commanders and glorious struggle.[52] One can imagine him wondering what he was doing in upstate New York whittling sticks by contrast.

Whatever the case, he followed the declining Union fortunes of war with anxiety and an increasing sense of obligation.[53] Finally, he enlisted not quite ten months later. As Fred went off to war, Emma, then living in New Jersey, abandoned her own pursuits— and a love interest there soon to go sour—to come live with Lizzie and the girls. Emma was forty-one years old and unmarried when she arrived at the Lockley household, now relocated from Troy to Albany.[54] In fact, her bad luck in romance may help explain why she responded with such alacrity. It also may explain some of her ill-temper, which bubbles up in Lizzie's letters from time to time and in Fred's responses to them. Notwithstanding her periodic ill-temper, Emma was always there for her brother, and her presence now proved indispensable. She became an important source of financial stability with her work as a seamstress and milliner, and she showed genuine affection to Fred's three girls by his first marriage. Toward Lizzie, twenty years her junior, Emma displayed a cool but companionable-enough attitude most of the time, just as she had with Fred's first wife Agnes.[55] She and Lizzie slept together in the same bed most nights, but there was occasional friction and, to judge from how Lizzie described Emma's recurring petulance, not a little jealousy.

The Lockley household eventually settled in a small, two-story apartment building on Lark Street in Albany. It seemed almost always in continuous motion, thanks to Fred's three young girls, who were, in 1862, all under age ten. As Lizzie's Civil War correspondence shows, she welcomed her new situation. Taking on Fred's household with its three girls gave her purpose. As the correspondence also shows, she was deeply in love with Fred, who may, at twice her age, also have served as the father figure she had wished for through large parts of her childhood.[56] But she was also uncertain about her new station. The girls were young: Josephine (Josie) was the oldest, having just turned nine in summer 1862; Emma Louise, or Dollie, was seven and a half; and Gertrude, whom Fred and Elizabeth refer to in their correspondence as "Gertie," "Tute," or "Tutie," was barely five.

As her letters show, Lizzie often reveled in the joys and affections of parenting three young girls who embraced her as their own mama. Just as often, she worried about her limitations as a mother, especially to three girls who could flummox her at times and who were not technically her own. "O! I feel so weak and incompetent; that at times I fear I did wrong in undertaking to care for and watch over these precious little ones," she told her diary in early January 1863. She then added, "My love for them grows stronger and stronger daily."[57] Fred had little patience with such doubts, believing her to be exactly the kind of mother he wanted for his children. "I repose implicit confidence in your maternal love, good sense, and firmness to feel that the children are being well trained and well cared for," he told her a month after her diary entry.[58] Still, as Lizzie noted with trepidation, she was only ten years older than Josie, the oldest daughter.[59]

The strongest theme running through their Civil War letters is Fred's need and dependence on Lizzie and his love for her, his three girls, and his sister Emma. Equally important is the reciprocal love, constancy, and attachment Elizabeth and his family in Albany provided him through their letters.[60] As Fred noted after being away only a month, "A letter from you is the greatest treat I have—it is like a message from heaven."[61] He felt the same way almost three years later, declaring, "Your letter symbolizes, impersonates and reproduces—all the magic charms of connubial bliss and all the extatic [sic] fervors of romantic courtship. Missus your letters are welcome."[62] Lizzie almost always commented on the joy of receiving his letters: "They are as precious as gold dust."[63] Indeed, few things could cheer Fred more than letters from home, including those from the children and news about them.

Just as people do today, Fred and Elizabeth built intimacy with openness, disarming honesty, mutual caring, sincerity, and unconditional love. Lizzie created intimacy through reminding Fred that he was needed and remembered by writing to him consistently, twice a week, and lacing her letters with references to home and children, to how much she missed him and wanted him (even through sexual innuendos), with references to the community and their place in it, the look of snowfall, the children gone sledding, what Emma and the neighbors were doing, and how they achieved small successes in making ends meet. Intimacy was also born of her attempts to refrain from complaining—and apologizing when she did complain—which mirrored his frequent resort to descriptions of camp life and then apologizing for a lousy letter because it was "all military."

The Lockley correspondence is full of family references, and the children are rarely absent from their exchanges.[64] In 1860 children (defined as people under the age of fifteen) constituted one-third of the U.S. population.[65] In the race to write the history of the war, historians and novelists have often overlooked them. But they should not be overlooked. As photographs from the Civil War era show, they were ubiquitous, and they were equally prominent in the correspondence of Civil War soldier fathers and families. Fred and Lizzie were no exception. As Fred wrote often to his three daughters, they wrote frequently to him. He had to be thankful the war never put them in physical danger, the way many Southern and border-state children and their communities were endangered by marching, clashing armies. But Fred and Elizabeth did consciously seek to protect Josie, Dollie, and Gertie, especially from deprivation when money grew scarce and when hard choices about such things as food, clothing, and heat had to be made.[66]

It is clear from his letters that Fred struggled with his inability to help raise his three daughters because of his absence. He frequently offered advice relating to them, and on her part, Elizabeth often asked for it.[67] When Fred did suggest guidance on child rearing, it was rarely directive, but on occasion, it could be, especially if he disagreed with Lizzie on approach or resolution of a problem. His vehemence at those times may have masked his frustration at not being present at home to discuss the matter more thoroughly as much as it reflected his confidence in being right. Such were some of the frustrations of Civil War correspondence. Issues and crises with children often had to be resolved in the moment, but letters could take days to arrive, and an exchange of letters, although framed like conversations, could take a week or longer.[68] But Fred prevailed in being an ongoing presence in his children's lives. Lizzie told him often how excited his daughters were to hear from him and how they would run screaming through the house to find him if they thought he had come home. He had succeeded in putting his love into writing.[69]

Despite a penurious condition during the war, Fred and Lizzie clearly subscribed to emerging middle-class values of domesticity arising at midcentury. It was reflected in Frederic's literary aspirations and sense of apt decorum, in Lizzie's determination to always dress properly for visitors or when going out, in their hopes for betterment after the war, and in their attitudes toward the children. The latter was exhibited in their emphasis on affection over

The Setting

rigid discipline and on the family as the haven from an unfeeling world. To them, their children were objects of care and constant sources of emotional satisfaction. Indeed, one measure of how well Elizabeth—and Emma—kept the household on an even keel emotionally and psychically is the lack of anxiety exemplified by the children. On that, Lizzie seems to have done a creditable job, notwithstanding what she may have confided in her letters to Frederic when her own confidence faltered.

Whatever face Frederic wished to put forward to the children, he could become as despondent as anyone at times, and he would sometimes admit to being blue. Even as what he wrote might take a darker turn, however, he invariably ended his letter on an upbeat note. In a recent study of common soldiers, one historian argued that they embraced adaptability—pragmatism, as he calls it—to navigate the moral dilemmas and potentially devastating psychological effects of being caught up in so horrific a situation as the Civil War, one that seemed so at odds with their fundamental values as Christian citizens. He credits what he calls "cheerfulness," or the soldier's determination to remain cheerful, so he might maintain psychological equilibrium and avoid falling into a pit of despondency. Cheerfulness, he declares, was—and is—a triumph of willpower. Indeed, outward displays of cheerfulness might be interpreted not as evidence of contentment but rather of inner turmoil and confusion.[70] If so, Lockley's letters provide ample confirmation. Fred was repeatedly overoptimistic in his interpretations of Union defeats or hopes for Union victories. However gloomy he became, he invariably emerged from it, often quickly, with adaptability if not outright cheer.

Frederic's ability to sustain cheerfulness in the face of fear, hardship, disappointment, and outright sadness could be attributed in part to the English custom of maintaining the proverbial stiff upper lip. Whatever the case with that, maintaining composure—"elasticity," as he called it—was, for Fred Lockley, clearly a component of manliness. His sense of manliness corresponded on one hand to the ways most Civil War soldiers saw it: characterized by bravery, patriotism, perseverance, fairness, courage—how he described the way Captain Charles Maguire[71] took hold as leader of his men in fighting at Harris Farm—and on the other hand in maintaining dignity amid hardship.[72] Elizabeth understood his need to live up to expectations, especially his own. As she put it, "O! I am not anxious to have you fight although I suppose you would never be satisfied were you to come home without winning a few laurels."[73] At Harris Farm, laurels seemed in short supply while fear and destruction were manifest. But as his attitude at Harris Farm and as exemplified in letters home reveal, manliness also meant doing no less than his part.[74]

Whatever conventional notions of manliness Frederic believed should govern his actions, his letters show that he embraced two additional qualities that could be characterized as manliness as he saw it or, as one historian put it, as "flexible understandings of manliness."[75] Both established his humanity and set him apart from the brutish callousness of the war. One was compassion, exhibited so often in his actions that it had to have been second nature to him. The other was his unshakable faith in intellectual refinement and interest.[76]

Fred Lockley cared for sick and injured comrades often, and he visited friends and fellow soldiers in field hospitals once his regiment was on the move in Virginia with Grant.[77] One incident, in which he shared fried chicken with two officers who commanded his deep respect, he recorded in his memoirs and is particularly insightful. As a sergeant major, Lockley said he enjoyed freedom of movement most enlisted men did not. When Gen. George Gordon Meade established his headquarters in an abandoned mansion, the surrounding grounds had been scavenged already, but Lockley, "foraging for No. One," snooped among some barrels and found a hen "which had hidden herself away to escape violence." When he found the pullet "well fleshed," he determined to have a chicken fry. An accomplished cook, he roasted the bird and began to dine, but he ate little, "knowing there were others as badly in need as myself." Putting his meal in a tomato can, he hunted up his regimental commander, Maj. Edward Springsteed, whom he found "so exhausted" he could barely speak. "Major," he said, "a fried chicken laid before you just now would exactly meet your case."

"Don't talk about fried chicken," the wearied Springsteed replied. Bring him a cup of coffee and hardtack and "I'd give a month's pay."

The Setting

"Major, I can do better than that," Lockley replied and spread the nicely browned chicken before his astonished commander. Lockley then invited Capt. James Kennedy (a lieutenant at the time) to join in, "and those two brave and deserving officers (both killed, alas! a few weeks subsequently) ate the meal with an enjoyment I cannot describe." If it is "more blessed to give than receive," then "I can vouch for the truth of this saying," he resolved. "The pleasure I felt in seeing those two patriot warriors refresh body and soul was worth a farm."[78]

An even stronger element in Frederic's sense of manliness was intellectual attainment, to be not only well-read but also able to draw lessons from reading and study to apply to life generally. To Lockley, familiarity with classical or well-respected literature— Homer, Shakespeare, Macaulay, Lord Byron, the Bible, Enlightenment writers, poets, historians, and novelists—separated the true man from the brute. He prided himself on his knowledge. His superior learning must have shown itself quickly, for less than two months after enlistment, his companions called him "professor." He felt the intellectual desert around him acutely—"A man possessing any refinement of sentiment—my taste for culture—is sadly out of place among soldiers"—but he must not have lorded it over his comrades because they all seem to have liked and respected him. Frederic often noted how well he got along with the officers, but even more tellingly, Elizabeth recorded what fellow soldier, Lt. Fred Mather, in Albany on visit, had told her: "He says that F is beloved by everyone."[79]

Frederic's ability to forage; his camaraderie with fellow soldiers, which enabled him to ward off a sense of loneliness and despair; his attitude of going along to get along, especially with superior officers, even those for whom he had little respect; and his ability to draw from his own personal background and deep reading among Enlightenment authors and others all enabled him to sustain his optimism. He celebrated not the strictures of organized religion but rather a faith in nature. Life was imbued with romance, and human life reflected the natural order. He embraced Voltaire's belief that anything contradicting the normal course of nature was not to be believed. He advised that Elizabeth not read the Bible as an unthinking acolyte but as a discerning reader who asks at every turn: does this jibe with how a human being could be expected to act rationally? "Read the Bible—not as a religious duty," he counseled. "Read it for mental aliment. In reading it use human judgment. Don't accept Saul as a pattern because he was accepted by God. Estimate his character by his actions—and judge him by the rule of human conduct. Shake off every trace of intellectual pupilage." As he admitted, "I am somewhat rude as a Bible commentator—but I prefer to be guided by my own interpretations."[80]

All these things sustained Frederic during his three years as a Union soldier, and his low points were never so grim that he contemplated desertion. None of his letters, nor his memoirs written later, indicate he ever saw desertion as a way out. To Lockley, desertion would have been unmanly.[81] Still, desertion was much on Frederic's mind toward the end of the war. It was too daily an occurrence not to be. The growing rate of desertions from the Confederate lines at Petersburg and the ritualized public executions of recaptured Union deserters—at one point, occurring every Friday—saw to that.[82] Frederic held no animosity toward Confederate deserters coming into Federal lines in spring 1865, but he had thoroughgoing contempt for what he considered disloyal "big bounty men" who deserted from Union lines. "We lose all human feeling towards such dastards and traitors," he wrote. "A Johnny we can respect—and regard as a brother soldier."[83] Yet, he could have sympathy for a Union soldier who deserted with reasonable cause, namely the tyranny of a commanding officer. Like most Union soldiers, however, Lockley resented those on the home front who did not voice wholehearted support for the war.[84]

A consistent desire for the war to be over courses like a refrain through Fred and Lizzie's three-year correspondence. Fred took being a citizen soldier seriously. He disliked military discipline and what he perceived to be the assault on his democratic individuality. He detested the army's brutal punishments and indifference to the welfare of enlisted men, and he chafed at the army's love affair with useless pomp and circumstance. When he said he wanted the war to be over, he consistently qualified that wish. It should end only on terms that would guarantee it would never have to be fought again. Lizzie, who became ever more politically aware and energized as the war wore on, felt much the same.[85]

Fred Lockley thus remained at his post and served out his term until mustered out in June 1865.[86] A naturalized American citizen, he was devoted to the Union, and he felt that devotion fervently, but he was never a committed abolitionist. As one historian put it, "Genuine concern for African Americans seldom preoccupied a population that remained profoundly prejudiced." Moreover, if Union-soldier attitudes toward Blacks were more pragmatic than altruistic, as another historian put it, and if most Northern soldiers thought of Blacks as children—sincere, earnest, and innocent but inferior in maturity just the same—then Fred Lockley was a typical Northern soldier.[87] If most Northern soldiers felt little or no obligation toward freed Blacks and contrabands and either dismissed them as someone else's problem or worse, hated them with racial malice, however, then Lockley was not typical. Writing years later about his regiment's early months in defense of Washington in fall 1862 but using journal notes he had made at the time, he recalled the following:

> We pass these sable laborers twice daily on our way to the drill ground. The women and children with what few idlers happen to be about run to the creek in the rifle-pit, that divides their camp from the road, to see the soldiers. It is painful to witness the repulsion that holds the races apart. These colored people are here as our auxiliaries and fellow-workmen. They fall forests, grub up roots, delve the soil, terrace the hillsides for roads and build bridges. But for their help, a good portion of this labor would fall on the troops. They are accommodating neighbors, too; many a little service in cooking and mending their women perform with cheerful alacrity. Still their presence is repugnant. We shout curses and ribald insult to them as we pass by; we make indelicate gestures to the women; we relieve our loathing in sotto voce ejaculations of unconfined disgust. Our regiment is new to the service, truly; but that is a breach of discipline, which I, as a non-commissioned officer[,] strive to restrain.[88]

Lockley also dismissed the charge that such people would not work. "Without theorizing on the matter," he said, "it may be stated as a fact that a squad of these contrabands . . . would do more woodchopping and shoveling earth in one hour, than a detail from our regiment of the same number would do in half a day. I have watched these contrabands by the hour. Their work was lightened by song or hilarious guffaw, and the heat, which oppressed us northern soldiers, had no debilitating effect on them." He also noted a seeming irony. "These colored laborers were free men now, while we were in bonds, (bound to the country for three years at any rate)."[89] Although a false comparison on many levels, it reflected Frederic's sense of constraint.

In place of prejudice and contempt, Frederic was curious and sympathetic. Condescending he may have been (although he was capable of that with his white comrades as well), he enjoyed their company, especially if he could teach them to read and write. If he did use words typical of his times, such as "sable" and "darkey," he never used truly derogatory epithets of that era toward them, as some of his own Seventh New Yorker comrades did.[90]

To Lockley, as to many others, emancipation was a means to an end. If it could end the war sooner, all to the good. But Lockley did not consider it an essential war aim. "Any permanent settlement of the slave question will suit me," he wrote early on. "I don't want to have this trouble again recurring ten or twenty years hence. Finish the war! And send us home—that's all I ask."[91] As if to underscore the point, Lockley never mentioned the Emancipation Proclamation in his letters home when Abraham Lincoln announced it in September 1862 and again when it went into effect the following January. Still, he found slavery repugnant, even before the war, and he consistently showed sympathy for contrabands and other African Americans during the conflict. Unlike some of his comrades, he was never cruel or derisive to contrabands and those formerly enslaved. In fact, he grew to respect their open hearts and desire for learning, which appealed to his belief in self-improvement.

Like most Northerners, Fred Lockley accepted without much question the inferiority of African Americans, but such inferiority emerged not from innate inadequacies but from circumstance. He had seen slavery up close in St. Louis and New Orleans when he worked flatboats on the Mississippi River in 1849. "The slave atmosphere that surrounded me was repellent to my taste," he recalled years after observing it in Saint Louis, but "I was not qualified to fill the role of abolitionist or reformer . . . so I held it the part of wisdom 'to hear all and see all, and say nothing.'"[92] He simply thought it something he could do little or nothing about. To Lockley, African Americans never had the chance to escape their condition while enslaved, had never had a shot at wider opportunities. With such opportunities, however, they might join the ranks of labor competition among the free. Thus, whatever sense of their inferiority he might have held, it was due to their present disadvantages and not born of his own need to feel superior. But he gained from the experience. Such notions toward African Americans would influence his attitudes toward American Indians after the war.

Frederic maintained his dignity in the most degrading of circumstances: filth, ill-health, poor food, exposure, lack of bathing opportunities, lice, no clean clothes, physical toil at the limits of endurance, violence, lack of refinement or sophistication, loneliness. Hope and constant contact with his wife and family through correspondence seem to have been the main reasons why. He possessed a sense of himself as a writer and hoped to turn his Civil War experiences into published writing. More important, his letters to Elizabeth show an increasing sense of his making a meaningful contribution to the war—as commissary, as sergeant major, as records keeper and adjutant, as someone respected for special skills, and ultimately as an officer and judge advocate. All that powered his determination to survive his enlistment term, return to his family, and get on with a better life.

For Elizabeth, it was important to be sympathetic and supportive; to ask for his encouragement, support, and confidence; and, especially, to confirm his faith in her ability to do the right things as wife, mother, and head of household in his absence. Maturity in the relationship is revealed in the deepening unconditional faith they had in each other, evidenced by her ability to chide or tease him and growth of his sense of boundaries with her—how critical he dared be. He was clearly her intellectual superior—he was too well read and had absorbed what he read too well not to be. But when he was too critical of her, as he sometimes was, it undermined her sense of self-confidence, in addition to her trust in his sympathies and support for her. That in turn undercut her ability to assure him and give him what he needed most: a sense that, as he navigated a very unstable world, he had a stable home life to look forward to while he was away. He depended on her as his anchor; she needed his assurance that she provided that anchor.[93]

In August 1862, however, Elizabeth and Frederic could see none of this ahead of them. As their correspondence shows, they took it a day and a letter at a time, riding the ups and downs of hope and despair, of enthusiasm and despondency, of impatience and fortitude. Amid it all, the lived experience of two individuals, very much in love during turbulent times, shone through.

2

Days of Roman Heroism
August–September 1862

Frederic's first letter announced his enlistment the same day he was formally enrolled in Company I of what would become the Seventh New York Volunteer Heavy Artillery Regiment. It was addressed to Lizzie's aunt, Maria H. Mair of Schuylerville, New York. Not quite forty miles northeast of Albany, Schuylerville was a small village then and remains so today. Located in Saratoga County, New York, it dates from before the Revolutionary War and holds prideful claim as the site of the British Army's surrender following the Battles of Saratoga in fall 1777. To the Lockley family, it was important as Aunt Maria's home and the place of Frederic and Elizabeth's courtship and marriage. "I have enlisted," he announced to the widowed Mrs. Mair, "and Lizzie is reconciled to her fate." Elizabeth may have been doubtful, but Fred was not.

The following letters show the roller coaster of emotions, likes and dislikes, family concerns about money, disagreements about religion, and feeling out of Fred and Lizzie's relationship that emerge during the early days of his enlistment. Early on, Fred's letters were full of enthusiasm for his new adventure. He even declared he felt no homesickness. Such zeal and heady independence quickly dissolved into longing for home and confessions of being a grumbler, even as he cared for sick comrades and lamented ill treatment of formerly enslaved people who worked as contrabands near camp.

Dear Madame,

I have enlisted—and Lizzie is reconciled to her fate. The spirit of
'76 is awake again—the whole country is aroused—recruits are
pouring in actually faster than the recruiting officers can take
down their names. It is believed by many that in a very few weeks
the second call for 300,000 men[2] can be filled without having
recourse to the obnoxious draft. I have not gone to barracks yet—
but have passed the medical examination and shall report myself
there tomorrow. The regiment is already eleven hundred strong—
and we expected to be ordered off next week.

. . .

Capt. Springsteed[3] (the capt. of my Co.), a very pleasant officer
who has seen service—promises some office when the regiment
is properly organized; and officers and men begin to know each
other. I suppose they make this promise to every man who desires
one. But I am content to wait[,] feeling satisfied that the same law
that governs organic matter controls moral qualities—they find
their level.

I saw three or four of my subscribers from the Victory[4] yesterday
in Troy—they had just enlisted and were having a good time with
their bounty money.

I wrote my sister[5] last evening to invite her to come to Albany.
I hope she will reach here before I leave. Lizzie has screwed
her courage to the sticking place—but I fear it won't stay there.
Like Bob Acres' valor, before long I expect it will be oozing
through her fingers' ends.[6] She said a brave thing this morning. I
happened to ask her if she did not hope the surgeon would reject
me on the ground of physical disability. "No," she answered with
emphasis—"I would rather take my chance of having you come
back safe—than know you to be unsound."

Have not the days of Roman heroism returned?

Very Truly Yours

[small, oval-shaped photo pasted to letter in place of signature]

Fred Lockley and his regiment were housed in the Albany barracks for a few days before embarking down the Hudson River to Jersey City Landing. Despite the presence of guards, Frederic left the barracks at least once to take his knapsack home to be filled with various items, mostly food, but he was not allowed to leave the barracks again to retrieve it. On August 19, the day his unit marched to the governor's mansion and then to the wharf, he bolted from the ranks to collect it. As his regiment waited several hours at the wharf before boarding ship, Frederic lingered at home—long enough to miss the regiment's transport. But luck was with him. He was able to catch a faster vessel and arrived ahead of his unit at Jersey City no worse for his absence.

At Jersey City, soldiers in his unit were assigned new uniforms and "handsome new Springfield rifled muskets, of which we were not a little proud."[7] From Jersey City Landing, they waited to board train cars to cross the New Jersey countryside, hurrahed all the while as they passed through cheering crowds. Ultimately, they reached the outskirts of the capital, and Frederic took time to detail his journey in his first letter to Elizabeth on August 24.

Camp Alexandria, D.C.[8]

Sunday Aug[t] 24th 1862

My dear wife,

I know you are anxiously expecting a letter from me—but I really have had no time to write to you before. This is Sabbath morning. We have at length reached our destination, and I propose to give you a brief recital of our adventures so far.

After leaving you on the dock at Albany I went quietly below; thinking I might as well begin soldier life at once, I laid my knapsack down for a pillow and enjoyed a good night's rest. I hope you did the same. The boat reached New York about nine. I called upon M[r] Fry,[9] and then went to M[r] North. Elizab[h] Hill[10] accompanied me to Jersey City, where I found our reg[t] lying off in the stream, while the 16th Maine[11] were taking the cars. She talks of paying you a visit next Saturday to stay over Sunday with you. Make her welcome, for she takes a lively interest in you and the children. At Jersey City we received our muskets, Springfield pattern—a very light and beautiful arm.[12] We started about 6 p.m.—were well rec[d] all thro' N.J. and reached Phil[a] by 2 in the morning. The whole reg[t] was marched from the ferry station into a spacious refectory where we found a sumptuous breakfast spread for every man. We learned that the patriotic citizens of this place regale every union soldier on his way to the wars with a cordial welcome, and a handsome meal, sending him on his way rejoicing.[13] We sat down on the curb stone till day light, and then piled into a lot of freight cars fitted up with benches—and started upon our next stage to Baltimore. We reached there at 2 p.m., and quitting the cars marched thro' the city to the Southern depôt. Loyal demonstrations were showered upon us thro' the whole march. Arrived at the depôt, we loafed around for three or four hours, which interval a large number of our men occupied in getting drunk as fiddlers.

Our next journey was to Washington (38 miles) where we landed about midnight. We were marched into a building which looked like an exaggerated barn, and here we were told to take our quarters for the night. The men took the matter good humoredly. The 16th Maine had taken possession of one side [of] the building—so we stacked arms—set a guard—dis-cussed the blessings of a soldier's life, and then spread our blankets for sleep. As the boys had made such free use of liquor, our colonel prohibited all access to the city—so all that remained to us was to loiter about until we received orders to march. Towards ten o'clock our colonel ordered the regiment to pick up and form in line for marching. It was intensely hot—our knapsacks were heavy— and we had a march of nine miles before us. Our company was the third in line; and as we stood heavily laden in the broiling sun waiting for the stragglers to be bro[t] up into the ranks—we saw the two companies in our front unpack knapsacks and load them into government wagons. Without orders our company lost no time in unstrapping their knapsacks and sitting down on them. By and bye, the colonel appeared and ordered us to march. Our captain (who is an excellent man, by the way, and a good officer) rated us for acting without orders, and ordering knapsacks on our backs, marched us on our hot and dusty way. The labor was immense. Nine miles in that intolerable heat, with the sands scorching the soles of our feet, while our comrades marched lightly ahead was

August–September 1862

too much for us untried soldiers. We began to straggle—some jumped into street cars, some hired passing vehicles—and all were discontented and unsoldierly. As we approached the limits of the city of Magnificent Distances, our orderly made a contact with a darkey teamster to carry those damned infernal knapsacks for a shilling apiece, and I was the first to fire mine into his wagon. After advancing five miles we halted and broke ranks—and to have seen the poor devils throw themselves down begrimed with dust and sweat, and panting with parching heat, would have moved your tenderest pity. Several fainted—some rushed to the hydrants and poured water over their heads and breasts—while a dozen benevolent darkeys were unable to satisfy our demand for more water. I made for a handsome residence on the corner of the street, and rung at the bell, being unwilling to wait till the clamors of the others were silenced. The proprietor seeing my uniform banged to the inner hall doors and the inmates closed all the blinds. "Boys," I halloed, "here's a secesh house, they've shut the doors in my face." "Batter his doors in," shouted a number of voices, and half a dozen approached to put the demand in execution. Our lieutenant stayed the tumult promptly—and Secretary Seward happening at that moment to approach in his carriage—we gathered around him, gave him nine rousing cheers—and receiving his congratulations, were restored to good humor. After a rest we resumed our march—and arrived in Tannelytown[14] late in the afternoon. We were halted in the woods, our baggage and commissary stores dumped upon the grass, and a thousand hot, hungry and tired men left to shift for themselves. Arms were stacked—knapsacks selected—some men were detailed to fetch wood and water—the quartermaster giving out stores axes and other implements to provide us a meal. I and several others set to work to build a fireplace to boil water for coffee. No one volunteering for cook, the office fell upon me, and I was kept busy till dark, distributing plates and drinking pans—and serving out rations to the entire company.[15] Tents were raised—and by nine o'clock we were all ready for bed.

At 2 the next day we were again ordered off, this time to Fort Alexandria in Maryland.[16] I should say three companies—the rest of the regiment being destined for some other place. Our captain

ordered us to strap on knapsacks, the weather still blazing hot—
but the boys were ahead of him. While he was at the colonel's
quarters—we piled our baggage into some empty commissary
wagons, and found musket, cartouche box—havresac [*sic*], and
canteen just as much as we wanted to carry. The distance was seven
miles—we halted for rest t[w]o or three times by the way—and
reached the encampment just at dusk. The same performance of
selecting baggage and raising tents had to be gone thro'—but as it
was late we determined to cook no supper that night. Imagine our
satisfaction when we saw the Rhode Island 10ᵗʰ come rushing into
our tent with abundance of fragrant hot coffee—and two barrels of
ship crackers. The Rhode Island tenth leave for home tomorrow—
and Co. I take their place in the fort—we move in when they leave.
Our regiment is being divided up into small parcels for garrison
duty. We are to be a heavy artillery regᵗ. and shall be exercised in
both artillery and infantry drill. I have been busy all the forenoon
in building a fireplace—and cooking for the boys a blowout
of soup. I sent to a neighboring farm house for potatoes, and
onions—and the captain complimented me by telling me it was
the best soup he had ever tasted. I had the choice offered to me
by the orderly as being either cook or corporal—and as I prefer
to learn the duties of a soldier—I decided upon the latter, so my
culinary career is ended. This doesn't preclude me getting up an
occasional extra dish for my own mess—when I get the materials
for furnishing one. Uncle Sam furnished his soldiers abundantly—
our rations are just double in amount what I can eat. I have just
been called from my tent to stow away 184 loaves of bread—what
we shall do with it all I cannot conceive. We can trade it to the
farmers for milk and vegetables—so we have the prospect of good
living before us. I have not time to write more—but will write to Mʳ
Duncan[17] and other friends in a few days. We have not [been] paid
our last $50 dollars bounty yet—when I receive it I will forward it to
you. I hope my sister has reached Albany—and is happily installed
in your household—Write on receipt of this—address Co. I 113ᵗʰ
Regᵗ. N.Y. Vol. Fort Alexandria D.C. My love to the children—I will
write to each of them pretty soon—I send some stamps—as I have
more than I want. Give this letter to Mʳ Duncan and Mʳˢ Bull[18] to
read. I think I shall like soldiering—but we have [had] a laborious

disagreeable time in getting here. My best love to you—pet—I hope to hear from you soon—I don't consider myself out of reach of home.

With affectionate regards to Mrs Bull and other friends—I am very devotedly Yours

F.E. Lockley

Five days later, Frederic posted a short note to Elizabeth to say they were on alert. The Second Battle of Bull Run[19] was underway, and they could hear the booming cannon from their post among the burgeoning defenses of Washington DC. Even as Frederic and his regiment had been making their way from Albany to the Washington DC area, events in northern Virginia had moved with stunning rapidity. As Union General George B. McClellan withdrew from east of Richmond, Robert E. Lee, now head of the Army of Northern Virginia, had moved swiftly north to engage Gen. John Pope's Army of Virginia.

Fort Alexandria D.C.
Augt 29th 1862

My dear little Pet—

I have only a few minutes to write you a brief note—as we are on the alert—the camp being full of war's alarms. It is reported here that half a dozen of Pope's dragoons passed our fort, fugitives from a lost battle—who state that the enemy is only seven miles distant—and likely to advance in this direction. This has set our colonel to work. At 2 a.m. we were called to arm—10 rounds of cartridges served and a strong picket force posted outside the gates. We are also busy practising on the big guns—and only ask a couple of weeks preparation in order to give a good account of ourselves. Our boys behave well—and are perfectly willing to be called into action. My health and spirits are excellent. I am ashamed to tell you that I have not felt home sickness one moment. That is yet to come, perhaps. There is nothing in soldiering yet that appears so very formidable—we have excellent grub and abundance of it—there is actually more wasted in this one company than would suffice to feed all the poor of Troy.

I have very comfortable quarters—mess with seven non-commissioned officers—have started a private cook-house, and "fix-up" a number of little extras which have purchased a high opinion of my culinary attainments from the members of my mess—But since this alarm of attack we are kept so busy with artillery practice and infantry drill—that cooking will have to go for the present.

My love to my dear little pets—I will try to write to them on Sunday. I enclose $23—there is yet $27 due. Please to put $27 to the amo' and put it in the savings to the credit of my sister. I hope to hear from you pretty soon—and am anxious to get a N.Y. paper from you. A new reg' encamped in our sight yesterday—they say it is the new Troy regt. The weather is cooler—and remarkably fine. This is a very desolate country—if we see a soul stirring—we suppose him to be a rebel scout.

Love to my sister and my dear little lonely wife—

From your devoted husband
F.E. Lockley

As he adjusted to soldier life, Fred began receiving Lizzie's letters with news from home, including that his sister, Emma, had arrived to help with maintaining the household. For whatever reason, none of Elizabeth's letters to him from 1862 and early 1863 survive, so we cannot know for sure how she responded to his saying he felt no homesickness—yet—but she could not have been pleased.

Camp Alexander
Aug' 31ˢᵗ 1862

Ma plus chére Femme

As I handed my last letter to the Capt. to send to Washington[,] I was overjoyed to receive your delightful epistle. I heartily thank you for the unaffected expression of such unsurpassed love and devotion—it is most pleasing to my feelings—but you must learn to acquire <u>fortitude</u>. The sacrifice is asked of you by your country—and a cheerful and unflinching compliance is becoming on your part. I reflect that the term is but short—and every day that passes tends to make it less.

We are full of bustle and excitement here—being in momentary expectation of attack. The non-commissioned officers have been pracitsing on the great guns—and most of us are familiar with the exercise. We had a squad of Pennsylvania cannoneers from Fort Massachusetts sent to the fort to lend us a hand in its defence— but late last night they received sudden orders to march to Chain Bridge[20]—and their place is supplied by an equal number of New York artillery. Yesterday a severe battle was fought near here— the incessant booming of cannon was heard thro' the livelong day—and at evening it was reported in the fort [that] Pope and Stonewall Jackson had had a heavy fight at Fairfax C. H. that we had lost 15–000 killed wounded & prisoners—and were victors of the field.[21] Jackson is hemmed in between McClelland's and Pope's forces—and it is thought his entire army will be destroyed. Rebel reinforcements are expected to be sent on to him—and it is with these gentry that we are preparing to deal. Like Jordan—this is a mighty hard road for rebel travel—innumerable forts bristle all the way from here to the Capital.

Last night there was a call to arms—Gun squads (six to a gun) were told off and ordered out with overcoat and blanket to lie by their guns. I had been out on picket for 24 hours previous, to watch the river (Potomac), and had already turned in and fallen asleep. I arose at the call—seized my musket (each man has been served with 40 rounds of cartridge) and spreading my blanket on the sod in my station at the cannon—threw my overcoat over me and was sound asleep. On Friday night while on Picket—I saw a party of horsemen approaching—and went out and challenged them. They proved to be the major and adjutant of our regiment accompanied by the Lieut-colonel of a Pennsylvania cavalry reg.ᵗ which had been cut up at Manassas the day previous. Five hundred men rode past me on their way to an adjacent farm where they reposed overnight—four hundred of their number being left behind them on the battle field. They were an intelligent well-spoken set of fellows—and seemed perfectly indifferent to the sad fate of their fellows. I don't understand this singular fact—but a camp life seems to alter a man's nature. To take a man from the refinements of home—and all the careful police protection of the comfort and security of life—and then to plant him here where havoc and desolation surround him—and his social standing is reduced to a level with the lowest and most ignorant—one would think would disgust him with life. But it has no such effect. Our minds adapt themselves to circumstances without an apparent effort—and we go in for superficial jollity and enjoyment just as naturally as water runs down hill. You will dislike me, I know, but I must repeat that I have not felt one moment's unhappiness or longing after home since I left you—and when I was abruptly woke up last night and ordered to take my station at the gun in expectation of momentary action—I went and lay down there and fell asleep with no more emotion than if I had moved from one bed chamber to another.

I rec^d another delightful letter from you this morning—together with a Journal. I am pleased to learn that Emma has joined you—she will be a great comfort and help you. The boys are equipping for picket service, it is raining steadily—and they will have a wearisome twenty-four hours of it. Great vigilance is demanded of us, which makes our work pretty constant. Please send me six stamps—I have had to supply my whole mess with them. Love to all—and a thousand embraces to my little loving Sweetheart.

Thine

F.E. Lockley

In a follow-up letter of September 2, Frederic said he had more leisure, now that Stonewall Jackson's threat to the capital had diminished.[22] His company would not be detailed to bury the dead at Second Manassas, but it had already lost seven deserters. The regiment's companies had been split up among forts north of Washington, with Frederic's Company I along with Company B assigned to Fort DeRussy.[23] As for himself, Frederic set up a small cookhouse outside the gate and prepared mess. Three days later, he acknowledged receiving more of Elizabeth's letters amid bustling military activity and life in a tent camp.

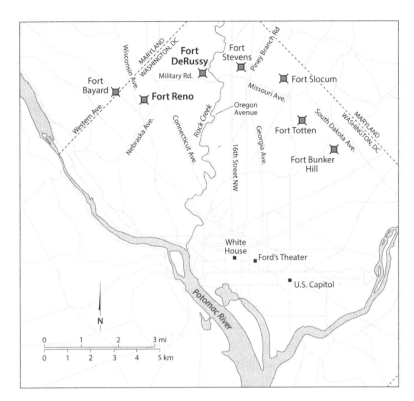

MAP 1. Forts that made up the northern defenses of Washington DC included
Fort DeRussy and Fort Reno, where Frederic Lockley was assigned from
August 1862 to May 1864. Created by Bill Nelson.

Fort DeRussey[24] Md

Sept 5th 1862

My dear Wife

I received your third letter a few days ago and was disappointed to
learn that you had not received two letters I had previously written
you. I have since learnt that letters for the East are held over in
Washington several days—I suppose to prevent the publication of
news—therefore it is fair to conclude that they have come to hand
since.

   . . .

    Events are thickening around us. At our former encampment,
Tanelly town[25] ab[t]. 4 miles from here—Sumner's & Banks's divisions[26]

are now stationed, and more troops are pouring in incessantly. Some of our boys were there yesterday—and myriads of horse, foot, and artillery there assembled fill them with wonderment. But the condition they report the poor fellows to be in is truly pitiable. Officers with their uniforms soiled, threadbare and ragged—and whole regiments of men shirtless, shoeless, and vermin-infested— their sole baggage one strip of canvass to protect them at night.[27] And with this example before us—for us to complain of hardships seems the grossest ingratitude that man can be guilty of. What we waste from our abundant rations—these poor war-worn veterans would be happy to gather from the dust for their sole nourishment.

. . .

I will attempt to describe to you a life on "the tented field." Our tents are exactly six feet square, sloping from a ridge pole six feet high. Into this tent five men are quartered—but to make things more comfortable we have seven. The reason is as follows. When we are messing in the fort seven of us gravitated together—and finding things worked together harmoniously—we have been unwilling to break up—and so continue to bed and board together. Two are sergeants from Rensselaerville[28]—very respectable—well-behaved young men—whom it is a pleasure to be associated with. The third is Orderly Sergeant (the highest non-commissioned officer who will soon be promoted to 2d. lieut.[).] This man is a study—a thorough soldier, having almost the entire care of the company—and stern as Ajax in his disciplines. But in his social hours the merriest dog you ever heard of. The next is commissary Parker,[29] a useful man having access to the stores—but one whom I think the least of. The fifth is a Corporal Joe Rogers[30]—rough—genial and whole-souled. He is like a character of Dickens—and presents a specimen of genuine human nature. He and Commissary Parker are the providers of our board— like last night they bro'. in some superb secession chickens, and at this moment Joe Rogers is out with his haversack to gather a mess of peaches for supper. Then there is a young lad who will not be shook off.[31] I am greatly attached to him and he to me—he is lippy and fast, but ingenuous and entirely free from vice. When we came to tents—as none of the adults would give up the number of his mess—I informed this lad that the disagreeable necessity of his changing his quarters existed—that for him to stay with us was a physical impossibility.

He acquiesced—but failed to act. He always presents himself at our mess—and sleeps outside the door of our tent. I call him our <u>Fidus Achates</u>,[32] but the joke is lost upon these Latinless dogs.

Well this family you may suppose renders our tenement somewhat crowded. If you could peep into the confined space when we rise at roll call in the morning, and see the confusion of muskets, accoutrements—blankets, overcoats—and other endless litter you would give up the idea of tidying the room in utter despair. Like all men (whose natural instinct (as Fanny Fern[33] says) is dirt) not one ever thinks of putting away a thing. After roll-call every morning, while these sluggards are loafing ab'. smoking their pipes—or hanging around the cook's log fire, I am kept busy for one good hour—packing away Knapsacks (they serve us for pillows of a night) folding up blankets—airing overcoats and <u>charing</u> up generally. The inevitable untidiness and discomfort of such a mode of life sometimes quite discourage me—but then I grow indifferent, console myself with the determination "to let it went," and don't care a—.

The weather is lovely—balmy sunshiny days—and cold dew-bedrippled nights. The health of the company is excellent—with the exception of one miserable counterfeit of humanity who takes a pleasure being sick and haunting the encampment with his spectre looks. War alarms thicken around us—we drill industriously—and only ask to be let alone another month. Then we shall be ready for the foe. It is not likely we shall be attacked by the rebels here—but we are in danger of sympathizers. To guard against this we have strong pickets posted out 2 miles on the road—have the camp vigilantly guarded and sleep with our rifles by our sides. It may be bad taste—but I would rather have my wife to hug.

We all rejoice that we have enlisted—not that as predilection for military life is so prominent—but because from the way things have taken—we should all have been hounded into it—and have lost the bounty by our delay. I am greatly obliged for your newspapers—when I directed you to send them so particularly, I supposed there would be a scarcity of them here—but the reverse is the case—so one Newspaper a week is all I will trouble you for.

Devotedly Yours

F.E. Lockley

Robert E. Lee had begun his Maryland campaign, which would conclude with the Battle of Antietam on September 17 and Lee's retreat the next day. From his defensive post on the northern edge of Washington DC, Frederic was optimistic and noted an abundance of new Union recruits.

Fort De Russey D.C.
Sept. 9th 1862

Why what is the matter wife? Not a letter for the last sixteen weeks! I can't stand it—so it's no use talking. Give me bread and beef enough, and a letter <u>twice</u> a <u>week</u> from home, then I am good for one rebel, <u>sartin</u>. But if you pretermit my inspiration from home, it is like depriving me of the light of day. Something is wanting—I lose my elasticity—take to immoderate smoking, and let my arms go rusty. Do not neglect me—I humbly beseech you. . . .

. . .

Our vigilance in camp is somewhat abated—a man is allowed time to breathe again now. The unending march of Federal forces without sight of our camp still continues—since last Thursday over 300,000 men have marched by and the cry is 'Still they come!' Reports reach us that 100,000 rebels have crossed into Maryland, that Pennsylvania is invaded, that Ohio is menaced, and that the rebels['] forces are overrunning Kentucky.[34] The feeling here is that it is all perfectly right. Let the devils spread themselves, as we have been doing lately—while we concentrate our scattered forces—which are increasing in numbers at the rate of ten full regiments a day. By and bye, when we turn on the foe, we will administer such a home-thrust as shall send him howling to his gods! I admit that such a policy seems like letting the lion in to see if you can turn him out again—but there are occasions when the lion may come upon you and overwhelm you—and then your only policy is to take time enough to make a sure thing of him.

We hear that the whole northern States have gone crazy with the military fever—that every man capable of bearing arms is off to the war. I pity the poor girls—what will they do? You are fortunate in having secured your victim—altho' he is away to the war. For I hold that it is better to have the prospect of his future return and enjoyment than the very slim chance of matrimony which the present market affords.

I've had my hair cut so short you couldn't take hold of it with your teeth. Love to Emma—may she be gifted with the spirit of early writing.

F.E. Lockley

Frederic wrote to his children often, but few of those letters survive. This one, to his second-oldest daughter, Emma Louise "Dollie," may have been saved originally by Elizabeth but was ultimately preserved among the family papers of Frederic's daughter Gertrude.[35] In this letter, Frederic, who speaks to Dollie as he would to an adult friend, described two colorful scenes from camp not found elsewhere.

Camp De Russey, D.C.
Sept 9th 1862

My dearest little Dolly Dumpling,

Because I have delayed writing to you till last, you are not to suppose that I love you least. To make amends for the delay I will try and write you the nicest letter.

First, I must tell you of an excitement we had in camp last evening. About dusk a fugitive slave came into camp and reported that a secessionist had come into their quarters, whom they suspected of being a rebel spy. I should tell you that just below our fort there is an encampment of wood-chippers from Maine who are busy cutting down all the trees for miles around to give us a chance to shoot the rebels with our big guns, if they should deem it prudent to approach. Well, quite a number of escaped negroes have attached themselves to these Maine boys, to whom they have given quarters, and they help them to chop, and make themselves useful generally. It was one of these negroes who came to the camp to report the secessionist. Our lieutenant immediately sent a sergeant with a file of men to arrest him and bring him to Post head quarters. We all ran to hear the examination. One darkey charged him with having served in the rebel army—another charged him with having been one in a conspiracy to kidnap the witness, and a third testified that he had been lashed by him. The accused declared himself innocent of all these charges, said he was a carpenter, and had merely come to get employment as a wood-chopper. The lieutenant held him in custody till the return of Capt. Jones,[36] who, on his return, heard the evidence over again—deemed it unreliable, and discharged the prisoner from custody.

Yesterday morning, we had a big fat man come into camp, having a policeman with him, who charged our boys with having stolen six of his chickens the previous night. No one had been outside our lines except ten men detailed for picket, and four of them had been stationed near to his house. The tents and haversacs of these were examined but as no chickens were to be found it was concluded that Co. P was innocent of the charge.

It is exactly three weeks to-day since I left home and although the time has past [*sic*] pleasantly enough, it really seems like three months. Mama tells me that you are good girls—and are going to school again. I shall be so glad when you will be able to write me such nice letters as Mama does. But then I don't want to stay away from home all that time. Some think we shall be discharged before our time is up—which is not unlikely—as the war will certainly be finished during the coming winter. Still I do not allow myself to hope any such thing for fear of disappointment.

I am corporal of the guard to day, and I will tell you what I have to do. The orderly sergeant gives me a list of names who are to mount guard for the next twenty-four hours; that is—the detachment is divided into three squads and each squad watches for two hours. It is my business under the direction of the Sergeant of the guard, to muster the different relief every two hours—and take them round to their different posts—so that the men who have been watching for two hours can have rest for four hours—when I shall call upon them again.

I wish you could see us drilling out in the field—you would laugh to see our motions. This morning while we were on duty and even deployed in line—our cook happened to pass along the road, and one of the boys called him to speak to him. When he had nearly approached our line, our orderly gave the command (just for fun, you know,) "Charge bayonets! Double quick, march!" Our two ranks levelled bayonets—gave a deafening yell, and charged in the direction of the poor cook, like a set of crazy fellows. He seeing the line of bristling steel, levelled at his ears, and approaching rapidly towards him—turned round to run away—but caught his foot and fell. I and the man in my rear fell over him, and the men next to me for mischief threw themselves upon me, and in an instant the poor frightened cook had about fifty men piled on the top of him. When we let him crawl out he swore at us some, and said if it was intended for a joke he couldn't see it.

My warmest love to your Sisters, my little pets are always in my thoughts. I shall write to Mama altho' I have had no letters from her I don't know how long.

Your loving Papa

F.E. <u>Lockley</u>

3

It's All for Our Country
September–November 1862

Only two weeks after declaring he felt no homesickness, Frederic admitted to being homesick. Noting that Elizabeth's letters were his greatest pleasure, he was disappointed by Emma's concerns, apparently about money, but he urged Lizzie not to suffer materially because of his absence. Likely reflecting their continued hopes for a short war, he assured her optimistically that he would be rewarded for his service after the war. Amplifying on the story he told Dolly about contrabands, he decried how his fellow soldiers treated the escaped former slaves employed around them and then related a comical incident of spilling ink on his head. With that, he inadvertently foreshadowed a degree of ineptitude that would haunt him—with near-fatal consequences—while on campaign in Virginia two years later.

Fort De Russey D.C,

Sept 13th 1862

My dearest Bride,

The date of my letter reminds me that it is just one month since I enlisted. Dear me! my time of service will run out before I shall realize that I am away from home. I have made up my mind to a great sacrifice—and I fear I shall have to re-enlist for another term of three years before I shall be satisfied that the sacrifice has been made.

Your little trivial note enclosed in my Sister's very sensible letter suited me to death. Byron remarks that the vibrations of the electric chain of sympathy cannot be accounted for—that a small

44

field flower may send a man's thoughts coursing thro' ten years of his past experiences. So that small unstudied piece of elegant pensive triviality came upon me with such a freshness—it at once resuscitated in my mind those happy hours spent at your Aunt's, and all those glorious rides in the stage home, with the sun gilding my early journeyings and my mind dazzled and circumfused with speechless love, that, not withstanding I write amid the den of this crowded and noisome guard house my mind is full of the home and peaceful atmosphere of Schuylerville.

Sept 14th A ludicrous incident interrupted my enthusiasm yesterday. I had placed my small ink bottle against the wall for security, and some one moving, upset it. I then placed it in my cap and laid my cap down before me. The guard at the sally port immediately after singing out, "Turn out the guard!" (This is called out by the guard when he sees a general or a field office approach, that the sergeant may have the guard all posted to present arms as he enters the fort.) I threw my cap upon my head, and the ink (like Aaron's oil[1]) ran down upon my head and overflowed my neck and ears.

I sent a letter to M[rs] Bull a day or two ago. Directly after sealing it, we had a crowd of 260 contrabands marched into a meadow adjoining—and yesterday our 2d lieut. went to survey a road to Washington. Those darkies are to do the work and, I suppose, we white folks are to boss the job. . . . It is painful to see with what harsh feelings, our troops regard these helpless timid fugitives. All kinds of insults are shouted to the poor wretches as they pass them, and they hound and chase them worse than a Southern planter. . . .

This is Sabbath afternoon—the weather is lovely—I am sitting in the shade of a peach tree as I write this—half a dozen of Co B's men are playing cards round the spring—our boys are all wiling their time away in their tents or the fort. I was on guard yesterday—and snatched but a few moments' sleep last night under one of the big guns. This afternoon I feel used up and slightly homesick. I long to run home to spend the afternoon with my wife and little ones and return early to my duty tomorrow.

The major held inspection this morning (I and twenty others being on guard escaped.) Quarters were cleaned out—arms and accoutrements burnished—and the men all compelled to have a general fumification of clothes and persons. A new commissariat tent has been raised to hold stores—and two of our family— the orderly & commissary sergeants take up their abode therein. This makes more room in the tent for us—which will detract greatly from our discomfort. Did you receive $23 in a letter from Ft. Alexander—you have not mentioned the receipt of it. There seems to be some trouble in getting goods here—if you have not despatched my box you need not do so until you hear further from me. If it is already gone well and good.

I hope you are not uneasy about the future—Emma's letter made me feel quite unhappy. It is not unlikely that some provision will be made for the families of the men who are in the reg^t.—if you wish information—Mr Duncan can obtain it of Geo. Dawson or Hamilton Harris.[2] The rent is paid to Nov. 1st. Emma Pays Oct 1st. Do not suffer I beg of you—because I should be quite melancholy if I tho't you were in want. You will not move before Nov 1—and we will see by that time what turns up. Write us a good busy letter on rec.^{t} of this—a letter from you is the greatest treat I have—it is like a message from heaven. Tell the children that the major bro^t. a deserter from Co. B into the fort yesterday—with his hands handcuffed behind him—he is going to send him to head quarters at Tanelly town to be tried and he tells him he will be shot. I would rather be shot by the enemy. Love to the dear Children—Emma says she is proud of them. They are so well-behaved. Good bye dearest—I send a kiss to all of you.

F.E. Lockley

Frederic delighted in receiving her letters, but ill health had invaded camp, and he was tasked constantly with caring for the sick. For the next three years, he would administer to the unwell repeatedly and bolster others' sagging spirits willingly. One comrade— Stephen Treadwell[3]—would acknowledge that such care from Lockley saved his life.

September–November 1862

Fort De Russey D.C,
Sept 19th 1862

Ma chére petite Femme,

You are better than good—you overwhelm me with your gracious
favors. Three delightful letters in one week, falling as the gentle rain
from Heaven upon the place beneath. My greatest pleasure is to
receive letters from you—my next greatest pleasure is to write them.
This latter pleasure I have had to forego lately—as all my spare time
has been devoted to nursing my sick tent-mates. It has been very
sickly with us lately—fever and ague and diarrhea being the principal
cases. Yesterday—at roll call our sanitary condition began to be quite
alarming—⅓ of our number were reported unfit for duty. The weather
had been murky for some time previously—and it was raining then—
our sick men were lying between damp muddied blankets on the
steaming round: every tent you looked into some flushed & feverish
countenance met your gaze. I took it upon myself to inform the Capt.
that he would have all his company down sick if he didn't compel his
men to floor their tents. Setting the example, I and Corp^l Jo[e] Rogers
(a sort of Mark Tapley[4]—one of the best fellows in the world) went to
a neighboring farmer and represented to him how the case stood. We
told him we must have boards somewhere and were willing to pay for
them—but we must have boards. He took the hint. He made some
halting professions of his willingness to oblige us all in his power—and
to prove it—pulled down his barn and sold us the old boards at 2c/a
foot. The darned critter knew that if he hadn't done so—he wouldn't
have had a board left on his farm by day light the next morning.

The weather is delightful again this morning—cool refreshing
breezes, bringing health & healing on their wings—and dry floors
to our tents have already worked a wonderful improvement in the
health of the camp.

The talk in camp is that we are likely to be stationed here
during the winter. You needn't dread to witness rejoicings at the
news of victory, there is not much danger of your husband's life
being sacrificed as the price of it.

With love to the young ones. Emma and the old 'oman I am
very distinctly yours

—F.E.L.—

A week later, Frederic observed that soldiering was an "uncomfortable, loafing kind of life" that he would be glad to get shed of. "Still, I greatly prefer it to the book business." Food and plenty of it kept him in good spirits. Responding to her fear that he was deprived, he asks, "Do you call duck—roasted and stuffed, purchased of a negress, a privation? Do you call apple pies, and cakes and excellent butter procured of the sutler privations? Are rations of pork—and beef (salted and fresh) vegetable soup, rice, excellent fresh bread, potatoes, and coffee furnished by Uncle Sam, are these privations? I will wager you an even sixpence that there is more good provisions wasted or left in the cook's hands by our mess of 4 men—than would suffice to feed your whole family." With that, he enclosed a letter to be sent to his mother in England.[5]

Frederic had been writing home regularly and somewhat voluminously about his life in camp, and he did so again in early October to paint a scene, innocently enough, of soldiers gathered to discuss the Bible and religion only to have a thoughtful discussion dissolve into badinage. Till now, most everything between himself and home had been upbeat, but this letter opened a clear rift with Lizzie and his sister Emma, who took religion more gravely than Fred and his comrades. His purpose, he would later say, was simply to relate stories of camp life and not to take religion too seriously, but the clash of views with those at home signaled a growing tension, one perhaps less related to the spiritual than to financial concerns.

Fort De Russey D.C.

Oct. 9th 1862

Ma chére Femme

On Tuesday morning last I found myself in the woods, and[,] thinking of home[,] the disposition to write to you came upon me. I expected a letter from you that same afternoon (we receive the mail at 3 o'clock) and having no writing materials with me, I concluded that rather than travel thro' the scorching hot sun for stationery, I would defer writing 'till the next war. Alas! All the warm and brilliant images that then peopled my mind, have exhaled and gone to heaven. Your delightful letter came, a metaphor of the writer's constancy—and I seize an hour in the cool of the morning to hold sweet commune with you. I write in the lee of my tent which throws a few feet of shade, and a refreshing breeze fans my face, forming a delightful relief from the oppressive air which reigns inside. One of my tent-mates, a Serg[t] Treadwell—after a long and severe sickness, has resumed his duties this morning—and now Serg[t] Fault[6] is down sick. These sick men keep me busy.

If I were seated by mine own hearth[,] I could not be in a position of greater safety than I am here. Our reg.[t] forms part of the second brigade for the defence of Washington north of the Potomac. This throws us entirely out of range of the conflict; and our officers seeing that we are in for a good time, are purchasing iron bedsteads and hair mattresses and are further engaging board at the neighboring farm-houses for their wives during the winter. The talk in camp is that we are to build log huts for quarters during the winter; and when Spring returns to gladden the earth, how much of the belligerency of the rebellion, think you, is likely to remain?

The subject of religious exercises was discussed in our tent some two weeks ago—on the occasion of an attempted revival by Serg[t] Richwine[7]—and one or two others. We have a large proportion of decent men in our company—who at home would be decent church going folk, and when the subject was introduced[,] they spontaneously advocated the experience. I am good humoredly labeled "The Professor," and Serg[t] Richwine referred to me for aid in exhortation. I fully favored the proceeding—while at the same time my stomach fairly sickened at the miserable burlesque vision present to my prophetic eye—basing my arguments on the ground that the practice of religion tended to induce decorum, to repress gross habits, and to make us a generally more decent and sober community. Our orderly being present, a man with searching eye and preponderating weight of character, burst out into an immense oath, and added, "Corporal, is that the strongest case you can present?" (This was said in good humor.) Serg[t]. Richwine attempted some penny whistle argument, but could not obtain a hearing. Corporal Berry[8] commenced a digression on the conversion of S[t] Paul and was requested to <u>bottle up</u>. The discussion then assumed a miscellaneous character; some found Jonah and the whale a stumbling block, and others objected to the morality of God counselling the Jews to borrow valuable articles of their Egyptian neighbors for the purpose of purloining them. Finally[,] we fetched up in geology, and demonstrated from the testimony of the rocks that the mosaic account of the creation was an old wife's tale, and became so hilarious and profane, that poor Sergt Richwine had to leave the assembly. Finally a motion made by Corporal Berry as follows: "Whereas, seeing that this present assembly is composed of such a d——d hard set of sinners that there is no possible redemption, therefore, be it resolved that henceforth we keep perfectly still on the subject of divine exercises in order that the almighty may not know that we are here." This motion was carried with unanimous acclaim and amid vociferous applause, and Corporal Rogers happening to drop in with a bottle of excellent Bourbon whiskey which he had just confiscated from the sutler, we all took a quieting nip around, refilled our pipes, and declared there was no sense in being a soldier if you couldn't have some fun.

My three tent-mates are sick—Riotous living and little to do I expect is the cause of their ailments.

Yours faithfully

F.E.L.

Next day, before receiving any response to his previous letter, Fred noted that a visit to Elizabeth from the Reverend Morrow was undoubtedly pleasant, but "do not let him exercise too great an influence over your mind. Remember there is a terrestrial as well as a celestial sphere."[9] Lizzie was already pure enough for heaven. "He lies who says you are not."[10]

In the meantime, he rejected outright his sister's suggestion that she and his family move to New York City, where Emma and perhaps Lizzie, too, could find work. Such a move would be expensive, foolish, and unrewarding. He noted instead that Mr. Duncan, a local Albany businessman, said a fund was being raised to help families of Union volunteers. She and Emma should rely on that plus his army pay. Sickness in camp persisted, meanwhile, and was now affecting him. He faulted bad water from an impure supply.[11]

Then, having received Lizzie and Emma's reaction to his story of Sergeant Richwine and his tentmates' Bible discussion, he responded angrily. He was not feeling well and admitted to dyspepsia, so it was bad timing, but his illness did not stop him from saying she and Emma placed too much confidence in Sergeant Richwine and not enough in his own spiritual judgment.

Fort De Russey D.C. Oct 19th [1862]

My indignant little Pet,

Your letter came to hand yesterday—welcome as ever. As I feel unwell to-day, I have taken a dose of Herrick's pills, and begged off from duty one day. The boys are all on the parade ground undergoing inspection, so as I have a serious charge hanging over my head, I tho't I would devote a leisure hour to the vindication of my character. The substance of the matter seems to be that I was indiscreet now to write you a slightly exaggerated acc[t]. of an informal meeting held in my tent on the subject of adopting religious services in camp. Whereupon you incontinently fall into a fit of incoherent wretchedness, telling me you were shocked at such sentiments, and begging of me not to try to influence any to believe in them. Emma swells the hue & cry by adding that when I write that I am the means of throwing ridicule on a worthy man, who tries all his influence to infuse a religious feeling in the men. [M]y wife is in a perfect agony for my safety both ["]in this world & the next." I gravely wonder what 'tis all about. "Sentiments!" "Ridicule!" "Agony for my safety!" What sentiments? What ridicule? Re-peruse my narrative, and if you can find one word of mine casting dishonor upon God or Religion you shall have my head for a football.

I enclose a brief extract from my diary, wherein I have expressed my views upon the cause of camp vices. Read it, & tell me whether my views are sound. If their soundness is admitted, you will at once perceive that the law governing camp life is too general & irreversible for any influence that I may exert to be sufficient to remove. My comrades are not children or fools to be led in whatever way a self-appointed leader may seek to direct them. A proportion of them are men with a force of character fully equal to mine own, & instead of making myself obnoxious by walking apart and proclaiming myself one pure man amid a community of sinners, I prefer to follow the apostle Paul's precept "and be all things to all men."

My sole intention in furnishing you such a narrative was to daguerreotype a camp scene for your amusement. If your feelings are so delicate that you cannot witness the asperities of life without pain and dejection [then] . . . it is your duty to infuse into them a healthier & robuster tone of vitality. . . . I wish to be indulgent to you, and would shrink from no sacrifice that might contribute to your happiness. Still, it is your duty to remember that the wife is subject to the husband, and, considering the disparity of our age and experience, I am not unreasonable in requiring you to pay some little attention to my wishes.

Oct 20th—Monday

I am on guard to-day—I am not well—but there are so many of our Co unfit for duty thro' sickness, that I cannot well beg off. I am satisfied that our spring is impure—which causes such general bilious affections. I first quarreled with the bean soup—then with the fat pork—next with the coffee, and abstained from the use of these each in succession. I now go to the creek for drinking water—it is a long walk—but pure water must be had at any cost.

I have been reading over your letter & Emma's addendum, and the sense of hasty & unjust judgment strikes me most forcibly. Have you no more confidence in your husband [than] to believe that he has become so reprobate and graceless that your mind is agonized with fears for the future welfare of his soul? Emma blames me for "throwing ridicule on a worthy man." Before you make a charge, you should have sufficient evidence to maintain it. Where does she get her "worthy man" from. This same Serg[t]. Richwine is one of the purest counterfeits of humanity that ever passed into circulation. Belshazzar[12] was weighted in the balance & found wanting—this man has been weighed—and there is found to be nothing of him. He is in debt to almost every one in camp—he Jeremydiddled[13] one young lad out of $26[00]. The other day he slipped into our tent & stole a pie. When we had an alarm the other night—he was so scared that he fouled himself, and then went on his knees to pray to God for deliverance! Would I cooperate with such a

man in rendering the sacred observances of Religion a hissing &
a reproach thro' the camp? When I join with scoffers in ridiculing
the pious efforts of a good man, it will be when my mind is greatly
changed from what it is. . . .

I love religion in women and children, but not an excess of it—
not so that it cramps or distorts nature. And if any man or woman
comes to you with the story that you are a miserable sinner, and
that all your humiliations and acts of devotion are insufficient
to reconcile you with an offended Maker, on my authority you
will tell him that his doctrine is a lie, and he a blasphemer of the
Almighty. . . .

Ten years from now you and I shall substantially agree in our
views. A prophecy—mark the fulfilment. Love & Kisses, Sweet
wife—My letter will bore you to death but it serves you just right.[14]

F.E. Lockley

The weather soon changed, but Frederic's spirits remained
upbeat, although he regretted that Elizabeth and Emma worried
so much about making ends meet. He should get paid very soon and
urged her again not to go without. As for himself, he ate high on the
hog—literally, after putting his butcher's skills to use on a runaway
pig. Without commenting directly on emancipation, he commends
President Lincoln for trying to end the war through negotiation.
All he wants, he says, is an end to the conflict. It was a conviction
in which he remained steadfast, although he would grow to want
peace only if it resolved forever the issues of secession and slavery.

Fort De Russey D.C.
Nov 6th 1862

Ma chére femme,

I am on picket to day, and write this under serious disadvantages.
The wind is blowing great guns up at the fort, and the weather is
cold; but here in this hollow, we are sheltered from the assaults
of rude Boreas, and with our roaring big fire, manage to keep
ourselves comfortable.

Your letter with Emma's addenda damped my spirits
considerably—I cannot bear to think that you are going to feel

the grip of poverty this winter. We are to be paid in the course of a few days, I believe, that will put $20 in the Chamberlain's hand for your use—you must lay in a store of fuel, flour, potatoes and butter to last you the winter thro'—don't for God's sake go short of wholesome food. Here we live upon the fat of the land, and if I tho't you were in want I would be truly unhappy.

A day or two ago Corp. Rogers and I were on picket, and a small detachment of choice porkers ran by our post on the double quick. Probably their instincts told them they were contraband of war. You would have laughed to see our instant execution of the skirmish drill. Without a word two or three headed them off, while Rogers (who is the most successful forager in the company) seized the finest in the squad—rolled him over—and crammed his havresac down his throat to stop his confounded noise. In an instant we had his throat cut, and poor piggy rolled into the ditch out of sight. As soon as we deemed it safe—I went and dressed him and he turned out 60 lbs of the choicest pig meat you ever saw. There have been fine times in our camp since, but the fun of it is that notwithstanding 25 of the company know of it—not a word has leaked out in the officers['] ears. Soldiers are poor neighbors, I eviz.

Emma expresses surprise at Liz. Hill's strange behavior—but there is nothing to wonder at. Except one who was a sensible consistent woman [his former wife, Agnes], these four sisters are inscrutable—wayward—unstable. Their good intentions never outlive half an hour. . . . Emma was extremely foolish to make such a time because I happened incautiously to say one day that I felt unwell. If you had seen me putting away pork steaks and fried potatoes for breakfast this morning you would have saw there was no danger of my dying just yet. After that little sick spell, I have been as ravenous as a wolf. . . .

. . .

It is reported that Seymour is elected—So be it.[15] I should not have voted for him—but we shall see how it results. Any <u>permanent</u> settlement of the slave question will suit me—only I don't want to have this trouble again recurring ten or twenty years hence. Finish the war! and send us home—that's all I ask. . . .

Your's affectively
F.E. Lockley

As his regiment received new uniforms and waited to build permanent structures for winter, Fred said he would send more money home soon, especially the twenty-five-dollar state bounty still owed him, in addition to two months' back pay.

Fort de Russey Novr 11th 1862

My chére Femme,

I rec'd a letter from Mr Duncan yesterday—which I enclose (of course you will not mention such to him). He states that you are out of coal & flour—which he proposed buying for you without delay. It would be far pleasanter if he would pay you the balance due you— and you purchase as you think fit. Our pay rolls were made out some two weeks since, and two months['] pay is promised us this week—but there seems to be great irregularity in Uncle Samuel's financial proceedings. The $25 state bounty is still unpaid to a few members of Co's I & B; I am told that at head[qrs] the residue of the reg[t]. have been paid. A month ago our capt collected all our certificates for the purpose of having them cashed, and since then he has never alluded to the matter. I don't know whether I have previously explained to you that the money was paid to the regt. At midnight during their passage down the river to New York—but some who were sleeping and those who were absent missed it. I am assured the money is safe—but I am anxious to get possession of it.

Our major is building his winter q[rs] but we have not yet commenced—as no orders have been issued—and we are unwilling to expend money or labor until we have something definite to work on. We are all sick of our present position, and would be very happy to be ordered into active service—but there appears to be no doubt that we are doomed to winter here on the summit of this fortified hill. On every side defensive preparations are in progress—new roads—extensive rifle pits connecting fort to fort, batteries to command every hollow, while the unceasing stroke of the axman is denuding the country of miles of noble forest trees, which are felled and suffered to lie on the ground to rot. At our picket posts we take our axes and cut & slash into the noblest oaks and chestnuts & hickories & pines, and burn up a cord of wood a day at every fire just for amusement. I am getting to be quite a forester; my hands are blistered and sore with the axe helve, but I haven't chopped off any of my toes yet. . . .

. . .

To-day an extra blanket and a p^r blue pants (artillery uniform) were delivered to each man.[16] We have a camp stove in our tent and now that we have got rid of our sick man with his bed forever spread under our feet, we can sweep up of a morning—have our meals in comfort and feel something like keeping house. . . .

The weather is so pleasant that I am tempted to take a run to the creek and have a bath—it is slightly hazardous—but you do get so nasty lying ab^t o'nights in the dust and the ashes that if you don't wash once in a while. . . .

With warmest love I am very truly yours

F.E. Lockley

On Sunday, five days later, Frederic was reminded of how much he appreciated Elizabeth when his nineteen-year-old tentmate, Jimmy Van Benthuysen, who insisted on calling him "Mr. Lockley," shared with him love letters Jimmy had received from various girls. "A love-letter affords a rare insight into character," he observed. The letters of one girl he found shallow. "They contained o." But those of another reminded him of Elizabeth because "the tone of her mind so closely corresponds to yours."[17]

Dreaminess aside, he was infuriated three days later that she received so little assistance from the Albany community. "The promises of support for families of volunteers held out as an inducement for men to abandon their families for the defense of their country" were, he thought, "very cavalier," and her list of market prices was "perfectly afflictive."

Conditions at the fort, meanwhile, were miserable. "It has been misty and drizzling for the last 4 hours and the fort is trodden into an adhesion paste," he wrote on Wednesday.[18] By Saturday, the rain of four hours had extended to four days, and conditions had gone from uncomfortable to insufferable.

Fort De Russey D.C.
Novr 22^d 1862

Ma chére Femme,

We have had a rain storm for the last four days. Our tent and blankets and clothing are saturated; our cook house burnt down yesterday and rations are served to us uncooked. Our stove will not draw and the tent is filled with pungent wood smoke which acts upon the eyes like vinegar. If we take refuge in the street we are up to our ankles in mud—and the sleety rain beats thro' the closest attire. We have spent the whole forenoon in trying to keep a fire—we turned the stove upside down—tried it at the front of the tent and the rear thereof—tried it with the stove in the street & the pipe inside but in no way could we coax a fire. At last by accident we [dropped word] a plan—by having the stove the reverse way of the pipe—on the same principle that if you want a hog to go forward you pull him by the tail—and by our keeping constantly at whittling wood as fine as lucifer matches, we have managed to fry a slice or two of fat salt pork for dinner. I have seen far worse times at sea—so I put quietly up with the discomfort— read Homer—smoked incessantly—and lent a hand to the house work—but, oh Lord, what a relief to my feelings it would have been to have uttered a terrific scream, kicked the blasted tent over, and quarreled with the first man I met. The comfort of the thing! And this is our prospect for the winter. Well! it's all for our country. But, a word in thine ear. If I get safe and sound out of this scrape, the country will have to be in fearful straits before I voluntarily take up arms again in her defence.

. . .

Your's as ever
F E Lockley

4

Not Exactly a Bed of Roses
December 1862

In Albany his sister had failed in love again. "Emma's long agony is over," he observed on November 26, "the bubble has burst! . . . Tell her not to cultivate Irish beaux in the future." In an earlier letter, he had admonished Lizzie for describing her letter writing as "unfinished." "My taste may be bad," he offered, "but that point is not in question." Her letters suited his taste perfectly. He would sometimes grow more critical, but for now, her letters "are graceful, delightful, finished." His comments on her letters would vacillate between rather severe criticism and, like this, unrestrained praise, depending largely on his mood.[1] Just now, he would have none of Lizzie's self-criticism. "You are a young thing—loving—inconsiderate—wayward. Love letters from such an one are not required to be _finished_!"[2]

Tomorrow would be Thanksgiving, and he hoped they would have the traditional turkey. "We have so marauded our neighbor's hen roosts that anything in the shape of a fledged biped is rarely to be seen."[3] By early December, they had passed Thanksgiving separately, neither enjoying much of a customary feast. Adding to the gloom, his regiment had been found next to worst in inspection, so they were busy cleaning guns and straightening up, and they were sick of their tents. Nonetheless, he wished Lizzie well on going to Schuylerville to visit her aunt and grandma.[4]

In early December, Fred reported himself in good health, but "the weather is cold as Greenland," and, not allowed to build log huts, they still lived in drafty tents. "You would have laughed to see us at reveille this morning. The wind blew down the chimney—and the fire wouldn't burn our beefsteak & cold potatoes were frozen together so hard that we couldn't cook them. The water was frozen solid in the bar'l—and while we were fighting all these difficulties the drum beat for inspection. These are the blessings of a soldier's life—and when I get home[,] I can sit in that arm chair of your's and tell tough stories by the fire side." He regarded the president's "statesmanlike and moderate suggestion" to extend emancipation to 1900 a readier means for ending the war "than all the masterly combinations that Gen Burnside's skill can devise."[5]

Then came the first serious flares of discord between home and camp. In a time before faster communication, letters were all they had, but some letters were delayed in arriving, assertions could cross in the mail like ships in the night, not yet absorbed by their recipients, and sharp feelings, otherwise moderated by reflection, might not be shared in a timely fashion. Trust and forbearance became the glue to hold it all together.

Such was the case in an exchange that pitted Fred's momentary but ill-considered fanciful embrace of military life and wish to escape the cares of family and home against Lizzie and Emma's very real concerns for making ends meet. Letting his literary self take flight, he expressed his feelings at length but set it aside long enough to realize he had gotten carried away. He forwarded both letters anyway and was then surprised by the alarm they provoked.

It all started innocently enough with a letter from Lizzie that placed him in a scene of idealized domesticity, no doubt reflecting her concept of marital bliss. Recoiling at the prospect—and the idea of having reached middle age—Fred was at first dismissive but then lapsed into an expansive wistfulness.

Fort De Russey D.C.
Decr 10th 1862

Ma chére femme,

. . .

I have been greatly amused with your domestic grouping of future felicity. It is perhaps an effective composition—with the multitude it would pass as quite a respectable <u>stock</u> picture— lacking in originality—but combining all the features (with a little filling out of details) which excites the venerative bump in unlearned rustic minds.

An evening family circle seated round the table in a humble but decent apartment, with tidiness and housewifely thrift for its prominent characteristics. The "husband and father" is of course seated at the head of the table, dressed in preposterous costume, with an opened volume before him, which might be Shakspere[6], but is generally accepted as the Bible. He has a breadth of brow with mechanic faculties well developed—but no loftiness to it. His spectacles are raised from his eyes—and his right hand is raised as in act of speaking. The gude wife is seated at the other end of the table, where she Gars[7] old stockings [to] look amaist as new, and her reverent, submissive look, indicates her devotional character, and that in her husband she beholds an oracle, who, when he speaks, must have no dog bark. Representations like this scattered broadcast thro' the land afford ground for cheap rhetoric about the virtue of the peasantry, and the felicity of rural pursuits.

I pray thee do not mock me, fellow student; I sit for no such picture. A comfortable arm chair—cheerful little parlor—the husband and father (aught—baugh—bother!)—some sublime part—matronly wife (you sly puss!)—three bright eyed girls (yet, too bright eyed by the whole Fourth of July to figure in that scene)—needle-work—crocheting—Git eout! I shall throw up my dinner! . . .

I mailed my last letter to you on Sunday—day cold eno' for Spitzbergen Straits. At night, the guard tent being crowded with half frozen men, and the air filled with smoke—I wrapped myself up like an Egyptian mummy and paced up and down the silent fort. Your domestic scene occurred to my mind, as a puny whistle contrast to the grim and imposing sublimity of historic war. In Rob Roy,[8] Sir Walter Scott makes one of his heroines declare that men have an instinct for fighting, as women have for domestic pursuits. It would seem so. From the age of Cain to President Lincoln, no leaf of the world's records is unstained by human blood. No greater monster stalks the earth than horridum Bellum—death, devastation, and misery follow in his all-pervading tracks. But the monster possesses an irresistible fascination—which appeals to all the chivalry and gallant inconsiderate adventure in a man's character. Here we see nothing of its more revolting features, altho' the stern reality of the thing is bro't home to our every sense.

But this clear frosty night, with the silence of death around me, save the occasional sentinel as he paced his lonely round . . . my ideas fecundated; and for two hours I paced the post, living again the days of my youth—In my early studies, where I have read of the heroic achievements of such soldiers as Alexander, Caesar, Marlborough and the Swedish Charles, I have been fascinated with the magnitude of their fame, and sighed for the profession of arm[s] as a glorious career. Who can read of the irresistible tread of Cromwell's Ironsides on fields where Death reaped his abundant harvest; or of the stern, unwavering advance of Napoleon's grim veterans and not feel his every pulse on fire with the grandeur of the subject? It is all wrong, I admit. War is a mere whited sepulcher whose exterior strikes the eye with its flimsy varnish, but within is full of rottenness and dead men's bones.

As I say, on this lovely night with elastic spirits and teeming brain I gave full flow to my excited thoughts, and with the halo of patriotic warfare surrounding me, and the poetic background of wife and children to complete the picture, all the sublime elements of hoar antiquity, distance, vastness, and human endurance gave elevation to my feelings, and I felt "It is good to be here!"

But in an undertone ran the contents of your letter thro' my mind, and while it jarred my feelings, it gave diversity to my reflexions. "Comfortable arm-chair—" "husband and father"! is this indeed so near? In years I suppose I am approaching mature manhood—but my sentiment has by no means kept pace with my physical progress. I feel myself still a boy—elastic spirits—unabated activity—love of frolic—mutability of character. Then why poke "husband & father" at me, and maliciously superannuate me in a "comfortable arm-chair?

D—the arm chair! Give me a blanket for my bed, a tent for my habitation, and these trackless untrodden solitudes for my abiding place. To me they possess all the lofty sublimity, and the sacred romance of those indefinable wildernesses where the unknown Jehovah first revealed himself to the Patriarchs of Israel.

. . .

. . . My feelings are young—my spirits volatile, exuberant—my health, perfection.

Then if you unseat me from my gilded chariot, and just remind me that a certain petite dame and three bons infants will persist in claiming me as "husband & father"—still that does not dispel the bright hues of my fancy. Here, entirely removed from the cares of the world, with the every day routine of domestic life tinged with the fairy outlines of the enchantress Distance, in my wife I recognize no humdrum, thrifty, painstaking dame, economizing her scanty income, and her faculties absorbed in the unceasing endeavor to "make both ends meet." Rather she is my consenting deity, my Calypso of the grot, the inspiration of my day dreams, and the halo of my night thoughts. And I feel the poet's devotion towards her—her lips are dapping with the fragrance of cinnamon—her virgin breasts are twin fleeces crowned with rubies, and her pine white hands the delicate filagree that surround the King's throne. And those bouncing, romping, bread & butter eating girls, rude as Boreas and wild as the mountain deer, they assume the character of the fugitive passagére creatures of prolific Nature—sent upon this earth to grace its surface and laugh their brief hour away.

Here his letter stopped. He did not mail it. Rather, he finished it two days later, admitting, to Lizzie and Emma's eventual distress, that he was unsure of taking a new position that might lead to a promotion—and more money he could send home.

Decr 12th

I was on picket yesterday and did not find opportunity to finish my letter. This morning before the relief came out I was taken quite indisposed and found considerable difficulty in dragging over the hills to camp. I always tell you everything altho' I know it is foolish—but don't for goodness' sake go and publish it in the Journal and distress the minds of my friends by representing to them that I am at the last gasp—I have deliriously laid off to day in heaps of soft blankets and by to-morrow or the next day expect to resume duty again. Commissary Parker[9] has grown into disfavor— the Captain has offered me charge of the commissary stores. I am

uncertain whether I will accept the trust or not. We are all bustle—
the men are building their winter <u>halves</u> Corporal Joe is out in the
woods with a fatigue squad cutting lots, and teams are employed
hauling them to camp. It seems beyond question that we are now
the Seventh N.Y. Heavy artillery we practise on the big guns every
day. I am ashamed to trouble you but I must beg 4 postage stamps.
We are promised pay this month.

Don't indulge in the romance of "pent up feelings"—they don't pay.

Peter Wart. (to command.)

In Albany, Lizzie and Emma received these two letters with puz-
zlement, judging from internal evidence in Fred's response to their
reactions. Why would he decline the commissary and a probable
promotion that might bring desperately needed cash? Four days
later, he told of taking charge of the commissary, but Lizzie and
Emma did not know that when they crafted their response to his
first two letters.

Dec 16th 1862

Ma chére Femme,

In my last I was incautious eno' to tell you that I had taken quite
unwell on picket, and had dragged myself home with difficulty. On
arriving in camp I disembarrassed myself of rifle, cartouche box—
blanket, havresac &c and incontinently threw myself down, my
desire for the rest being huge & importunate. An unadulterated
<u>loaf</u> of twenty-four hrs. duration which I enjoyed with insatiable
avidity, put me entirely to rights. The next morning I arose and
betook myself to work.

. . .

Sergt. Richwine has resigned his stripes and will be reduced to
the ranks. His wife writes him that her two children are sick, and
her hand lamed in consequence of the dye in cloth uniforms.
She has been making soldiers coats. Commissary Parker has been
promoted to Quartermaster serg^t. and I have taken his place.[10] It
is a position of considerable difficulty—but it relieves me from
military duty—and I thought I would try it for a short time. I feel

quite used up this evening and write with as much grace and facility as an Irish kitchen maid. We have had a severe rain and wind storm—our canvas shrunk—the windward pins drew out (the pins are strong oaken sticks with a shoulder which are driven into the ground and a loop is passed over them) and our d—d tent capsized. Sometimes such a disaster is very funny. Your house raises from over your head—your stove is capsized—your blankets muddied, your guns rusted—everything helter-skelter—and your tobacco lost

I am as full of troubles as Job. The cook is sick—the cook-house is burnt down—we are building our own tent—and the company has to be fed as usual.

. . .

Don't sympathize—we have very happy times—the weather—with now and then a storm is indescribably lovely. Love to sister & kids–

Yours in all love and trust

F.

Although we do not have Lizzie and Emma's actual letters, we may judge with fair confidence the shock and apprehension they expressed in them from Fred's responses on December 18 and especially December 21. He began the first letter to note that his correspondence might become more infrequent simply because he had so much to do. When he resumed his letter on Sunday, December 21, he had finally received Lizzie and Emma's response to his overwrought letters of December 10 and 12. Reacting defensively, especially to Emma's cynical parodies, he claimed they took him wrong. He would be more circumspect in the future. But from what he quoted and paraphrased from their letters to him, Lizzie and Emma were clearly fearful of not having adequate resources to confront the coming winter. They could not sympathize with his wistful fantasies nor fathom his reluctance to accept a promotion, a promotion they were unaware he had accepted.

For now, despite conceited self-pity and an inability to resist cuffing Emma, he would try to make amends.

Ma chére Femme,

For the next week or two I fear my letters will be infrequent and unsatisfactory—I have no leisure. We are all up to our eyes with building—and in addition to this our company cook is sick, and there being no man capable of taking his place—I have undertaken his duties.

Decr 21st

. . . In my last I think I mentioned to you that I had accepted Commissary Parker's vacated office. I have done so at considerable sacrifice of personal comfort, being urged by the whole company to assume its duties they feeling that confidence in my integrity that an impartial distribution of stores will be secured. Parker was so unaccommodating and lethargic that the duties were grossly neglected. There is a considerable improvement in the men's rations already. But, personally, I derive no benefit by the change, whatsoever. I am pleased that I can be of service to my fellow soldiers—but I thereby sacrifice every moment of leisure, together with those delicious dreamy idealizations which have transfigured my tho'ts for hours together. I dislike hurry—business—preferring solitary reverie—a master author—and the sweet company of home musings. In the midst of these regrets, I receive your letter—with an addition to the following effect by Emma—

So you have a chance of promotion, and why don't you accept it? We have been trying to imagine your reason for hesitating. Lizzie says she tho't it was the office you wished for before you left here. I wish you could get it. I should be so glad for the honor of the thing. Not that we care for the increase of pay: money is no object to us. Our souls are above all mercenary considerations. All the associations of our present life are filled with poetry, so there is no room for worldly cares to enter our minds.

I cannot see the application of this piece of undisguised ill-humor. You require no assurance from me that if it lay in my power to help you in any way—I would shrink from no labor to accomplish it. Because I sacrificed every domestic delight at the call of an imperilled country, proffering life and limb for the preservation of her institutions, I do not see that I lay myself open to ill-tempered reflections upon the position I have placed you in. I have been educated in the old classic faith that a man's life & services are due <u>first</u> to his country—and <u>then</u> to his family relations.

. . .

This will find you at Schuylerville—I have no humor for sentiment—I will confine myself to commonplace prose in future. <u>Nota bene</u>. In common with Commissary serg^t. the duties of Captain's clerk are heaped upon me; and this same Sabbath afternoon while writing this letter to my wife, I was called off to write four letters for the captain. This brings me almost to dusk and jaded at that. I was much pleased with Josie's very sensible little letter. I will write to Dolly in a few days in answer to it. I have lots of news for her.

You will acquit me of all desire to quarrel with my friends at home, or with any one, but I must produce another passage from Emma's extraordinary letter. It is as follows:—"Lizzie appreciates the beauty of your poetry, too: the next letter you receive from me will be an epic poem on seeing some coal brought to our door." I don't know what my sister's precise intention in writing the foregoing might have been, but I read it with the same sensation as I should receive a painful rap of the knuckles. I submit that it is not generous to twit me with your privations. Mine is not exactly a bed of roses, exposed on the summit of this bleak hill in a miserable canvas tent, with the water freezing solid by the side of the stove. And it certainly is no addition to my comfort to have produced before me in acrimonious spirit the sufferings of my family in addition. To you my dearest, fondest wife, I appeal. Do you wish to cast slurs upon my provisions for you . . . ? My relation to you has been so delightful; it is mixed up in my mind with a warp of such gorgeous tissue that when I give loose to my retrospective imagination, I unwittingly transcend the bounds of sober sense and vault hither and thither at the mere bidding of aerial thought. And my confidence in your indulgences and unswerving obedience is so unreserved, that I never pause to criticize and ponder what I write. I rapidly photograph the vagrant images of my brain without regard to whimsy or reason, satisfied that you will read them with favorable construction, and thus it is a happiness to me to unravel my soul to you. But if these letters are exposed to unsympathising eyes, and a torrent of ill-humor is voided upon my gabardine in consequence—this familiar intercourse shall cease, and I will endeavor to write in a strain more suited to my audience. I trust my sister will not take offense at what I have said; it is written in no unkind spirit. I must quit as it is growing dark. God Almighty bless thee and make thee fruitful and multiply thee, that thou mayest be a multitude of people. But not till after I come back—mind! Not till after I come back! A merry jovial Christmas! . . .

F.

Taken as a whole, the exchange reflected Frederic's desire to satisfy youthful illusions of military gallantry and his desire to be part of something momentous. He was also reluctant to let go of the fanciful world of literary construction—of "aerial thought," as he put it—a world he still hoped to be a part of himself. He had already written one novel, and he had spent much time doing his own translation of Ossian. He hoped to write more. Also wrapped up in the exchange were Fred's insecurities—about age, about lack of accomplishment, and perhaps most of all about the wisdom of leaving home and family. The latter was a theme that haunted his correspondence throughout the war, and like other soldiers, he would assuage his guilt by claiming a higher duty to country.

In fair spirits, Fred began his letter of Christmas day describing the merrymaking in camp and telling Lizzie more about Richwine's financial scrapes. Still smarting from criticism of his own poor fiscal decisions, he tried to explain why he enlisted and then encouraged her to be her own kind of patriotic soldier.

Fort de Russey D.C.
Decr 25th 1862

Ma chére petite Femme aimable,

I intended to have written you a good long letter to day—but it is already 7 o'clock p.m. as I commence it. Our men have been drinking pretty freely, and Capt. Shannon[11] (being officer of the day) has kept me busy in errands to and fro. The inhabitants around here are all <u>secesh</u>; and as one of our Co. got stabbed to-day; without strong precautionary measures there was great danger of our men running amuck, and raising Hell's delight. I have stayed in camp, but have been so busy all day that I have not had time to feel lonely. x x You wish to know my duties as <u>Commissary</u>. They consist of taking charge of the receipt, the preparation, and the equal distribution of the men's rations—and also being custodian of quarter-master's stores. I cut up the fresh meats (4 times in 10 days) and supervise their cooking. I deliver a loaf to every man daily—weigh out coffee and sugar, and assist the cook in serving the impetuous hungry crew at meal times. So far I have given entire satisfaction.

I mailed a letter a few days since to you to the care of your Aunt—supposing you would spend Xmas in Schuylerville. In future please address your letters to Battery I, 7th Reg[t]. N.Y.I. Heavy Artillery, Fort De Russey, D.C.—that being our new designation.

By-the-bye, why do you spell frozen with two z's—and writing with two t's? Am I saucy?

I must tell you of Serg[t]. Richwine's troubles. To-day he was reduced in the ranks—and deprived of his sword and stripes. These are his offenses. When we were at Fort Alexander, M[r] Cuyler, editor for the Albany Express[,] called to see us and received several parcels of money from the men to convey to their friends. Richwine had left all his bounty home with his wife; but, being a fool, tho't he must do as the others did, so he applied to a young lad for $30 to give M[r] Cuyler, assigning as his reason that he had not time to go to his knapsack for it. The boy lent it to him,

supposing it would be ret.ᵈ to him in a few hours. Since then he
has been running in debt to the sutler and borrowing money of
one and the other until he is over $50 in debt. Latterly he got up
a subscription to buy the orderly a watch—and rec.ᵈ a few dollars
toward the fund which he has appropriated to his own use—and
the orderly had to pay for the watch which Richwine had ordered.
All these Jeremy Diddler tricks coming to the knowledge of the
Major he recommended his reduction to the Colonel—and today
(Christmas-day) he was reduced accordingly. In addition to all
these troubles his wife & family are sick—she had a basket of
clean clothes burnt up while [she] was ironing. x x You say that
every body expresses surprise at my having left my family in an
unprovided condition, and you add that you cannot bear to hear
people talk in that way. I suppose for the reason that it leads you to
question my judgment. Now, putting all romance and patriotism
aside, I will show you how great a pecuniary sacrifice I have made.
In the first place you know that I greatly disliked my business, and
was willing to make any change for the purpose of getting well
rid of it. It was an uncertain business besides. Well, say my clear
income amounted to $600 per ann. If I am away from home two
years (longer than I expect to be) my earnings would have been
$1,200. Now see what I earn as a soldier the while. Bounties $200—
pay $312—Clothing $80—Board $150. total $742 showing a loss of
$458 during the two years.

On the other hand we could not expect to escape our share
of the burdens of the war—had I waited to be drafted (as there
seemed a chance of it) I should have had to leave home without
any bounty. Accepting our share of the burdens you reduce
your style of living to the amo.ᵗ of $100 per ann. And also rec.
benefactions from your friends. And we have a reversionary
interest from the fact that whatever future public benefits may be
offered, those who fought in the war will always be preferred. So
don't get impatient—don't become unpatriotic—but bear your
cross cheerfully—and never doubt the wisdom of your husband's
judgment.

It is after taps—and I shall have the sergeant of the guard at
me for keeping my light burning. But I must laugh at your dream
a little. You talk of my appearing to you in your midnight visions

haggard & careworn. Such dreams don't amount to much. I have gained twelve pounds since I left home—and am as light hearted as a cock-robin.[12] And that further clause that "after a great while I came to bed—and would not talk to you but turned from you and told you not to trouble me.["] I laugh. I suppose you believe that. Old lady—don't believe you will escape so easily. You will have to take the tightest squeezing that ever you passed thro'. I intend to woo you Soldier fashion—and that is none the gentlest.

The men have returned to camp and are drunk and fightable. They are talking <u>fight</u> outside my tent so strongly that I can't keep track of what I am writing. So abruptly Good bye. Will write to Emma anon. I enclose a letter to Dollie. Warmest love to all. I prithee write regularly—and I will engage to send two letters weekly while you stay in Schuylerville.

> Sweet nymph! In thine orisons
> Be all my sins remembered![13]
> Whoop, jug! I love thee!
> Thine—desiringly—impatiently—fondly—truly
> F

Two subsequent letters finished out the year, neither as upbeat. So busy was he during the day, he told Lizzie on December 28, that he had to write at night, sitting uncomfortably at a box and writing by candlelight with "continual interruption of men coming rushing in to sit and talk." They were building a rude hut for winter, "a miserable shanty 8 ft by 10 with rough unhewn pine logs for walls, with our clothes and equipments hung around the house like the contents of a junk shop."[14]

His last letter of the year, written on December 31, his thirty-eighth birthday, was even more downbeat, provoking what he termed "gloomy retrospection" about his age and lack of accomplishment, linked as that was to Elizabeth's continued worries about money, which depressed him. "I am distressed that such weighty cares burden your shoulders."[15]

Interrupted the next night in finishing the letter, he could no longer resist the holiday merriment of camp. Having imbibed, he ran hither, almost activating the sentinel guard. Next day, he stated, "I have vowed not to touch whiskey or tobacco for the next three mo⁵." When he admitted to having been "tightly slight" on another occasion, he had tested Lizzie's tolerance. Her father had openly avowed temperance, and she had absorbed his convictions.[16] Her letter does not survive, but he quotes her as saying, "I shan't love you, nor let you kiss me if you taint your breath with disgusting liquor."[17] Under her influence, and his own self-restraint, he became more of a teetotaler as the war wore on.

5

We Must Ride the Tempest
January–May 1863

For his part, Fred would grow more inured to a soldier's life during the coming year, although not without peaks and valleys. For her part, Elizabeth, with her strong embrace of religious faith, would strive to maintain the household and contest his irreligion. That in turn provoked his appeals for her to find solace instead in "the eloquence and sublimity of nature" and to remember that "God is not a Scotch Presbyterian."[1] But throughout, they missed each other terribly.

Perhaps sensing the importance of the historical moment, Lizzie began a diary that she would keep most of the year. "I propose recording a few facts," she said with her first entry. "How very differently this year opens from the year that has just fled," she said. "Last New Years day Fred was at home with us, and all seemed bright and happy. Alas! What great changes a few months will show. The 19th of August, he went forth with the 113th Reg to fight the battles of his adopted country. Home ties were strong, very strong! I hoped they would prevail," she admitted. "Perhaps that did not seem patriotic, but so I felt." Nonetheless, "He could not see his Country suffering and not fly to its aid."[2]

"What I suffered in giving him up," she observed, but then added hopefully, "I am highly favored in hearing often from him; and have every cause to be thankful, in that his health has been preserved and his not being called into action. O! God do thou watch over him, & guide him."[3]

While Lizzie lamented her loneliness in Schuylerville—"I can not be gay when the being I love most on earth is absent"[4]—Fred continued his commissary duties, braved stormy weather, and contested boredom. "The article of news is entirely worn out here; we hear o, we do o and we know o."[5] And, he grew lonely himself.[6] But he bluffed his way through, remarking on curious events, such as his comrades' determination to defend a former slave and his family from recapture if it came to that.

Fort De Russey D.C. Jany 21st

Ma chére Femme

We are having a severe rain and wind storm which has been raging for twenty-four hours. All military duty is suspended—except camp guard and picket; even the cook is drowned out—and I have had to serve out uncooked rations to the men. The soil here is of that clayey nature that the least rain causes thick pasty mud, to walk in which is like wading thro' birdlime. We all stay in our quarters, and wile the tedious hours away with reading, smoking, card-playing, or writing home to our friends. Card-playing I have an instinctive horror of—especially by daylight. I have been reading and smoking till I became wearied, and as a last resource I throw myself on my bed to shut my eyes and think of home. I suppose you are comfortably housed at your Aunt's by this time, and cannot afford to expend a thought upon me. I write pretty often for the purpose of retaining a hold upon your memory—but still the apprehension weighs upon me that the task I assign myself is a difficult one.

For since of womankind so few are just;
Think all are false, nor even the faithful trust.[7]

I cannot tell you what ideas have been entertaining me this morning. I fancy the time of my service expired, and me thrust ashore at Albany. I give some boy a small gratuity to show me the way to Lark St. Arrived at my home, I enter, and find the matronly object of my affections, and her three blooming daughters all seated variously employed around the table. A coarsely clad soldier enters the apartment, his features bronzed, his hair short and grizzled. It is a singular fact that we are all turning grey as old father Time here. Young men of twenty-four are becoming grey as their grandfathers. . . .

. . .

An interesting incident occurred yesterday. There is a worthy old negro comes to our camp to gather clothes for washing, whose wife and two young sons are owned by a man in Rockville, Md. who is now an officer in the rebel army. Last night in the midst of the storm he abducted his wife & children, and brought them safely home in a wagon to-day. It is not likely any attempt at recovering them will be made. His house is near one of our picket stations of eight men, and our Serg^ts have all promised him that if any attempt to molest him is made that they will protect his house with bullet & bayonet. If ever there was a happy colored individual this man is he.

I enclose a long letter to Gertie. My affectionate regards to your Grandma' & Aunt. You must write me twice weekly. No excuses will avail—Give me some of the gossip of the village. No flirting with former beaux. Keep clear of the cabinet maker—for possibly the <u>Root</u> of the matter is still found in him. I have been reading Homer he does not believe in women. I mailed a letter to Albany last Sunday. Love to Emma

Your's paternally & connubially

<u>F.</u>

Throughout January and February his letters faithfully arrived in Albany twice a week. Lizzie saved them all, although at one point he urged her to destroy them.[8] Whether by accident or neglect, none of Lizzie's letters survive until mid-May.[9] Much of what she said in those lost letters is revealed nonetheless in his answers or reflected in sentiments recorded in her diary.[10]

Both Fred and Lizzie could be jealous of what they wrote. Fred, for example, did not wish her to share all his letters with everyone. When she said her grandmother wanted to read them, he thought not. "You know what a happy time she'll have!" But "let us propose a compromise," he said. "If she wishes it, I will write an occasional letter to her crammed full of wisdom and the clearest sense, and then as a relaxation from the effort I will fire nonsense at your head by the bushel."[11] She, too, could be jealous of their correspondence. "Emma & others were not pleased because I chose to keep the contents [of one letter] to myself," she told her diary. "I usually read F letters to them all, but I sometimes have one which I think he intends only for me. Therefore I only read it."[12]

In mid-February, he wrote a long letter over two days with a disquisition on Solomon and his wives, camp news, and the weather. He then suggested playfully that perhaps they should write to each other only once a month. "While you are spending your time writing to me you might be sewing soldiers' clothing, earning money at the rate of two cents an hour; and while I am writing, I might be studying 'Casey's Tactics,' and preparing myself for a future brigadier general." Kidding aside, he declared: "Military honors may go hang. My ambition runs not that way. Sooner would I devote one brief hour to the company or the cogitation of my little wife—than take part in the grandest military pageant that ever dazzled the eyes of the vulgar. I am no soldier and do not wish to be."[13]

In other letters, he urged her to avoid religious doomsayers. "Whenever you hear a miserable quack exhausting his powers of language in depicting the horrors of hell, rise and leave his presence," he admonished.[14] "Our God is a God of love!" They were lovers, and "lovers are like kings—superior to all law, rhetorical or statute."[15]

Whatever his thoughts on love, God, Solomon, and religion, finances always intruded.

> Fort De Russey D.C.
> March 1st 1863

Wife,

I finished my muster rolls by two-o'clock this morning, and
feel as slim as tho' I had been drawn thro' a very narrow tube.
I hate writing—in fact, all sedentary pursuits, and when you
come to impose sixteen hours' a day of that work for three days
together—il en suffit—it suffices. We are promised four months'
pay about two weeks hence. I shall then be able to send Emma
$15.00 of her loan—in addition to your allotment. I begin to feel
quite uneasy about your future. What you receive from me is
not half sufficient to support you; and I really do not feel much
confidence in your sign. The considerable rise in the price of
commodities, too, adds to your difficulties, and I can see no

present prospect of improvement. Thinking of your troubles is a continual care upon my mind; I have a horror of your suffering for any necessary. Tell me unreservedly how you push thro! or I shall imagine worse than the reality perhaps. I do not wonder at the country growing sick of the war, its burdens begin to press; but it is no part of patriotism to leave the work incomplete. I am as sick of the business as any one, but I am good for my three years, rather than have to fight this battle again.

Your letter suggested to me that I have been married two years yesterday. It seems nearer twenty. As you say, it has been a most eventful period. You nobly and courageously declare that you are willing to encounter whatever fortune Providence may have in store, being cheered thro' all with your husband's sustaining love. That's my rare Puck! When I courted you—when I was carrying you home as my bride, and while I revelled in the rich fruition of your chaste affections, there was ever a sombre back-ground to my feelings prophetic of the approaching day when the country would demand me of your love. These forebodings are realized.

. . .

The sacrifice is severe—but I do not yield it grudgingly. Were I home now, following my inopportune calling,[16] I should hate and despise myself. Peddling figs in a hurricane! In the name of the Prophet no!

. . .

We must ride the tempest out as cheerily as possible—placid seas and sunny ilses [isles] await us.

. . . Jimmie is asleep in his bunk—he returned this morning from 48 hours' picket—thoro'ly beat out—not having slept a wink the whole time. He is such an incessant chatterbox—that we are glad to have him out of the way. . . . I shall tire you with my small talk. Your letters all rec^d. (with the exception of the one not (!) in the parcel.) <u>Ah perfide</u>! Always welcome—cherry-delicious. I wish it could rain wife's letters. By and bye, I will come home sweetheart, and take them unsyllabled and warm from your fragrant lips. Good bye—love—dove—jade—chére amie

Your's possibly

<u>F.</u>

Throughout most of 1863, Frederic sustained optimism for the success of Union arms despite serious reverses, and he found most of his soldierly duties tolerable, even pleasing. But memorizing artillery tables was beyond him. When his officers directed that an hour a day and a class meeting three times a week be devoted to such study, he conceded, "If it were only Political economy, now; or biblical criticism, or philology, or grammar, or poetry, or half a dozen other congenial topics—I could go with gusto . . . [but] . . . ranges, elevation, weight of charge, time of flight, pah! I want you to come and learn the tables for me."[17]

He had also become chief letter writer in camp and was feeling "quite hackneyed" as a result. "I have acquired (in some way) the reputation for being a facile writer, and my opportunities for airing my epistolary ability are more numerous than agreeable. I have written three or four to-day (business letters—you know— short) and I don't know how many more are promised." He would be glad for better weather, so "I may hide myself in the woods and hollows and have respite for contemplation and reading."[18] Elizabeth did similarly on occasion. In January, she told her diary, "Staid home to write a letter for a woman to her husband in the army."[19]

When he took command of the Army of the Potomac in January, Gen. Joseph Hooker instituted various reforms. In addition to improving the food, sanitation, and medical care, Hooker kept the men busy with drills, tactical studies, dress parades, and brass bands to improve esprit.[20] Units like Frederic's Seventh New York felt the increased emphasis on discipline and drill, although by April, he had secured a position that exempted him from regular duties. He frequently participated in camp routine anyway. He had signed on to be a soldier, and a soldier he would be.

[Letterhead] 7th New York Vol. Artillery, Col. L.O. Morris

Company I

Fort De Russey April 8th 1863

Your's all with unmitigated delight received. I am so uninterruptedly employed, that I really can find time to correspond with none but you my pleasant helpmate. This hurried time will not last a great while. We have taken to drilling in real earnest. There is an _esprit du corps_ excited among our non-commish which will either keep me busy along with them or strand me as a d—d fool.[21] That is a position I am not ambitious to fill. We have school three times a week, where our lessons in the scientific principles of artillery are rehearsed; and we have two daily drills on the service of the piece. I as corporal act as gunner—but when the Serg[t]. is on duty, I fill his place as chief of the piece. All the men have to be instructed in their duties by the chief—while the commander stands at a distance and watches the execution. Should you happen to go astray in any one little detail (such as whether No. 3 passes the sponge or rammer to No. 1 with the right hand or left, or the relative distance in inches of the cannoneers from the _epaulement_ and the gun carriage) you run the risk of having the Major yell to you in the hearing of the whole garrison; "Chief, on gun No. 7! You are drilling that detachment wrong!" Any price such as this to pay for blunder, could not fail to make a man industrious.

It is true my military services are all voluntary, since my position as commissary & captain's clerk exempts me from other duties— but I cannot bear to fall behind the others and be looked upon as a mere steward & scribe. If war is the business of savages—so long as I adopt _war_ as my profession, let me be respectable in my attainments.

There is one reflection I wish to make here. When my opportunities of observation were less intimate, I had an instinctive misgiving of the demoralizing consequence of military life. When I used to see young innocent boys leaving their father's homes, to mix up with violence, profanity and the other many camp vices—I feared for the injury that would be inflicted upon society, and deemed that the loss of public virtue would be even more disastrous than the loss of life and treasure. But since then I have found that the law of _Compensation_ rules here as well as in all other social relations. When our regiment was first got together and we started on our way South, a rougher and more unpromising heap of materials you never saw gathered together. All the vices of civilization were represented with strong delegations. I would rather encounter the perils of an open field fight with the foe, than go thro' the terrors of that car ride to

Washington again. But now all this ruffianism has vanished. The hardest cases have become, in many cases, the best soldiers. So that if some ingenuous youth became corrupted, there is no doubt that as many mauvais sujets[22] will be reclaimed from their evil practices—so in the long run it is possible that our social morals will not suffer so severely after all.

I regret that I have not time to write you an interesting letter. While I was drilling on the 10 in. siege mortar this afternoon I was sent for by the captain to make out two muster rolls (we are to be inspected on the 10th inst.) and I have been busy on them ever since. It is now 9 h. 30 m. P.M. As for corresponding with any other living soul—just at present it is impossible. I hope to have more leisure ere long.

Your's beyond redemption.

F.

In Albany, Lizzie hit another low. "O! I feel so unhappy! So desolate so lonely it seems as if I could not endure it." She was eager for the war to end so Fred would come home, so she followed the war news closely. "It is reported that our forces captured Charleston, but I put not faith in it," she told her diary. "I only hope it is true; the longer the war lasts the more misery it brings[.] Of course, the right must prevail! If for a time treason and rebellion seem to triumph, it is nothing! . . . With God on our side who will be against us."[23]

On a more immediate level, Lizzie feared for her poverty, and sometime in mid-April, she shared her distress with Fred. Her letter does not survive, but she confessed to her diary, "I do not know why it was, but today as I walked through one of the dark miserable streets I felt as if poverty was most repulsive. The thought that it would be possible for me ever to sink to such a state made me shudder. We are poor enough & sometimes gloomy thoughts take possession of my mind, and I picture to myself the last dollar spent, and nothing in the house wherewith to satisfy the children[']s hunger." But then, as it often did, her faith bred resolve: "But I chase away these fearful forebodings, know[ing] & feeling that a kind Providence ruleth over all who will do all things well."[24]

In another letter, she apparently told Fred of an encounter with a rude neighbor woman and how it bothered her, especially now that they had moved to a poorer quarter. Again, her letter does not survive, and she did not record the circumstances of the encounter in her diary, but Fred's reaction to what she wrote was visceral and said much about his views of class distinctions and best conduct in personal relations.

For De Russey D.C.
April 19th 1863

Chére Epouse,[25]

How frequently one will bring trouble upon himself when he least thinks of doing so. You have been and gone and evoked a judgment which you little tho't to have visited upon your head for any act you have committed. But, in this predicament I say thou stand it. Your last letter liked me not. I propose to devote a few moments to an analysis of its contents.

One serious cause of regret in my mind is that my leaving home should have necessitated your removing into a low, ignorant neighborhood, where the persons with whom you are brought in contact are sullied with those many vices which poverty and ignorance rarely fail to engender. Rudeness, meddlesomeness—slander, dissention, are a few of the evils which beset you. But they must never reach you. You must never suffer yourself to come down to the level of the people whom you daily encounter. You live within yourself. It is not necessary to make friends of any of this class of persons—you are not responsible to them for your conduct; you take no interest whatever in any impertinent opinions that may be expressed upon your domestic habits. Do not listen to them. The approval of such people you do not covet or ask for, while their malevolent cousins can work you great annoyance. When Christian came to the encounter with Apollyon,[26] he was armed with impenetrable steel thro' which his enemy's fiery darts could not reach him. Your integrity and conscious moral greatness, place a defense between you and these froward women; you are of the same race but with different habits—their scrutiny of you is not shrunk from but is totally disregarded.

This ordeal of poverty is for your benefit. Your moral caliber is to be tested, and you will come out unscathed and purified by the process. Never give way for one moment. Abate no jot of heart or hope. Draw strength from your own soul, cultivate serenity and equanimity of temper. Fortune's gifts are unjudgingly distributed, and precariously held; rate them at their just value, and you will scorn the giver.

These apothegms slip glibly from the pen, but it is hard for a young thing like you to adopt them as rules of life. I do not ask worldly wisdom of you, I want nothing inconsistent with a character where grace, purity, charity and juvenility are found. Still, under your present circumstances you must live to yourself; be reserved but unaffected, and let popular opinion affect you as the waves affect the rock. Your character has yet to be formed (as the character of all has at your age,) and I wish you to cultivate the quality of dignity—not starched, obtrusive, civic, counterfeit—but graceful—affable, yielding, defensive. Be sensible to public approbation—without effort court it; but hold slander, malignity, and impertinent talking as beneath a sober thought. "'Tis a quick lie," says the gravedigger, "'twill away from me to you.["][27]

Therefore this idle slander authored by the misguided woman without a name, with which you have defaced your last letter, is reproduced in bad taste. It is not worth repeating. It is low billingsgate. It has none of the sacredness of home—none of the poetry of domestic affections, none of the odor of feminine gentleness and purity. It was like a nightman.[28] I had to burn the letter to rid myself of its influence. (All your others are carefully preserved.) What she says does not amount to much—so the less attention you pay to her malicious inventions—the less your peace of mind will be disturbed.

. . .

I enclose a letter for Dumpling.[29] It is getting dark. I must close—our doors are open—and the camp live pretty much in the street now. . . .

Good bye—love to Emma & self

F.

When President Lincoln replaced McClellan with Ambrose Burnside in November 1862 and Burnside proceeded to make costly blunders at Fredericksburg and in the pathetic "mud march" of January 1863, morale in the Army of the Potomac plummeted. With Hooker instituting orderly administration and greater attention to the needs of the troops after being made commanding general of the Army of the Potomac in late January, morale improved. By April, with Grant threatening Vicksburg as never before and Hooker preparing to confront Lee in Virginia, Northern hopes soared. Thus, Frederic wrote to Elizabeth of "the general patriotic uprising of the people" as a "most encouraging symptom." It was, he said, "more predictive of eventual success than three victories." But victories would be welcome also. When she received this letter, Lizzie observed, "Fred . . . feels quite encouraged, and thinks that all is going on well as regards the war." With her usual caution, she added: "I trust so indeed."[30]

Soon after, Hooker had his chance to defeat Lee and his Army of Northern Virginia but lost it in the six days known as the Battle of Chancellorsville.[31] Despite being outgeneraled by Lee, Hooker remained in command for the time being, and Fred remained optimistic, as was his wont. That the explosions in battles should produce rainstorms he found a worthless theory, but his belief in Union arms and prospects for conquering the Confederacy were as resolute as ever. He even saw the Battle of Chancellorsville as a Union victory. His captain, William Shannon, had a more accurate assessment, but Lockley would have none of it, and he grew angrier at secessionist sentiment from Mary, his sister in England, and the people of Schuylerville, where Lizzie had gone on visit for eight days.

Fort De Russey D.C. May 10th 1863.

Ma petite Femme,

Vot you tink now, eh? Are the federal arms striking home thrusts? Do the <u>rebs</u> show signs of faintness from their long agony? As the French said at Jena, I do not believe in a fighting Providence; but Napoleon's apothegm is vindicating its truth. God is on the side of the strongest battalions. As I can gain purview of things, our cause never looked so hopeful. Banks[32] opening the country and driving the foe at every encounter; Vicksburgh isolated and the enemy's communications with Texas cut off; Dupont still confident of reducing Charleston;[33] and our gallant army in Virginia flushed with success, and merely pausing to gather strength for a second overwhelming assault upon Lee. And behind all this another immense army gathering for the field; while the determination of the country is unabated, and the resources of the nation in prodigal abundance. Does this savor success? Evidently the rebels are approaching exhaustion. Famine is spreading thro' their land; their whole military strength is in arms; their credit gone, taxation ten per cent of their entire possession, and the people sick of the fratricidal desolating conflict. Does this point to a not distant suppression of the rebellion? I fear to be too sanguine; but I cannot see how it is possible for the ill-starred confederacy to hold together during the present year. Political laws govern them despite all their desperation, and since the object of their iniquitous ambition is defeated—their recognition as a sovereign power—a speedy collapse is inevitable, and the rehabilitation of our national integrity.

Your letter reached me this afternoon. I am sorry that my interrupted correspondence has caused you any uneasiness. I supposed from your saying that Emma would open my letters—that you did not intend to have them sent after you—consequently as I had but little leisure, I did not persevere to write to you. From this I will communicate with you semi-weekly as usual—you must try and do the same.

I see you have been visited with the same rain storm that has hung by us for the last five days. We had a theory here that the heavy long continued firing at Fredericsburgh [sic] has caused the storm. An opinion was advanced that the concussion produced an electric effect upon the clouds—causing them to discharge their vaporous contents; while others held that the effect was due more to chemical than mechanical forces, and that the charging [of] the atmosphere with such immense explosions of salt-petre would lower the temperature and thus cause nebulous condensation. The extent of the rain storm proves these theories to be worthless.

You would be pleased to see our camp now—we have got it in handsome order. We have planted cedar trees between each house—sodded round the walls—interlaced grape-vines in the shape of trellis work round our porches—and strewn our street with stones of milky whiteness. We have cleaned and graded all the approaches to our camp—and it now presents quite a cheerful thrifty appearance. Cleanliness before Godliness, is a wholesome rule in the army.

You probably have seen that Gen. Heintzelman has joined Hooker[34] with a strong re-inforcement. We fully expected to have been ordered to proceed with him, and were pleased with the prospect of having a chance of seeing active service, but since we are still kept here, we have now inclined to the opinion that we shall take no hand in these Rappahannock battles. There is no doubt that these forts require to be manned with troops who can serve the pieces with some effect, and I do not see what artillery regiments are to be found to replace us.

I am very unfortunate in my friends—save yourself and my "Yankeeized sister."[35] I can find no one who is worthy of the free government which the nation is pouring out its life streams to maintain. My sister Mrs. D.[36] denounces this as a "cruel, revengeful, fratricidal war," and stigmatizes our heroic devoted Generals and officers as "a set of harpies preying upon the very vitals of the nation." Friend Duncan (in a letter to hand from him to-day) which is refreshing from its tone of nonchalant indifference, wishes the difficulty settled some way or other (it matters not how) "and if the Southern states want to live apart from the union, let them go!!" Not exactly. This country is not going to commit suicide just at present. But of all the species of pestiferous copperheadism—preserve me from that type of the unpardonable sin ruling in classic Schuylerville. My views fire at your words. "I hear nothing here—no body takes any interest in the affairs of the nation." Of course not. The federal arms—at fearful expenditure of life, are winning successes—therefore these traitors have no interest in present affairs. Every advantage is grudged—and passed over with moody silence. Let the rebels, however, achieve a success, however trifling, see then how alert they are! This vivifies them into warmth and animation—and their croaking predictions of the futility of the war profane every ear they gain access to. I would like to put all such in Charleston, and let Dupont's iron-clads fire at them.

X x x This is a very exciting time—the exact result of Hooker's engagement is canvassed in every particular. Capt. Shannon has just been in—and spoken as follows: "Corporal, I have been reading everything relating to Hooker's engagement that I could get my hands on—and I have arrived at the conclusion that he has been licked like the devil." I reply: "If your expression conveys the idea that he has been badly beaten, I do not see it. As I understand the case—he was foiled in his main endeavor, but he inflicted more damage upon the foe than he himself sustained—and Stoneman's successful raid is entirely our gain."[37]

By and bye the lieutenant comes (a much esteemed officer) with smiling looks—the precursor of good news: "Hooker has crossed the river again," he tells me, "and Lee has sent to Hooker for medical stores for the wounded." This is glorious. With the poverty and defencelessness of the entire state exposed by Stoneman—Hooker re-inforced with 30,000 fresh troops to fully engage Lee whose connections are severed—Genls Peck and Dix to advance upon Richmond and capture their capital almost without a blow.[38] I can see nothing to save the rebel army from utter rout and demoralization. I fear to form expectations too sanguine— since we have tasted of disappointment so often—but the programme I have here marked out seems so reasonable that I do not fear to expect decisive results from the conflict occurring this month. Abate no jot of heart or hope—we shall come out right yet.

Emma speaks very highly of the breeding and docility of my children. I am pleased to think they receive so good a training at your hands. Perhaps you are not fully aware how largely the character is moulded by the influence of the mother. . . . Love to my treasured womankind.

Yours thro' thick and thin

F.

6

Your Letters Are My Meat and Drink
May–June 1863

"He writes so encouragingly of the war," Lizzie noted yet again in her diary the same day she wrote the following letter to Fred, the first to survive. "[He] thinks [the war] must certainly end during this year. O! that it would."[1] That she shared his hope but not quite his confidence she betrayed only to her diary, not in her letters to Fred.

Financial worries continued to trouble them both. "I know that my allotment is totally insufficient for your support," he wrote, "how do you raise the remainder?"[2] It was a good question, one Lizzie could not easily answer. The Albany community was supposed to help, but that support was given reluctantly when it was given at all, which angered him. Nonetheless, he had sent her $40, a tidy sum with which she paid many debts, although, as she told her diary, "This does not leave us much to live upon."[3] As with most of her letters, Lizzie's was full of domestic news about the household and neighbors.

Albany May 13th 1863

My dear Husband,

My letter must necessarily be short as it is after <u>taps</u>. If I were to give you a programe of my proceedings for the day you would feel satisfied that I had not idled much precious time. I discover quite a difference in the ammount of labor I have to perform since Emma went to the shop to work. She works hard. I am afraid her strength will not admit of it the walk is long.—we live near Washington Ave. and her place of business is on Brodnay [Broadway] near Clinton

Ave. 8 O'clock is the hour she goes to work. She comes home to tea but, not to dinner, then returns and stays till 9 P.M. I wish the place was nearer for her sake.[4]

Your delightful letter was received to day; so full of hope and encouragement, it did me much good. it does indeed look brighter and I hope to see the programe you have laid out followed up. if so the end is not far distant. Stonewall Jackson was I believe to have been buried today. What a pity his energies had not been directed in the right course for he was without doubt a remarkably smart man.[5]

I received your pay yesterday $40 half an hour after getting it I disposed of $24 for rent; that pays up all to the 1st of May. now I feel clear, I have no other debts to pay. I make a point of paying for everything I buy at the time I get it, and what I can not have I do without. Fred I am going to send you a box I have wished to do it for a long time, but had not the means; now that I have become suddenly rich, I am anxious to send you a few little articles. I will not send till you write, as I wish you to tell me of anything you should like. There may be little necessaries that I should not think off [sic] do not fear asking for what you want.

Do I approve of your indulging such visions of me? I think not! I wonder what next you will dream, eh? That I have cleared off with this disgusting piece of humanity, and left the kids to take care of themselves I suppose. I shant promise what I will do if you stay away too long. This much I will say it will have to be a very handsome man that I go with. I am only writting nonsense, troubling you to read what is neither sensible or profitable whereas you might be better employed. I shall not detain you much longer. I had almost forgotten to say that I received a letter on Monday from you. I am glad you completed it at last[.][6] it would have come a little more speedily if you had known how anxious I was to hear from you. I intended to have you address them here, have Emma open them and then send to me, but it is all over now, and I shall try to recover from the loss, if I hear semi weekly as usual. So you have suffered some from home sickness or wife sickness, I have had a few quite severe attacks of the same disease. We must occasionally expect them. all that can be done is to nerve our selves up, and shake off the feeling as quickly as possible. The children have all been promoted at school, of which they feel quite proud. I am pleased with the progress they are making. Can you immagine your baby Tute (I guess you can claim the honor of her paternity) reading little stories with quite difficult words in them very correctly too. She often plays studying and in this may acquire considerable knowledge. It is such a comfort to think they are all in such good health. I shall try always to write 2 times a week, when you disprove of my letters tell me so dear Fred I shall not be offended. Emma sends love also the kids. Good night

Most devotedly yours
Lizzie

Josie sends this little scrap of the cat and the sparrow

A day later, Albany rejoiced at the return of the Sixteenth New York Infantry from its two-year enlistment. Mustered in from small towns surrounding Albany in May 1861, the Sixteenth New York had seen service at various postings, including the Battle of Gaines' Mill in June 1862 during the Seven Days Battles, where it had lost heavily as it did also at the Battle of Crampton's Gap (part of the Battle of South Mountain) three months later. More recently, it had fought at Fredericksburg with Burnside, endured the Mud March, and lost men at Chancellorsville. For her part, Lizzie found the city's celebrations depressing, although she attempted to take the children to see soldiers returning from various units in subsequent days. In her diary, she confessed, "One thing has had a tendency to make me miserable, the ringing of the bells the firing of cannon and Millitary music which I have heard nearly all day." She did not see the returning soldiers that day, she said, "but those who did tell me they never saw anything which made them feel sadder. Out of a whole Regt. only 260 returned, how plainly this shows of death, of sorrow and weeping. There must have been some glad hearts to greet them, but how many many more sad ones. . . . They were ragged and sunburned to a fearful degree."[7]

Fred, meanwhile, was amused, both by his sister Emma and by the men in camp. Emma, he said, "reminds me of her way of getting rid of her nieces when they were babes. If the child began to squall, she would toss it about and talk nonsense to it for awhile, but if it persisted in being troublesome, she would corner the maternal relative, make her give the young one her breast, and then go off satisfied with her accomplishment of a great work. In the same way with me. She has been promising me in my impatience the solacing words of my fluent dame." Lizzie, Emma had said, "is writing to you, so your coveted allowance of sweet words will be delayed no longer."[8]

As for life in camp, he asked, "What do you think our men are doing at this precise moment. <u>Pelting each other with bread!</u>" Each man received a loaf per diem (about one-and-a-half pounds), "and now the weather is warm we do not eat half our allowance. In this way barrels of stale loaves have accumulated on our shelves, and to-night some inventive genius started the idea of having fun with them. Loaves gyrate past my window thick as hail. I have been looking at the sport for the last ½ hour with the greatest enjoyment. I have sixty loaves in the Commissary tent I wish some one would come and steal." As the air filled with bread missiles outside, he observed, "I could not help drawing comparisons between our superabundance and the rebel's scarcity."[9]

A week later, he plunged from frivolity to anger and despair over what he considered Capt. William Shannon's tyranny and the wrong done to several men in his company, including one of his favorites, twenty-year-old Jimmy Van Benthuysen, a printer by trade who refused the captain's order he and others believed unjust.

Fort De Russey D.C.

May 20th 1863

My dear Wife,

I owe you a thousand apologies for my long neglect, but I have to plead such constant occupation of late that I have had no moment of leisure afforded me. Our last pay was rec.[d] two days after the muster and pay rolls were made out—and on Saturday last Capt. Shannon received some new blanks with instructions to have them filled out immediately as the regiment would receive two months' more pay as early as possible. I commenced upon them forthwith— wrote all day on Sunday—and have only just finished my task [on Wednesday.] What renders the work so tedious quadruplicate blanks have to be filled—and this involves a great amount of labor.

I merely write you a few lines this evening (it is now 10 o'clock) because I know you will be daily disappointed at my failure—tomorrow I will give you a good long letter.

Your ever-welcome messages come regularly—you improve in your love letters. I have had time to read your last two but once over—I promise myself the treat of poring over them to-morrow. Your sister's portrait I like—I must refer to that tomorrow.

Don't talk about sending a box I prithee. We already have more things than we can stow away—I am abundantly supplied with clothing, and have the opportunity of getting sundry little extras from the officers' mess—which make our fare tolerably liberal. There is nothing that I am in want of except my wife. If you pack yourself in a box and send it along—I would feed upon you to satiety.

Our little friend Jimmy is under confinement together with five others of our company on charge of mutiny. I will give you the details of the case tomorrow. . . .

F.

Two days later, Fred fulfilled his promise of a longer letter along with details of young Jimmy Van Benthuysen's arrest.

Ft De Russey D.C. May 22 /63

[No salutation]

We have had quite an excitement in camp. For a long while past the restraint of severe discipline has been relaxed, and the men have abandoned themselves to intoxication and absence from camp to quite a demoralizing extent. I have presumed to speak to the major and Capt. Shannon about the growing evil—but they have not seen the necessity of tightening their loose control—both officers have told me they would not give a d—for a man who does not get drunk once in a while. Whether the fact of the sutler being a near relative to the colonel induces them to allow his unrestrained sale of poisonious liquors, I do not know. But certain it is our military efficiency has become seriously impaired of late.

At length the evil assumed such proportions that our Captain resolved to put a sudden stop to it. The most rigorous measures were adopted—severe punishments instituted—and a sort of discipline established that reduced the whole command to the condition of slaves. The men were naturally restive under such rule, and an ill-feeling was engendered between officers and men. On Sunday last this culminated in a collision. There being brigade inspection that day—the men were released from fatigue, and were ordered to thoroughly clean and scrub out their quarters, polish their arms and accoutrements—and be spic and span clean to fall into line at 4 p.m. About ½ hour before that time one of the houses was found to be uncleaned—the occupants thereof being on duty. He read off the names of six (our tent-mate Jimmie among the no.) and they being cleaned for inspection refused to do it. This being reported to the captain he ordered them into confinement, and they were lodged in the bomb proof. The lieut. then went to them and demanded of them if they refused to perform the duty required of them. They re-iterated their refusal. This being communicated to the Capt. he became possessed of ungovernable fury. He buckled on his sword—and thrusting a loaded revolver in his coat sleeve rushed to the fort livid and trembling with rage. He ordered the prisoners out of the fort; they were conducted into his presence by Corporal Joe [Rogers] and a file of men with loaded rifles. Being halted before him—he inquired of them if they would clean the house for inspection on his command. One of the prisoners answered that the Regulations forbade any menial service being imposed upon a soldier—that to clean another person's house they held to be menial service, and for that reason they held themselves justified in refusing to perform it. At this answer the unbounded rage of the Capt. became terrible. He drew his sword—denounced them as mutinous G—d d—d sons of b—s, said he would as soon shoot them as look at them—and raising his sword stood ready to cleave the nearest man down. It is the undoubting conviction of all who witnessed the scene that he would have slashed and shot them, had the men not succumbed. His fury intimidated them, and they cleaned the house under a guard. They were then remanded to close confinement to await trial by court martial on a charge of mutiny.

Perhaps this occurrence was none of my business—but it absorbed me. . . . I proposed to carry a complaint to the colonel—

signed by the n.c. officers of the company. . . . I did not wish to urge my brother non-commish against their wills—so the next morning I submitted the complaint to my friend the officer. . . . He assured me the case was a good one. . . .

But . . . on my return to camp I found the wives of two of the mutineers sitting in the Officers' tent, come unexpectedly from home on a visit to their husbands. . . . Capt. S. naturally unwilling to have these men go home and circulate stories about his brutality, went and released the two men—and as this could not be done without unfairness to the others—he ordered the liberation of the other four prisoners.

This determined me to delay my complaint until some other similar occurrence.

One of our Serg^{ts} having tendered his resignation, the captain was kind eno'h to offer me the promotion. I declined it for reasons sufficient to myself, and Corp^l Rogers has been recommended to the colonel for promotion in my stead. . . .

Ah! This war is getting to be an intolerable nuisance. Would to God it were over! . . . I have not become a submissionist yet.

Goodbye pet . . .

Very respectfully

Your obedient humble servant

Peter Cray[10]

Lizzie noted upon receiving this letter how Fred was in uncommonly low spirits, but his cheerfulness had generally returned two days later. Still, he devoted much of his letter to lingering dissatisfaction with his captain.[11]

Fort De Russey D.C. May 24/63

Ma chére petite Femme,

I have risen at 4 o'clock to have a cool hour to write to you. Dr Johnson said that he had never come across but one book that had taken him out of bed earlier than his wont. But the phlegmatic litterateur does not tell us how many hours intended for the rest he devoted to writing billets doux. The major wishes me to do some writing for him to-day—so this hour before <u>reveille</u> will probably be my only opportunity. The weather is dreadfully warm—I have returned to my former love, the delicious creek which laves the base of this hill. I spent half the day down there yesterday—bathing in its tide and lounging on its verdant banks. There has been considerable talk of our regiment being removed, and we have been almost in daily expectation of receiving the order to march, but now that Hooker appears to be inactive, and a raid by Stuart's cavalry is threatened thro' here—it is probable that we shall be kept here for some time yet. I am happy to report to you that I have recovered my customary cheerfulness, and am again reconciled to military discipline. But it is well to remember past occurrences—and some day the buried dead may be resuscitated to bear testimony against the living.

There is a singular spirit animating the minds of our non-commissioned officers—at least one half of them are ambitious to be reduced. One reason is the growing unpopularity of our captain; and another, and more controlling reason[,] is the difficulty experienced by the mal-contents in learning the science of artillery. Serg[t]. Frost[12]—a highty-tighty English soldier who served for 18 mo[s]. in the Crimea, to-day is reduced to the ranks at his own request, because of his unwillingness or inability to apply himself to the study. Corp[l]. Rogers has been invested with his sword. Another corporal obtained leave of absence for a day to see his brother in Washington as he returned home with his regt. and has since been arrested in Baltimore as a deserter and is now confined to Fort M[c]Henry. With him is a private from our co—named Joseph W. Kirk, son of one of the firm of Carpenter & Kirk, drapers in Albany, also arrested as a deserter. This young man left camp under singular circumstances. A couple of stylish prostitutes came to visit Co B. officers mounted on excellent horses. When they left this Kirk must needs follow them to Washington. He applied at a neighboring house for a horse to ride offering \$5[00] for the use thereof, but being refused followed after them on foot[,] overtook them and spent a happy time with them, getting gloriously inebriated as a matter of course. We fear this interesting pair will be apt to get severely punished. I am sorry for Joe—as he is a good soldier, and a harmless peaceable fellow.[13] Capt. Shannon doesn't anathematize that frail sisterhood much. Two other corporals insist upon resigning, and the captain is at his wits' ends to know whom to appoint in their place.

. . .

Do not send a box I want nothing but milk and fresh vegetables—I will give you trouble eno' yet—if that's what you want. Write longer letters—longer letters write—I send some candy money for my dear little pets. Both Mama and Auntie give them the best report. You mustn't have any. Without love or desire or interest—I am alienatedly Your's

F.

Flushed with his success at Chancellorsville, Robert E. Lee convinced Jefferson Davis and most of the Confederate military high command that a successful invasion of the North might have the best chance to further Southern war aims. The Army of Northern Virginia had thus begun marching north in what would culminate at Gettysburg in early July. Lee's venture north put Frederic's regiment on heightened alert. With the danger rising, they experienced some desertions, which he expected to be severely punished. Lizzie, meanwhile, could do little more than remain hopeful and observe from afar. "I do try to be cheerful," she told her diary, "but beneath it all there is our one sad thought, the knowledge that my dearest Husband is away, and that I may never see him again."[14]

Fort De Russey June 3^d. 1863

My dear Wife,

I am getting sick of addressing my letters so constantly from Ft. De Russey. Don't you wish we could have a change, so that I might have fresh scenery to describe, fresh incidents to narrate, and fresh manners to portray? We seem on the eve of a change. Rebel movements being anticipated thro' this quarter, the utmost attention has been directed to the defences and their garrisons. We have had five inspections the last two or three weeks, yesterday Gen Barry (the chief of artillery) paying us a visit.[15] Strong reinforcements have been sent us both of cavalry and infantry—

the roads are blockaded and heavily picketed, all communication with Washington stopped except for military purposes, and we, heroic defenders of our nation's capital (!!) admonished to be ready at the first tap of the drum, to fall into our places, and give the advancing rebels particular Jesse.[16] We have fooled with these big lumpish guns so long—heaving them out of battery—and going thro' the motions of loading them, and then heaving them in battery, and pulling the lanyard as tho' we were firing them off—that we actually are impatient for an opportunity of displaying our skill upon these pieces. If any reasonable sized force of rebels would obligingly come within range of our guns, thus affording us a chance of blowing a few to the elysian fields, what a big thing it would be! Our military heads are making great preparations for a brush—of course I can see that the utmost vigilance is necessary, but I have no idea that we shall be called into action.

I think I mentioned to you that two of our men had deserted. One of them returned last evening having run the guard at Washington—the other is still held in durance vile. All their clothing was sent back to the qr mr yesterday, so they have o but what they stand in—and they will have to take a trial by court martial, where their sentence will probably be severe. Deserting now is a pretty difficult business.

You remember old Major Williams[17] who was sent after our reg^t as a deserter with bracelets on—I saw the old fellow yesterday. He tells me he is likely to get his discharge for physical disability. This is a shrewd game. He was discharged from the 2^d. N.Y. Art.^y for the same disqualification, then he enlists again, pocketing the heavy bounties, and when it suits him, slips out again on the same plea. The man had a pleasant time eno' as colonel's cook—with plenty of contraband help—but was diseased with the John Bull mania. Old Hengland! He loves not wisely but too well. With the feeling which the action of our loving cousins has aroused in the American mind, the braggart dotage of the old nuisance rendered him the butt of his company. In his kitchen—he had the busts of Washington & Queen Victoria placed vis-à-vis. I suggested to him that such propinquity was a desecration. The immortal champion of Freedom by the side of a representative of a race of fools whose greatest quality has been prolific breeding, and whose prominent characteristic is a German greed of salary, I regarded as an insult to the genius of our political institutions. Royalty! Augh! baugh! bother!

. . .

Your letter reached me this afternoon—I read it on my way to headquarters. At present there is no living chance for a furlough—when the present excitement shall have abated—I will then do my best.

Your's affectionately

F.

Lizzie wrote two letters in three days, both expressing her loneliness and her wish for him to secure a furlough.[18] She took the girls to Troy for the day and worried about Jack, whom she identified as her cousin, a mischievous member of a New York regiment.[19] Accompanying her second missive was a letter from Frederic's sister Emma, who declared the "Secesh" of New York had made her an abolitionist.

Albany June 4th

My dearest Husband,

I was so thoroughly worn out last night, that it was impossible for me to write. Firstly I did not rise yesterday till about 9 O'clock having a very disagreeable sick headache. Then I had promised the children if I was well enough, I would take them to Troy, as I had disappointed them the day previous; so feeling slightly refreshed after drinking a cup of tea, we made preparations to leave by 1 O'clock in the cars. Such a set of crazy children, I could scarcely keep them within bounds. They received a very warm welcome, which made them feel at home directly. I left Tutie with them while I went to call on a few old neighbors. Mrs Wooster told me that she asked one of the Officers about Jack, and he said that he was never out of mischief, and that he was very cowardly—when they were in expectation of a battle he with ½ doz others were sure to cut up some caper that they might be sent to the RipRaps. He is there now I believe[.] at some time the enemy had been throwing shells into their entrenchments, and one of them not happening

to burst Jack picked it up and called to ½ doz men who happened
to be near to come and see some fun and before they were aware
of his meaning he threw it with all vengeance upon the ground,
but strange to say it did not explode. How long his confinement is
to last I know not.[20]

I brought Tutie home with me, knowing she would not stay as
contentedly as the others. We were both tired enough to go right
to bed with out any ceremony. How strange it seems to have the
family reduced to two. I do not like it. I would rather have a family
of a dozzen than such a small one.

I have commenced cleaning house and was in hopes I should be
able to finish while they were all away, but I have had some sewing
brought in which must be finished this week, so housecleaning
will have to wait a little longer. I called to see Emma yesterday. Her
ankle is improving fast. She will I think be able to walk home by
Saturday.[21]

Your letter just received. I have read it twice. Your letters are my
meat & drink. Without them I should famish and die—how every
word is treasured. More precious to me than gold dust or sparkling
diamonds. Tute the little trollop is pulling my hands, tickling me,
and shaking the table in a fearful manner. What shall I do with her?
Bundle her up and send her to you? She knows she is the only one at
home, and therefore seems to consider that she has a right to do just
what she has a mind too. I do not feel like checking her. I am glad
she is not an only child, for she would certainly be spoiled. I bought
her a nice india rubber ball, which she ammuses herself with.

. . .

You are a funny man Fred, according to your talk[.] you take
very little pains to please [and] still you get along as well, if not
better than others.

O darling I try to think as little as possible about you comming
home, but the thought of such unalloyed pleasure will sometimes
creep in, and fire my veins with new energy and for the time being
I revel in an atmosphere of perfect happiness; it intoxicates me—
it is too much. O! why do I let my thoughts dwell upon it. I feel
that it is dangerous to do still I can not help it. You have assured
me that you would try to get a furlough, and I doubt not but you
will succeed. I must conclude this hastily as my work is crowding—

much as I enjoy these little pen and ink conversations I would
rather it was verbal. Rain would I think be quite acceptable to our
farmers here. Tute sends love and kisses. I will be saucy and say
none to you. May Heaven's richest blessings be vouchsafed to you
my dearest Husband.

With love and truth
Lizzie M. L.
[Albany]

[June 7, 1863]

Dear Fred

I am waiting patiently for my letter. I suppose it will come when
you have time to write it. We are disappointed to find we shall not
see you for I did begin to think it possible that you might get a
furlough, but it seems we must wait still longer. how I do hope you
will come home before the summer is over, for we all want to see
you. I came home last night the first time I have walked since I hurt
my ankle, and it seems real nice to be in the bosom of one's family
once more but I wish you were here to share it with me. what a
pleasant party we should be. I suppose you will remain at Fort de
Russey some time longer yet but I don't feel afraid the rebels will
attack you[.] I don't think they dare to[.] A young man from the
22^d (returned) regiment[22] spent the evening at Mrs Owen's last
week, he says their regiment built the forts you now occupy. I had
a long talk with him but did not agree with his sentiments he is
a strong democrat and call[s] this a nigger war Mr. Burke never
made an abolitionist of me but the Secesh of this state have. Fred
if it is not an impertinent question will you tell me what kind of
a letter you write to Mary in answer to her precious copperhead
epistle. I hope you did not shew the least sign of disgust at the war.
Don't give way one jot keep up faith and hope in the good cause;
all war is cruel[,] tyranical and despotic, but if ever a people had
just cause for war we have[.] don't doubt it for one moment all will
be well. I want to see you.

Your loving Sister Emma

7

Would You Fancy the Surprise?
Mid-June–Mid-July 1863

Frederic found military drill so wearisome, he often struck off into the woods to commune with a more lenient nature. There, he found contraband Blacks—former slaves—who labored in the area on behalf of the Union Army cutting wood. When Frederic asked if he could teach them to read and write, his major objected, but he worked with them anyway.

Fort De Russey D.C. June 10

My cheap wife,

Your letters used to come o' Tuesdays—now they reach me a day later—comment <u>fait cela</u>?[1] I have the pleasure of receiving one before me this afternoon. Do you know that I have stayed from Artillery drill this morning for the purpose of writing to you. You cannot conceive the mechanical dulness—the wearisome routine of military drill. At least, in this way it impresses me. There are some who enter into the spirit of the thing, devote their whole energies to the execution of a movement and attain that grace and ease and precision in drill which give to military performances their principal effect. But I cannot reduce myself to the level of a machine. To stand immoveable so many inches from such a place—my feet at a certain angle, my hands hanging in such a position, body erect, shoulders square, head & eyes to the front, gaze resting on the ground 15 paces in advance—and thus to stand like a statue—if a bee should alight on your face and sting you—you are not to move a muscle—augh—this wearisome dull constraint, is opposed to my religion. Youth, lightness—grace

99

naïvaté,[2] the impulsive motions of a bird, unconstraint, debonair, unstudied—naturalness—When the British sloop ship <u>Birkenhead</u>[3] (I think was her name) was foundering at sea with a detachment of troops on board, the officer in command drew them up [in a] line on deck—and there held them till the waves submerged that gallant band of men. This may be soldier nature but it is not my nature. I hate uniformity—it is against nature. She made no two blades of grass alike, and do you suppose she meant two men to stand alike?

I have things exceedingly easy—as you say—I take little pains to please—and still get along as well as the rest of them. Every chance I have I scamper off this hill to go and wander along the sedgy shores of the creek—or clambering up the masses of rock watch the impetuous miniature cascades as they expend their petty fury. A fresh delicious breeze always inhabits the spot—and I linger there with my mind filled with images from the freshly read pages of Homer & Byron.

Sometimes I strike out thro' the forest—and stay and converse with a gang of contraband woodchoppers who are working for a wealthy farmer in the district. It is interesting to listen to their history. One has a wife and five children in Shenandoah, Va— whom he left behind in his exodus for freedom. He cannot write, of course, and is waiting for the success of the federal arms to liberate the state—that he may venture to return for his wife and little ones. Another is from Roanoke, N.C., escaped on board the federal fleet at the time of the capture of the island. Two are emancipated slaves of the district. All seem to enjoy their condition of freedom—are industrious—contented—and busy with plans for the future. I one time tho't of teaching these darkeys to read and write—forming a class and devoting two or three evenings a week to them—there are a hundred contrabands around our camp—all anxious to learn. But our major, who is a young man and has not come to his senses yet, objects to it; he is unwilling to encourage any d—d abolition business in his command. I enter their huts sometimes, take the sable students' soiled books—and make them rehearse their lessons. They are docile—persevering— and anxious to learn—but not apt. The emulative vivacity of our northern children does not show itself in them. No wonder—what development has it had?

War is all wrong—but to do a great good it is necessary to do a little harm. Removing the bonds from these four millions of God's creatures—will justify the spilling of considerable precious blood. Then there will be work for the philanthropist. To educate these neglected wretches—to inculcate maxims of healthy morality—and fit them to attain the level God intended for them. There will be work for my girls—and they live in a fortunate epoch.

But where have I lost myself? We are carefully taught by our officers that a soldier is a mere block of wood—that to think is not his attribute. Yet I have been guilty of the insubordination of figuring out our political future! Oh—when this cruel war is over!

. . .

How did les enfants enjoy themselves [in Troy]? I suppose they have effectually forgotten me by this time. Very respectfully your's

F.

Lizzie was more than sympathetic both for accompanying him on a ramble in the woods and for joining him in instructing the contrabands.

Albany June 15 1863

My dear Husband,

I am sorry my letters do not reach you as early as they used too sometimes I have been to blame, but I do not always go to bed with the stomach ache. I will try Fred to manage it so that they shall reach you earlier. I have no news to communicate[.] everything progresses as usual. I get a little work occasionally for which I ought to be grateful, and I trust I am, last week and the week before I earned six shillings. if I could earn 6/ per week it would be a little addition to my income. We get along nicely I often wonder how it is. I think I can never doubt again. a merciful and gracious Father reigns.

I know drill must be insufferably dull—how I should like to ramble with you, these warm days, everything would be novel and interesting to me; I am so glad you can find a place of retreat where you can enjoy nature, and nature's God. my heart throbs in pity for those poor ignorant blacks, it is not at all strange that they are dull, surely what development has it had? I only wonder they have as much intellect as they have beaten neglected and despised as they always have been. I wish your Major would consider that it is duty to encourage and assist all in his power the instruction of these poor neglected beings. I should like to assist you in the work. My letter must necessarily be short this time. . . . come come h-o-m-e

Lizzie

If Lee's invasion of the North made a visit home impossible, it also heightened Frederic's contempt for copperheads.[4] Heated marches by day and interruptions by night as he attempted to write his letter also had something to do with his pique. As Confederate Gens. Richard Ewell and Jubal Early moved to take thousands of Union prisoners at the Second Battle of Winchester[5] in the early stages of Lee's invasion of the North, Fred brimmed with contempt toward a fellow soldier who tried to argue on behalf of constitutional rights for Clement Vallandigham and other Northern Peace Democrats.

Fort De Russey D.C. June 14 / 63

My dear Wife,

When a man, or any man, or any other man sits down to write late in the evening of a hot June day after a fatiguing march, he cannot be expected to be in condition to produce any thing very startling. I should properly defer my letter till to-morrow, but perhaps I may find some other impediment then. While I am writing this there is a queer old fellow from Cohoes, a perfect copperhead—one whose contrariness has passed into a proverb—is standing in the door-way doing his best to involve me in a political argument. He of course is a great stickler for the constitution, and thinks the ostracism of Vallandigham an outrage upon our national rights.[6] I tell him (out of mischief of course) that just such men as he and the two Woods[7] and Gov. Seymour[8] ought to be hung without regard to the constitution—we are in arms against our foes whether in front or rear—and all whose actions proclaim hostility to the country should be destroyed, and we will see what the constitution says about it when we have time. He expresses himself a staunch supporter of McClellan[9]—and it is a singular fact that every man who inveighs against the justice of this is infallibly a supporter of little Mac. This affects his loyalty in my mind on the principle that like seeks like.

We are full of war rumors again. An attack is daily expected—we hold ourselves in constant readiness for action—and twice during the present week, have been summoned from our beds by the beating of the long-roll to man the guns. I cannot believe that there is the remotest chance of our having a visit from the foe. It is now past 10 o'clock—I have been constantly interrupted—so I shall have to be brief in consequence. Capt. Shannon has brought his wife and child out with him and they are staying in camp. I enclose a letter for Dollie—Gertie's birthday will soon be here. No show for furloughs at present. Wait till the present month expires, I will then see what can be done. Will give you a good long letter next time. With best love to wife & sister.

I am devotedly your's
F.

Even as tensions mounted for everyone as Lee and the Army of Northern Virginia made their way north of the Potomac toward what all anticipated to be a clash of some sort with the Army of the Potomac, Frederic remained ever the optimist. He saw Lee's invasion as having aroused "the spirit of '76" and given "Fighting Joe" Hooker a chance to engage the rebels successfully on Northern soil.[10]

June 18, 1863
Fort De Russey D.C.

Ma petite Femme,

I am a day late in my letter and shall [have] to write you an unsatisfactory one at that. We have had inspection again—the sixth during the last 30 days—besides our weekly inspections in our quarters. I am sick of them. We call our's a band box reg.—a paper collar reg.—a kid glove reg. We are here for ornament—not for service. Pet lambs from the capital of the Empire state, of course, we must not be classed with the common run of soldiers. Our guns are bright as burnished silver—we have never fired a shot at a rebel yet; our uniforms are made of the finest cloth; our brasses and accoutrements are polished and stainless. Our drum corps serenades the president, and if my general happens along, as a matter of course he has to inspect The New York Seventh. Possibly it is fun to them—but to us it is death. To day the mercury stood at 93°, and the atmosphere almost suffocation; and most fervently we desired rain. Harnessed up with knapsack—havresac and canteen—with forty rounds of cartridge—and rifle and bayonet—trudging thro' the blazing sun—the dust flying in clouds—the march was truly distressing. Numbers fell out of the ranks—some fainting and some overcome—and when we were drawn up in battalion line—they dropped out so numerously—that the inspection was hurried over—and the companies dismissed. I didn't suffer much. I carried no load—checked it thro', you know—and had just as much credit as the rest. To-night it is raining—the first rain in forty seven days. How delicious! I feel tempted to go and wallow in it. It is dripping thro' the roof down my neck and my seat is swimming. We have had the most dreadful claps of thunder—and the largest hail stones I ever saw. The air is deliciously cool—and there is a chance of breathing again.

We received two months' pay yesterday—you will acquaint me when you receive your allotment. There has been very little intoxication this time, for the reason that the men were kept busy cleaning for inspection—and we are kept in so strictly that there is little chance of roaming round. The military position is satisfactory. Lee's attempted invasion of the North shows his desperation—and Hooker is taking every means to catch the rebels on the wing. The spontaneous uprising of the people in defence of Pennsylvania shows the true spirit. Notwithstanding the mouthings of Copperhead orators, it is manifest that the Spirit of '76 still exists. Love of country is a deeper feeling tha[n] state pride—and when the foe sets foot upon our borders immediately a determination is aroused to drive the invader back.

I have to close hastily as taps are beating—and we have strict orders to extinguish lights. Love to all–

Your's constantly

F.E.L.

Having received the previous week's letters, Lizzie recoiled at something he had enclosed in one of them and at his suggestion that Vallandigham and other Peace Democrats might be hanged without regard to the Constitution, but she successfully navigated Josie's suggestion that she acquire a baby of her own.

17 Lark St Albany N.Y.

June 24 1863

My dear Husband,

Your letter of last week, which was a day late arrived on Monday to my great satisfaction and peace of mind (am a great fidget if your letters do not happen to come just at the usual time. . . .) I also received another pleasing message today O! aint you ashamed. No! I did not put that into my purse, for safe keeping but destroyed it immediately. Such things ought never to be preserved. I fear the remedy you suggest [for Vallandigham and others] would be worse than the existing troubles. . . . What do you think is Jossie['] s greatest trouble? That I do not get a baby. Last night she dreamt that I had got one; and was sadly disappointed upon wakening to find it was naught but a dream—she cross-questions me equal to a lawyer—upon the subject. She says she is sure we some of us know where they come from—her Aunt [Emma] & I told her that we had never had any therefore we should not be supposed to know anything about the matter. Mrs Duncan being here she appealed to her, but she proved to be as ignorant as we were. She says they can not cost so much for she saw a woman with one yesterday, and she is sure she is poorer than us. She thought she had gained her point, when she had suggested getting one, as a surprise for you, when you came home to see us. Would you fancy the surprise? Eh! Not exactly.

. . .

I should like your picture in your uniform, but I suppose there would be some difficulty in getting it. I find I am running of[f] the lines and must light the lamp. The lamp has been lighted some time; I always devote a few minutes to reading to the children before putting them to bed. They are in bed now, and cutting up so many pranks that I know not what I shall write. E[mma] has not got home yet. I was at the shop today, and I read part of your letter to her. So your tent mates are having visitors? I wish some friend would go from here to see Mr Lockley. I think it would do his heart good to see an old friend. You think yours a pet Regt that you are for ornament instead of service. You are doing service; if you were not there some other regt would be needed.

. . .

I received the $20 dollars today. I will defer building the brown stone house.[11] I will I think wait till you return. . . . Tutie insists upon it that the 4 of July is her birthday.[12] She is independent enough if that is all.

Yours devotedly, E.M.L.

With the intention of playfulness—and perhaps a touch of augury—Frederic suggests that should he "conclude to turn up my toes, and get quietly stowed away under the turf here, you wouldn't be so badly hurt." She might be better off with a fallen hero who doesn't return home than with "a lusty warrior . . . rude as Boreas." He is teasing, of course, and asked, "Is this badinage touching on a prohibited subject?"[13] Indeed, it was. "I am not pleased at you for talking as you did about turning up your toes," she wrote after receiving his letter. "I have cried over these fine words. . . . The very thought of such a thing chills my inmost soul. . . . I know you said it mischievously but I can not bear you talk thus about such a subject. What would life be to me if you were taken away?"[14] Otherwise, she said they expected high times for July 4th. She would get firecrackers for the girls.

Frederic and his fellow soldiers defending Washington remained on alert as Lee made his way north toward Pennsylvania, but they were as much in the dark about ensuing events as anyone. "Oh, for some stirring news! Something achieved that would indicate this war is not to last alway. . . . Of course you see the papers daily, and take a lively interest in the progress of the war," but for him to discuss it in his letters "is only a dull waste of space, as the opinions I express are obsolete—so rapid is the passage of events—by the time my letter reaches you."[15]

Events were indeed moving rapidly. President Lincoln and Gen. in Chief Henry Halleck had replaced Joe Hooker with Gen. George Gordon Meade, whose responses to Lee's movements were to crescendo at Gettysburg. On the first day of the battle, Frederic and the Seventh New York remained on high alert.

Fort De Russey July 1 / 63

My dearest Wife,

When I dispatched my last letter to you, we were in expectation of being called into immediate action. The whole garrison were in the fort, where they were kept constantly for forty-eight hours— and the Major said twenty-four hours could not pass without our being in the midst of the fight. The rebels captured a wagon train of 150 wagons about eight miles to the north of us—and a number of their scouts and spies were captured in our lines. Their intention of marching upon Washington seemed imminent, and the numerous forts which protect the approach to the Capital, were ready and waiting to make mince meat of a certain proportion of whatever forces might attempt the emprise. The enemy has concluded not to undertake the task—so a portion of our garrison are released from their confinement—four gun detachments merely being kept at their posts. The inactivity of our army seemed inexplicable until I learnt the removal of Hooker— this seemed a most disastrous proceeding on the eve of action too. But I see the public prints anticipate no evil consequences—and Gen. Meade brings such a glorious record to sustain him, that we may still fairly hope that some advantage may still be taken of this incautious movement of the foe.[16]

I received a letter from Mr. Duncan yesterday—he is still doing prosperously—but is despondent about the result of the war. I grant our present rate of progress is enough to discourage more patriotic men than he—still I can see grounds whereon to base my

hopes. I want Vicksburgh to fall however—and I want Gen Dix and
Foster to enter Richmond. With good generalship the rebel armies
spread as they now are could be destroyed to a certainty. I expect
to hear of stirring movements before long.

. . .

To day has been a scorcher enough. Serg. Joe and I left camp
(against orders) and had a truly delicious swim—we then went
berrying and picked a gallon of the finest blackberries—and
gather[ed] the same quantity of cherries. How I do enjoy these
escapes from camp where life is so constrained and harsh!

. . .

I wish I had some news to send you—something pleasant to
fill this sheet with. I have been busy with muster rolls till noon to-
day—and feel wearied and used up. My labor is finished once
more—I will try and send you a satisfactory letter next time.

. . .

Your's truly

F.

Elizabeth watched developments at Gettysburg keenly, and,
despite her young age and inexperience, in her next three letters
she commented on the war and the fates of generals as sagely as
any subsequent historian might.

Albany N.Y.

July 1 1863

My dearest Husband,

. . .

Your very welcome letter was received this morning. Every word is
precious, no matter what mood it is written in.

. . .

I do not sympathise with you dear Fred the monotony of your
life is tedious in the extreme. The same round of duties to perform
the same faces to look upon daily I wonder not that you tired of
it and desire a change. The change I ardently hope and pray for,
is the end of this wicked and cruel rebellion. I do indeed take a

deep interest in the progress of affairs. dead must be the soul who does not take an interest in the Country at such a time as this. I have no patience with the indifferent. They have no right to be so. My Father takes deep interest in this war. We do look daily for something startling something decisive on our side, but it comes not. It is said that Hooker has resigned I have not seen the truth of it confirmed. it does seem as soon as they begin to know something of the state of affairs, and we look forward to their accomplishing something, they resign or are removed. It looks as if they had not found the right man yet to command our armies.—kind heaven send him speedily.

. . . How I wish I could convey myself to your camp and their [*sic*] circulate about unseen by all eyes but yours. O Fred I want to ask you something. I have saved up $10 by laying by little sums at different times. This you know is to defray your expenses home; now that you cannot come just now would you advise me to put it in the Bank? perhaps I shall be able to save enough to pay both ways if you can not get your half. at any rate do not let the expence deter you for a moment.

Good bye love. Most truely
Lizzie
Albany N.Y.

July 5 1863

My dear Husband,

E[mma] and I sat down to write half an hour ago, but we got talking and well nigh forgot how time was going. Now that I have commenced I know not what to say I am perfectly barren of ideas. I want you to come home and impart a few to me.

So you have finished your muster rolls! I am glad for that—it is quite a fatiguing job. I have no doubt you were all sadly disappointed after waiting so long in the fort, that you did not have a visit from the enemy. I do not think they will attempt to go to Washington now.—our late news is good Gen Meade successfully drove the enemy back at Gettysburg—suppose Gen

Meade proves to be the right man[,] the <u>Washington</u> of this war, it does really seem as if but little will be accomplished while they change commanders so frequently—but let us hope for the best. I do hope this war will end while Lincoln holds the presidency for if a democrat is elected I should look for a patched up peace, that would not last 10 years. Much grief and sorrow as their is in the land I should not like this war to end, till it ends satisfactorily.

. . .

I am glad that you can occassionally steal away and enjoy nature in all her freedom and loveliness. I quite envy you your cherries and berries. They are so extravagantly dear that we can not think of getting many.

. . .

Truely Lizzie

Albany N.Y.
July 8 1863

My dearest Husband,

I have no doubt you had a jolification over our good news yesterday. Vicksburg has at last fallen! It seemed almost too good to believe, but it is nevertheless true. Next thing we want is to take Richmond and Port Hudson.[17] I was so excited and so delighted over the good news that I could scarcely sleep last night, we have been so successful too in driving back the foe at Pensylvania[.] Gen Meade's name is in everybody[']s mouth; all seem to think we have at last found the right man. The tide seems indeed to have turned in our favor completely. These defeats will have a telling effect upon the rebel cause, will they not?

I got the Albany Journal last night but will send it to Pa and get todays N.Y. paper for you as there will be a more particular account in it, fuller at least. I intend sending a paper to my sister Maria.

. . .

I am writing while the dinner is cooking. Emma is coming home today to dinner, which is a rare thing and I want to complete this hasty letter that she may mail it for me on her way back, so you must excuse all omissions and abruptness. Gertie's letter I received a few minutes ago, she has not come home from school yet but will be not a little proud when she finds a letter from her dear papa awaiting her; dear me the cannons are firing away at a great rate and the bells ringing right merrily. I cannot immagine what's the matter perhaps they have received news of the capture of Port Hudson or Richmond. (I doubt whether you will be able to read this I am so excited that I cannot hold my pen.)

E has just come and says it is not another victory that they are firing for, merely because they are so glad of our news yesterday.

Emma says she would hugely enjoy a picnic in the woods with you, so would I so would I. E is waiting for this. Adieu Adieu Yours forever

Lizzie

As joyous as the Union victories at Gettysburg and Vicksburg were to her, Lizzie took a more compassionate viewpoint in her diary. "It was heart cheering to see the change in people's countenances" around Albany "instead of looking sad as all have for some time past," she wrote privately. But, "Oh how many sad homes there will be; for these great victories are not won without great loss of life, on both sides."[18]

8

I Am at My Old Lunes
July–September 1863

Fred would not write to Lizzie again for almost two weeks, blaming the hot weather for his ennui and saying he might have to put her on "half rations" of correspondence—that is, one letter a week. The weather may have contributed, but he failed to write mainly because he was involved in—and then despondent over—the attempted court martial and removal of Capt. William Shannon, whom he and others thought arbitrary and despotic. Lizzie protested his threat of diminished correspondence. "Do you mean to starve me to death?" she asked, noting that letters were delivered free now.[1] Why not take advantage of the fact? Frederic remained disaffected throughout the summer, however, largely because he and the other noncommissioned officers continued to feel Shannon's repression.

On July 15 Lizzie lamented the violence in New York City and admonished him for writing so infrequently.

Albany N.Y.

July 15th 1863

My most dear Husband,

I shall not send you any more petite envelopes. It is a temptation to send me short billet doux when I am hungering and thirsting for a long letter;—it is so long since I had the pleasure of receiving one that I should esteem it a great treat; I know my letters do not merit such answers. still I would exact them if I could. My spirits are so depressed today that I feel as if nothing could arouse me. I am an enigma to myself; one day I feel cheerful & hopeful and think all will come out right; the next I am perfectly miserable. I think it is high time this war was over; and in fact I am ready to find fault with everything[;] nothing looks right; such a fit is on me today. I think my reading of the disgraceful and fearful riot in N.Y. was the cause of it today.[2] O! how dreadful I never heard of more barbrous actions among the indians, it makes my blood run cold to think of it. N.Y. is very democratic is it not?

The draft is being enforced in Troy. I hear that there was danger of a riot today, but trust it is untrue. I believe the draft for this place has been postponed; imagine us here in the midst of a riot. I saw by the morning paper that the 7th 8th and 81st Regt had been sent for; from the seat of war. it does not mean your Regt does it? I would much rather know of your going into battle where you if killed would at least stand a chance of being decently deprived of life [and] not kicked and stoned to death as many have already been; O! I feel so sorry that such unheard of outrages should have been committed in the noble empire state. Will not the rebels hold jubilee over the news.

. . . [rest of page torn and missing]

The war news today is good. Lee has escaped however. I was in hopes they would not let him recross the Potomac. I never heard such lying as the Richmond Examiner is guilty off[.] They in the most glowing terms tell of the splendid victory gained by them over the "God abandoned sons of Yankees" "Lincoln and his rascal Ministers turn pale" ["]Army of the Potomac annihilated trampled under foot" all is done I suppose to keep the rebels from despair surely they are not so ignorant as to be duped in that way.

No letter today Fred. I shall say to you as Emma once heard a woman say to her children, "if you do not so and so, I will appear to you in a dream." Would you like me to appear to you in a dream? I must not be stinted in my supply of nourishing delightful epistles, never say they are tedious, no matter what you write it is all deeply interesting to me. . . .

[The rest of page is torn and missing, but a fragment adds:] Get a furlough as soon as you can. I will joyfully welcome you. I have much to say to you when you come home you will find it difficult

to get away from me much when you do come. I shall tag after you,
see if I don't

God bless and protect you my own dear Husband
Mostly lovingly

Lizzie M.L.

"The poor negroes have suffered terribly," Elizabeth observed
two days later with more news of the draft riots available. "The men
were killed, their habitations burned and their wives and children
left perfectly helpless." She reported some rioting in Troy and fears
of the same in Albany. And she was tired of "half rations." "I shall
openly rebel. One letter a week indeed! I don't agree to it. I wont
have it. I'll write twice a day to you, if you try that. No! No! No!"[3]

She had been sewing busily for the family, and with the children on a six-week holiday, she, Emma, and the girls would visit
her grandmother and aunt in Schuylerville. Emma needed the
change. "E is generally very desponding. I try to cheer her up
sometimes," but without success, she said. Emma felt neglected
"and thinks no one cares for her." Fred should write to her more
often.[4] "Cousin" Jack was in worse trouble, "in jail in Alexandria
poor boy." "He says he is perfectly innocent [but] he does not say
what he is accused of."[5] News of Jack's troubles came by way of a
letter to Emma asking Fred's sister to send $20 so he might travel
to Troy to be discharged. Although disturbed by the boy's plight
also, Emma was less sympathetic. "This all makes me very miserable to think of that misguided boy languishing in prison and none
to help him out," Emma wrote to Fred, "but his letter does not
deceive me of course. I know how innocent he is, and as to his
love to me it never was very great."[6]

Meanwhile, Lizzie said their friend, Mrs. Owens, was having to
visit her husband in jail because he had overstayed his furlough.
"When you come I shall take good care you return at the expiration of your time," she said, "for I should not fancy visiting you in
jail." Then she seemed to pause at the thought of his really being
home. "I shall feel as bashful as a new bride."[7] In his next, Fred
wondered about her bashfulness. As for Jack, like Emma, he had
little sympathy.

[No salutation]

The mail to-day was brought into camp by Lieut. O'Hair[8] just as
we were falling in for 4 o'clock drill. I happened to be out of the
ranks at the time—so I seized the whole bundle, appropriated one
delicious missive to myself, and distributed the rest to the eager
expectant men. How unspeakably welcome are these messengers
from home! It is true they do but provoke the feelings they excite:
where the robust hungry affections ask for the clinging throbbing
wife, or the tender obedient child, we have but the echo of a
murmur, the simulation of a kiss. . . .

On reaching the drill ground, the instructor Serg[t] Treadwell
broke ranks to afford us an opportunity to read our letters. The
mail was a large one as it had failed the day before and almost
every man was made happy with a letter. If one had had time to
contemplate the scene—there is no doubt it would have afforded
interest to see us love-famished soldiers recumbent on the grass,
devouring in every variety of attitude, the messages from our loved
ones at home. I am always among the most highly favored ones. A
loving amiable intelligent lady-like correspondent, her letters are
ever pleasing for their variety and delightful for their exuberant
love. On my return, you say, you shall feel bashful as a new bride.
The feeling will become you; but I forewarn you that your coyness
will not [prompt] me to let you off as lightly as when you were first
a bride. Shall you ask it?

We are having delicious weather. The thermometer at 65° and
nights cool as October. I am recovering my faculties of expression
again in a measure. I am sorry you dwell so constantly on my
coming home on furlough. I am inclined to think you will be
disappointed. I have no doubt that we shall be discharged next
spring. The news from the southwest continues glorious—we are
rapidly approaching the end of the war—the rebel armies are
reported to be so thoroughly disaffected and demoralized that
they are melting like ice in midsummer. You say, "I wonder how
long a person can endure." Can you endure and still survive until
next March or April? Try. It is wearisome I have no doubt: but
the endurance is not all cast upon your shoulders. I suffer some

from wife—home and civil liberty sickness. Yet I manage to eat my rations—and keep my flesh up.

[hand pointing] I have recovered my 'earing[9]—but one of my front upper teeth has broke—I shoved the end of my thumb through it the other day—or rather the end of my thumb nail. The break is not visible to the naked eye—but it is one of the ravages of time. I shall return home to you a broken down old veteran—a fitting candidate for the soldier's home.

Let me once get you within my grasp—I will make manifest to you my physical debility.

. . . As for Jack, he must work out his own salvation.

. . . Sergt Mather[10] will call upon you in a few days—I shall send my watch by him—it wants cleaning. I dropped it in the creek about a month ago. Good bye Sweetheart. Love to sister and the kids.

Very devotedly Yours

F.

As August faded into September, Lizzie and Fred's correspondence grew newsy and intimate. In one missive, Fred admonished her for crying herself to sleep. "Tell me whether you have gained or lost flesh—I like plump rotund figures. I don't know why Lieut Mather should describe me as stout—I am spare as ever. I am in splendid health—flesh hard as oak—weigh 155 lbs."[11] In other letters, he shared a comic scene of the men debating grammar, and in another he detailed a raucous episode of escaped horses galloping through camp and undue punishment for an unoffending newspaper vender.

Sept 2^d 1863

Chére femme affectionnél,

Your <u>billet doux</u> came to-day. Your old lunes are upon you, I see. Love is still the burden of your song. . . . Will you never tire of declaring your devotion?

. . .

Our camp has been like a horse-fair all day—the varying equine scenes and spectacles presented would have charmed the eye of

Rosa Bonheur.[12] Twenty-seven hundred horses escaped from their guard at Rockville Md. and scouring wildly over the country came upon Ft De Russey in clouds like a flock of pigeons in a migration. Our men have had the greatest fun in catching them and galloping them barebacked up and down the hill. They are still wandering about the face of the country in squads suffering for water.

Much obliged for your remittance. I shall keep it—altho' I know you want it worse. While I write the serg[ts]. are having an amusing discussion—and refer to me to decide. The question is whether the noun Molasses is singular or plural. I pronounce that it is plural in form—but singular in use by universal sanction. Serg[t]. Faulk dissents. I cite an example. Suppose you have a plate of buckwheat cakes before you—and some spotless virgin inquires if you will take molasses—how would you address her—"I will take a few, if you please?" or "I will take a little?" He puts on a profound look and says, "I will take many." This is so characteristic of the man—huge as he is—good-natured—sterling and a grass feeder[13]—that we recognize the humor of his answer and burst into eclats de vire.[14]

Excuse my nonsense. I have to fill my sheet. Good bye

F.

September 21, 1863

Ma chére Femme,

We are deprived of news here, thro' some misunderstanding with the vendors. Our papers are brought to camp by the post mail carrier—an enlisted man of Comp[y] I. There is a diminutive little hunchback at Head quarters who eats with the men, and sleeps anywhere, whose pitiable deformity has won the sympathy of the colonel. This dwarf obtained the Colonel's permission to supply Ft de Russey with papers—and they were refused to Clarence Tuthill our mail carrier. The dwarf mounted a big horse and came over on Saturday last with papers—but he committed the fatal mistake of selling to the men first. He sold out before he thought of the officers. Lt. Col. Hastings was wrathy and forbade him coming to the fort again—under pain of the guard house if he disobeyed.

but the dwarf, thinking the license of the colonel superior to the prohibition of the lt. Col. ventured here the next day. Immediately he was arrested—confined in the guard house and a thirty-two pound ball fastened to his leg. The poor little object was kept in that condition 'till night—when he was released with the admonition that if he again offended he would be showered. This has kept him away—and Clarence not being able to obtain them (the colonel's veto not having been removed yet) we are without news; and to be without papers here is like being at sea—we are entirely isolated.[15]

I must describe the punishment of showering to you—it has only been inflicted once, and that was upon an incorrigible offender yesterday. I have mentioned to you that we are seriously annoyed by the unrestrained sale of poisonous liquors at the sutlers. Particularly after pay days—the camp is demoralized. The colonel being interested in the business—he allows this enormity to exist regardless of the trouble occasioned. So since the officers at this post are unable to remove the cause—they resolved to restrain its effects—and a variety of punishments have been inflicted to prevent drunkenness. Private Shipley[16] (the man operated on yesterday) is finely educated—a deep thinker, a lucid speaker, a graceless infidel, and a bitter unrelenting satirist. He has grown disaffected, and has taken to drunkenness. Good usage being exhausted, the lt col. ordered a shower yesterday. To receive this the culprit is seated on a low board—his arms tied to the posts of a square frame, and his head thrust thro' an orifice. A barrel filled with water is placed two feet above his head with a hinged plug in the bottom; this is raised at the word of the officer of the day and down comes the deluge—plentiful as the unguent which overflowed Aaron's beard. If it wasn't that there is a chance of surviving—I would prefer being thrown into the liquid element—to see the sudden shock communicated—and the convulsive gasping for breath—indicated sensations anything but agreeable. "The worse use you can put a man to," says an old political apothegm, "is to hang him." I have found a worse use yet you can put a man to—make a soldier of him.

. . .

We had a sharp frost last night and to-day the air is quite brisk. It is a delightful fall day, and I just feel like setting out from Ft. Edward[17] to follow the shores of the Great Hudson until I arrive at the classic walls of historic Saratog! Take a pencil and compute how long a space would elapse after my feet touched the western terminus of the bridge which spans the river's limpid wave before I singled out a nondescript semi-Grecian cottage entered its precincts—and clasped the goddess that dwelt there in my arms.

Ha! There's no use a talking! Tantalus for his crimes was immersed in water to his lips—but when he sought to drink—the water sunk beyond his reach. Sisyphus was doomed to roll a heavy wheel up a steep hill which ever overmastered his strength ere he had half ascended its side—and rolled to the bottom. I am doomed to be continually craving the embraces and enjoyments of a dear loving little wife—but a geographical space is interposed to keep us asunder. All's well that ends well.

F.

Lizzie had sent him a picture of Josie, his ten-year-old daughter, but in his response of September 9, he asked for a picture of all three girls. She obtained it quickly, sent it to him, and was glad to learn he approved of it. Reminded of their courtship three years earlier, she admitted to having been naive to his initial overtures, although her grandma and auntie were quite aware of his intentions. She continued to sew to make a little money but thought his commander a humbug for not allowing him to come home on furlough.

Albany Sept 24th 1863

My dear Husband,

. . .

I received your very welcome and pleasing letter Monday. I am glad you like the girl's pictures[.] I thought I would not tell you that I had sent the three, but give you an agreeable surprise. I think they all give promise of being fine looking women. Dollie is I think the general favorite, altho Emma will have it that Jossie is superior. I am not able to decide between the three sometimes I think one and then another but I am perfectly impartial, one is just as dear to me as the other. Of course they all have their faults and need to be tutored occasionally[.] Mrs. Duncan and I were discussing the subject the other day and she told me that she thought it would be difficult to find another such good family of children as yours don't you feel proud? I do.

I see by Emma's letter that you have moved your quarters. I should think it quite necessary, your castle being rather too well ventilated for the uncertain weather we must now expect. Greatly disappointed as you may all be; I hope the rumor of your going to Texas is not true. I should give up all hope of ever looking upon your face again if you did. I think I shall accept of your invitation to go as laundress.

. . .

I had not heard that Ed Graces was drafted. truely! tis such fellows as he who ought to go first. I wonder how his wife will feel in regard to it. Our draft here was postponed if I am drawn I will certainly try to get into the 7th Artillery (I wish they would draft the women.) . . .

I think Genl Heintzelman is a humbug! I wonder if he would not like to see his wife & family if he had been away 13 long months. I have no doubt he sees his family daily well! Well! That is the way of the world. There is no use in grumbling. I think if you had a different Captain you would stand a better chance of getting a furloug[h] The idea of my being able to get anything to do in W—n[18] will I supposed gradually fade out of my mind. I am still sewing for Miss Van Olinda she is to return next Monday.

. . .

You "feel like setting out from Ft Edward and following the broad shores of the Hudson till you arrive at a nameless village." I do not like the place[;] still a portion of the time spent there will always recall some of the happy moments of my life much as I used to watch and long for your coming[.] I rather dreaded it[;] you know why? when I look back it does not seem as if three years had nearly passed since these events transpired just 3 years ago the 9th day of this month since you told me those few words which I so innocently repeated at dinner to Auntie & Grandma. When she exclaimed to my great astonishment that she bet he was after Liz. I laughed at her, tossed it of[f] lightly and thought no more of [it] till you reminded me of it in the evening on our way to Church. What a vast deal of attention I paid to the sermon that evening I could not even tell where the text was to be found. enough! we'll discuss these important matters more fully when we meet. Adieu God bless you.

Lizzie

Tis too bad that you are deprived of the news. I will try and send you papers more frequently.

Frederic wrote the day before in a quite discouraged mood, or as he put it, "I am at my old <u>lunes</u>." New recruits were arriving. He liked their quality, but what happened to them under "the iron despotism of military rule" disheartened him. He understood the necessity of it, but he regretted the scene just the same.

September 23rd 1863

Ma chere[19] Femme,

Your's reached me yesterday your complaint that you received but one letter last week arose from the fact—I suppose—that I was delayed in sending my letters. I believe I have dispatched two weekly. I mentioned to Emma that we were expecting another batch of recruits. They arrived in camp on Monday—19 of them—a splendid sct of fellows. We are getting a very superior set of men now—which is attributable to the fact that the draft hauls into its meshes a class of men who would not have volunteered. It is really grievous to see so many intelligent young men bro'. from their free homes and attired in their various civic garbs—marched into camp, the dull ungracefull blue suit thrown upon them, and the free and fearless air of the citizen crushed out of them by the iron despotism of military rule. I can appreciate the priceless value of Liberty—now if I never did before—it is worth every sacrifice to preserve—even the mustering of armed bands, and the subjecting [of] the citizen to the rigors of the camp. It is worth this sacrifice because Army Regulations govern us for but a season while our liberties if once parted with we become slaves for life. But, oh! what pen is there to describe the injustice—the abuse of paltry despots—the demoralization and moral abnegation of the victims! The normal state of society is peace—beneficent Peace—and ere long the irradiant Goddess will again visit our blood stained borders—but during this murky eclipse, while the fratricidal demon of War is free to disturb all harmonious relations—and ravage and pollute every thing that comes in his way—our only portion is to silently endure.

I am at my old lunes—they affect me periodically. Individually I am well treated—well provided for and blessed with unflagging health. If an inscrutable Providence would only please to take to himself a heavy, puffy self-important fool—a thrice double ass whose oppugnable dullness chafes me unendurably—or if the Provident would create him a Brig. Gen. in five minutes or devise any mutation that would rid us of his presence at this post—then with what freedom and elasticity I could respire! But the whirligig of time brings about its own revenges.

I understand the draft has been delayed in Albany. I pity any poor devil constrained by adverse Fate to loaf in camp for his country. What a way to vindicate right. On my emancipation from thraldom I intend to join a universal peace society.

I have nothing to write you to-day. I am so constantly at my pen that I am weary of wielding it. Still I prefer this counting house work to drilling. I solemnly swear that if I live to get away from the sound of a drum—that the first one I ever meet in the streets at home I will knock a hole in it.

We have just had another visit from the Sanitary Commission[20] agent. The old dame is an exaggerated Santa Claus. She has left the Officers' room bestrewn with flavorous preparations— such as syrup—dried fruits and so on—also lots of pillows— comforters—linen rags—besides a profusion of Books and religious publications. The religious publications were distributed with unsparing hand thro' the camp—they being of interest to man's immortal soul; all the other inconsidered trifles, which merely serve to gratify a man's carnal wants, were sedulous[ly] appropriated by the officers.

I write this while his royal Nibbs is at Fort Stevens on Court martial—it is about time for his return—so I will pretermit my clandestine confab with you and resume business. Did the letter containing an enclosed note for my mother reach you? You have not alluded to it. How is Mrs. Smallwood—she is not destined to make old bones Good bye mum

Your's devotedly

F.

[P.S.] Opposite to our quarters the Saratogians dwell—their habitation a wall-tent. They are a quite neighborly set of fellows— all Christians—occasionally they raise their voice in divine harmonies—their taste is so novel that we draw round them to gaze with wonder. They are dull, however—and carry no great weight. A French boy—named Gauther[21] was caught asleep upon his post last night—and is confined[.] he is to be tried by Court martial for the offence. He is a good Soldier—a lively companionable fellow—and all grieve at his misfortune.

Lizzie battled mice, and as she wrote her letter of September 27, a snap in the pantry announced there was one less to nibble her stores. She shared Frederic's contempt for dominating officers, especially after hearing his story of the hunchback newspaper vendor. "I think locking up of that poor deformed creature perfectly outrageous," she declared. "It plainly shows their ignorance. . . . I despise these upstart tyranical beings who wear the garb of Officers but sadly disgrace their profession."[22] Frederic felt similarly. His was always the citizen soldier's point of view. Nevertheless, he had made his peace with Captain Shannon and wrote discerningly of the new recruits in camp. However resigned he was to make the best of things, he deplored the intellectual desert he thought surrounded him.

Sept. 30th 1863

Ma Petite Femme,

If I fill this sheet, it will furnish you with epistolary aliment sufficient to last you for three weeks. I feel a trepidation as I look down the page. I am exceedingly busy—the close of every month visits upon me lots of writing . . . [but] our respected Company commander is at Washington [so] I thought I would e'en let company writing go for an hour or two—while I talked a little nonsense to the <u>old 'oman</u>.

I am much interested in Josie's education. I do not, by any means, want the young one's mind overtasked, but I am unwilling that the present opportunity should not be used to its fullest limit. I have no doubt that her studies in school are arduous enough to engage all her faculties—and I do not wish to have her mental task increased—but these studies, be it remembered are merely the <u>means</u> to education—they discipline the mind, and lay out the charts and channels of human knowledge, but in themselves—they contain no wisdom. Grammar, for instance, teaches the proper use of words; with its assistance we can employ language fearlessly and gracefully—as a skilful fencer is able to wield freely and defend himself with his sword, but Grammar alone contains no wisdom. It arranges the weapons—it drills the forces—it opens the road.

<u>Education</u> is thus derived. <u>E</u> signifies, out of, proceeding from—and <u>ducere</u>, to lead; and its literal signification is to lead or draw out. To educate, therefore, is to draw out a person's intellectual powers. In order to do this—the process of thought must be enlisted, and this is best developed by supplying matter for thought. With young people this is best accomplished by profitable reading.

Oct. 1st It is folly to enter into depth of argument here—interruption is so incessant that I cannot remain at the same work an hour together. I had just started upon my letter yesterday—when commissary wagons from hd qrs. arrived bringing ten days' rations. Then Capt. Shannon returned from court martial, and set me to work on Company reports—and so I was kept busy until midnight. The mail has just arrived—bringing him a letter from his wife—so while he dwells upon that precious missive, I come to my quarters to make one for you. I expect to hear him calling me every minute. We have grown to understand each other better—we get along far more harmoniously than before. He is dull, obstinate—and is the incarnation of untruth; a man of false character and unscrupulous as a pickpocket—choleric as Achilles and variable as Eolus.[23] But he is human—speaking generically—I rub up against him all day long—hair est un tourment (to hate is a torment) he is my superior officer, and opposing him is a fruitless business. Besides these he finds me exceedingly useful to him— and that if he wants service from me, he must take the right way of me. So all these considerations seem to remove all asperities—and we jog along with much less opposition—if not with greater love.

. . .

We are having truly cold weather—a frost nearly every night. This time last year we were driven away from camp during the middle of the day by the flies the dust and the heat. I do not like the camp half as well since we have had so many fresh faces crowded upon us. They are bully men—we are fortunate in having such excellent material to fashion into soldiers—but they are rough. A man possessing any refinement of sentiment—my taste for culture—is sadly out of place among soldiers. By a mysterious law of nature they abandon themselves to vice and frivolity. Drinking, gambling—sleeping are the occupation of most of their leisure hours—their reading, beyond the newspapers, is generally of an impure nature. Anything instructive, elevating, religious—is turned from by common sympathy. Yet our men are first rate fellows—loyal citizens—good soldiers—and generally intelligent. Save Lieut. Mather there is not a man in Comp. I that ever thinks of opening Shakspere except to look at the pictures.

. . .

You will weary of this—and I must close Good bye

9

Hope Is the Anchor of the Soul
October 1863

Frederic started his last letter on a Wednesday. By Friday, October 2, he had received promotion and transfer to the adjutant's office at Fort Reno.[1] The change threw his life into disarray, but he welcomed it. Fort Reno offered greater potential for advancement, and besides, it provided escape from his dominating captain.

Fort Reno D.C. Oct. 4th 1863.

Ma chére Femme,

The change you invoked for me has been vouchsafed—I am detailed as clerk in the regimental adjutant's office. I came here on Friday, and shall act as assistant to the sergeant major—he has been instructing me in my duties, and very soon I shall be able to run about. My removal is a serious cause of annoyance to Capt. Shannon, as the filling of his comp[any] with recruits causes considerable work. He is detailed on special duty on general court martial—and is consequently unable to devote much time to the requirements of the comp[y]. Hence his annoyance at the loss of my services. It is a singular fact that we have not a good writer in the whole camp—and when I took the signatures of the various Squads of recruits assigned to Comp I, I looked with considerable interest for some one fair specimen of calligraphy. In the last squad among the crude variety of autographical combinations, I detected one fair signature. This I showed the captain—the writing was neat and finished; he approved it and remarked that he should have to use that man. So when the official order was handed him detailing me for duty at Head quarters, he immediately sent for this man,

126

to install him in my place as company clerk, and Serg[t]. Berry I understand is to perform my quartermaster duties.

I was warmly congratulated by my brother non-commissioned officers on my happy escape from Fort De Russey—there are some excellent fellows there—and I parted from them with sincere regret.

I am going over there this morning to pack up so as to have my things transplanted thither tomorrow. I am living a vagrant life at present—I am quartered nowhere, my rations to last till the 10th inst. have been sent to Ft De Russey—and I get my meals wherever there is the best show. I patronize the hospital steward for my breakfast—get my dinner perhaps with the teamsters at the barn— and sup at some of the Company cook-houses. The adjutant must get me quarters soon—or I shall wear my welcome out generally.

I have wanted to get here—there is some chance of advancement—besides being a far more pleasant post. My pay is not increased at present—but that will come anon. Serg[t] major Treadwell who was appointed at the organization of the regiment, was promoted to Aide de camp with the rank of 2[d] lieutenant; and he has since been advanced to acting ass[t] adjutant general, with the rank of 1st Lieutenant. The vacancy created by his promotion was filled by a Corp[l]. O'Brien[2] who was promoted to serg[t]. major and he has since been advanced to a lieutenancy. He was succeeded by a Corp[l]. Norton[3] who still retains the office—but in the event of his promotion there will be a chance for me. Fort De Russey was so secluded and away from change that one stood but a slim show there for anything beyond comp[y]. promotions.

This is a miserably dull letter. The fact is my mind feels so unsettled this morning that I cannot fix my thoughts upon my theme . . .

Love to Emma and the kids. Good bye missus

F.

Lizzie, meanwhile, was reaching her breaking point; she had not seen Fred in more than a year, and the subject of a furlough home coursed through all her letters. Still, she and the girls carried on.

Albany N.Y.
Oct 9th 1863

Dear Fred,

My having earned three shillings this morning does not warrant my
loafing the afternoon away does it? Conscience plainly whispers no
still I do not feel inclined to listen to her voice this time. I would
give worlds if I possessed them to spend this most magnificent
afternoon with you, I would go without eating for a week; I could
endure any penalty that might be inflicted upon me but tis all of
no avail, the unpleasant conviction faces itself upon me that it is
impossible at present to enjoy each others society.

When you first left us I used to flatter myself with the thought
that you would be able to come and see us at the end of 6 months,
or a year at the farthest. Surley! Hope is the anchor of the soul. I
have several times of late met persons who at a distance bore so
strong a resemblance to you that my heart would thrill with an
estacy [*sic*] of delight, quick as a flash the thoughts would dart
through my mind perhaps it is he it is possible another moment is
enough to suffice and I go on my way more weary and dispirited
than before; the sudden elation of spirit only tends to make me
experience my utter lonliness. I wish I was stronger minded, less
afraid to meet the cold indifference of the unsympathising crowd.
These stirring times that we are now passing through are fitted to
develop and draw out the latent energies of the mind, if there are
any to be drawn out.

I feel this afternoon as if I could enjoy an intelectual feast[.] I
would like to go with you to some retired spot, and have you read
Shkspeare to me, <u>King Lear</u> would suit my taste well; It is utterly
impossible for me to get time to read, as I wish. I snatch an hour
occassionally but so many duties and cares await me that I feel as
if I was stealing time. . . . I am anxious that the children should
improve their time, and will do all in my power to lead them, ask
with me dear Fred for help from on High to enable me to do my
duty faithfully. No one can be so well fitted as an own Mother to
watch and guide them every step in youth, and it is impossible to
fill her place but Heaven helping me I will cheerfully do what I
can. . . . Tutie came home from school today feeling very proud.

The teacher pronounced her the best reader in the class that is of the girls; there was one boy I believe equal to her. Each one of the kids is head of her class. Gertie after an absence of several days had to go to the foot of her class, but she again took her place at the head the first day she went. Last night I gave her a taste of gin for a little ailment, and she felt quite funny, her sisters told her she was drunk, and she did not like it at all. She is like me she does not require but a very little to make her quite merry.

I so often wish you had one of the kids with you for company, but the camp would be rather an objectionable place for a child. I shall not let sister Emma know that I wrote this letter or she would think I was going crazy. Mrs Owens Husband has been exchanged and is now with his Regt I believe; ill fortune seems to follow him, on the way to this Regt the train of cars carrying him thither took fire and he lost all he had, and just escaped with his life. This is the second time he has lost all. Before[,] he lost his musket and was obliged to replace it. I shall look for a letter as usual tomorrow. I think all my friends have forgotten me. I get letters from no one. I do wish Pa would write.

I have not finished house cleaning yet but I got so tired out yesterday that I thought I would let the rest go till next week. While washing is what I dread most I have not tried it yet.[4] I suppose you have house cleaning time occassionally. I hope you like your new quarters. Are there any Ladies at Headquarters? Tell me who are your tent-mates and all about them. I had your little habitation at Ft De Russey all pictured out in my mind and I do not like to feel as if I know nothing about you in your new abode.

My kind regards to all enquiring friends

[PS] I feel inclined to tear this up. There are so many errors that I will not undertake to correct them all. Don't you wish I would not write unless I wrote more sensibly?

Your foolish Wife
Lizzie M.L.

At Fort Reno, Frederic still rustled his grub at the hospital and slept in his office, but his mind was active on a scheme to bring Lizzie to camp and provide board for the officers. In fact, combined with trying to deal with Lizzie's loneliness, it seems to have been overactive with a plan to sell fresh berries in Washington during summer.

October 13th 1863

[No salutation]

Cannot you restrain your impatience a little? What makes you so crazy to see me? What good would it do you? Sooth to say, I divide with you in a measure your impatience for a re-union—but Time will be our only restorer. Let us trust that his flight will be speedy.

I have had busy thoughts since my last to you—and just to fill this sheet I must give you the benefit of some of them. Talking an evening or two since with Lieut. Mather on things in general—the subject of boarding the Officers for the winter was introduced. He and two or 3 other officers board with the drum major who has his wife and family here—and has built him a snug little house. The reg^t. Commissary Serg^t board a few other officers—the rest get their meals at a poor comfortless hotel. To day the two companies who have been doing guard duty on Mason's Island returned their bringing six more officers to be provided for. In addition to this— when our companies get filled up as they will be during the winter two additional lieutenants to each company will want a table to sit down to: evidently the accommodations already provided will be insufficient. The idea just struck my mind, what if I were to build a house and have the old woman out and take half a dozen officers to board, how would that work? It would require considerable outlay—and I must first get permission of the colonel to build. The modus operandi I can yet see into—if the thing proves practicable, should you like it? the men are moving from their winter quarters into barracks, and their stockades left standing would be quite a start towards a house. I should require considerable help—and if Col. Morris approves my plan I could get a detail of men to build it for me. the task would keep you busy—but you could have help eno'. Emma of course would be willing to come—also, your brother, perhaps would like to try Dixie land for awhile.

By the bye—here's another thing in relation to your brother. I intend next Summer—God and the elements favoring, to rent a little place in Pennsylvania Ave fit it up tastily—and set you behind a counter therein, with a fabulous amount of freshly gathered blackberries every day. The demand for them in Washington exceeds the supply—and they perish ungathered here by the hundred bushel. Just set all the children and idle grown girls around here to gathering berries—and send in a cart load twice a day to you to dispose of—you would be kept busy measuring them out to eager customers all the livelong day. But you must be careful what money you take—don't let them put counterfeit off upon you. Rightly attended to—a constant supply of nice fresh fruit furnished you—attention and business tact on your part—and during the season of six weeks while they abound—a small sum might be netted out of which I could buy you a calico dress.

This is all premature however.

I received your letter this morning—you are unusually attentive—You cannot send me enough, tho! Your small talk—as you persist in calling it—still has charms for me. Love to Emma and the kids. You need not lay in your winter's fuel for a week or two—that we may see what comes of my project.

Frederic

Lizzie responded gleefully to the prospect of going to Fort Reno to cook for the officers, as Fred suggested, but she was full of questions.

Albany Oct 18th 1863

My dearest Husband,

I know not how to commence. Your letter furnished me a full supply, for busy thoughts you may be sure. Go to Fort Reno and be with you, a whole family once more? I say the words over half a doz times in an hour, still I can scarcely comprehend their meanings. How should I like it? I have no doubt should the thing come to pass there would be many difficulties for us to contend with; but I am perfectly willing to meet them all. I should have your sympathy and love to sustain me under them, and I should be happy. Tis a momentous step and there is much to be considered as you of course know, but we are unable to judge in the matter, and will trust entirely to you, knowing that you will do all in your power for our welfare and happiness. Do you think I am competent? They would not expect to have everything just so, would they? I know they go in for good living.

How novel our life would seem there. Here we so seldom have a man come to the house, that we do not know how to behave. I do not mean that we are so attentive; but we are almost shy; then to go among such a number of them how great the change. I am too much confused to write half what I want to say.

. . .

Yes! Fred I want to go to you; live the alloted time and it is short enough, I want that our lives should glide on in unity and joy together; we can not afford to live so many years assunder. I trust the Colonel will fall in with our plans[,] consent to it and give you all the assistance in his power. I am so impatient to receive your next letter! If this project should fail I should feel even more miserable than now. The faint hope having been excited in my mind of a reunion. If you see that the thing is practicable, you will find employment enough in planning matters. How soon should we go? You have not said what we should do with the kids and the sticks[,] leave them behind? Eh? Emma says she fears there would be no way for the children to go to school. In what way do you think my brother could employ himself there?

. . . May Heaven smile upon your plans.

Most truly

Lizzie

All such plans collapsed, however, when Fred was ordered back to Fort DeRussy thanks to Captain Shannon's intrigues to secure him as quartermaster sergeant.

Fort De Russey D.C. Oct 18[th] 1863

My chére Femme

I am uncertain whether it is Mendels[s]ohn or Haydn who was in the habit of attiring himself with the utmost exactness, and placing a valuable diamond ring on his finger, which had been presented to him by some crowned head; then he could sit down and produce those divine melodies which have charmed the universal ear of mankind. He had the organ of <u>order</u> largely developed; and his attribute where it can be readily indulged, is productive of great enjoyment. But oh Lord o' massy! what could such men do here? Dirt, and disorder, and chaos are all-pervading.

I should have told you that I am returned to my company "by order of Col. L.O. Morris, Special Orders No. 238. Octr 17th 1863, F.L. Tremaine Adjutant." This order was issued in consequence of my having been promoted to company quartermaster sergeant, my new duties of course requiring my presence with the company. We are now filled up to our maximum standard 147 enlisted men; my duties consist of directing the preparation of food and the serving of the men. I also have charge of the quartermaster stores. This is a responsible position, and Captain Shannon thinks me the man best calculated for the trust.

My return to my quarters—where I find an accumulation of two weeks' litter and <u>laizzer faire</u> perfectly disgusts me. The table is so nasty I cannot fancy my grub off it, the bread box (an empty ammunition case) is choke full of mouldy portions of loaves—the towels are foul—the plates and cups strewn hither and thither. Just returning as I have from civilization and sporadic elegance, the untidiness here affects me disagreeably. I objurgate my friends' habits—they are amused at my annoyance—and Serg^t. Rogers humorously remarks "didn't I tell you you'd catch rats when the old man returned?"

I resolve to <u>clar</u> things up a bit. I take water to the cook house to heat it in order to scrub the table first thing. But the range is so filled with kettles and boilers that I have no chance to heat it. I become discouraged. Cleanliness is a virtue—but fidgettiness more than annuls it. I take towel and soap—and go down to the creek, resolved to be clean in my person—even if the house remains filthy. So on this bright October Sabbath morn, I sit down to write a rambling letter to you—and philosophically resolved to let things <u>went</u>.

There is a game being played between Captain Shannon—the quartermaster, and the adjutant, with regard to my possession. The Captain has played a good card and carried me off. But I expect to be back to headquarters again before long. The regimental commissary sergeant is complained of as being miserably inefficient. I must admit that I covet the position, but of course can only wait the course of events. Q.M. Serg^t. Parker told me the other day in confidence, that the quartermaster wanted to get rid of him—and that I should be appointed in his place. This is likely to occur at any moment—and you need not be surprised at my having to report another change to you. My pay is now $17 per month: the pay of the reg.^{l} Com.^{y} Sergt. $21 per mo. besides considerable pickings. My position is interesting, however being bandied about between them.

Our barracks are nearly completed—and we shall probably move in about a week from now. I shall be glad of the change—for I have grown perfectly disgusted with our shanties. Strict police regulations will be observed and although crowded we shall be clean and orderly. The men will be fed in the mess house—their plates and cups washed for them—so they will be relieved of that nuisance.

A distant cannonading which has reached our ears for the last three hours tells of a third battle being fought at or near Bull's run.[5] This heavy dull booming has a melancholy sound—every report is perhaps the herald of death dealt to patriot soldiers. We have had two reverses upon that blood stained field! I cannot bear to link Heaven's name with these scenes of carnage; but I trust in the genius of Meade—the indomitable spirit of our soldiers, and the justice of our cause for success in this encounter.

We have inspection tomorrow—and I have to turn out to exhibit myself. I thought to have been rid of this nuisance for one while. I gave away my old clothes when I was detailed on daily duty in the Adj^t's office—I shall want them again now.

Good bye—Lieut. O'Hair wants me to board the officers at this post—they are half starved at present. I shall have to send for the old woman yet. Love to Emma and the kids.

Your's devotedly

F.

A trip to the capital left Frederic disgusted and embarrassed to be seen in uniform there, so lured were the soldiers into mind-less entertainments and dissipation. Sleeping arrangements with his tent-mates were not much better, but he did outsmart the rats that lived with them.

October 21st 1863

Fort De Russey, D.C.

Ma chére Femme,

I was in Washington yesterday; it was late when I returned, and I was too tired to write. Like a big goose I forgot to take Miss Van Olinda's address with me[6]—so I was deprived of the pleasure of calling upon your friend. I dislike going to that city much, it is so cheerless to walk along those interminable streets without a friend in the place; and the level to which soldiers have fallen is so low, that one is hardly treated like a human being. A soldier's visit to Washington is generally an occasion of visiting some of the innumerable haunts of impurity and dissipation; the amusements provided for them are of the lowest character: mammoth women and seven legged calves, and exaggerated melo-dramatic performances and <u>sich</u>. I feel ashamed of my uniform—and am glad to get back to bury myself in camp.

By the bye—I don't like the present style of bonnets. I am undecided whether they most resemble a coal hod, or a water spout. The sight of so much perambulatory dry-goods affects me with home sickness—and I do not recover the tone of my mind for two or three days.

My removal to Fort De Russey will rather interfere with my calculations of having you out this winter. It is a folly to discuss such a matter while affairs are in so unprepared a state—we must wait a little, and see what turns up. Now that my pay is a little increased, instead of giving you the benefit of it, I propose to apply the amount to paying my expenses home—and will certainly try to spend next New Year's home with you. I have been restrained hitherto in consideration of the expense; but my desire to see you all is so vehement—that the gratification will be fully worth the cost—and I am determined to gratify our mutual wishes. I intended to have spent the 4th-of-July with you—but the pleasure is yet to come.

The company has just gone down to the parade ground to drill under the tuition of the Sergeant. I have straightened up the house a little. It would horrify you to tell you the condition of our beds. Last fall Serg^t. Falk had some bed sacks sent him from home—these he had filled with straw—and he and his brother sergeants had quite comfortable beds. But after a year's almost constant use, the straw has become so broken up and the bed sacks so worn that if one ventures to touch them—the broken straw filtrates thro' like pepper from a pepper-box. For this reason we leave them severely alone. Joe and I sleep together—and the bed having worked about half a foot from the wall—he complains that one half of his body comes in contact with the bare boards. Joe is very fastidious in his bed—if the rain or the wind beats on him thro' the night—I can have no rest with him till all the available shirts and trousers in the quarters are stuffed into the holes. He also finds the scanty ration of bed afforded him a subject of complaint. I offer to change places with him—but this he declines on the ground that our bunk being six feet above the floor, the person sleeping outside—if he moves any in his sleep is apt to fall out—and the sudden fall in the dark upon a miscellanea of boxes, camp stools and old boots is apt to be disagreeable.

I must tell you how I spited the rats the other night. They will drink a whole pail full of water thro' the night if we leave it uncovered, and it[']s quite annoying to have to run down to the spring before the dawn in order to wash your face. This night I thought I would best them—so I covered the pail of water with a heavy ammunition box—put the grub carefully out of their reach and then extinguished the light and lay down to sleep the sleep of the righteous. Such a racket as the rats made all that night was a caution. They knocked our cups and plates off the shelves—pulled every article that was movable over—and then extending their search, commenced running in the most lively manner over my face and chest. This was unpleasant.

The next night, I put two whole loaves in the cupboard— and fetched a pail of water for them; the bread they demolished except the thin crust which they tunnelled out—and the water pail they emptied. I had a quiet night's rest thereby. I was amused at a similar compromise made with the flies by the orderly one evening during hot weather. I had given him some blackberry preserve, and this delicacy so attracted the flies that he could not eat his supper for them. He is an enthusiastic naturalist, and admitted their right to a meal equally with his own. But in order that their lives might not be sacrificed to the action of his jaws thro' their persistent adhesion to his victuals—he spread a slice of bread with the savory paste—and laid it on the table for their especial delectation.

. . .

Please send me a quarter's worth of stamps—I will send you the money pretty soon.

Your's

F.

Fred and his comrades had moved and now had new and better accommodations, where he was again taken with the poignant scene when he distributed the mail. He then noted, disingenuously and almost as an aside, that he and seventeen others had been detailed for duty "a few miles north of Baltimore" as security for the off-year elections. Understandably, Lizzie failed to guess that "North of Baltimore" was code for a furlough home.

Octr 28th 1863

My Dear Wife,

You complain of feeling an uncertainty about my locale. Relieve yourself of that incertitude; we have moved into the barracks—and are established for the winter. Our hundred and forty men make a tolerably lively hearth—there is no fear of our suffering from dulness. I have all along preferred the idea of thus living—the building is roomy and commodious (20 ft x 100) well lighted and ventilated; the police arrangements excellent. The Orderly has a room 15 x 10 ft partitioned off for his quarters, with whom I am at present living. This he intends to furnish with a few necessary articles—and while it separates him from the crowd it admits of his living in entire comfort. . . . When the mess house is finished my quarters will be there—and my functions consist of taking charge of all the stores quartermaster and commissary. I have the most desirable berth in the whole company. I rank next to the first sergeant.

I wish you could have seen the distribution of the mail to-day. For some reason it failed to come thro' yesterday, and the men were ravenous for letters. I received about a hundred letters from the Mail carrier, a delicate charming little missive from you amongst them—and proceeded to the barracks to distribute. The throng that gathered round me to hear the names as I called them—the ready voices in answer and eager hands outstretched to receive them. The satisfied looks with which they received them, and the dejected look of those who were neglected—and then the quiet that prevailed as each man with absorbing interest read the precious effusions. These moving illustrations of the power and permanence of the domestic affections, are touching to behold and show how strong is the influence of <u>home</u> upon us all.

. . .

I am detailed for duty a few miles north of Baltimore with seventeen men, to take a hand in the Election to come off next Tuesday, so I will deprive myself of the delights of your correspondence until you hear from me again. . . . We are ordered to report thither without arms—merely wearing our waistbelts so I presume our duties are not of a belligerent character. It is not certain whether we leave here tomorrow or Saturday. I am pleased with the change and will inform you fully of its incidents.

. . .

Your's connubially

F.E.L.

"He says he [is] going a few miles north of Baltimore to aid in the election," Lizzie recorded in her diary Halloween night, "and does not want me to write till I hear from him again. I do not understand why he is going to aid in the election." She had to wait a week to understand, but understand she did Sunday night late, November 9. "O! what a happy! Happy! week this has been," she wrote two weeks later. "Fred came unexpectedly after we had gone to bed. About 11 o'clock the door bell rang, twice before I arose, then the shutter rattled. I jumped up and called out who's there. A voice which I at once recognized answered, 'Come and see.' I was not long in obeying the summons. This solved the mystery. A few miles north of Baltimore meant Albany."[7] After fifteen months gone, Fred had finally come home on leave.

10

A Rather Scandalous Affair
November 1863–January 1, 1864

Fred Lockley was home to Albany for eight days, from November 1 to November 9, not including travel time. "I went with him in the afternoon" the day he left, Lizzie said, "and he had some photographs taken." They said goodbye about 9:00 p.m., and friends accompanied him to the train. "E[mma] and I walked home feeling desolate enough."[1]

Almost certainly with Mrs. Owens's husband having been jailed for overstaying his furlough in mind, Lizzie worried that Fred would be punished for overstaying his, but he wrote instead of how warmly the regiment welcomed him back. To her diary, she confided, "O how long and dreary last week seemed after Fred left. It was like putting out a bright light."[2] In their letters, they both noted how inadequate writing was after being together in person. "I fear I shall be a negligent correspondent for some little time to come," Fred warned on November 18.[3] Lizzie agreed. "Writing seems so unsatisfactory."

Albany Nov. 22nd 63

My dear Husband,

I feel very much as you do about writing; it is so unsatisfactory, compared to the delights of the week spent in each other[']s society. I want to throw my pen down, make a dash at you and blind you with caresses. aint that sensible. I ought to be more dignified and reserved, shouldn't I? but I am not tis what I long to do half a doz times a day (and night too) for a few nights after you went away I would without knowing it reach towards you; forgetting for a moment the truth. Emma and I both being rather a cold nature scarce ever put our arms round each other.[4]

The day is lovely. The air bracing, and the sun shines in so pleasantly that our parlor looks quite bright and cheerful, all that is needed is your presence to make us all very happy. I can hardly persuade myself that you have been here although in thinking of it I feel that there has been a break of one short week, in the monotony of our present existence one bright and hallowed scene in the panorama.

The children have just come in from S.S. and are singing away as happy as birds. long may they be free from care. I often try to picture their future if their lives are spared but we know not what it will be; probably altogether different from what we think. They are all smart, and possessed of good dispositions. I do not fear for them.[5]

I am glad your Captain has promised to approve all applications for furloughs. I want all to have a taste of domestic bliss. it will fortify them to endure the remainder of the term, but you have made a mistake Fred in computing time. The 19th of this month it was 15 instead of 16 months [since he went away]. There is a very neat thrifty German woman living next door to whom I have never spoken more than twice. The day after you left she saw me in the yard and spoke unto me. "So your Husband's been here, and gone again. O well, it is too bad, but you must just think that every night makes one less." I fancy that you are rather a favorite Fred. If you were disagreeable & unfair they would not hail your return with so much pleasure, even if you do dispense the grub. You are pleased with your picture. I think it perfect, although a triffle dark. You could dispose of many, I have no doubt if you had them.

. . .

Thursday will be Thanksgiving day. I hope I shall not be too busy to go to church; last week I had scarcely time to think. I was up every night till 12 and 1 O'clock. I would not do so, but we must make hay while the sun shines, all the work seems to come at once. . . . One thing I object to [is] <u>stinted rations</u>. I shall miss one letter per week sadly. They constitute a part of my food. I will not be unreasonable though. but write as often as possible. . . . Goodbye pet.

Lizzie.

November 1863–January 1, 1864

Despite his regiment's enthusiastic welcome, Fred was not glad to be back. He was stifled in promotion, unhappy with his current position, and disgusted with his officers, including the chaplains. Lizzie said Jack was apparently in jail for some criminal offense. As with most of his circumstances, Fred could do nothing about it. He had the blues.

Fort De Russey Nov. 21/63

Ma chère femme,

I am sorry my delay in writing caused you so much uneasiness—as I explained in my last I allowed a feeling of indifference to lead me to procrastinate. Content yourself with one letter weekly until I gain more leisure and I will promise to be punctual.

I saw a young man a few days ago who was in the Second N.Y. Reg^t. He says that Jack was in jail in Alexandria on a charge of burglary. He was released when he saw him—and he [is] staying in that town without visible means of living.

I had some talk with Lieut. Scripture,[6] our regimental quartermaster, a few days ago, in relation to the appointment of a q.m. serg^t. vice [as a substitute for] Parker promoted. He has a serg^t. from Co. C acting in that capacity, but not appointed. He said he was ignorant of my feelings in relation to the appointment—but had supposed that my recent promotion in my own company, would render me averse to another change. He should have a vacancy he tho't before long—and if I wished it would appoint me with great willingness. I told him my preference lay in that direction—and I have his promise to take me the first opportunity.

The position I at present hold is an honorable one and a responsible [one], but very unsatisfactory. The moral control exercised over the men by our chaplain and officers is so lamentably defective, that we lead a life little better than savage. Gambling, profanity and profitless indolence seem to be the sole pursuits of our leisure hours. I declare I am discouraged. Among my own immediate friends in the company, I can awaken no feeling of solemnity—no taste for profitable occupation. Religion is scoffed at, and the charms of reading turned from. Our orderly—

altho' a most estimable man having a mother whom he reveres
and sisters whom he loves—has been brought up such an entire
stranger to religious influences, that the name of the Creator has
no sanctity for him, and the sublime legacy of the Hebrew laws is
as a tuneless instrument. The dull-witted Joe I am utterly disgusted
with. Invariably when I spend a leisure moment in reading to him,
whether the Bible or Skakspere or Homer, he falls incontinently
asleep. These speak a tongue unknown to him.

I read of Chaplains whose ministrations are acceptable and
profitable; preachers who mingle religion with the concerns
of life, and appeal to the better feeling of men whom they are
appointed to teach. But our Chaplain is a nuisance—Without
energy—attainments or talent, addicted to tippling and a lover
of loose conversation—he has become a standing butt for the
regiment. His mouth alone would turn a man's thoughts from
religion. Lecherous, misshapen—tobacco stained and breathing
corruption. What woman could receive a kiss from such lips and
not nauseate to death?

Our lieut. Colonel, John Hastings, a fat solemn self-important
little man—made a humiliating exhibition of himself two or three
days ago on review. The fame of the Seventh has been spread
around Washington as a crack regiment, and on this occasion
a large concourse had been drawn together to witness our
evolutions. Such a display of incapacity as the man displayed was
probably never witnessed in the field before. It is a rule in tactics
that a wrong command shall not be executed. The men knowing
their business stood still as he gave one command after another; he
got them mixed up, and it was out of his power to extricate them.
Col. Morris who witnessed the performance recommended his
deputy to study tactics and ordered battalion drill every morning
at head quarters to give him an opportunity of acquiring some
knowledge of his duties. Thus through his ignorance—we have the
satisfaction of trudging thro' the mud daily.

. . .

I must quit—had a wretched day yesterday—raining incessantly.
To day it is pleasanter but cold. My health is excellent—but I have
a tendency to suffer from the blues. I will try and write to Dollie

this evening. Love to Emma and the young ones—time flies swiftly along. How blessed the day that shall restore me to your arms.

Devotedly your's

F.

Nov. 22

I did not complete my letter yesterday: when I sat down to write this morning, I found some one had borrowed my ink. This is the best I can procure.

From rain and the blues, Fred grew ecstatic about the southern climate ten days later, so in contrast was it to the winters in upstate New York. "The weather is delicious," he wrote on December 2. "Frosty nights and bracing sunny days" encouraged him to walk beyond the interior line of rifle pits at Fort DeRussy where he had a clear view north into Maryland. Trees all around had been felled for construction or firewood and to provide open fields of fire for cannons and muskets, but even at that, Frederic noted, the country was "not a desert." Amid a few farm implements, two or three cows grazed on a small holding in the distance, and a child running about provided movement in what otherwise seemed "a still life"—a still life that would remain notably undisturbed until Confederate Gen. Jubal Early showed up with thousands of troops to confront Union forces seven months later. For Lockley just now, however, the weather could be volatile, as he made clear in other letters, but for today, he said, "Give me the sunny South!"[7]

Otherwise, military life for the Seventh New Yorkers was tedious. In Washington that day, the last section of the Statue of Freedom was being installed on the Capitol dome. Gun salutes from the forts surrounding Washington were to accompany the installation, but the soldiers had wearied from delay. "Every fortification in the defences of Washington will fire a salute of thirty-five guns to celebrate the raising of the statue of divine Libertad upon the dome of the national Capitol," Frederic told Elizabeth. The men, waiting for the signal from Fort Totten "with guns loaded and lanyards ready," were "cold and hungry," he added. "It is now

2 o'clock—and they wish the statue of the benignant deity any-where but where it is."[8]

Fred's affinity for the southern climate was fleeting. Two days later, he complained about his toes being cold as he sat writing a letter in his unheated tent. A tentmate suffered no such discom-fort, however. "Sergeant Treadwell is busy writing to his lady love; no doubt the ardor of his feelings keeps him warmed." Fred did not lack ardor, although he would warm himself more effectively "by the big stove outside my door." Still, after Lizzie said she wished only to blind him with caresses but instead her arms went empty in bed at night, he responded, "You sly jade! in your dreams you turn your enfolding arms in search of your husband but he is not present." She should be patient. "The happy hour of re-union is approaching when we shall meet not for eight fleeting days and nights—but for temporal perpetuity—that is, for the remainder of our lives."[9]

In his next, Fred wrote at length to compare the evangelizing of the Apostle Paul with the wisdom of Shakespeare's Polonius and the effusions of King Solomon. "Busy as you are, do you ever get time to speculate on these matters?" he asked, then admit-ted, "I am somewhat rude as a Bible commentator, but I prefer to be guided by my own interpretations." Then, almost as an after-thought, he turned abruptly to report a rape in camp.

We had a rather scandalous affair in camp last night. Some of our officers getting drunk at the Sutler's—Capts Murphy (Co. A) and Jones (Co. B)[10] went to the Widow De Moranville's house— and one held her down while the other proceeded to commit vio-lence upon her. A soldier's wife living adjacent raised an alarm—the guard double quicked down the hill to the scene—and the game of the two patriot centurions was up. But for the feelings of the wom-an's child—a bright girl some 5 or 6 yrs old—who was disturbed by her mother's cries—I hold the affair outrageous.[11]

Having not received this letter yet, Lizzie worried more about how the South treated Union prisoners. "Every paper gives worse & worse accounts of the cruel and barbarious treatment our pris-oners receive at the hands of the Rebels. Fiends from the lower regions could not act more wickedly." It made her blood boil. Some way should be devised to rescue the prisoners. "Starvation," she declared, "what could be more horrible."[12] When she did receive his letter of December 8, she regarded the rape as "a most horrid affair. What demon could have possessed them to treat a woman in such a shameful way." Camp, she thought, "is no place for a husbandless woman."[13]

Fred wrote subsequently of having to stand at inspection without coats in the intense cold of a blowing wind even as his comrades, with enticements of $890 bounties and thirty days' furlough, entertained the idea of reenlisting.[14]

When Lizzie learned of this, she insisted he dare not reenlist. But it was Christmas Eve, and she was otherwise lighthearted. "The children have gone to bed as happy and light hearted as birds," she wrote. "They feel confident that Santa Claus will remember them. They have talked so much about what they would like, and what they should expect and their wishes being moderate, I shall be able to gratify them to the fullest extent."[15] Two days later, she wrote how pleased the family was on Christmas day, even the dour Emma.

Albany N.Y.

Dec 27th 1863

My dearest Husband,

I have commenced writing with the children all buzzing about the table. Tis very near their bed-time but they insist upon staying up till the clock strike the hour. Tute sits close to me, looking earnestly up into my face as if she would read the thoughts I pen here. as my pen glides smoothly along, she exclaims how nice you write Mama. she is quite a little flatterer; and knows well how to play her cards. The children were all highly pleased with their Santa Claus presents. They had long talked about wanting Bibles, so I bought one apiece for them. Tutie's contains 4 small engravings one The hand writing on the wall that just suited her. That history perfectly fascinates her. She never tires of hearing it. ask her what you shall read, and her usual answer is Belshazzar.[16] But I have strayed from my subject. I think I was talking about what Santa Claus brought. lead pencils with rubber on the top, slate pencils, a round comb for Tutie[,] stockings. for Dollie candies etc.

I was not forgotten either. The kids bought me a little emery bag to sharpen my needles such an affair as is appended to your needlebook, only that mine is in the shape of a <u>rouare cap</u>. E[mma] gave me a nice warm pair of gloves and a slice to turn my pancakes with. Christmas morning Emma said well! You have all had presents but me surely Santa Claus has forgotten me, but she was slightly mistaken. The children had with their money bought a nice lead pencil like their own, and I knowing it would give her pleasure bought a small book of poems entitled <u>In war time</u>.

I need not tell you how constantly you were in my thoughts all through the day and how I longed to have you near to share our pleasures. I do most humbly trust you shall spend the next xmas with us. God grant this war may be at an end ere that time. We all went as was expected to Mrs Blake's, and spent a much pleasanter time than we anticipated. nevertheless I should have enjoyed 3 or 4 hours reading at home much more.

. . .

I see reenlisting is very rapidly carried on. it shows no lack of spirit on the part of our brave soldiers. but $2000 bounty would not induce me to give my consent if you wished to reenlist—No! No! I could not endure even the thought of it[.] But I need not trouble myself for I know that your term of service is long enough to suit you. You will have done your part fully when you have served 3 long years. . . .

Would that I could throw my arms around you and tantalize you all in my power. my dear Husband

Lizzie M.L.

New Year's Day, along with his birthday, afforded Fred a chance to consider what he had and had not accomplished in life and to wish the war were over. A well-prepared plan to have Elizabeth come cook meals for the officers foundered when Captain Shannon rejected the idea. He wondered if it wasn't just as well. As if in mocking parody, he caught a ride on a bread wagon to avoid a muddy march back from inspection only to have a wheel fall off in a heavy rain and require a disagreeable repair.

January 1st 1864

Ma chére Femme

A happy new year to you! I know one essential element is
abstracted from your happiness, the presence of your husband;
but it is to be hoped that the year just dawned will witness the
extinction of the Rebellion and the return of us citizen soldiers
to the hungry embraces of our wives. These holiday times visit us
here with an indescribable feeling of restlessness. Mud, disorder
and discomfort prevail; the same monotonous round characterizes
our holidays, as our working days. And we know that at home are
bright eyes and cheerful faces, and pleasant chambers and troops
of friends. As through a glass darkly we see the whole thronging
busy festival of this great Natal day of time, its joyousness and
exhilaration are feebly communicated to us; and we are here in the
Mud; stale—listless—unprofitable. Curse upon all wars—and upon
this fall my direst maledictions.

I thought to have surprised you this New Year's with an
invitation to camp. Our officers have no means of eating their
meals in comfort; they have neither cook nor dining room. Lieut.
Niles[17] suggested to me to build a house, have my wife out, and
board all the officers at this post—some eight or nine in all. He is
an impulsive dashing young man—fond of good living—and the
idea of having comfortable meals afforded him, rendered him
energetic in preparing the details. He procured the Colonel's
consent to your living in camp—he even canvassed all the
officers (except Shannon) who were pleased with the promised
chance of comfort[.] he selected the site for the house and made
arrangements with the qr m^r for the transportation of stores. The
only difficulty in the way was Capt. Shannon.

In advance he [Niles] and I both knew that it was an
impossibility for him [Shannon] to act humanely. To disoblige is
his instinct. He is one of these petty, jealous, moody, overbearing
men—that he must go counter to his fellow man's interests. To see
a man enjoy himself immediately furnishes him with employment
to mar it. Lieut Niles in approaching him paraded all the
corroborative testimony, showed him how the arrangement would

conduce to the officers' comfort—and asked his consent to your being admitted and provided for. He refused.

I have no doubt it is better that he did so—for had he consented—I should surely have sent for you—which would involve considerable outlay. No sooner would this unsocial brute see you comfortably established—and the officers decently provided for—than his malign instinct would compel him to upset everything—it is beyond his power to leave well enough alone. If the devil doesn't get this fellow it is no use having one.

Yesterday was my birthday—always a retrospective unhappy day with me. As year after year passes swiftly by me—filling out the brief allotted space of man's existence leaving no improvement and unmarked with profit; when I contrast what man's nature is capable of, and indistinctly conjecture the many sources of delight of which God intended us to partake, and then turn to what life is—

Well, after all things might be worse;

So read your Bible, Sir, and mind your purse.[18]

We had inspection and muster yesterday at head quarters—it rained and the line was not formed in consequence. After muster, when the company were about returning, I dropped out—and repaired to the quartermaster's where I waited for the bread wagon to ride home. the roads were fearfully soft it was raining heavily—and as we labored along drawn by six patient mules, I was hugging myself on having escaped a disagreeable march. Suddenly a fore-wheel came off—and the axle buried itself in the mud. The wagoner and I were alone—no help within reach—and there was some heavy lifting to do to get righted. I almost wished I could run off and leave my companion to his task. He jumped out of his saddle and I out of the wagon and both repaired to the "source of all our woe."

You have heard of the profane swearer who lost the tail board out of his cart, laden with apples when he was ascending a hill. The neighbors gathered to hear him swear, thinking the occasion would prompt his sublimest efforts. But the occasion was past his powers—he succumbed in silence for he felt his inability to do justice to the subject. It was so with us. My companion commenced a slight peroration, which I interrupted by suggesting that he wanted a pole to lift with. He acquiesced, and I climbed the ascent which bordered one side [of] the road to seek a hickory pole, while he descended to the run to fetch some fragments of rock for a fulcrum. We were on the military road made by our former friends of the 31st N.Y. which is substantially terraced round a congeries of hills. We replaced the wheel on the axle—but we acquired some mud in the process, and when I resumed my place in the wagon and we again took up our journey, my mind was visited with shrewd suspicions whether I had gained any advantage over my pedestrian comrades.

   . . .

I must quit as I am called for. I will write to Emma in my next.

Goodbye

F.

11

This Morning That Boy Was Buried
January–March 1864

The routines for both Fred and Lizzie were broken abruptly by physical misfortunes. For Frederic, it was a punch in the abdomen from what he identified as a "rebel cow" that charged him while he walked a trail leading to camp. For Elizabeth, it seems to have been far more serious, possibly a miscarriage. Internal evidence is unclear, but her being confined to bed for more than a week, having to see a doctor, suffering what she described as "a goodly amount of pain," her weekslong effort to regain strength, and a subsequent letter from Frederic, most of which was destroyed at some later date for apparently "being private," indicate an intimate dimension to her illness.

In her first letter written since the onset of her "illness," Elizabeth came as close as she ever would to identifying the malady.

Albany N.Y.

January 10th 1864

My very dear Husband,

This is the first time I have been up to sit a minute since last Sunday. it really seems good to don a dress once more, and I feel truely thankful that I am able to be up so soon; although to tell truth it seemed a very long week to me. I have suffered a goodly amount of pain during the time, but they tell me that I do not look the least as if I had been sick; my looks slightly belay [belie] them; for I feel as if I had been ill for a long time. The Dr has just been in and congratulated me upon being up[.] he cautions me strictly not to be too ambitious. he says that I overrate my strength and may easily be thrown back again if I am not careful. I feel just as if I should like to cast aside all anxiety[,] go up to Schuylerville and loaf for a fortnight. I wish some kind angel would drop $50 dollars into my lap as I sit here but I have said enough about my unworthy self.

I have suffered more anxiety on your account, since hearing of your distressing accident, than I ever did upon mine. . . . (I was so tired that I could write no more I have been lying down for 2 hours. I want to finish this poor effort before evening)

I was so disappointed at not receiving a letter from you yesterday that I fancied all sorts of dreadful things concerning you. I do trust and hope that you are not suffering from the effects of your encounter with that most unamicable creature who dared to remain in your path when ordered to go. E says she should have thought she would have had more respect for the Federal uniform. No doubt she was of Secesh proclivities[.] if I do not get a letter from you tomorrow I shall think my worst fears are realized. Thank God! for your narrow escape; I shudder to think it might have proved a fatal blow. . . .

I have news for you. Mrs D presented her husband with a boy yesterday morning. Thursday afternoon she came up to see me it being dusk before she prepared to return[.] I tryed to prevail upon her to remain till E came home that she might accompany her back, but in rain I feared she would fall; and so she did, causing her illness sooner than was anticipated, but the Dr told me that it did not do any mischief. The children have all seen this little stranger and pronounce it the dearest little thing they ever saw. Tutie came in her eyes sparkling and her cheeks aglow with the fresh air. O! Mama! Mama! I wish the Doctor would bring you a little baby boy like that. "Ain't you sick enough?" Mrs. D was not sick so long as you. They attribute it entirely to her fall. They think the Doctor was so sorry for her that he brought it. Dollie says I guess Mrs Duncan was not sorry that she fell, if she had not, she would not have got her dear little treasure.

The children are at Sunday School. They are all as healthy as little bucks. They go sleighriding and enjoy themselves generally. Josie was my little nurse and she proved herself quite trustworthy sometimes. I did not need more attention than she could bestow, but I have got through thus far.

No need of my saying how sorry I am that the delightful surprise you hoped to give us was nipt in the bud.[1]

I must not write much more or I shall tire you.

E sends love. God bless and keep you my own dear Husband

Your wife

Lizzie

Frederic had not received this letter yet, but he had received a letter from Emma dated January 8 in which his sister alerted him to Lizzie's health problems. Emma's letter does not survive, and how much detail she disclosed was not reflected in Fred's letter of January 11, but he did express relief in a short note three days later after receiving Elizabeth's letter of January 10.

Jany. 11th 64

Ma chére Femme

I am a day behind with my letter to-day. I commenced one to you yesterday—but broke down. I suppose my faculties were frozen up. We have been having very severe weather—thermo 10° below. We are certainly better protected against such inclemency than we were a year ago—but even now our heating and ventilating arrangements are of the most primitive character. Our barracks are built upon sleepers laid upon spiles, which raises the building from three to six feet above the ground. This keeps it dry and well-aired, but when the weather becomes too cold, we find fresh air in excess of our requirements. The seams in the floor gape about ½ an inch, and as we have not laid down our carpets yet, the current of air is so steady that 2/3 of the time we are not conscious whether we have any feet at all. The newspapers are filled with disastrous records of fatalities caused by this unprecedented frost. Soldiers freezing to death in their tents as far south as the Mississippi. We have escaped accident in this way except in the case of one man who, getting drunk on New Year's night, lay out and had his two feet and one of his hands so badly frozen that they had to be amputated.

I am interrupted by the arrival of the mail boy—Emma's letter of the 8th arrived. I do trust to hear more favorable accounts of your health by the next mail. All is well with me.

Good bye

F.

Frederic had begun—and perhaps finished—another letter on January 11, apparently in follow-up to this one and a rereading of Emma's letter of January 8. "My dear wife, I am up to my optics in pay rolls. I have hardly time to get my meals. So you will excuse my cutting you off with a shilling," he wrote routinely enough. But he then added, "Your letter together with one from each of the children reached me last evening. I was immeasurably pleased with so many loving communications. You are exceedingly—" Here, the letter is cut off. A note on the back reads, "I destroyed the remainder of this letter, it being private and confidential." The handwriting is Elizabeth's, and the letter was likely severed sometime later, perhaps years later, as she reread the family's correspondence, including all the letters she and Frederic wrote to each other during the war.[2]

Still fighting despair, Lizzie wrote again on January 13. Whatever her illness, and especially if it was a miscarriage, she nonetheless expressed disappointment at Captain Shannon's rejection of Frederic's scheme to bring her to camp to cook for the officers.

Albany N.Y.

January 13th 1864

My dearest Husband,

I delayed writing this morning hoping the postman would bring me a cheering—and—inspiring missive from you. but he has passed and I must wait with patience the coming morrow. Would I were not such a simple Simon. I have had the blues these two days and try as I will I can not drive them away.

Emma received a letter from you on Monday. I should think letters have been delayed. a person may be sick for a week and get well again almost before the news goes a distance that may be traveled in 17 hours or less.

O! tell me why it is I am so very very wretched today. I can not restrain myself. I feel as if it were impossible to live on in this way. my heart is well nigh breaking. I want and crave affection as the hungry man does food. if I do not get it I am miserable. E does, and has done all that was necessary for me while I was sick[,] willingly I know[,] although she was sometimes hasty[.] I do not think she meant to be; but withal there is such a want of affection that it chills me and I doubt whether she entertains any love for me; but I may be mistaken she is not demonstrative. I am a poor weak little piece of humanity or I would not notice these things. Shall I ever be strong minded? I fear not. You will be disgusted with me Fred, but you must not [be], you must forgive these occassional outbursts. I want love and sympathy and to whom should I go if not to thee. I could endure any toil or privation if blessed with your loving presence, but this cannot be. It sends a painful thrill through me now when I think how happy we might have been if your scheme had proved successful[;] what a hateful selfish tyrant that man [Shannon] is I wish he would get tired of military life and resign.

. . .

I must not write any more[.] I know I have already wearied you out with such a doleful letter, don't think I am often in such a mood. I am never as happy as of yore, but strive to be cheerful and courageous. I know you have much more reason to complain than I separated as you are from us all. I often think of this. I will not have to read this over for if I do[,] I know I shall destroy it. I enclose a few stamps. I shall be glad when I can venture to walk out in the bracing wintry air. Probably in 2 or 5 days I shall be strong enough to try it. With deepest devotion.

Lizzie
The kids are well & boistrous as ever

Frederic sent a short note on January 14 acknowledging her letter of January 10, the first he had received since learning of her illness.

My dearest Wife

It afforded me inexpressible satisfaction to receive a letter from you in your handwriting. This is a poor compliment for Emma, I admit, but she will understand altho' I am very grateful to her for her promptness and attention to me during your severe illness, still the sight of your own welcome and familiar characters spoke to me of improved health, and removed a great weight of anxiety from my mind. I deeply sympathise with you in your suffering—and trust that you will speedily be restored to perfect health. I will write you a long letter on Sunday. I merely send this that you may be assured that all is well with me

    Love to all

Affectionately yours
F.

"I commenced writing last night but was unable to go on," Lizzie wrote on January 17, still low in spirits. "I do not know what is the matter with me[.] although able to be about, I suffer a great deal of pain, and am very weak. I am so impatient to regain my former strength and health that every day seems like a week. I thought I would certainly go out yesterday, but I loafed all day. I arose late[,] dressed myself and laid on the bed the greater part of the day."[3]

Lizzie was not alone in her low spirits. On the same day, Fred still chafed under Shannon's control and wrote of being overlooked for several promotions, any one of which might have provided freedom from his dominating captain.

January 17th 1864

My dear Wife,

Two of our lieut^s. are splendid fellows—O'Hair and Niles. Sometimes these two officers and our serg^{ts} will get together compare notes and derive inexhaustible amusement from our keen and scathing analysis of the character of this moral abortion. Appreciating a generous free and easy and estimable man, we have presented to our moral sense such a repulsive aspect in the notable doings of this haughty commander.

Tuesday Morning

Before reveille'—dark as nimbus—muddy as the Serbonian bog[4]—and raining heavily. I have been to the Mess house working for an hour—have just called the cooks and now take a few minutes to finish this epistle to you. Things don't shape to my mind whether it is my fault or my misfortune I don't know.

Returning to this post from the Adjutant's office threw me into the bleak shade entirely away from advancement. I told you that the quartermaster had promised me the first available vacancy that occurred in his office. Since then he has filled both commissary and quartermaster sergencies—and I have been overlooked. Also I was considered as standing fair for Sergeant major in the event of change recently Serg[t]. Major Norton[5] has been promoted as a serg[t] from Ft. Kearney[6] is filling the office. This is the inevitable effect of being absent from the spot.

> Time hath, my lord, a wallet on his back.
> In which he puts alms for Oblivion.
> Those alms are good deeds past.[7]

The drummers are arousing the garrison with their tintinnabulant din. I must be brief for the mail boy will be here in a few minutes. I do hope before a great while to be able to regain my philosophy and equanimity—so that I may write you a few discursive letters. I write to no one and no one—save my loving wife and sister writes to me.

Take good care of yourself. I wish it were possible for you to spend a week or two at your aunt's to recuperate. . . .

Love and rapturous kisses

F̲

Although not having received this letter yet, Lizzie anticipated his mood, writing on January 18, "I think you are not in the best of spirits yourself, Fred." She admitted to being weak and suffering "a great deal of pain" even yet. Hearing this, he wrote on January 20 of hoping "your disease is not ineradicable." He added,

"Pleurisy is a disease of which I know but little—tell me whether your medical attendant promises you a radical cure."[8]

Lizzie's next two letters were more upbeat. She told of a gentleman friend of her sister-in-law Amelia ("Minie") who came from California and gave each of the three Lockley girls a five-dollar gold piece. She reported that Minie was earning $11 a week operating a machine in a lace store in San Francisco and that Fred's sister Emma was entertaining the idea of going to California herself but would not go until he came home for good. Lizzie also reported the sanguine effects of the otherwise unfortunate news that, while sledding, a group of boys knocked down Mr. Bull, a neighbor friend, and broke his collarbone.[9] "Mrs. B says it has done him good[,] that he is as pleasant as a May morning."

In his next,[10] Frederic told her of having taken a long walk into Maryland, where "the effects of the war are truly disastrous." The slaves, he said, "have all fled from their masters, white help is not to be procured, and the stillness of desolation seems to have settled down upon the place." He would write to Emma in a day or two. As for her going to California, it would undoubtedly improve her circumstances, and she might make friends, "but it would be a complete isolation at first." As for himself, he had no intention of living in New York after the war and enclosed a description of Florida's salubrious climate.

By the end of the month, Lizzie had regained considerable strength, including assisting with a bazaar on behalf of the Albany Sanitary Commission, sewing for hire, and caring for the girls, all of whom were well, save Gertie who she said was afflicted with growing pains.[11] "I tell her she has as many aches and pains as an old lady. . . . She eats her share, and plays as usual but is full of pains. first her throat, then her side, then her ear, and her head . . . I think her rapid growth is the cause."[12]

Although finances were tight, she downplayed it. "Money is not flush with us," she said, "but do not feel worried about us[;] we will get along." Still, she exchanged the gold pieces Amelia's suitor gave the girls. "I received 56¢ on the dollar" and put the money in the bank "till they should need it," which she said they would come summer. He got the gist—they needed more money—so, transfer to the adjutant's office and promotion to sergeant major on February 1 were most opportune; they offered double benefit: a pay raise and escape from Captain Shannon.[13]

February 1st 1864th

Ma chére Femme

I just snatch ten minutes from my overwhelming duties to tell you "I still live." I am back in the Adjutant's office, if you please! My friend Serg'. Major Norton, having been promoted to Lieutenant, I am detailed to fill his chair, and if found competent, shall probably be promoted to the vacant <u>posish</u>. But, oh, my! Yesterday, (Sunday) I was busy from 4 in the morning till 11 o'clock at night, so unceasingly that I could not find ten minutes to address my little wife. This pressure of work is only periodical—I shall work my way clear in a few days, and will then have leisure to address you at length. My position is a very desirable one, if I can work my way into it. Pay $23 per mo. Besides a first rate chance of being Adjutant, with the rank of 1st lieutenant. But, hold—you are going ahead of your time. Excuse haste. Love to all. I shall come out right yet.

Devotedly
F.

Fred was working eighteen-hour days. "Official rolls neatly tied with red tape haunt my mental vision," he confessed.[14] Lizzie regretted he had to work on "the Sabbath" and worried about the strain on his eyes, but money woes continued to haunt them at home, where Emma leveled sharp criticism at Lizzie for spending money on travel to Schuylerville to visit her aunt and grandmother. Emma, Elizabeth reported, disliked Albany and was "exceedingly unhappy & discontented." With Lizzie and Dollie in Schuylerville, Emma, she said, was so low-spirited, "I fear she will mope herself to death alone." Lizzie wished he would write more often. "I crave letters more than I do food."[15]

For his part, Fred was most unhappy with Emma's complaining about poverty in the children's presence. "It is very annoying to you—and will produce a most pernicious effect on the character of the children. I want their childhood to be all sunshine and

cheerfulness—it is as necessary to their healthful moral development—as light is to flowers." Incessant harping on poverty "will
haunt their dreams," he warned. Recalling his impoverished youth
in London, he declared, "I speak from personal experience. . . .
Never speak of poverty and wretchedness in the presence of the
children."[16]

Still, his family's poverty was real, and so was his. At times, he
could not even afford to mail his letter. "I wrote a letter to you
two or three days ago—and have been constrained to keep it by
me waiting a stamp. . . . I have been perfectly destitute—without a
cent, and my friends in the same state of impecuniosity—we could
not assist the other."[17]

In a two-part letter, Lizzie observed their third anniversary (February 28), noting they had yet to spend the date together as a married couple. In the second part, she told of returning to Albany
with enough money from her grandmother to pay several debts.

> Schuylerville N.Y.
> Feb 28th 1864
>
> My dearest Husband,
>
> Today is the third anniversary of our marriage. We have not yet
> been vouchsafed the pleasure of spending a single anniversary in
> each other[']s society. You probably remember the first one, you
> were snowed in at the North Pole, and I by way of celebrating the
> event sprained my anckle, and was unable to go and meet my sister
> who came to visit us. The second was spent cheerlessly enough by
> me at Albany while you were still farther away than the year before
> and where am I today? where are you? How ardently I wish we
> could be blessed with each other[']s love and presence this day. All
> that we can do is to look forward with hope for the future.
>
> Your communication of the 23rd reached me on Friday. I
> clutched eagerly enough at it when the boy brought it. every
> word is precious I have read it half a dozen times. I shall look with
> anxiety for your next letter. I most fervently hope the indisposition
> you felt when you wrote has passed of[f] and you are yourself again
> only keep your health and I will strive to be content.

Albany March 1, 1864

At home again once more. We left Auntie's shortly after 11 A.M.
yesterday and reached home about 7 O'clock in the evng. I feel
tolerably well tired out this morning but a day or two will set me
right I think. I fancy I am stronger than when I left home. I did not
work while I was gone and visited very little so I had every chance
to rest and gather strength.

Grandma and Auntie were both generous to me. G—gave me
enough to pay my Doctor's bill, pay E[mma] $5 that I owed her
and buy a new stove. I found Emma and the babes well. I must
make my letter very brief as I want to go down street this morning.
I will write soon again. We feel half afraid that you do not get all
our letters tell me if you received the stamps I sent you. I am going
out to pay the Doctor this morning.

O Fred I am dying for a long husbandly letter, do write as soon
as you can.

Your hateful tyranical Wife
Lizzie

By March, Frederic had gained control of his work in the adjutant's office and had the time to relate the particularly sad fate of
a new recruit who died of illness just before his parents came to
visit him in camp.

March 4th 1864

Ma plus chére Femme,

I am undertaking what I rarely succeed in—that is to write a long
letter by lamplight. I have been so uninterruptedly occupied since
I last wrote that I positively have not had five minutes to devote to
you.

There is a quantity of work still awaiting me which cannot afford
delay; but the Adjutant has gone to Washington—to the theatre—
and while he is enjoying himself I thought I would also enjoy
myself by holding a quiet confab with you.

You must not suppose I am going to kill myself with such
constant application. I believe I have already explained to you the

reason of the great access [he may have meant *excess*] of business at these head quarters, and this multiplication of work coming on us just at the time when the Adjutant's force was in a disorganized condition, the administration here now established have had a hot and heavy time to pull through. I begin to see daylight. Another week's work, and I shall have time to breathe—I am so entirely in arrear with my correspondence that I fear I shall be denounced as an ingrate by all my friends. I have incidents enough to file a long and entertaining letter to your respectable Grandma' as soon as I can save time to write it.

Talking of incidents one occurred to-day of so affecting and dramatic a character, that I am induced to relate it.[18] One dreadfully cold evening of last week, as we were busy at work in our comfortable well-warmed office, we suddenly heard a great alarm outside, which was followed by a lieutenant of the 117th N.Y. entering with the information that he had eighty-five recruits for the 7th. This was giving us a snug little job—besides being very interesting for the poor fellows outside who were dinnerless and supperless.

A receipt has to be given for the men—and to enable the adjutant to do this the roll has to be called. With drilled soldiers this would be about five minutes work—for they stand in line— preserve perfect silence and answer to their names promptly. But these raw recruits are troubled with such restlessness and have so much chatter, that a satisfactory roll call is impossible.

While the poor shivering wretches stood out there answering their names one sick looking lad came to report to the Adjutant saying he was too sick to stand. "What is your name?" "Gates." There was confusion—the keen wind blew the lamp out—and the Adjutant's teeth chattered. "Here, Sergeant Major," said that Officer, "take this man, Wee gaits[19] to the Officer of the guard—he will find quarters for him." The joke was unconsciously perpetrated by the Adjutant, but it tickled me hugely—and we have had many a hearty laugh over it since.

This morning that boy was buried. I sat busy with my morning report when the solemn cortege passed our windows—the coffin draped with the national flag—and preceded by our superb regimental band—the company following without arms. As the slow procession passed, the band uttering a wailing symphonious lament—a phantasmagoria of images crowded upon my brain where the boy's home was pictured and the melancholy incidents leading to his death—formed with affecting vividness before me. As I was thus imagining the scene—as a drama was transpiring without—which sounds strangely like one of the Poet Ossian's gloomy imaginings, the procession was met by a wagon containing a citizen and his wife who had come from Schoharie co. New York to visit their son who had lately joined the army. The name of the dead soldier they did not learn so they drove on to camp to behold their boy. Here they learned that their son's corpse has passed them—and they were even denied the melancholy satisfaction of witnessing his funeral.

I must quit—writing by lamp does not suit my eyes I will draw up to the fire take my pipe—and shut my eyes to keep them warm. Good bye

F.E. Lockley

While in Schuylerville, Lizzie saw that her grandma and Aunt Maria were incompatible living under the same roof, so she advised them to separate. Her grandmother would move to Northumberland when the weather warmed, and Lizzie would eventually visit her there. In the meantime, she bought her new stove for $10 (more than $180 in 2022 dollars) but told Frederic the girls had sore throats. Gertie, the worst, would sleep with her and Emma that night. "In some of her ailments sleeping in Mama's bed acts like magic."[20]

Four days later, she admitted she and Emma found his story of Gates, the boy who died and whose parents missed his funeral, so affecting they both wept over it. "How many such similar scenes are daily enacted in the army. You frequently read about them." Otherwise, they all went to the bazaar and stayed until seven-year-old Gertie, soon bored, was ready to exclaim, "If I was not so heavy I would walk."[21]

Fred reported that their major general, Samuel Heintzelman, was finally granting furloughs (raising her hopes he would get one) and that he had received back pay, but he went from dearth to overabundance when the paymaster gave him a $50 bill. Fearing to send it through the mail, he did not know what to do with it. He sent $5 instead and waited until a trusted friend could deliver the rest to her in person.[22] He found that person three days later in the form of Sgt. William Faulk who, he alerted Lizzie in a letter written in early morning, would come to see her the following week on furlough home. He asked also that she give Faulk a copy of his novel, *Arthur Frankland*, written and published before he left England sixteen years earlier. "In sober discourse with Lieut [Frederick] Mather one evening, I was indiscreet enough to mention that such a narrative had proceeded from my pen, and now nothing on this earth will content him but he must see it."[23]

In a second letter written that evening, Fred playfully expanded on her threat to pinch him if he were within reach. "To the expression from 'intense desire' that I could be present, you naively add, 'I but seldom let such feelings get possession of my mind.'" Seldom? he asked. "I have not received a single letter from you during the last nineteen months, wherein the sentiment has not been expressed as conveyed. . . . 'Seldom let such feelings get possession of my mind,' indeed! If I thought they were ever absent, I would incontinently renounce all faith in womankind, and sell out my fee simple in your domestic professions." "Bide your time!" he counseled. "The term of military service is rapidly passing (not half rapidly enough however), [and] I shall be restored to your hungry arms before you know of the fact."[24]

Meanwhile, four months' pay issued at one time had unleashed chaos in camp.

March 19th 1864

Ma plus chére Femme,

Who writes to you more often than I do? two letters a day! I shall tire you surely. I have just sent Serg^t Falk's furlough over to him— the Quartermaster's dept a large handsome frame building 30 ft x 50 ft—is just across the way from the Adjutant's office—and as it is just half an hour to dinner time I thought I should spend the leisure in writing to you. Serg^t F will carry this.[25]

. . .

Pay day has swept through our Reg^t. again like a hurricane. Sixty-three in the guard-house; forty absent without leave—seven reported deserters (they may turn up again, however,) and a number of non-commissioned officers reduced in the ranks for drunkenness! On guard mounting to-day an unpleasant incident occurred. First Serg^t Philip Jenkins[26]—battery F. having been entrusted with $200 of recruits' money, went to Washington—got on a spree—spent and lost all his money—and was absent from camp three days. This occurred, too, while the captain was home on leave of absence—and the company was left in his charge. The Colonel ordered his reduction to the ranks and I issued the order yesterday. Being detailed for guard this morning, he was marched on to the parade ground with the detachment, and left in the line as a common sentry. As I passed along the line, to count the number and verify the details previous to turning them over to the adjutant, my eye happened to catch his, and he changed countenance in an instant. . . . Feelings of humiliation and chagrin gained such mastery over the man that he dropped his musket, reeled from his place, and had to sit down to recover himself. The $200 he lost the men of his Battery have subscribed and applied to repaying the recruits, but the Col. is so indignant at the man's unsoldierly conduct, and weak betrayal of his trust—that he has ordered his pay stopped until the amount is refunded.

. . .

You must excuse me for my thoughtlessness in sending you an overweight letter—I had no tho't of doing so. I want a few more stamps, missus—I am borrowing of my friends.

I have nothing more to say. 1st Serg^t. Rogers has been quite sick these three days past. I intend going over to Fort De Russey to see him this afternoon. Capt Shannon is home on ten day's leave. The weather is magnificent. I shall fill my pipe—look over to-day's paper—and answer calls which are incessant here.

You will go to church to day

Nymph! In thine orizons

Be all my sins remembered![27]

Emma will have to excuse me—I am not in mood for writing to day. Good bye duck.

Your ever true love

F.

12

I Left Josey Standing on the Stoop
March–April 1864

As he grappled with his adjutant's work, Frederic attempted to explain to Elizabeth the significance of the reports he so fastidiously compiled every day. He noted having received an Albany recruit, "a well-behaved lad," but he had to let another Albany boy, Oscar Bigelow, go for carelessness in the office. Bigelow, an eighteen-year-old student from Troy, New York, had enlisted as recently as January and would be killed five months later while on picket duty at Cold Harbor in early June.[1]

Frederic then imagined dropping in on her for breakfast or having her pass by and bestow a "sunbeam glance" upon his quarters.

March 22^d 1864

Petite Femme,

The days have increased so considerably that Reveille is now beaten at a ¼ to six. I do not generally rise till about ½ past six—get to work at a ¼ to 7—consolidate the morning reports by about ½ past seven—then take fifteen minutes for breakfast—and copy the report fairly out upon a broad sheet. Just for fun I will enclose you a regimental morning report within a couple of papers which I will mail you to-morrow. Every ten days these reports consolidated from companies into regiments—from regiments into brigades—again into divisions and still further into corps d'armée are sent to the Adjutant' General's—and so admirably is the system perfected that he is enabled to see at a glance the present condition of our armies—those effective for the field—how many sick—how many on extra or daily duty—how many absent besides having a compendious history of the last 10 days furnished him by the remarks in the margins.

We have a son of Mrs Corliss in our regiment—lately joined named Rosswell B.[2] He is in one of the new Batteries—Batt^y^ M—and seems a delicate well behaved lad. I have not made his acquaintance yet. I had to ship young Oscar Bigelow—Jack's dear friend. He knew so much—was so dreadfully fast—that the Adjutant would not have him in the Office. It is a pity boys can't get from seventeen to twenty two without growing through the intermediate period. I write in great haste—so have no time to pause to select my subject. Say! It wouldn't be so bad if I could just step in this pleasant crisp March morning—take <u>dejeuner</u>[3] with you—warm my shins by your fire <u>unguart d'heure</u>[4]—talk matters over a little—then get up give you a kiss, and come back to this pleasant cozy office. I think you are very unaccommodating in keeping yourself so unattainably recluse. Won't you just drop in as you pass—light us with your sunbeam glance—and then disappear like a Grecian deity—diffusing celestial fragrance around your path? A la bonne heure![5] Till then! Aye—then!

F.

"Yes, I'll 'drop in as I pass, and light you with my sunbeam glance,'" Lizzie responded on March 27, adding, "and I tender to you a very cordial invitation to partake of breakfast with us tomorrow morning if you will." His having raised the possibility of furlough, she said, "I have been thinking what a nice thing it would be if you could come home this spring." Then, as she contemplated it more, she said, "Won[']t you try to get a furlough? . . . <u>tell them I am not well 'tis time and must see you</u>, if that is not sufficient reason, I know not what to say." She'll pay his way if he will come. "<u>Come home! home! home Do come</u>."[6]

Frederic appealed to her to be more buoyant in spirits, but his own were vexed when things fell apart in the adjutant's office for him one morning.

March 25th 1864

Petite,

I have a little leisure this morning, so propose to devote a few moments to you. They are having target practice in the Fort, and the big Guns as they give tongue almost shake the windows out of the house. The adjutant is out at the Target, taking observations of the effect of the shells; he seems to be doing a big business there[.] he has sent in three messengers—two of them to demand men and building implements to put up the target (twice blown down) and the third messenger requiring stationery and some cigars.

What is the matter with the woman? Always ailing? Always melancholy? Can't you indulge an occasionally cheerful feeling, and just by way of change write to me when in buoyant vein? I cannot see the sense of such mental prostration. The feeling must be repressed—and I interdict to recurrence.

I find myself in but poor condition for writing. I am teaching a clerk my duties, so that in case of sickness or absence there may be no derangement in the Office. To day I set him to work upon the morning report—and let him lose so much time in enquiring his way along—that I got belated, and it would not prove. This is an annoying dilemma. The report must go in. Guard must be mounted, and the various routine business—such as details of men for the Quartermaster, to guard prisoners to Genl. Court Martial—to chop wood for the colonel, to build the chapel, that your business is apt to drive you. This happened this morning; in spite of myself I became a little flurried, sent the morning report in unfinished, left the men at a support arms on guard mounting when I should have brought them to a shoulder, and finally, I became so annoyed that I lost temper and have not recovered my equanimity since.

The weather is lowing—and it is beginning to snow again. As I write there is a curious piece of business being conducted in the Office. Yesterday—the Colonel directed an order to be issued convening a Board of Officers to determine and regulate the pricing charged by the Regimental tailors and bootmakers. This matter has been a subject of complaint for some time past because those men who get relieved from duty to do tailoring and shoemaking relapse into drunken habits—become dirty and undisciplined and charge exorbitant prices for their work. The colonel thought to convene a board to take testimony—and determine prices. Maj. Pruyn[7] and Capt. Jones[8] form the board—Capt Bell[9] having been summoned to attend at Gen. Court Martial. Maj. Pruyn—a dry old stick—is submitting a poor shoemaker from [Company] G. to a series of interrogations on the cost of the stock, and the length of time required to do a piece of work while Capt Jones and the Adjutant will relieve the poor fellow of his embarrassment by some sly cut at the Major's inquisitiveness. I do not think much good will result from the action of the Board.

Have I told you that my friend 1st Serg^t. Joseph L. Rogers has had a very dangerous attack of measles which came near using him up? I went to Fort De Russey on Tuesday last when I found him so ill that he had scarcely strength to speak to me. Three brother sergeants were charged with the care of him—and the women down the hill sent him an occasional preparation of some kind. As I sate by the bedside of the poor fellow, I fully realized the discomfort, and sickness in camp. The room was small—the beds were chaotic—the floor nasty—the stove running over with ashes—and a rubber blanket fastened to the window excluded all light and air. These barracks are a poor institution.

Did you receive five dollars in a letter one day last week. I don't remember your having acknowledged the receipt of it.

Good bye—a duller letter the befogged brain of man never produced.

Yours
F.

Two days later, Fred attempted to write Lizzie a love letter, but unwanted interruptions intruded, one from a drunken man demanding a pass and a second from another soldier wanting to know the time. Assuming the demeanor befitting the adjutant's office, he dismissed both with contempt.

March 27th 1864

Ma chére Petite

It is possible that as I write this to you[,] you are inditing a loving epistle to me. If we could only hit upon an identity of ideas we might render our intercourse very pertinent. This present mode of interchanging thoughts is insufferably slow—thoughts warm and fervid from the brain cool during their transmission three hundred and odd miles by mail. You will have to adapt telegraphing as the only medium suited to my impatience. Even that is unsatisfactory. Human language conveyed through a metallic medium is deprived of all its fullness, its melody, its natural sweetness. What is the annoying click of the instrument to the dulcet tones of a loving wife's voice? A poor representative, in sooth. Indeed, since I have grown fastidious—I find something wanting even in the tones of that much coveted voice. Words are but air—and, Talleyrand says, their object is to disguise thoughts. They please the ear; soothe the feelings, and while away the vacant hour. But to the soul starving for love, they are but faint symbols of the wealth of enjoyments they mellifluously represent. One clip of the slender waist; one pressure of the swelling bosom—one nectarous draught from fragrant lips!—away, woman! Do not madden me!

What business have you putting such wanton extravagant thoughts into my head, as I sit here solitary in these head quarters, when Mars has driven many pleasured Venus afar from our presence? . . .

I suppose I was going to indulge in some fine writing which fortunately for you is nipped in the bud by two or three ludicrous interruptions. Our man comes in evidently the worse for liquor—a bugler his companion making frantic motions to him from the outside to return. I have become so ineffably disgusted with drunkenness—seeing the lamentable effects of it produced every day—that I have but little patience with drunkards. He wants a pass to Washington—a preposterous request. I tell him I cannot give him one and continue my writing. He urges my compliance—I invite him to leave. The man having his sense steeped in alcohol gives me some insolence—I hail the Officers of the guard, and have [him] placed in the guardhouse to learn manners. Another taps at the door. I bid him enter. He comes in without removing his hat—and asks me what time it is? Yankee like. I answer him his question by asking him another. I demand of him whether he has been nineteen months in the service and has learnt no better than to come home on that trivial errand? He tells me he has been but two months in the regiment. Then, say I, it is time that you were soldier enough to know to take your hat off—and not mistake the Adjutant's office for a town clock. But for a harsh, brusque exterior—discipline would be overrun. But my heart and sympathies are with the soldier when he behaves himself or shows himself a man. We have had numerous changes of late—2 Companies C & H have gone to other posts from this fort (the ninth replace the 4th N.Y. the 4th has been divided into two regiments and have gone to the front as infantry[)]. Sixty three recruits arrived to-day. Our regiment is more than full. I am sure you cannot read this letter—it is written miserably. Your buttons and needles and thread were received—many thanks—also some stamps yesterday.

Good bye—love to the kids—Your's affectionately.

F.

On March 30, Lizzie wrote her response under attentive eyes.

Albany March 30th 1864

Two letters this week, and the week only half gone. Who knows but two more will come to gladden me ere the week is done. Your letter of the 25th reached me yesterday, that of the 27th today, both respectably long and most interesting. altogether of a different style from the poor trash I send you. I would most gladly mend my ways for I know my letters are insufferably dull and low-spirited. you justly chide me for my melancholy. I am ashamed to think how very poorly I have enacted my part forgive me my faithful and trusted husband and I will with my heavenly Father's aid shine to do better in the future. Can you trust me?

I hope your clerk will prove an apt scholar so that in any case of emergency he will be able to perform your duties. . . .

I am anxious to know the result of the board convened to determine and regulate the prices that tailors and shoemakers should charge. I think they will find it rather a difficult matter to arrange.

Dollie who has been watching me for some time, has come to the conclusion that I do not treat you fairly by sending you such small sheets, when you send me large ones.

I grieve for your friend Sergt Rogers, who is so ill. I can picture to myself the discomfort and wretchedness of sickness in camp. May you be spared that trial. We have great cause for thankfulness when we consider how good your health has been since you left home.

Say! what are you accusing me of? putting extravagant thoughts into your head. I deny the charge. I am innocent you know I am. if I dared I would prefer the same charges against you, but we will not quarrel about it. we are both perhaps more guilty than we are willing to allow. I think and dream continually about you coming home; and so much have I thought about it that I am prepared to see you at any time. do you think I am taking leave of my senses?

I thought to be able to devote a quiet hour to you, but I had scarce commenced as I was aware that the Philistines, no! the children were upon me school having closed an hour and a half earlier than usual. Jossie is writing her composition Dollie is working examples in arithmetic, and Gertie the little romp is rip[p]ing out some work which was not properly performed. but she does not like work, she does not seem to think it right that she should be called upon to assist her sisters she will not relinquish her baby privileges.

I am in a quandary. Mr Davis has raised the rent 1 dollar per month. The house as it is is not worth that amount. Much as I dislike moving I would rather do so if I could find a suitable place, than to stay here unless he will make some necessary repairs, but houses are very scarce and I know it would be very difficult to find as much room in a more agreeable neighborhood as we have here. Therefore I suppose we can do nothing but stay. . . .

31ˢᵗ Snowing, hailing, and raining. again this morning, yesterday it was the same. March is going out rather stormily.

. . .

The war is not over yet but everybody is looking anxiously forward in the hope that Grant will prove superior to any who have preceeded him. Heaven grant him wisdom and success in what he undertakes. I see by the paper that he says he will take the Rebel Capital at all hazzards. . . .

Solely yours

Lizzie

Ulysses S. Grant's appointment as lieutenant general would have profound consequences for Frederic and the Seventh New York Artillery Regiment, but for now, Fred took advantage of leading Lizzie on playfully, writing, "What a preposterous old lady you are to be ever harping upon my coming to see you this spring!" In reality, he would be home for ten days within a week. But first he sent another letter describing conditions in camp, especially the fleecing of new recruits, adding, again deceptively, "You can live without seeing me sixteen months longer can you not?"[10]

April 3rd 1864

Ma chére Petite femme,

Much obliged for quite a long interesting and affectionate letter yesterday.[11] When the mail carrier galloped past the window of our Office yesterday, I felt certain he had a letter for me—so I sent the Orderly up after the Adjutant's mail. He returned with quite a hand full of letters—but <u>nary</u> one for me. 'Twas annoying but it could not be helped. I was very busy—and tried to employ my thoughts upon my work, but I felt something wanting—the customary letter from home had failed. By-and-bye, Maj. Pruyn's young son, came with a letter in his hand—my wife's characters I know by instinct—the mail boy had placed it in the wrong box. I breathed freely against.

While I write this the band is playing[,] the drum corps rub-dubbing—and a general hilarity prevails. One of the newly organized batteries (M) are presenting Adjutant Hobbs[12] with a handsome horse and housings. It pleases them, and it does no harm to any one. They are troubled with a plethora of money—

they cannot spend it fast enough at the sutlers—they cannot lose it fast enough at cards—the English sailors after a distribution of prize money bought gold watches and fried them—these adjective recruits do as simple a thing—subscribe their money for their Officers!!

Cash is abundant here—every new arrival of recruits brings a golden harvest into camp—some old soldiers will misbehave themselves for the purpose of getting into the guard house—and when a recruit is thrust in there, they go through him—clean him out entirely.

Q.M. Serg^t. Falk has not reported yet—he has overstayed his furlough four days. What can have happened to him? I had to report him a deserter to-day. I anxiously look for his arrival in camp—I recommended him so strongly to the Quartermaster—it was upon that that he received his appointment and I feel quite hurt to think that he should behave dishonorably. A man who deserts while absent on Furlough adds to the offence of dastardy, the manner of violating trust of abusing a privilege. When I skedaddle it will be at my own neck—I will never act ingrate to the general who favors me.

I suppose you are quite sick of my incessant discussions of camp affairs—what's Hecuba[13] to him or he to Hecuba?—and wish for the time to arrive when I shall take up with the Bible again—and inflict some more Bible commentaries upon you. My views are somewhat heterodox I evis [evince]; but I take common sense for my exponent. Because an old nuisance who lived five thousand years since tells mc what I know to be a lie—am I bound to believe him? Give me good morals—and fair legislation—and I don't care whether the Prophet Moses or Prince Beelzebub is leader.

Your Grandma is better, I am pleased to learn[14]—the picture you give me of your aunt's domestic affairs is truly lamentable. What can become of your poor helpless Grandma? Your aunt is a very worthless woman to act in the unfilial manner she does. I do not like her for it. Her good qualities are not as counterpoise to her sins against mother and country. Have any of you written to Amelia Hill yet? I should like you to write to her if you have not yet.

After dinner I am going to De Russey—Serg^t Joe has sent in an application for Furlough—a trip home will do him good after his severe sickness.[15] You can live without seeing me sixteen months longer can you not? How does Emma like getting into harness again.

Love to Sister, Kids, and old 'oman. I would give five cents for a kiss from you—it should be a huge one.

Your's

F.

Neither Lizzie nor Fred corresponded further for two weeks, ten days of which Fred spent in Albany on furlough. On April 17, however, both "take up their pens" to correspond again and find writing a poor substitute for being together. The call of home remained strong, as Fred's mental image of his ten-year-old daughter, Josie, waving goodbye from the front step made clear.

April 17th 1864

<u>Ma chére petite Femme,</u>

I promised to write to you to day and I don't know what to say. I have not settled down yet. There is such a difference of feeling between the impatient desire to visit home—and the return from thence, that I cannot yet collect my thoughts to correctly estimate the matter. Again resorting to the unsatisfactory medium of communication of addressing from a distance is perfectly repugnant to me. I can derive no satisfaction from it. Everything is pleasant here; I was well received on my return to camp; work is light at present; my health and spirits good; but it is difficult to settle down to the monastic dullness of camp life.

I was interrupted by a visit from the Chaplain. Our Regimental hall now being completed (an edifice capable of containing four hundred seats) religious services on the Sabbath are held therein. His ministrations meet with poor acceptance, and he came to complain of the sparse attendance at divine service to-day. Liberty being guaranteed to the citizen by one of the provisions of the Constitution, of course, no military law can override this by compelling a man (soldier or civilian) to attend religious exercises against his will. The colonel, in order to drive the men to church from choice, some time since issued an order to the effect that those who neglected attending divine worship should be marched in the Fort there to listen to the reading of the Articles of War. But this order having fallen into disuse[,] the men avail themselves of the liberty of straying away from camp after Sunday inspection, and the poor Chaplain is left to preach to empty benches. Out of civility to the Chaplain I wished to be virtuously indignant—but the reflection that I also was one of the offending parties, restrained my denunciations, and I could but express my surprise at the apathy which pervades men's minds in regard to truths of such momentous importance.

I learned yesterday that we are indebted to M^r. George Dawson for the appointment of the very sufficient chaplain who has care of our souls.

It has been raining ever since my return. I reached camp at 1 o'clk p.m. on Friday last. The weather shows signs of clearing off but the roads are in a wretched state. I feel quite uneasy about Sergeant Joe—his furlough expires to-day. I fear he will have a severe fit of sickness. I reported this morning ten absent sick on Furlough. Going home seems to be dangerous.

Shall you write to me to-day? Seeing I cannot have the blooming dame herself—I must repair to her soft effusions for solace and support. Wife, wife! Every letter lessens the number that separates me from a final return to your arms.

I hope Emma's neuralgia has left her. Love to sister and kids. I left Josey standing on the stoop watching my retreating footsteps—is she there yet? I am going to dinner have you anything good to eat?

With warmest love, I am your's devoted as ever

F.

In hers of April 17, Lizzie reported considerable sickness in the neighborhood. Although she noted none for her family, she followed up to say some folks were improving but the mother of the family they shared their house with had been diagnosed with smallpox, occasioning a round of vaccinations for herself, Emma, and the girls.

Albany N.Y.
April 21st 1864

My very dear Husband,

The postman has this moment handed me your letter. I looked so eagerly for it yesterday. I cannot immagine why it was behindhand just because I was so very impatient to get it I suppose.

A week today since you left us. no I verily believe tis a month. I share with you fully in your dislike of writing but feel thankful that we can avail ourselves of this mode of communication[,] tame and unsatisfactory as it is.

Am happy to hear that you reached Camp in safety, and found all agreeable there; I have no doubt it takes some little time to settle down to camp duties after a visit home. I felt quite unsettled myself after you left. housework did not look in the least interesting but I have once more settled in the harness, and have been so busy this week that I feel well nigh tired out. E[mma] goes to the store daily[;] her neuralgia has almost left her I think but she has got a very disagreeable cold, which does not make her any better tempered[.] for a few days she was more agreeable but tis the old story again. I shall abide by your counsel. Shall not seek a quarrel but allow her to pout if she chooses to do so.

Mrs. Drysdale's sickness proves to be smallpox. I have kept at a distance since the Dr. told me so. he at first thought it was typhoid but he came in this morning to tell me to the contrary. At his suggestion and advice we have all been vaccinated, both Josie & Dollie took a fancy to faint while undergoing the operations. I am not frightened, although I always have dreaded that disease above all others. her's is a very light case indeed and the Doctor thinks we may all escape. God grant it may be so. We are congratulating each other that although it had been next door we had been fortunate enough to escape. Would it not be well for you to be vacinated Fred? I do not want you to feel uneasy about us Fred for I shall let you know at once if we are any of us taken ill. We are in the hands of a merciful Father and I am willing to trust him He doeth all things well. I did not hear how Willie Duncan[16] was yesterday but the day before the Dr gave more hope for him.

Do you know that you left Grandma's letter to her son here. I will enclose it with this. Send it to someone if possible. I do not know what she would say if she knew that it was still here. I must not write more or I shall not get this in in time for the mail. Write just as often as you can you know how fully [I] appreciate every word. I supposed I have as usual spelt 14 words errant. Pardon them and me to[o]. Naughty but loving wife

Lizzie M.L.

PS Jossie is not standing on the stoop still

A few days later, Lizzie said they all felt poorly from their vaccinations, but each of the neighbors seemed to be improving. Emma was writing to him all about it, she said, and her letter was "so filled with naught but talk of illness and disagreeable things. . . . I will say no more upon the subject."[17] In her next letter, Lizzie said two of her aunts came to visit, bringing a supply of foodstuffs. Her Aunt Maria Mair from Schuylerville even suggested she would like to board with Lizzie and the girls come winter. "I do not want her but I can not well refuse her." Lizzie pleaded, "Advise me what I must do." She noted also that the children were eager to hear of how his lecture to the regiment went.[18]

"My lecture, which you [and] the young ones take such an interest in, was neither a failure nor a success," he responded. "I had a full house (perhaps 350 auditors) and a number of whose judgment I believe to be honest, assured me they were much pleased with the performance." His subject had been the poet Lord Byron with, as he said, "a critical and biographical framework." But, "it went off dull. With sundry exceptions—my audience was too illiterate to appreciate the beauties of the poetry I read to them—or I failed to render [the beauties] apparent." As he said, "If every one is not as rapt as I am—I become annoyed—and cannot keep my thoughts upon my subject."[19]

None of Lizzie's letters from May 1864 survives, but from his responses one sees that she had told of ongoing dissatisfaction, both with their house on Lark Street and with Albany generally. "If you think the dampness of the house affects your health," he advised, "move by all manner of means."[20] But he urged her to hold on in Albany until he returned home.[21]

He also advised against allowing her Aunt Maria to board with them. "It will be generally disagreeable to you—you will be snubbed—and contraried—and be pooh-poohed as a mere child, and it will be difficult for you to maintain your position as mistress." And this, he said, she must not forfeit.[22]

FIG. 1. Frederic Lockley at about age thirty-seven in a photo likely taken
the day he married Elizabeth Metcalf Campbell, February 28, 1861.
Folder 1, box 2, Fred Lockley Papers and addenda, 1849–1958,
Huntington Library, San Marino, California.

ground of physical disability.
"No," she answered with emphasis,
"I would rather take my chance
of having you come back safe than
know you to be unsound."

Have all the days of Roman
heroism returned?

[...] a monument not as
I am like the merchant who sends
a delegation, I have no need to say

Best regards to Mr [...]
Lizzie desires love to her Grandma
and Uncle. I hope the chain is found
[...] and [...]

[...] truly yours

Albany Aug't 15th [62]
Mrs M. A. Main
  Dear Madame
            I have
enlisted and Lizzie is reconciled to her fate. The spirit of
76 is awake again the whole
country is aroused recruits are
pouring in actually faster than
the recruiting officers there can
take down their names. It is
believed by many that in a
very few weeks the second call
for 500,000 men can be filled
without having recourse to the
involuntary draft. I have not
gone to Barracks yet but have
passed the medical examination
and shall report myself there to

---

commence. The regiment is already
eleven hundred strong and we expect
to be ordered off next week.

Lizzie received a letter from
her father this morning. He is
at present in Shortsval. He
complains of business being dull.
He has been offered an appointment as Colporteur for the Bible
society salary $500 a year and
expenses paid. He does not say
whether he will accept it or not.

Capt. Springstead, the capt
of my Co is a very pleasant officer
who has given us some promises
some office when the regiment
is properly organized; and officers
and men begin to know each
other. I suppose they make this
promise to every man who desires
one but I am content to wait

---

feeling satisfied that the same
law that governs organic matter
controls mental qualities they find
their level.

I saw there a few of my old
comrades from the [...] city yesterday
in Troy. They had just enlisted
and were having a good time with
their bounty money.

I wrote to my sister last
evening to invite her to come to
Albany & hope she will reach
here before I leave. Lizzie has
secured her cottage to the [...]
place but has it won't stay there
[...] Col Ostrander before long
I expect it will be coming through
her [...] works. She said a [...]
thing this morning. I happened
to ask her if she did not hope the
surgeon would greet me on the

FIG. 2. (*opposite top*) Pages 1 and 4 of Fred Lockley's letter of August 13, 1862, to his wife's aunt, Margaret H. Mair, announcing his enlistment. He has appended his wedding photograph as his valedictory. Folder 13, box 2, Lockley Papers, Huntington Library, San Marino, California.

FIG. 3. (*opposite bottom*) Pages 2 and 3 of Fred Lockley's letter of August 13, 1862. Folder 13, box 2, Lockley Papers, Huntington Library, San Marino, California.

FIG. 4. (*above*) Agnes Jeannette (nee Hill) Lockley, Frederic's first wife and mother to his three daughters: Josephine, Emma Louise "Dollie," and Gertrude. Born about 1832, Agnes died of a spinal tumor on March 4, 1860. Courtesy John Frewing.

FIG. 5. Frederic's older sister, Emma, ca. 1862. Born in London in 1821, Emma immigrated to the United States with Frederic in 1851 and came to live with Elizabeth and his three daughters in Albany in early fall 1862 after Frederic's enlistment. Courtesy John Frewing.

FIG. 6. Josephine "Josie" and Emma Louise "Dollie," ca. 1862. Josie, born June 10, 1853, would have been nine and Dollie, born February 19, 1855, would have been about seven. Courtesy John Frewing.

FIG. 7. Fred Lockley wrote of the rousing welcome he and other newly
enlisted New Yorkers received when they reached Philadelphia on their way to
Washington in August 1862. The Cooper-Shop Volunteer Refreshment Saloon,
located near the Wilmington & Baltimore Railroad, provided food and services
to hundreds of thousands of soldiers during the war.
From *Frank Leslie's Scenes and Portraits of the Civil War.*

FIG. 8. Alfred R. Waud, a London-born artist and illustrator, made numerous sketches from the field during the Civil War, including *Barlow's Charge*, a depiction of the Seventh New York Heavy Artillery Regiment's assault on Confederate lines at Cold Harbor on June 3, 1864. Courtesy Library of Congress, Civil War collection, LC-DIG-ppmsca-22448.

FIG. 9. Fred Lockley and the Seventh New York occupied trenches like these along the North Anna River during Grant's Overland Campaign. Civilian photographer Timothy O'Sullivan took this view as a wet-plate glass negative on May 25, 1864, to show the shelters soldiers improvised for protection against sun and rain. Courtesy Library of Congress, Civil War collection, LC-DIG-stereo-1s02548.

FIG. 10. The Chesterfield Bridge, where Telegraph Road went over the North Anna River, is shown in this Timothy O'Sullivan photograph taken on May 25, 1864. The view is from the south looking north to the upland where David Crawford, a Seventh New York color guard, was killed by a Confederate sharpshooter as he and Fred Lockley attempted to wrap up regimental colors. Courtesy Library of Congress, Civil War collection, LC-DIG-ppmsca-33359.

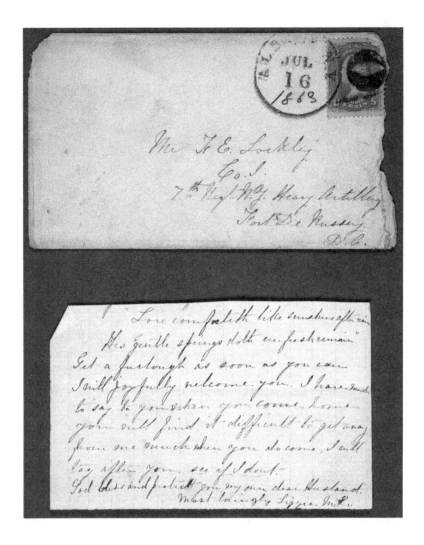

FIG. 11. Elizabeth addressed this envelope to Fred Lockley at Fort "De Russey" on July 16, 1863. Bearing a canceled three-cent stamp, it contained a note with lines from verse and a directive for him to get a furlough: "'Love Comforteth like sunshine after rain / His gentle springs doth everfresh remain.' Get a furlough as soon as you can. I will joyfully welcome you. I have more to say to you when you come home. you will find it difficult to get away from me much when you do come. I will tag after you. see if I don't. God bless and protect you my own dear Husband. Most lovingly Lizzie M.L." Folder 3, box 5, Lockley Papers, Huntington Library, San Marino, California.

FIG. 12. This photograph of Elizabeth was taken in Leavenworth, Kansas, sometime after the Lockley family moved there in 1869. Fred's letters mention receiving at least one photograph of Lizzie during the war, but its whereabouts are unknown. Courtesy John Frewing.

FIG. 13. The three Lockley girls are shown in a photograph probably taken in 1864. If so, Emma Louise "Dollie" (*standing at left*) was nine; Josephine "Josie" (*seated*) was eleven or twelve; and Gertrude "Gertie" was six or seven. Courtesy John Frewing.

FIG. 14. (*opposite top*) "I have not felt so light-hearted for weeks as I do tonight," Lizzie wrote to Fred in this letter of June 22, 1864. It was the first letter she wrote after finally receiving word from him that he was alive and well while on campaign in Virginia after leaving the defenses of Washington DC in mid-May. Folder 3, box 5, Lockley Papers, Huntington Library, San Marino, California.

FIG. 15. (*opposite bottom*) The Seventh New York would lose again heavily at the Second Battle of Reams Station, depicted here during a third Confederate charge on Union lines (foreground). The battle was fought on August 25, 1864, southwest of Petersburg along the Weldon-Petersburg Railroad. From *Frank Leslie's Scenes and Portraits of the Civil War.*

Albany N.Y.
June 22nd 1864

My dear dear Husband

I have not felt so light-hearted for weeks as I do tonight. Oh darling I feel so very thankful to think you are still alive and well. I received 2 letters from you today, one dated June 10th Camp near Chickahominy, the other June 11th near Petersburgh. Oh what a relief to our minds to hear from you. Yesterday my courage entirely failed me I was despondent and wretched. I fancied there was no brightness anywhere but tonight I feel half a year younger. I am cleaning house, and while everything was in the greatest confusion, Mrs Winslow and Mrs Thomas came. I made them as comfortable as it was in my power to do. We had an early tea, and they went home. I slipped on my things and hurried down to Mrs Duncan to tell her the good news, she was very nearly

I will put them under my pillow go to sleep and dream of you.

You would like morning for tobacco or anything of the kind let us know and will gladly send it. Your letters read as if they were written on the field each letter I send I will enclose an envelope ... should it be sometimes difficult for you to procure them. O, your letters are such a comfort. Emma says tell him they are worth untold millions. You may imagine our joy at receiving three letters when we had only received one during a period of 5 weeks. I am glad you received our letters. The box has come to me from Belle Plain, your clothes and books which you sent in the little black trunk came safely, but that was forwarded from Washington I suppose. You ought to have seen the children's eyes sparkle when I told them I had two letters from Papa. Josie can not tell till dear Papa is able to write. I do hope my dear Husband your strength will not give way under this great fatigue. God bless you
Your loving Lizzie M.S.

1062.   The Union Line before Petersburg.
[FOR DESCRIPTION OF THIS VIEW SEE THE OTHER SIDE OF THIS CARD.]

FIG. 16. (*opposite top*) Photographer Timothy O'Sullivan took this view of Union works on the Petersburg siege lines. It shows the interior and northern wall of Fort Morton, looking south by west with canvas-covered service way and magazines at center, bombproof quarters at left, and gun platforms at far right. Courtesy Library of Congress, Civil War collection, LC-DIG-cwpb-00517.

FIG. 17. (*opposite bottom*) Timothy O'Sullivan took this subsequently damaged wet-plate view of the Petersburg siege line. Fort Morton is shown in the right-center background, Baxter Road crosses the center-middle ground, and a covered way leading to a battery emplacement is in the foreground. Courtesy Library of Congress, Civil War collection, LC-DIG-cwpb-01323.

FIG. 18. (*above*) This view taken by Timothy O'Sullivan looks south along Union lines at Petersburg with huts at left and a fraise of sharpened logs at right. At center is a latrine with log seat. Courtesy Library of Congress, Civil War collection, LC-DIG-stereo-1s02656.

FIG. 19. John Campbell, Elizabeth's father, is shown in a photograph taken in the early 1870s. An inventor and tinsmith, Campbell, born in Scotland in 1813, assisted Elizabeth as he could during the war while searching for steady employment. Courtesy John Frewing.

FIG. 20. Frederic was mustered in as a first lieutenant in command of Company I of the Seventh New York on October 10, 1864, and one month later was granted leave to obtain an appropriate uniform and try to recover company records lost at Belle Plain. This photograph was likely taken during his leave home in November 1864. Author's collection.

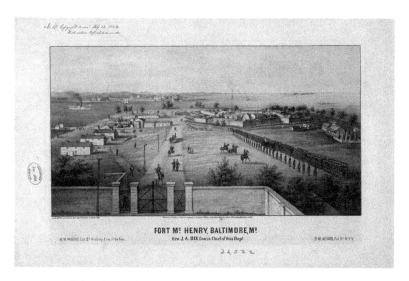

FIG. 21. When Frederic and fewer than one hundred other Seventh New Yorkers were reassigned from the Petersburg siege lines to the Baltimore area on February 22, 1865, they would spend two weeks guarding Union parolees at Camp Parole near Annapolis and then be reassigned to Fort McHenry to guard Confederate prisoners yet to be released. They would serve at Fort McHenry, depicted here during the war, until sent home in June. Courtesy Library of Congress, LC-DIG pga-08135.

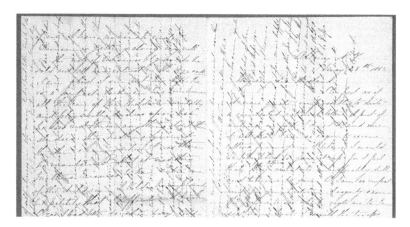

FIG. 22. Both Fred and Lizzie, but especially Lizzie, sometimes wrote perpendicularly across what they had already written to save paper and postage, as Lizzie did here with her letter of May 28, 1865, one of the last she would pen to Fred before he came home. In it, she tells of arguing with Mr. Duncan about how a father should act toward his children. Folder 3, box 5, Lockley Papers, Huntington Library, San Marino, California.

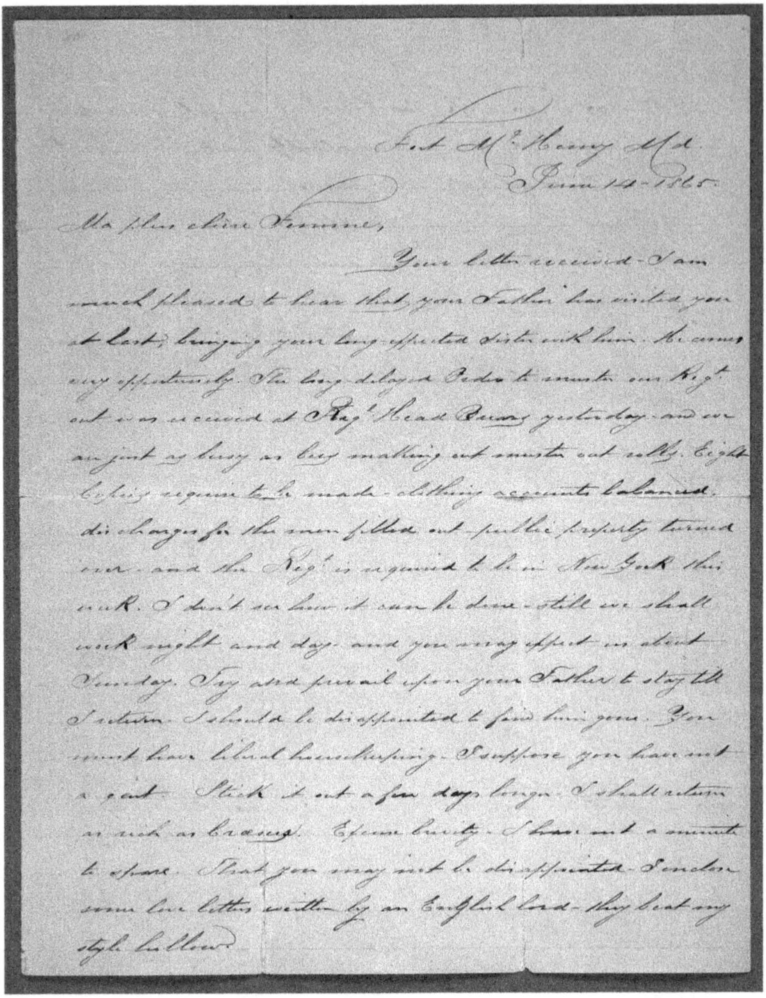

Fort McHenry Md.
June 14–1865.

Ma plus chère Femme,

Your letter received—I am much pleased to hear that your Father has visited you at last, bringing your long-expected Sister with him. He comes very opportunely. The long delayed Order to muster our Regt out was received at Regt Head Quarters yesterday—and we are just as busy as bees making out muster out rolls. Eight copies required to be made—clothing accounts balanced, discharges for the men filled out—public property turned over—and the Regt is required to be in New York this week. I don't see how it can be done—still we shall work night and day—and you may expect us about Sunday. Try and prevail upon your Father to stay till I return—I should be disappointed to find him gone. You must have liked housekeeping—I suppose you have not a cent. Stick it out a few days longer—I shall return as rich as Croesus. Excuse brevity—I have not a minute to spare. That you may not be disappointed I enclose some love letters written by an English lord—they beat my style hollow.

FIG. 23. "My last letter!!" is how Frederic celebrated not only his conclusion of thirty-four months in the Union Army but also fulfillment of his obligation to write home faithfully twice a week during that time. Of the letters he wrote, almost 290 survive, including this final missive of June 14, 1865. Folder 2, box 3, Lockley Papers, Huntington Library, San Marino, California.

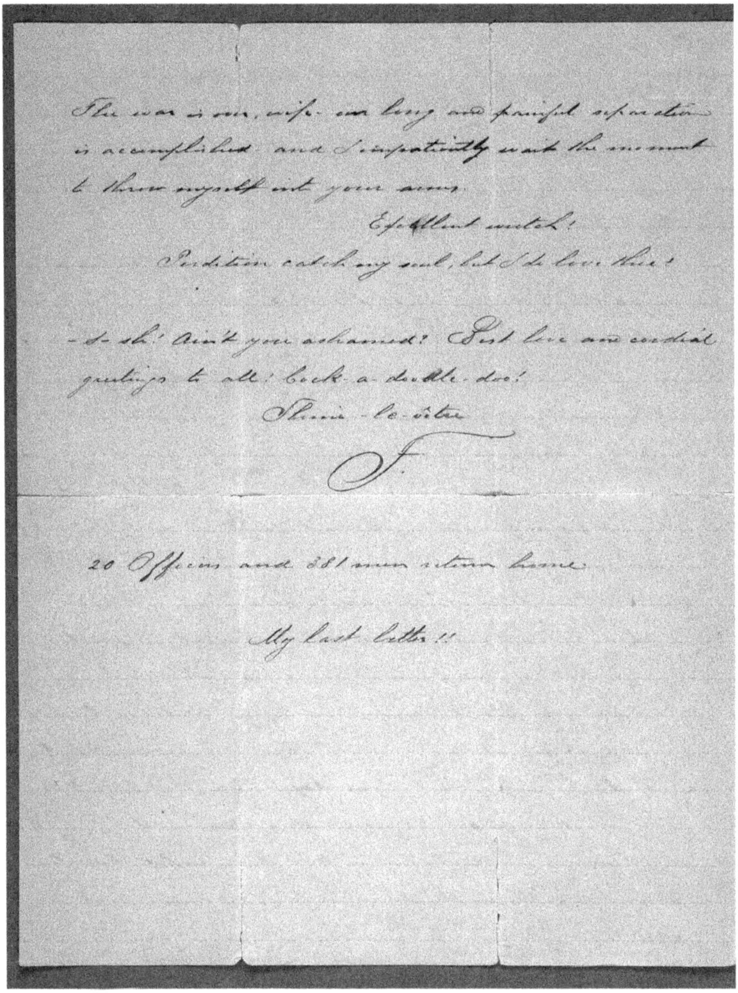

The war is over, wife - our long and painful separation
is accomplished, and I impatiently await the moment
to throw myself into your arms.

Excellent match!
Perdition catch my soul, but I do love thee!

- o- oh! Ain't you ashamed? Best love and cordial
greetings to all! Cock-a-doodle-doo!

Thine - le-âtre

F.

20 Officers and 881 men return home

My last letter!!

FIG. 24. The second page of Frederic's two-page letter shown in fig. 23.
Folder 2, box 3, Lockley Papers, Huntington Library, San Marino, California.

FIG. 25. Elizabeth and Frederic's only son, Fred, is shown here about the time
Fred was editor of the *Pacific Monthly* (1905–10). By the 1920s he was a well-
known newspaper columnist for the *Portland Journal* and an assiduous rare
book dealer. He would donate his mother and father's Civil War letters to the
Henry E. Huntington Library in the late 1940s. Courtesy John Frewing.

13

Sergeant Major! We Have Got Our Orders!
May–June 1864

Frederic betrayed little hint of how all Washington was astir as Grant prepared and then launched his Overland Campaign into Virginia. Despite the call-up of heavy artillery regiments all around him to be converted to infantry and sent south, he thought his regiment would be left in place. Still, he and his fellow New Yorkers itched "to have a hand in at the death" of the rebellion.

May 8th 1864

Ma chére Femme,

I wrote a long letter to Friend Duncan this morning—and have just returned from dress parade. The thermometer stands at 90° and it is almost too warm to think. Under such circumstances do not expect a brilliant letter. I suppose if I were with Lee or Butler[1] I should endure my share of the labors, but upon my word I do pity those poor fellows toiling in the scorching sun—herded together in such immense masses—and a vigilant treacherous foe watching his chances to assail them. This evening the news is, upon the author of despatches from the Medical director and chief quartermaster[,] that 8,000 of our wounded are on their way to Washington, and that Lee has been foiled in a most desperate effort to disorganize and break Meade's centre.[2] This is most favorable news—and augurs well for the issue of the strife.

I am pleased to have to write you for once in rollicking spirits. Do try and preserve good health and strength—I am never happy when I think you are ailing.

F.

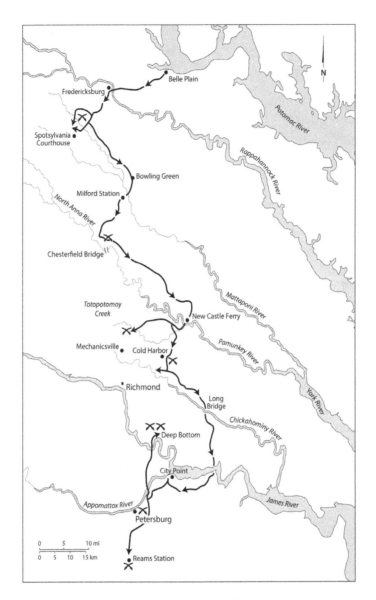

MAP 2. Map shows the route Frederic Lockley and the Seventh New York
Regiment followed during the Overland Campaign May to August 1864. From
top to bottom, crossed swords indicate engagements for the Seventh New York
at Harris Farm (near Spotsylvania), May 19; North Anna River (on Telegraph
Road north of Chesterfield Bridge), May 23–27; Totopotomoy Creek, May 30;
Cold Harbor, June 3; two engagements at Deep Bottom, July 27–29 and
August 13–20; before Petersburg, June 16; and Reams Station, August 25.
Created by Bill Nelson.

The Battle of the Wilderness over, Grant pivoted to Spotsylvania Court House. At Fort Reno, Frederic cheered the Union advances despite their frightful cost and noted that more units were being called up around him.

May 12th 1864

My dear Wife,

I commenced a letter to you yesterday—but the weather was so intensely hot I had not energy to achieve my task. This morning it is much cooler. It rained heavily yesterday—and the air is now charged with a dense mist. . . .

You seem apprehensive of our removal. I have heard nothing of it yet. The defenses of Washington are being thinned out rapidly. I have mentioned the removal of the 9th N.Y. Art[y]. from our brigade, and yesterday I learned of the 1st Vermont Art[y]. (3rd Brigade, Haskin's Div.) being under marching orders. When this regiment moves it will cause a further division in our Regiment, as I hear that one of their posts (Fort Stevens) which commands the Washington and Baltimore road, will be garrisoned by a detachment from the Seventh. We shall get split up into very small parties soon.

The war news is good, but we have paid an immense price for it. The loss of Gen.[ls] Sedgwick, Hays, Wadsworth, and thirty-five thousand men put hors de combat shows tremendous fighting, and illustrates the truth of our convictions, that the rebels would yield nothing without a desperate contest.[3] The news so far is meager and inconclusive, but it seems beyond doubt that Grant is driving Lee—and that Butler will very soon be in Richmond. So favorable a condition of things we have not had since the capture of Vicksburg in July last. Heaven sustain the arms of our intrepid warriors—vouchsafe help to our leaders, and make incisions in the foe!

Lieut. Mather is under arrest for going to Washington without a pass. . . . [He] will probably have to take a Court martial and be suspended from his duties three months or more.[4]

I know you must be sick of this camp gossip—but I really have nothing else with which to regale you. . . .

Much obliged for your Postage stamps. How is your health? Has
Emma's neuralgia effectually left her? Love to all. I will try and
write Josie a letter this week if the weather remains cool.

Au revoir, ma mignonne[5]

F.

Two days later, Frederic and the Seventh New York Volunteer
Artillery Regiment received orders in the middle of the night to
muster and march to Virginia. He was delighted with the chance
to be with Grant and have a shot at "lifelong glory," although he
knew Lizzie would not share his enthusiasm. Arriving in time for
the last of the bloodletting at Spotsylvania Court House, Frederic
and his regiment were to be foot soldiers. They would see terrible glory.

May 14th 1864

Ma plus chére Femme:

You make me quite matutinal in my habits; I actually arose
at five o'clock to indite this letter to you. Yours reached me
yesterday—I read it with much pleasure—it was cheerful—
sensible—and elaborate. But why this continued apprehension of
our removal. . . . We have renovated our office—the Colonel has
brushed his headquarters up—and we are just gay now for a quiet
summer of it.

Just after midnight this morning the act[g]. Adj[t]. came into my
room in a state of the greatest excitement, exclaiming "Serg[t].
Major! We have got our orders!" Waking up, my thoughts were
slightly confused, and I inquired, "What orders?" "Orders
to march! Get up—I want you to copy them for the Battery
commanders." And he was [so] nervous that he had to go the
whole length of the street to call up every officer at the Post.
Having dressed myself—and lighted a lamp—I found the following
letter—it is no order—lying before me.

Hd Quars. Dept. of Washington, 22[d]. Army Corps, Washington,
D.C., May 13th 1864. Lt. Col. Haskin, Comdg Division, Colonel,
The Maj. Genl. Comdg directs that the 1st Maine Heavy Art[y] Col

Chaplin, and the 7ᵗʰ N.Y. Heavy artʸ. Col. Morris, be prepared at once to take the field. The regiments will be provided with shelter tents, five days' rations and 150 rounds of ammunition per man. Be pleased to report at once at these headquarters, when the troops are ready to move. I am, Col, very respectfⁱ. your most obedient servⁱ. J.H. Taylor, Chief of Staff and Assⁱ. Adjⁱ. Genˡ.

I made ten copies of this interesting document, which Lieuts. Hobbs and O'Brien sealed up—and then mounted their horses to warn the commanders of the other posts. I went quietly to my bed and slept out the rest of the night. Early this morning I was awakened by the hilarious cheering of the men on the news being imparted to them that they were going. We have long been wishing for removal—garrison life is so monotonous and irksome—that we all feel as merry as boys at the breaking up of school. We do not know where we are going—most probably to join Grant's army. The news from the field of strife is truly inspiriting. Rebellion is receiving staggering blows; it will be a lifelong glory to have a hand in aiding our heroic chieftain in consummating the gigantic task he is so successfully prosecuting.

Do not be unhappy at this long dreaded news. Bear it like a Soldier's wife. For myself I have no fears. I will write you regularly. I do not suppose we shall start before tomorrow—it will take some time to cook five days' grub.

. . .

Excuse brevity again. I have lots of business on hand. It is a source of great satisfaction to me to think that I visited you in the spring. Love to Emma and the babes. You all ought to rejoice at my removal—as it will be the means of affording you more interesting letters. Good bye—my dearest pet—your love will sustain me thro' every privation.

Respectfully

Your obⁱ. Servⁱ

F.

Frederic's regiment left Fort Reno on Sunday, May 15, and arrived near Spotsylvania four days later. In his first letter from the field, he described their landing at Belle Plain[6] the day after leaving and their long march to and through Fredericksburg to arrive as reinforcements in the final stages of the fighting at Spotsylvania Court House. "Don't feel uneasy about me," he advised Elizabeth; "I think I can dodge the rebel shells." That was slim comfort at home, no doubt, although notwithstanding some frighteningly close calls, Fred would dodge the rebel shells and musket balls. Most of the men in his regiment would not.

In the Field Near Spottsylvania,[7] Va.
May 19th 1864

Ma chére Femme:

I must devote a few moments to you to relieve your natural anxiety—but my accommodations are so poor—I shall have to be brief. We left Fort Reno on Sunday the 15th and marched thro' a drenching rain to the wharf in Washington where we embarked. The following day we landed in Belle Plain near Fredericsburg[8] where we learnt we could obtain no transportation for our baggage—consequently everything had to be abandoned. Great coats—blankets—shirts—knapsacks—officers' expensive uniforms—commissary stores—strewed the camp and lined the road for miles. At least $50,000 dollars of property was abandoned by our regiment alone—when we encamped the next night those poor wretches had to sleep on the damp ground exposed to the skies with no protection but what they bore on their backs. Each man carried 60 rounds of cartridges—5 days rations—and half a tent.

At Belle Plain is an encampment of rebel prisoners where over 8,000 were kept under guard. Troops were pouring in every hour of the day on their way to join Grant's army; and when we started on Tuesday morning, we led a column of 10,000 men. We reached here, Fredericsburgh about noon—quite a respectable town in size—with substantial buildings standing upon a commanding height above the Rappahannock. We crossed the river upon a pontoon bridge. Every building—churches—hotels—dwelling houses—were filled with our wounded—and the agents of the Sanitary commission seemed omnipresent in their blessed ministrations. We made a forced march of 30 miles that day—and encamped near Gen[l]. Hancock's headquarters[9]—having travelled 16½ hours with an occasional rest. Being faint from garrison duty— the men straggled prodigiously—and hundreds gave out by the way. They have since come up however, and I don't know that the regiment has lost a man.

The next morning we were aroused at an early hour by the firing of cannon—and after breakfast were ordered to cross the south Anna river[10] to report to Gen[l]. Meade. On our way we met hundreds of ghastly objects—mutilated in every imaginable way— the trunk of one poor fellow lay in the road blown to pieces with a rebel shell. The artillery practice was terrific.

On reaching Gen[l]. Meade 's headquarters he ordered us into a rifle pit—there to await further orders. I had an opportunity of running about—the foe was not in sight—but their batteries were belching fire about a mile to the left of us. Only one missile came amongst us—and that blew a horse to pieces. Being held in reserve—we could tell nothing of the progress of the battle— nor what forces were engaged—but we afterwards learnt that our forces in charging upon the rebel position had been repulsed in the forenoon—but that in the afternoon we drove the foe four miles. At present I have no idea of the nature of our operations nor can I find that our officers have any clearer view—but we learn that everything is going satisfactorily. About noon we were marched back across the river into a piece of woods—where we are now encamped—holding ourselves in readiness for any instant order to move. Grant having gained an advance is busy throwing up earthworks—and Lee appears to be acting entirely upon the defensive. It is now about 11 A.M. and we have had no fighting to-day.

I don't like this mode of life—you have no idea of its fatigues and privations. I have always wished for a season's active campaigning—and now my ambition is likely to be gratified—it is a rich experience in a man's life—but you have a big price to pay for it.

My health is good—our fare consists of raw pork and hard bread with now and then a cup of coffee when we have a chance to cook it. I never supposed I could come down to such grub—

but I find I can eat it with the keenest relish. Rather than throw all my things away—I packed up a box—and delivered it to a Sanitary commission agent to forward to the Express office in Washington. I directed it to Friend Duncan. You will probably have a dollar or two to pay upon it—but I tho't that better than throwing all away. I have retained my greatcoat, half a blanket, a change of shirts and stockings, and half a tent, so I sleep warm at night and have suffered none at present. You will wash my shirts—one or two of them have been worn.

Don't feel uneasy about me—I shall get thro'—I have no fear for my health—and I think I can dodge the rebel shells. Our regiment on its first approach to the battlefield with the bleeding wounded pouring past us—showed good pluck—not an officer or a man betrayed trepidation. I am no soldier—don't claim to be— but I really felt no fear—singular—isn't it. Write as usual—your letters will reach me. Love to Emma and the babes. Good-bye—

Devotedly yours,

F.

In an all-too-brief letter, Frederic reported on rapid marches and "three or four" fights[11] in which they had lost one hundred men. There was much he did not tell Elizabeth, except to report that he was alive and well and to acknowledge her twenty-first birthday.

Camp near Newcastle, Va.
May 29th 1864

Ma chére Femme:

I wrote you from Belle Plain on Wednesday the 18th inst. Since then we have made such rapid marches that all postal facilities have been excluded. We are now within 15 miles of Richmond with an overwhelming [force]—Lee does not show himself—altho' he is in force near by. We have had a most harassing campaign so far—Strategy being employed more than fighting. Our regiment has taken part in three or four fights—we have lost a hundred killed. Capt. Morris[12] was killed in the first battle. I enjoy excellent health—altho suffer from the fatiguing marches. In a week or two it is probable we shall be in Richmond—then we shall live like civilized beings again. This is your birthday.

Goodby

Lockley would forward at least one letter to the *Albany Knicker-bocker* on June 5, probably written at the direction of his brigade commander, Lt. Col. John Hastings. In it, he admitted that forced marches, severe fighting, and rapid entrenching had "severely taxed" the regiment's energies, but as he told his Albany audience, "it is entirely out of place to complain." The Seventh had won "an honorable record," he wrote, but had "lost severely." He then detailed the count: only 932 men out of 1,850 officers and men who left Washington were now present for duty.[13]

He and his regiment had been through four significant clashes with the enemy—at Harris Farm on May 19, or what Frederic more often referred to as the fight at Fredericksburg Road; at Milford Station on May 20; at Totopotomoy Creek on May 30; and at the North Anna River, May 23–26—before the carnage at Cold Harbor on June 3. His next letter, his third since leaving Fort Reno, was written one week after his regiment's bloody assault at Cold Harbor. In it he told of several tragic deaths in the Seventh New York, not least that of Col. Lewis O. Morris, shot fatally while inspecting Union defenses the morning of June 4,[14] and of his companion, Sgt. Joe Rogers, as well as the wounding of his friend Lt. Stephen Treadwell.

The Seventh had been reduced severely in less than three weeks since leaving Washington DC, including more than five hundred killed, mortally wounded, incapacitated by wounds, captured, or, for a few, deserted. The Union and Confederate armies still confronted each other over a perilously small space at Cold Harbor as he composed the following letter, but he was fairly safe, the regiment having entrenched almost to a degree equaling the front lines in World War I. Fighting had resolved itself into an occasional thrust from one side or the other and otherwise a deadly duel of sniper and artillery fire.[15]

Remarkably, he had received three letters from Elizabeth and two from his sister, Emma, since leaving Washington DC in mid-May.[16]

Camp near Chickahominy, Va.

June 10th 1864

My dear Wife:

I know it is brutal to neglect writing to you so long—and you
suffering such anxiety on my account. But you must excuse me—
We are having it hot and heavy—and my opportunities of letter
writing are of the slimmest kind. We have been in this place eight
days—our reg^t. has suffered severely—and I don't see that we
gain one inch upon the rebels. I suppose you hear of our losses—
Col. Morris[17] killed—every member of his staff killed or wounded
and over 700 of our men killed—wounded or missing—Serg^t.
Rogers[18] killed Corp^l. Swinton[19] wounded in the shoulder—Lt.
Treadwell[20] wounded in arm. I have comparatively safe posish of
it—Col. Morris forbade me exposing myself in battle—so after the
first three or four actions—I quietly dropped out—and now my
quarters are in the rear with the doctors and the cooks.[21]

I have received three letters from you since leaving
Washington—with two enclosed from Emma—I have written two
or three to you—do not expect frequent letters until I get more
comfortably situate[d]. You need not be alarmed for my safety. I
am in good health now—but I have been almost sick for two weeks
past—this horrible Chickahominy water—and the irregularity of
our habits and diet, are enough to affect the soundest constitution.
I sent a box to you from Belle Plain—did you receive it? This is
Josey's birthday[22]—I hope to spend the next anniversary under
more agreeable circumstances and in her company.

Good bye—dear wife—your letters reach me. Warmest love to
Emma and the kids. When opportunity favors I will write you all
more fully.

Till then

Your constant loving husband

F.

Having determined that he could accomplish more against Lee
than ordering further assaults at Cold Harbor, Grant again wheeled
his army southeast on June 13, toward the James River and then

across it to converge just east of Petersburg. Lockley and the Seventh New York were part of this move. Their marches were hot and dusty before the Seventh crossed the James by transport on June 14. They then marched two miles more by moonlight.[23] They were part of Hancock's Second Corps, most of which crossed the James the next day. All were intended to join an assault on thinly manned Confederate defenses just outside Petersburg the morning of June 16. But delays and miscommunications delayed their efforts until the evening of the sixteenth and gave Lee time enough to reinforce his lines. Grant and Meade proceeded with the assault anyway. Frederic's regiment was part of the deadly results, with 425 more Seventh New Yorkers killed, yet to die of wounds, wounded, or captured. Frederic watched this assault from the rear with the artillerymen and medical staff. More attacks on ever-strengthening Confederate lines continued on June 17 and 18, but the Seventh was not much involved, providing him a chance to pen a brief note to Elizabeth to say he was all right.[24]

> Camp near Petersburgh
> Va.—June 18th 1864

Ma chére Femme,

Yesterday I received three letters from you making six in all since leaving Reno. I have written to you thrice—none of which had reached you at your last writing. Our regiment has passed thro' a scathing baptism of fire—we have suffered horribly—we are reduced from 1800 to 300. Grant seems determined to push things through at all costs. So murderous and exhausting a campaign is not recorded in military annals. I have escaped unharmed—but the sights and scenes of woe and suffering that meet the gaze at every turn are truly harrowing. I am sorry to have disappointed Josie in her letter on her birthday—but it was unavoidable. By and bye, I hope to have time to write to you all in full. I am going to spend today in collecting a list of casualties incurred in our last engagement—a melancholy duty—they will number at least four hundred.[25] My health is good—but I am almost worn out with fatigue. Under present circumstances I cannot write except now and then—to assure you that I am well. We have been 22 months

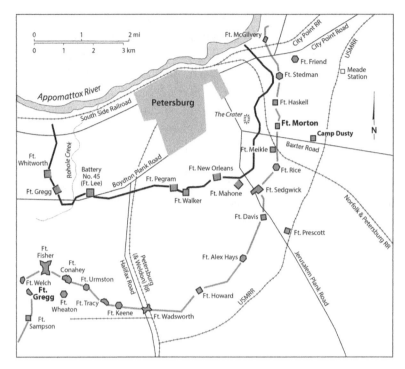

MAP 3. Union siege line along eastern and southern perimeter of Petersburg, including Camp Dusty near Fort Morton on the east and Union Fort Gregg on the west. Created by Bill Nelson.

in the service to-day. Love to Emma and the babes—am at all times pleased to hear from you. Good bye—your's devotedly.

F.

On June 20, after an extremely hot afternoon, the Seventh withdrew about a mile behind the Petersburg lines, where they received a backlog of mail and were allowed to rest. Either that evening or sometime before eight the next morning, Frederic finished a long letter to Elizabeth that reflected criticism rife within the regiment of their division commander, Francis C. Barlow.[26] Frederic also criticized overly optimistic newspaper reports of the Union army's supposed successes in the field, which contrasted markedly to what he described as "the daily recurring scenes of slaughter and mutilation."[27]

Camp near Petersburgh, Va.
June 21st 1864[28]

Ma trés chére Femme:

Another heavy mail came to camp yesterday—and two letters were my portion of the precious budget. On receiving such liberal and continuous favors from you—I cannot but upbraid myself for my inattention. But I know you will accept my plea of fatigue—pre-occupation, and inconvenience. We are having easier times now. Our army is beleaguering Petersburgh—the place is strongly defended, and the rebels dispute every inch that we gain. We lie out in the extreme front, snugly protected with heavy breastworks, but the enemy's sharpshooters are so persistent and annoying—that we meet with quite a number of casualties.

Before this reaches you, you will probably have heard of our disastrous charge of the 16th inst. which resulted in a loss of 500 men to the Regiment.[29] We are now reduced to 531 men. Lieut. Mather[30] was captured. Our division commander—Genl. Barlow—a very young man, appears to me to be rash; the way in which he used up his men is fearful.[31] This campaign is of a most murderous character. Genl. Grant seems to calculate no cost—and this culminating advance upon Richmond—is the make-all or mar-all of our fortunes. To protract beyond this present summer—the daily recurring scenes of slaughter and mutilation—is too sickening to be endured.

Our knowledge of the progress of events is confined to our own immediate sphere—so I would not be understood as speaking positively of our prospects—but I really cannot view the success of our operations in that favorable light in which newspaper correspondents seem to set it forth. Whatever strategy we practice, Lee always appears with some counter movement—ready to receive us—every advantage we gain is at such a fearful cost of life and limb that we pay the full value for it. We still have an immense job before us—but the entire energies of the country are devoted to its successful prosecution. The drain of life is repaired by daily accessions of strength, our army in numbers, determination and matériel, would seem to be irresistible—so I presume it is but reasonable to calculate upon ultimate success. Heaven speedily vouchsafe it.

Did I tell you that Jack's friend—Oscar Bigelow[32]—was killed in the trenches at Coal Harbor?[33] On one of our marches he brought George Swan[34] to me—whose regiment bivouacked on our route. Lieut Stephen Treadwell was wounded in the arm— Capt Geo. H. Treadwell is in the division hospital sick. These are all the officers of that name in the reg^t. The fact is the men had been so thoroughly beat out, with forced marches, exposure in the trenches and murderous charges—that they had lost their energies—and when they got into a tight place, they suffered themselves to be captured rather than expose themselves further by attempting to fight their way out.

You ask whether I participate in the battles. Since the first three of our fights I have been relived from that hazardous duty. Col. Morris instructed me to keep out of the fights—since if any accident befel me—the records of the Reg^t. would fall into confusion. So I have a comparatively safe time of it—my only risk being those cursed sharp shooters' bullets which buzz past a fellow's ears at a most venomous rate. But there are so many places in the State of Virginia where these bullets can strike without going through my body—that a man finally grows indifferent in regard to them. My health is good—but I have had all I want of active service. I enclose you an article from the Washington Chronicle which very correctly narrates some of our rapid marches. I am much obliged to Emma for all her attentions—she will excuse me writing personally to her at present—as these letters are intended for you all. My best respects to Mr. and Mrs. Duncan. The reg^t. has sustained an irreparable loss in the death of Col. Morris.

Continue to write regularly—your letters are an inestimable boon. Emma can send Mary's letter—it will doubtless reach me. Love to the babes.

Yours devotedly

F.

14

Soldiering in Its Roughest, Sternest Form

June–July 1864

Lizzie was undoubtedly relieved to hear that Fred was no longer participating directly in the fighting. But he was not telling her the whole truth. Just prior to the Cold Harbor assault on June 3, he had been hit in the shoulder by a shell fragment, injuring him no more than a bruise but enough to alarm Colonel Morris and convince the colonel to hold his sergeant major and chief records clerk out of the fighting as much as he could. "I hold the sergeant major responsible for the regimental records," Frederic recalled the colonel saying. "If he should meet with a casualty, our data will be in a worse state of confusion than ever."[1]

Fred also neglected to tell Lizzie that he did not comply fully with his colonel's orders, especially after Morris was killed. "I kept out of the active fighting till June 4th, when Col. Morris received his death wound," he explained. "Then to save myself from the suspicion of skulking I kept at the front, which I really believed to be the safest place, and where I enjoyed greater contentment of mind."[2]

Although death or mortal injury along the lines was constant, especially by sharpshooters and random bombardment, Frederic had been exceptionally fortunate. He might have survived the Seventh New York's bloody charge on June 3 had he participated, but more likely, considering the eventual devastation of his regiment, Colonel Morris's directive to stay in the rear saved his life then and in subsequent attacks at Cold Harbor and Petersburg.

"So I have a comparatively safe time of it," he told Elizabeth nonchalantly, admitting that sharpshooters' bullets were nonetheless "venomous." Indeed, they were, and already they had come close to taking his life. What he did not relate at the time but ultimately confided to his memoirs years later were three particularly close calls.

One of those occurred at Harris Farm on May 19. When his regiment hustled forward and turned abruptly to fire on Confederates pilfering a Union wagon train, Frederic and several other sergeants almost died from friendly fire. Upon advancing through spreading cedar trees and seeing the rebel soldiers, who began to flee, the Seventh's leading companies, without orders, halted, spun to the left, and let loose a volley. Several sergeants, including Lockley, positioned only four paces beyond the left of the column, were in direct line of fire. "It was done so suddenly," Frederic recalled years later, "that had I not instantly thrown myself on my face, I should have been riddled with bullets from our own men."[3]

Later that same day, Lockley had what may have been an even closer call. Many Confederate soldiers used Enfield rifle muskets, and Frederic said some Union soldiers preferred them to their Springfield rifle muskets because they supposedly had longer range.[4] "Seeing a musket lying on the ground, abandoned by some wounded soldier, I picked it up thinking it might prove serviceable."[5] Encountering Capt. Samuel Anable[6] along the line soon after, as he said later, "I fell to discussing the novel situation [when] a musket ball struck the barrel of my piece and glancing, whizzed past Capt. Anable's ear." Said Anable, "Those fellows have got a bead on us." Frederic said they both decided it was "a good place to get away from."[7]

Frederic related none of this to Elizabeth in his letters home, nor did he say anything about what might have been his closest call at the North Anna River on May 27. The Seventh was the last of Union forces withdrawn from the ridge overlooking the river's northern bank that morning, and "the fire of the enemy became so harassing" that Fred, like others, didn't wish to dawdle. Still, he said,

> I happened to be standing near the color sergeant,[8] when he knelt down to tie up his flag. To aid him in this dangerous work, I knelt by his side, and while tying my first pair of tapes, I heard a subdued groan from my companion, and looking up saw blood oozing from the top of his head. A ball had entered

his brain, and the poor fellow was at his last gasp. Our heads had not been two feet apart.

Frederic quickly shouldered the colors and fled.[9]

Through all this, Lizzie had written to Fred faithfully, as had his sister, Emma, but until this date, they had received only one letter from him, likely that of May 19 in which he detailed his regiment's departure from Washington DC. Throughout the summer, he said her letters arrived regularly, but only one of her letters seems to have survived from this time.[10] Having kept note of the battles and the Seventh New York's involvement, and knowing they had lost fearfully, she was joyous to learn he was "still alive and well."

> Albany N.Y.
> June 22nd 1864

My dear dear Husband,

I have not felt so light hearted for weeks as I do tonight. O! darling I feel so very thankful to think you are still alive and well. I received 2 letters from you today, one dated June 10th Camp near Chickahominy, the other June 18th near Petersburgh. O! what a relief to our minds to hear from you. yesterday my courage entirely failed me. I was despondent and wretched, I fancied there was no brightness anywhere. but tonight I feel half a year younger. I am cleaning house, and while everything was in the greatest confusion, Mrs Wooster and Mrs Thomas came. I made them as comfortable as it was in my power to do, we had an early tea, and they went home. I slipped on my things and hurried down to Mrs Duncan to tell her the good news, she is very nearly as much delighted as we were, no not quite but my heart fairly sickens when I think what an ordeal you are still passing through, you have suffered fearfully. surely such a bloody terrible war has never before raged. the loss of life during the war has been immense, when will this desolating tide of bloodshed cease. God in mercy grant that it may be ere long. How very melancholy is your duty that of collecting a list of casualties. To see your companions with whom you have so dwelt in happiness and peace, lie dead and wounded must be very very sad indeed. Poor Sergt Joe.[11] so young and full of life and promise it seems very mournful to think he has fallen. it will be a great grief to his friends. O! the sad and lonely hearts spread over every portion of the United States. Sometimes I think every other one I meet looks thoughtful and anxious. no wonder, these are deeply anxious times. We have had no very particular news within the last two days. Monday it was reported that all that was left of the 7th had been gobbled up by the Rebels, while they were acting as skirmishers, but this has not been confirmed therefore I am unwilling to believe it it is to be hoped it is only a rumor.

I wonder if Mrs Swinton knows where her Husband is wounded, in the last list of casualties, it did not mention where they were wounded merely gave their names. How does Mather[12] progress? I see that Gen Hancock's wound troubles him and that he is temporarily released from duty;[13] I did not know that he was wounded, should hope it was nothing serious. Would you like me to send you newspapers if so I would most gladly do it. Emma says ask Fred if he would like a straw hat tell him if he would I will send him the money to get one, or if you would like money for tobaco or anything of the kind let us know and [we] will gladly send it. Your letters look as if they were written on the field[.] each letter I send I will enclose an envelope or sheet as I know it must be difficult for you to procure them. O! your letters are such a comfort Emma says tell him they are worth untold millions. You may immagine our joy at receiving these letters when we had only received one during a period of 5 weeks. I am glad you receive our letters. No box has come to me from Belle Plain, your clothes and books which you sent in the little black trunk came safely, but that was forwarded from Washington I suppose. You ought to have seen the children[']s eyes sparkle when I told them I had two letters from Papa. Jossie can wait till dear Papa is able to write I do hope my dear Husband your strength will not give way under this great fatigue. God bless you.

Thine forever Lizzie M.L.

[along the upside of the last page] Emma and the kids send love. They are all asleep. I wish you could have a comfortable place to sleep in. ½ 12 p.m. I must go to bed. I have read your letters about 16 times. I will put them under my pillow[,] go to sleep[,] and dream of you.

Labeled "Tho'ts on the march," Fred's letter told of his regiment's having moved and marched away from Cold Harbor on June 13. Immeasurably thankful for her constancy in writing to him, he admitted that the army was growing discouraged. Having hoped to be in Richmond and to have defeated Lee by now, they were instead settling into a siege at Petersburg, which boded for a drawn-out campaign. Like others, he hoped that most of the hard fighting was over. Unfortunately for the Seventh New York, the bloodletting would continue.

Tho'ts on the march

June 27th 1864
Camp near Petersburgh, Va.

My chére Femme,

Another letter from you yesterday—dated June 16th. You still complain of having rec[d]. but one short note from me. I have written you six or seven letters at least.[14] I hope by this time most of them have reached you. Your epistolary constancy to me is an unspeakable satisfaction. I don't know what I should do without the consolation derived from your letters. The truth is we are having soldiering in its roughest sternest form—old soldiers all declare that this beats everything in the previous experience. Yesterday we had a day's repose—to-day we are moving again— only a little to the left however. But a move of a few hundred yards even causes a deal of work. We have fresh wells to dig, new bower houses to put up, brush to clear away, and defences to strengthen. There is no water here—the country is suffering from a severe drought—we have to dig thro' clay for the vital element— and when we get it—it is as thick as lime wash—and tastes of the roots of pine trees.[15] I have read of the sufferings of mariners and others from thirst, but never supposed that in a christian-habited land, a whole army could be reduced to the straits that we suffer.[16]

The weather is intolerably hot—the whole country is a scene of bare desolation—the shagged scorched and blasted forests which surround us exhale an odor which is perfectly sickening. We are all lousy—not a drop of water to wash a shirt in—the men are stale—dirty—and listless. The romance of Battle! The pomp, pride and circumstances of glorious war! Incessantly my friends and I are talking over the blessings of home—the inestimable delights of ever-blessed Peace—and we have come to the conclusion that the felon in a state prison—the troublesome mendicant whose instances [insistences?] you turn aside to avoid—the bogus ticket agent—each and all are far more reputable characters than the patriot soldier.

This sounds Fernando Woodish[17]—but I could sustain it by thousands of instances. Firstly his officers are harsh and unjust to him. The intercourse between a general officer and a private soldier indicates no human affinity. On one side it is harsh—despotic—unjust control—on the other side it is powerless unquestioning submission. On a march—the day is sultry—the roads choked with dust—the soldiers are parched, heated and foot-weary, we come across a deserted residence and there is a cool delicious well—we run in eager haste to fill our canteens—and a guard drives us away. The general wants water—his servants want it—his horses require watering—we can't have it. There is no sense of it—on this side is unquestioned power—we are the brute instruments of his will.

I am often amused at the staple of my thoughts during these horrible forced marches. We march 16 or 18 hours thro' a waterless country—we suffer exhaustion, hunger, thirst—and the brain becoming active from the physical excitement. Face, hands, and body are grimed with dirt—such a jostling set of dirty devils your imagination cannot conceive. Then I invariably revel in the luxuries of Duke Humphrey's dinner.[18] (You remember that favorite story of your Grandma's in Harper's Mag.) The epicurian feasts my mental vision spreads before me—would do credit to the profusion of Heliogabalus.[19] A cup of fragrant tea—just the right heat—slightly flavored with sugar and weakly tinctured with milk—a dish of chilled strawberries ripe and luscious—perhaps the aroma of a lemon originates in my brain—and I express its juicy pulp as I would nectar. Or I may revel upon more substantial viands—I am about to sit down to a table spread with cold ham—warm roast veal nicely stuffed—brown gravy, a dash of lemon juice and a profusion of vegetables. The whole scene is vividly depicted before me—my imagination is excited—but unfortunately the viands never cross my lips.

When we finally come to a halt for the night—it is late—no one can direct us to the water—we are tired out—and we throw ourselves on the ground dirty—jaded—hungry and thirsty as we are and sleep till sunrise unless earlier disturbed to resume our march. Let us pray that these masterly flank movements of Grant's are over. . . . I believe we are doing favorably. We have Richmond disconnected and shall soon assault Petersburgh. The officers say most of our hard fighting is over—we shall resort to the slower and surer effects of siege. Ans the pleasant letter from Emma—Love to all—Hope your health is good. Good bye-

F.

[Note in upper left-hand corner, p. 1]: Will you please send a small tooth comb—I keep my hair cropped close—and my body clean—but lice abound in camp—you cannot keep away from them.[20]

Two days later, Fred detailed the regiment's march to the James River. He noted especially the soldiers' thirst and his struggles with reconciling regimental records. Years later, when quoting some of his letters in his memoirs, Frederic added further detail, some of which is included here, indicated by brackets or in footnotes.

Near Petersburgh, Va.
June 29th 1864

Ma chére Femme:

We are having a little rest now. As I understand the position of things, we have the rebel capital and army in a pretty snug place, and quietly [hope] the results will be as profitable as fighting. We are slowly growing into the habits of civilized life again. Our camp has been policed—and laid out in company streets—tomorrow we have bi-monthly inspection and muster for pay—and our band discourses excellent music every evening. The weather has moderated considerably—if we only had water here that we might wash and be clean—all our troubles would be intermitted. You probably see our position discussed in the daily papers—and can gather from that source as intelligent an understanding of the matters as I can furnish you. I am busy just now with monthly returns—muster & pay rolls and sundry quarterly statements.

[You remember my deploring the abandonment of regimental and company books at Belle Plaine. Since then our only means of making any report of the regiment were afforded by the company roll-books and the morning report blanks, in the possession of the first sergeants. The latter were carried in their knapsacks, and as these were flung aside in our hurried march to the Fredericksburg Road fight,[21] nothing remained but the company roll-books. These simply give the names of the men composing the companies. From May 15th to June 23rd, one week since, the regiment has lost in various ways thirteen hundred men, of whom but trifling and fragmentary data have been preserved. The adjutant, like myself, was absorbed in the incessant labors of the campaign; and when a few hours rest was afforded, all were so utterly beat out—first sergeants and company officers included—that an attempt to collect needed information was futile. And, farther, we have lost so many captains and first sergeants that the source of information is destroyed. How all this confusion is going to be straightened out so that the accounts of the missing men may be settled, passes my understanding.

I have been employed the last three days preparing a list of the killed, wounded and missing, in the regiment, for the Adjt. General of the state of New York. It has been a laborious and vexatious task. No one has energy to assist me. The officers—what few of them remain—are either sick or demoralized, and non-commissioned officers are almost an extinct class.][22]

I commenced this early this morning—and now I resume it. It is growing dark. We have orders to pack and be ready to march— the rebels appear to have fallen away from our front—our march will be probably northward towards Richmond. I trust our long marches are over. The recollection of the painful scenes incident upon these labors is [harrowing][23] in the extreme. To see the hundreds of panting, fainting men and boys strewn along the road in various stages of exhaustion—grey-haired bowed old men—robust-looking men in the prime of life—and fair-haired boys prostrate and helpless in the broiling sun—faces begrimed with sweat and dust—clothes stained and feet swollen and blistered—these are sights that long remain impressed upon the mind. The craving for water is universal.[24]

During our last march—I suffered more intensely than at any other time. We left our encampment where a delicious little stream gurgled past our camp—and as I had no idea we were going to march over a mile or so—I neglected to fill my canteen. That day we marched ten miles without meeting one drop of water.

[I find relief from thirst, in a suggestion made to me by a sanitary commission agent, who with knapsack on back and staff in his hand, traveled along with the column. Said he: "You place a few grains of tea between your lower lip and your gum and keep them there. They become moist and keep the mouth sweet." He also supplied me with a pinch of the fragrant plant. I find the effect very pleasant and satisfactory.[25]]

July 1st

Now we are having a little leisure there is so much work found for us at division headquarters that I really have not time to finish this letter. I must send it half written as it is—the mail carrier is waiting.

F.

In his next letter, Frederic told of nearly being captured in an operation at the Weldon-Petersburg Railroad. The incident is known derisively as Barlow's Skedaddle after the regiment's commander, Francis C. Barlow, and his unit's disorganized flight during a Confederate attack on June 22. Fred was lucky not only to avoid being shot when fleeing pursuing enemy troops but also to get away. Robert Keating, author of the Seventh New York's regimental history, said more than forty-nine Seventh New York men were killed or captured in that encounter alone and that of the more than five hundred Seventh New Yorkers taken prisoner during the Overland Campaign and Petersburg siege, nearly half of them, wounded or not, died in Confederate captivity.[26]

Near Petersburgh, Va.

July 3d, 1864

Ma chére Femme,

This is Sabbath morning—tomorrow will be the <u>Fourth</u>! They are pounding away with cannon on our right, and have been all night—but the rebels have fallen away from our front. We are having remarkably quiet times—for over a week our regiment has not been engaged and the impression seems to prevail that our repose will not be disturbed for some time. The weather is again excessively hot, and our want of water for cleansing purposes is seriously felt. I manage to keep a clean hide—by filling my canteen—and washing my body with my silk handkerchief. I do certainly greatly miss the luxuries of clean wholesome water—a change of linen—and a cool retreat. But my health continues good—our stay here is but for a season—and a little fortitude will put me thro' my difficulties better than anything else.

Yesterday we had a distribution of stores contributed by the Sanitary Committee. Lemons[27]—can tomatoes and plug tobacco constituted the luxuries. This contribution was munificent in quantity—but when divided up to each man his share was very trifling. The care felt for and interest manifested in our comfort and well-being—which these philanthropic labors make evident, are very gratifying to the feelings. The box you received was sent from Belle Plain—but the Christian commission carried it to Washington. I received your papers and am much pleased with them. . . .

I came near being "gobbled" the other day—the affair was quite amusing.[28] On the 22d June the regt. had orders to move. I harnessed up and fell into the line of march. After proceeding about one mile, the division was halted in a pine forest—formed in an irregular line of battle—and the men ordered to lie upon their arms. Col. Hastings established his headquars. under an immense pine tree—the enemy's bullets whistled around rather lively but

I had considerable writing to do—so I spread out my papers and went to work.

Shortly an order came to detail 30 men and an officer for picket to connect with the skirmish line on our right. In the execution of this order the officer mistook his way—and felt his way clean to the rebel skirmish line. These received them with a shower of bullets which caused them to fall back precipitately. The Excelsior brigade on our right then gave way—and the rebels (concealed in the woods) sent in a volley which put them to flight. Our regiment next broke and fled—and the rebels were on them like a flash. This happened so suddenly—that I had merely time to snatch up papers—knapsack—haversack and tent and join the crowd of fugitives who were in confused flight. Our pursuers were close upon our heels—I could see the flash of their muskets through the trees—and every now and then a man would fall wounded. The bullets did zip around my head in a manner really disturbing to the nerves. After a chase of nearly a mile we emerged from the woods—and came across an advanced breastwork. Into this we piled and held the rebels at bay until our division formed—and the confusion was over. We lost from our reg^t. 2 officers captured—and 7 men wounded and 27 missing. We have had many a laugh about this since—but I had to fling my tent and haversack—containing four days' grub in order to save myself.

I have plenty of stamps at present. I bought ½ lb. cheese with your 25c /—money is no use here—you can put a dollar's worth of groceries in a snuff box. Warmest love to Emma & the babes. I have plenty of stationery now.

Your's devotedly,

F.

In his next letter of July 8, Frederic noted that a division from the Sixth Corps had been sent from the Petersburg lines north to intercept Confederate cavalry leader Jubal Early, who was then raiding into Maryland with some ten thousand troops and soon to threaten the capital itself.[29] Early's strike north carried the Confederate general to the hills and fields north of Fort Stevens and adjacent forts, including Forts Reno and DeRussy, where Frederic and his fellow New Yorkers had served unchallenged for almost two years. Frederic was correct to believe Lee had sent Early north of the Potomac to relieve Grant's pressure on Petersburg and Richmond. Suspecting that was Lee's intention, Grant was slow to respond to the threat but eventually sent veteran Sixth Corps soldiers in numbers great enough to defend Washington effectively. In fact, with President Lincoln looking on from the Fort Stevens parapet when the Sixth Corps division arrived in late afternoon on July 12, Gen. Horatio Wright's soldiers were just in time to thwart Early's Confederates. If Early had attacked that morning, when the capital's fortifications were thinly manned by new recruits, invalids, militia, and volunteers, he might have entered the city. But he had waited. Noted Elisha Hunt Rhodes, who was on hand with his Sixth Corps regiment, "Early was Late."[30]

Meanwhile, Frederic and the Seventh New York, which had vacated the Washington DC area in May, manned the siege trenches facing Petersburg and grew discouraged. As one historian termed duty along the line at Petersburg, it was "slow-motion torment for soldiers."[31] Indeed, discouraged and determined not to extend his term of service, Frederic rejected promotion to a lieutenancy.

Near Petersburg, Va.
July 8th / 64

Ma chére Femme

I wrote a letter to Emma yesterday and intended to pen a few lines to enclose to you—but I was so constantly occupied that I had to delay my enclosure 'till today. We are having such dreadfully warm weather, that a personage does not feel capable of any close application.[32] The mail carrier has just left the mail here, and tells me [he] has a letter for me over in his tent. I must endeavor to see it before I complete this—as there may be something in it I wish to refer to. A division from the Sixth Corps left here yesterday—to attend to the rebel forces menacing Maryland.[33] Manifestly the object of Gen¹ Lee in making this diversion in our rear is to relieve himself from the pressure which threatens strangulation here.[34] I trust his object will be defeated—the invading force probably does not exceed ten or twelve thousand—surely the populous northern states can attend to them. We think Couch & Siegel[35] will be slow if they do not capture the whole force.

I thought that when we got into active service, I should have so many stirring adventures to relate, that my letters would be elaborate and numerous. But I am still affected with the same indisposition to write—a mental lethargy dulls my pen—and I can get no discursiveness from it. However[,] you have taken me for better or for worse.

Your letter received.[36] Much obliged for your small remittance—it is foolish in you depriving yourself for me. Until the last week money has been of no use to us for nothing could be bought—but now we have a sutler to purvey to us—and any little inconsidered trifle goes to the purchase of some little extra. I always feel as if I were guilty of extravagance.

Your counsel recommending me to refuse a commission on the ground that I should have to be mustered in for three years—by a singular coincidence I have already complied with. I have been sold once. When I joined the army I had no idea that I should serve over <u>one</u> year—I tho't the six hundred thousand men then being raised would sweep the whole embattled host of rebels into the Gulf of Mexico. The burnt child dreads the fire! I think the war may terminate this year—it may last five years more. I will serve three years upon my original contract—but any further entangling alliances with the war dept. I respectfully beg to decline. The adj[t] proposed to me to recommend my name to the Governor for a lieutenancy—I hastened to decline the honor.[37] My patriotism is about <u>given out</u>. The principle of <u>War is wrong</u>—the soldier is degraded below the status of a decent man's dog—I would not enlist again to save the country from perdurable ruin. You will not like these sentiments—but I have had them forced upon me. Good bye—I wrote to Josephine a day or two since. Hope your health is good—mine is exuberant.

Very truly Yours
F.

15

An Epoch of Endurance
Mid-July–Mid-August 1864

Frederic was more upbeat two days later. In a letter to his nine-year-old daughter, Dollie (Emma Louise), who apparently disliked the capital M, he invited her to consider how things might be if she lived with him in the "nice little house" he had built for himself on the Petersburg siege lines. He then told her of having been caught in open ground under rebel shelling one night during the Cold Harbor battles. The incident occurred on June 5, two nights after the horrific assault of June 3. Having visited the field hospital behind the lines, Fred had lost his way back in the dark when the shelling commenced. As the bombardment intensified like "a fiery tornado," he wrote years later for his memoirs, he threw himself prostrate on the ground, "thinking I was less exposed to the iron tempest in that position." Still, "riven fragments were burying themselves in the earth all around me," and escape seemed hopeless.[1] Frederic also wrote to his oldest daughter, Josie, who had turned eleven this day. Unfortunately, that letter does not survive, but this one to Dollie does among Josie's descendants.

His descriptions to Dollie are remarkably lively and detailed, far more so than anything he related at the time to Elizabeth, for whom he intended this letter as well. The unpretentious tenor in which it is composed—father to daughter but so honest and devoid of condescension—says much about the way he related to his children.

My dear little Daughter [Dollie],

Before I commence I must apologize to you, I have commenced my letter with a kind of M which you dislike. It ran off my pen without premeditation. I will try not to offend again.

I could not sleep last night. This warm weather and the woolen clothing which I wear, has caused a slight rash to break out on my skin and thus it itches and irritates me in such a manner that it is a perfect torment. We cannot safely undress here. The nights are so cool. We have so little bed covering (my bedding consists of half a woolen blanket) and we are so liable to night alarms that all we can do when it gets dark is to take off our shoes, put them and our caps under our heads for pillows, pick out a clean spot and lay down for the night. Last night, I undressed—however—and as a consequence was woken up at 12 o'clock by the Adj. and the Regiment had orders to pack up. So while we wait for orders, I thought I will fill the interval by writing to you.

I finished a nice little house for myself yesterday. I wish you could see it. You would be charmed to live in it. It is not built of brownstone—nor bricks—nor weather board either. I must describe it to you. First I cut down six maple saplings about seven feet long with a fork or crotch at the upper end. This I sharpened at the lower end and drove firmly into the ground. Four of them for the corners of the house and two in the front for door posts. Then I cut a dozen more poles and placed four of them along the top, resting in crotch's to form the frame of the building. The others I tied about half way up the poles to help form the walls. As I had no string or rope, I tore up an old shirt, and these strips of woolen clothes answered the purpose very well. Then I sent some men into the woods to cut a whole lot of pine boughs with thick tufts of its hair—like verdure. These I hung over the transverse poles. They form quite a thick wall or screen—keeps out the sun's rays and gives free ingress to the cooling breezes. The roof is formed by tying a few light poles across the upper frame work and throwing a quantity of pine branches upon these which answer for a thatch. I suppose it never rains here. We have been out eight weeks today and have seen no drops of rain yet except one shower in Spotsylvania which wet me through one night when I was asleep without waking me. But if it should rain, I don't hardly think my building would be waterproof. There is one good thing, however, the rain would not be likely to injure my furniture.

Mama tells me (another nasty M) that you and your sister are all well. All progressing nicely with your studies. All in high spirits and enjoyment. It makes me happy to hear that you are so. We have had a wearisome time hitherto but now our labors are over for the present and we are getting comfortable. Our men have dug scores of wells and our supply of water is sufficient and of good quality. We have plenty of food and the sanitary commission furnished us with fresh vegetables which we hugely enjoy. Having leisure we can keep ourselves clean and this I find greatly conductive to both health and comfort. This being Sabbath morning, the Adjutant (a very worthy and pious young officer) wished me to read the Scripture to him. I read the 1st Book of Timothy and a few Psalms. He declared he never enjoyed the Scripture so much in his life before. Don't you think we are getting civilized again.

I must tell you of a rather dangerous night adventure I had while we were lying at Coal Harbor. I had pitched my tent in a piece of woods about half a mile in rear of the breastworks which the regiment occupied. They made a charge, drove the rebels back and advanced their lines fully a mile. This left me too far in the rear. So one evening I struck my tent—packed up and followed them up until I came to a pleasant rise of land where I pitched. Shortly after I had fallen asleep for the night I was awakened by a very heavy cannonading from the rebels which was accompanied with terrific discharge of musketry. To my horror I found I was lying just within point blank range. The air all around me was filled with screaming and reverberating missiles. Shells were bursting thickly around me, cannon balls were ploughing up the earth to the right and to the left and some rifle balls were whizzing over my body and plunging into the earth in every direction around me. There were plenty of small firs and a few rods distance where I could have thrown myself in and been safe, but the air was so dense with deadly missiles that I did not venture to raise my head from the ground. To offer the least possible mark to these dangerous messengers, I turned my head towards the enemy—piled a knapsack and blankets upon my head and shoulders and lay as close to the ground as was possible. For about an hour the devils kept up this ferocious fire. Two bullets perforated my tent and buried themselves in the ground a foot or so from where I lay, but I escaped without injury and when they grew tired of spending their ammunition I fell asleep and slept soundly till morning. I concluded this was not a safe place, however, and moved up to the rifle pits the next day. These rebels don't care whom they hurt. They toss their cannon balls about as if they were paper bullets.

I have written you quite a long letter. The first opportunity I have, I will also write to Miss Gertrude. Did Josey receive her letter? I shall address to you and you will be pleased to hand the enclosed note to Mama. God bless you my child. Love to your sister[s] and friends. Geo [probably "Ger" in the original] and Josey must try and write me a few lines.

Your affectionate father

F.E. Lockley

The same day Fred wrote his letter to Dollie, he sent a briefer note to Lizzie. It had less verve. "I am afraid you will think I am rather stinting you," he wrote, but justified the few letters he was sending her by saying his writing to others in the household made up for it. "Don't cut me short, however," he admonished. "I want my full allowance." His having to list the killed, captured, and wounded of his regiment contributed to his melancholy. The impact on the officer corps was particularly severe. A lieutenant, he said, "commands the regiment."[3]

He wanted to see one of two moves: "either into Richmond or back to the defenses of Washington." He got neither. They would move along the siege line three times in the next five days, including one move the very day he had written to Dollie.

Camp near Petersburgh Va July 15

Ma plus chére Femme,

It is high time I wrote to you—but I am in such an ungenial
humor—that I fear my letter will be unsatisfactory. We have
removed thrice since my last writing. Our first move was at
midnight on Sunday last—about four miles to the left—where
we rested one entire day in the glaring intolerable sun—and at
evening marched some four miles further to support a heavy
column of cavalry while they tore up some miles of the track of
the Weldon and Danville Railroad.[4] A fight was fully expected on
that occasion—but the foe submitted to the injury without offering
a word. This accomplished we returned to our bivouack [*sic*]—
slept till daybreak, and then marched here. Gen[l]. Grant has been
contracting his lines—and we are placed near to the fatal field
where we made our unfortunate charge on the 16th ult.[5] We hail
any change of encampment that offers with delight—trusting
that a benign Providence may direct our steps to a land where the
vital element of Water—flowing in limpid purity and abounding
plenty—may once more refresh our dusty and sun-scorched souls.
But all pervading and unfathomable dust—and a fervid, angry
intolerable sun—are the only material conditions vouchsafed us.

Two days since I took a towel and a clean shirt in my hand,
determined to find some pool or stream where I could have
a wholesome wash. I travelled and searched during the whole
afternoon but could find nothing but a fetid repulsive pool—
where on stepping into it, I sunk up to my knees in green pasty
mud. I attempted to wash my shirt—but took it back a great deal
dirtier than I started with it. Not a drop of rain yet. The whole
surface of the earth has resolved itself into individual particles,
and assuming to themselves (what the Poet Blair[6] adduced as
one of the contingencies of the absence of a creative hand) "an
indesputable right to dance," we live in a palpable atmosphere.
The Egyptian plagues could scarcely have been more grievous.
Dust everywhere—uppermost—and inexhaustible. The paper
I write on is gritty—my pen clogged—my mouth dried with the
palpable earthy solution—and my hair sticky—adhesive—unkept—
impervious. Oh! For a glorious wash! Never will I complain of mud

again. Moisture in any shape it may resolve itself into will ever be welcome to me in future.

July 17ᵗʰ I commenced this letter two days since intending to write you an agreeable, intelligent letter. But I have been interrupted with so much office work that I am defeated of my intention—and must hurry a few lines together as best I can. I have received no letter from you for just one week—so conclude the rebels must have anticipated me with one in the mail they seized upon. I have no energy to write. This is Sabbath afternoon—I have been busy during the last three days in preparing a list of the killed, wounded and missing of the regiment for the Adjᵗ. Genˡ. of the State of New York—thirteen hundred names. This I find a work of immense labor—and had intended to defer it till cooler weather. The officers (what few remain) are either sick or indifferent—and the non-commissioned officers are almost an extinct race—consequently my sources of information are rather interrupted. I write this in a state of painful languor—my lethean[7] senses are just sensible of dis-comfort, but without energy to shake off its influence. The division band is discoursing divine airs in the breezy distance— its symphonies fall upon my ears like solemn organ tones in an antique cathedral. I am just sensible of images of groined roofs—and delicate architectural tracery—and faded trophied banners—"the very atmosphere of peace"—and I am aroused in consciousness with the incessant clouds of dust which persist in invading the sanctity of our wall tent, and the constant booming of cannon against the devoted walls of Petersburgh. Oh this wearisome siege—this shadeless[8] in a sandy plain, this continued condition of intellectual vacuity—when shall they have an end? I will write no more—as I shall only infect you with my own discontented feelings.

Do not neglect your correspondence—I was quite disappointed at receiving no letter this morning. I wish you would send me a little darning cotton and a small dinner knife and fork in your next papers—send the articles separately.

. . .

A connubial kiss—sweetheart—albeit a sleepy one. I doubt whether your divine presence could arouse me.

Thine–

F.E.L.

In his next letter, Fred speculated on the death of his friend Joe Rogers, presumably killed during the June 3 assault at Cold Harbor. Rogers' body was never found despite a search for it by his friends from the regiment. Frederic would later ponder whether the effort to find Rogers was motivated by genuine concern for a comrade or for the $300 they thought Rogers had stuffed in his boots.[9]

More significantly, he described the disastrous charge against Confederate defenses at Petersburg on June 16 in which Maj. Edward A. Springsteed was caught in an almost impossible situation. Pinned down in a hollow during the charge, Springsteed and thirty-one others hoped to wait for darkness to make an escape following their 6:00 p.m. assault. Constant enemy fire took its toll, however, and some of the men waved hats and white handkerchiefs to surrender, although none dared stand up and move toward the Confederate line. Realizing their plan was to wait for dark, the Confederate commander, twenty-year-old 2nd Lt. Francis M. Kelso,[10] took his small command onto the field and forced the New Yorkers to surrender. When the ensuing commotion diverted Kelso's attention, Springsteed and a couple of others fled for Union lines. Of the thirty-two men trapped in the ravine, twenty-nine were either killed during the assault or died in Confederate prisons.[11]

Lockley watched the affair from the rear with a contingent of Union artillery. When he saw that a line of Confederates was approaching on their right, he announced to a nearby officer that the rebels were surrendering. "See the Johnnies coming in!" he shouted. "They're deserting." His companion observed the enemy's approach for a moment, then snapped, "Deserting. You d—d fool! They're surrounding us." Recalled Lockley years later, "Thus illuminated I thought that a good place to get away from" and ran for safety.[12]

N^r Petersburgh Va. July 20th / 64

Ma chére Femme,

Two long letters this week, after a long silence. I am exceedingly busy—and can only snatch a few moments—just to satisfy your impatience with the promise of doing better next time. . . . I

Mid-July–Mid-August 1864

do not care about writing to Joe Rogers' friends. If you write to
them again you can tell them that he won a high name for his
dauntless bearing and the unflinching performance of his duty.
It is a subject of doubt whether he was killed or taken prisoner on
the fatal morning of the 3ᵈ of June, 1864.[13] Several of his company
saw him fall forward upon his face as he was shot while charging
upon the Rebel works at Coal Harbor. Capt. Shannon (who must
be contrary) persists in his belief that he was wounded and taken
prisoner. I fear Friend Joe breathed his last that day. Frank Butt[14]
was captured along with three or four hundred others of our
regiment on the evening of the 16ᵗʰ June in an attack upon some
advance works near Petersburgh. The charge was badly planned—
and Maj. Springsteed is blamed for his poor conduct of it.[15] Our
regiment rushed into a perfect cul de sac—where retreating was
more dangerous than staying to receive the enemy's fire. When
Major Springsteed was called upon to surrender his command—he
hesitated—and bade his men reserve their fire until he sent to
consult with Lt. Col. Hastings. The result was some threw down
their arms and surrendered[,] some turned and fled of whom
a portion escaped—and a large number were shot down as they
ran. The storm of missiles which the enemy rained upon them was
terrific. Poor Frank stayed to be captured. I sincerely sympathise
with his wife[;] her case is indeed pitiable.

I trust your health is good—you never speak of it now. I fear
you are distressed for means—four months' pay is now due—
and I see no signs of the paymaster. Tell me how you weather your
difficulties. My health is good—but I do wish we could get into a
more human country. The desolation and drouth prevailing here
are truly depressing. Military movements light—our division is
out on fatigue work and the rebels are peppering them with a few
shells—but I don't believe they can hurt them any.

Excuse a short letter—time presses—Love to all.

Yours truly

[P.S.] Will you send me two or three stamps? I am a great trouble
to you

Fred wrote to Lizzie next on July 24. The short letter said that James D. Van Benthuysen, "my garrulous little friend," is about the only "old chum" he had left in the regiment from their days serving in defense of Washington. The boy, aged nineteen at the time of his enlistment in 1862, had escaped unharmed—and would survive the war—but, Fred noted, "his military experience has sobered him." The numbers were sobering also. "The company is reduced to 37 men—it numbered 153 on leaving Ft Reno."[16]

A week later, he told Lizzie of having marched north of the James River for reasons not clear to him at the time but, as he would learn later, as a feint to distract Lee's attention from the underground mine Grant's engineers set off on July 30 for the disastrous assault that came to be known as the Battle of the Crater. He noted having heard the mine's explosion under Confederate defenses at Petersburg, as had others, but not until later did he learn of the tragic events that befell the Union assault in its aftermath. Otherwise, he was taken with the beauty of the landscape around the James River, but the summer heat was so intense that half the column straggled. Describing the march back from the James years later in his memoirs, Frederic seemed to shudder at the scene, including his regret at abandoning one soldier by the side of the road.

We made a dreadfully fatiguing march back following the column; the mercury marked over 100° in the shade, and the extreme heat overpowered a large proportion of our force. Men dropped out exhausted and thickly strewed the road. One poor fellow, a recent arrival from the north, fell in an epileptic fit by the side, being terribly convulsed. In such times of extreme endurance the feelings become blunted, and the mere instinct of self preservation controls. In this case there was no help; no ambulance to call, no provision made for succor. I left the dying soldier on the dusty ground, and he was but one of a score of such reported "died on the march."[17]

Mid-July–Mid-August 1864

Ma chére Femme,

I have summoned up energy to pencil you a few lines—but the
prostration resulting from a heavy march yesterday added to
the intolerable heat of the weather will prevent me being very
discursive. On Tuesday afternoon [July 26] last we started on a
march and next morning halted on the northern bank of the
James river 5 miles below Fort Darling.[18] I have not yet learned the
object of the expedition nor what we accomplished—but from
the time we started till our return yesterday afternoon we were
incessantly employed in supporting skirmish lines—building breast
works or forming line of battle. Considerable fighting was doing
all around us in which the cavalry and artillery were principally
engaged—but I have not learned that we gained any decided
success. The scenery surrounding the James is delicious—green
fields and handsome residences[19] nestling in breezy groves—and
the wide abounding river flowing in inexhaustible abundance
past. We plodded past hungry—heated—fatigued and laden down.
What numerous exclamations of delight were uttered—and how
ardently we longed for the privilege of halting upon that blessed
shore—to drink our fill of the stream to luxuriate in its wave—and
to refresh our minds after the harassment—toil—and desolation
of this bloody war. But we hurried past this rare oasis without
one moment's pause. The heat was so intense that a number fell
sunstruck—more than half the column straggled—and after we
had accomplished about 12 miles we were halted about 3 hrs in a
wood where we found a cool well—and where we found shade. But
it was too hot to sleep. We had been on the skirmish line all night
exposed to a rattling fire of musketry—and were tired out—but we
sat and rested keeping ourselves from the penetrating rays of the
sun by a continual change of position.

Yesterday a terrific battle was fought before Petersburgh—we
heard the explosion of the fort[20]—and the incessant cannonading
but the 2d Corps (for a wonder) had no hand in the conflict.

I have received half a dozen papers from you this week, and one
letter, containing a brief enclosure from Emma. I have received the

½ dollar sent—also a fork and some thread—the knife was taken out—much obliged for all your kindness—I have picked up a good knife—so I can make out very well.

Jesse Rogers has written me—inquiring about his brother—I have no information to afford him so cannot write during this blazing weather.

Last evening on our reaching camp four days rations were issued and we were to prepare for immediate departure. Maryland was mentioned as our destination—but sudden orders revoking the march arrived—and we remain temporarily in camp. Excuse haste—the flies bother me to death—

Will write again soon

F.

In his next two letters, Frederic declared his health was excellent and that he got more than enough to eat, but the news was not encouraging. Three days later, notwithstanding sharpshooters' bullets and occasional shelling, he tried to make his letter more literary, but oppressive heat and merciless flies made it a struggle.

Camp Near Petersburgh, Va.
August 4th 1864

Ma chére Femme,

I rather stint you in correspondence of late—but it is almost unavoidable. I am driven to death with office duties—and the weather is so intolerably hot—that I have no disposition to write letters. Exposed as we are to the glaring sun[,] I am astonished that we preserve our health as we do—my health was never better—and I begin to feel quite at home here. It now transpires that our long march to the James River and back was a mere feint—to mislead Lee while Grant exploded his fort and charged upon his works. High expectations had been formed of this exploitation—and I see news was sent north that the affair was a decided success. But here we can see no advantage gained—two thousand five hundred soldiers were put hors de combat, and we have not advanced our lines one inch. I am getting discouraged—I can see no termination to this war. If we are to fight it out on this line (as Grant talks about) it will take more than the whole Summer to do it.

Your letters reach me regularly—in your next will you please enclose a small piece of india rubber? How is it you send me so many papers? I hope you do not buy them to send to me. We get quite a number of papers now we are settled down—and I am unwilling to put you to expense for my reading. The paymaster is ready to pay this Brigade—but our regiment is so revolutionized that one half the pay and muster rolls are not yet finished. There are so few officers that I am afraid it will be some time before they are prepared.

Maj. Springsteed and Capt. Kennedy are back again. There is a probability that we shall stay here some time.

Excuse brevity—I will write more at full when I have leisure. Hope you are well and doing well. Love to the young ones.

Your's devotedly
F.E.L.

Camp near Petersburgh, Va.[21]
August 7th 1864

Ma chére Femme,

I am going to try to write you a letter. If I succeed it will be under serious difficulties—the flies are tormenting—ready to devour me alive; the heat is intense, and I am subject to continual interruptions. This is Sabbath morning—the camp is alive with business: two days' rations are being delivered to the men—and the Quartermaster is making a large issue of clothing. We have fallen into the routine of camp life—guard mounting—drill-inspections, dress parade— and fatigue details—and are about as monotonous as when in garrison life at Fort Reno. We hear the almost incessant firing of the pickets—at intervals of every few minutes a heavy cannon from our lines gives tongue and belches a shell right into the enemy's midst. This sometimes provokes a retort—and occasionally a brisk artillery duel will ensue—but each party is so effectually covered—that little damage can be done. On Friday evening the enemy attempted to spring a mine—they failed—but the attempt was followed by a charge upon our lines. A hasty order was sent to our headquarters for the division to take a hand in—they marched at double quick to the scene of action but by the time they reached there the attack had been repulsed and the fight was over.

The newspapers are blathering about the esprit du corps of the army of the Potomac. How that Gen[l]. Grant is confident of success and the men devoted to the cause and impatient to be hurled against the enemy. Springes to catch woodcocks. A sicker set of wretches you never saw. A feeling of discouragement has become infectious. Our immense army has been wasted in battles and horrible marches until it is now too weak to work with; Petersburgh seems impregnably fortified, and our efforts to disconnect Richmond from the south have been unsuccessful. I am unable to see that anything has been accomplished by this campaign. Meantime, every day spent here is an epoch of endurance— intolerable heat—scarcity of water and no shade. The country is drifting rapidly in bankruptcy—and the "promised end" is disappearing in the dim and visionary distance. When newspaper correspondents prate about the élan and enthusiasm of the soldiers you must understand that the 4th Brig. is excluded.

Your letters all arrive—I grieve that your health is so poor—I trust that two weeks in the country will invigorate you—I arose early this morning—started two men away into infinite space in pursuit of water—who returned with a camp kettle full. I washed all my dirty clothes—cooked breakfast (we live well here) attended Guard mounting (9 o'clock) and then intended to devote to private writing. But my fortitude is not equal to the task. The glare of the sun distresses me and the flies are so pestiferous that my hands and face are literally covered with them. To write calmly— philosophically and wisely under such circumstances passes my powers. I should much like to write to your rebel cousin in Cincinnati[,] but you do not tell me his regiment—do you know that he is there still? I have intended to repay Mr. Owen's visit— but his corps is away in Maryland. My health is excellent—and notwithstanding the hot weather I eat enough to make a horse ill. As I write our tattered and blood stained flag flouts the hot breeze that fans these headquarters—and Jimmie Van Benthuysen treads his silent beat as sentry over the sacred presence of our commander. I think I have told you that Maj Springsteed had resumed command of the reg^t. After the futile interregnum which has ensued since Col. Morris' death on the 4th of June it is quite a relief to have the familiar and much respected Major amongst us again. He is an excellent officer and very popular with the men. Some boisterous friends of Major Murphy's have just arrived—so I will adjourn. Love to all–

Your's devotedly

F.

The Seventh New Yorkers, now so decimated, had entertained the hope they might return to defensive duty in Washington, but as that hope dimmed it seemed likely they would remain in the siege lines for coming months. Frederic dreamed, meanwhile, of family.

Near Petersburgh Va.

Augt. 10th 1864

Ma trés chére Femme,[22]

. . .

We are moving camp to-day. Our Brigade is commanded by a fussy Englishman—Lt. Col. Broady[23] of the 69th.[24] He seems to entertain the idea that the men cannot be kept sufficiently employed. He is forever putting up some job for them. Inspections, skirmish drill—fatigue details—his fertile brain is ever pregnant with some new project of folly. As I sit here I watch the whole camp in commotion. We are moving about one hundred yards to the right—and the men were up and tearing down things by daylight.

It is growing into belief here that we are likely to remain about here for months. There have been great expectations of going back to the defences of Washington, and the story was circulated that Maj. Genl Hancock had been placed in command of the Middle department.[25] But we learn by the papers that Genl. Wright is invested with that command, consequently there are but slim grounds remaining for us to build hopes of any return to Washington. Our progress against Petersburgh will be slow. The unfortunate repulse of the 31st ult.[26] Having defeated Grant's plans—will render him cautious and the enemy more wary. I presume we have a sure thing upon Lee. Their defensive powers seem now confined to two vital points—here and Atlanta. Success at either point will be ruin to the rebel cause. Sherman's operations before Atlanta appear to be successful—and Gen[l]. Grant may be willing to remain quiet and await the result of this co-adjutor's labors in Georgia.

. . .

I often amuse myself with the idea of a day's picnic with you and the young ones. We would try and re-produce one day of pleasant camp life. A bivouack under a spreading tree—with flowing water within reach, a hatchet to split firewood—a few culinary utensils—a haversack full of rations—and a newspaper and some tobacco. Why couldn't we live a soldier's life? It has its charms—but they are most attractive in the distance.

I enclose a small document endorsed "Memoranda" I may send you a number of such. Will you be pleased to file them away—I may need them for reference on my return home

I will trouble you no further Warmest love to all

Yours Respectueuusement[27]

16

No Sundays in the Army
August–September 1864

Less than a week after writing that a soldier's life had its charms—at a distance—Frederic and the Seventh New York were on their way with more than twenty-five thousand other Union soldiers in a forced march to a second rendezvous with conflict at Deep Bottom. Staging yet another feint against Richmond, Grant hoped to divert Lee's attention north so that Federal forces under Maj. Gen. Gouverneur Warren could attack the Weldon-Petersburg Railroad, a key Confederate supply line south of Petersburg.[1]

The Seventh began its march to City Point, Virginia, the night of August 12, a Friday. Many straggled and some succumbed to heat exhaustion.[2] After a swim in the Appomattox River the next day—their first bathing in eight weeks—they took transports to arrive at an active front on Sunday, August 14, what some said was the hottest day of the year. After taking leave due to the death of his wife, Gen. Francis Barlow had resumed command, but he was disappointed with his troops' lack of enthusiasm and ordered them into some woods as reserve. It proved a lethal assignment. Although behind the lines, Rebel shells exploded in the trees overhead all afternoon, raining deadly fragments and large tree limbs down on the men, killing four outright, mortally wounding another, and injuring ten others.[3] That night, it rained heavily, and, for fear of rheumatism, Fred Lockley did his best to stay dry. The weather cleared somewhat the next day when he penned this letter home.

Deep Bottom Va Aug 15th / 1864

My dear Wife,

I write this during a brief bivouack in the woods. We left our
Camp before Petersburgh on Friday last—it being reported that
the whole 2^d. Corps was going to Washington.[4] The troops were
in the greatest glee and marched to City Point—to embark in
transports—like schoolboys on a holiday. The distance marched
was but nine miles—yet the weather was so insupportably hot
that fifteen died from sunstroke on the road.[5] On arriving at City
Point—our division encamped for the night—then drew three
days['] rations, and hung and loafed around in the blazing sun till
4 o'clock in the afternoon, when we embarked—steamed out half
a mile and then cast anchor. We were in the Appomattox river—
which a short distance below City Point forms a junction with the
James river. Here we grounded—the rest of the transports slipped
silently off—during the night, and landed their troops at Deep
Bottom—this is a wooded section of country four miles from
Malvern hills and two from Gaines' Mill.[6] We did not get afloat
till 11 o'clock on Sunday morning—the 14th—we steamed to Deep
Bottom—disembarked[,] marched three miles—three of our
regiment dying of sunstroke on the road—and took our position in
line of battle right in front of the foe. We were not engaged during
the day—but were vigorously shelled by the enemy—our regiment
lost four killed and nine wounded.[7] The Second division made a
charge—and suffered severely—We do not yet know the precise
object of the fight—but the prevailing impression is that we gained
nothing by it. During the night it rained heavily—we were pleased
to see the rain but being in the open field we got drenched to the
skin. I laid my knapsack against a tree—sat down on it—threw a
rubber blanket over my head—and thus fared better than many
did. The majority—officers and men—threw themselves on the
ground and slept from mere exhaustion—pelted with heavy rain
the while. I have such a horror of Rheumatism in future years that
I never lie down in the rain. Once in Coal harbor[8] I lay down to
sleep—and when I awoke found myself wet through. It had been
raining heavily while I slept—so I do not hold myself responsible

for that. It is cooler this morning—but still dreadfully close. During our present bivouack we have cooked breakfast—and the men appear to be as fresh and jolly as ever. My health is excellent—and my spirits exuberant. Our regiment is thinned out fearfully—One hundred & sixty were present at roll call this morning—besides seventy-six reported as stragglers. It is just three months since we left Washington 1800 strong. Don't you think we have done a big business the while. . . . Best wishes—warmest love—conjugal kisses. My dearest wife, I love thee! Thine

F.

I enclose some more memoranda—be pleased to save them—I jot them down as I have time or opportunity. . . . Our pickets are firing like fun just in our front as I write—we may have another plus muss to-day.[9]

Four days later, Lizzie received his letter while visiting her grandmother in Northumberland, northwest of Albany, and offered to send him a silk handkerchief to soak in water and put under his cap to keep him cool while marching.[10] Meanwhile, Fred and the men of the Seventh spent much of their time on picket duty or under arms expecting to be thrown into the fray at Deep Bottom. This time, however, they evaded much of the action. Instead, they dug breastworks in a light rain that intensified into a heavy downpour overnight and continued all the next day, dampening belligerency on both sides and encouraging some friendly interchange between the lines.[11]

Although Hancock's foray at Deep Bottom accomplished little there, costing Grant three thousand casualties, some one thousand of them from Hancock's Second Corps, it succeeded as a diversion, allowing Warren's Fifth Corps to capture and hold part of the Weldon Railroad south of Petersburg. Warren's success would prove deadly for the Seventh New York, but for the time being, it meant withdrawal from Deep Bottom and a return to Camp Dusty, as the men called their defensive position outside Petersburg.[12] On their way, Frederic found time to write home.

[Deep Bottom]
Near Somewhere, Augt. 20th 1864

My dear Wife,

I have been spending the last two days in complete lethargy.
We have had rain until our craving for it is satisfied, and now
we are hoping for the sun to come out and absorb some of the
superfluous moisture. I wished you could have seen our sleeping
arrangements last night. Heavy rain penetrating everywhere,
and our only protection from it a couple of rubber blankets
stretched over four poles placed slatwise. I had washed all my
linen, including the shirt on my back two days previous—and they
remained packed wet in my knapsack. We were in momentary
expectation of moving, so I had everything ready for a start—and
lying down lightly clad in the wet—I became so chilled while I
was asleep—that I shivered in every member. One would suppose
that this would be enough to give a person a cold—but I arose in
the morning as fresh and sound as ever. I merely mention this to
show how much soldiers can endure. At home, I suppose, such
experience would lay a person up for a month with fever.

We are delightfully encamped in a large open pine forest—we
only want fair weather to enjoy it as a summer vacation. The
rebel lines are plainly in view—the pickets on both sides holding
amicable intercourse. Our men are coming into camp laden down
with green corn—they trade coffee and sugar for tobacco—and
report that the rebel soldiers declare that if they had their own
way they would never fire another gun at a union soldier. It seems
grievous that we should continue this murderous war, while such a
feeling animates the combatants.

I wrote you a few days since informing you that we left our
position before Petersburgh on Saturday last—the 13th and
cross[ed] the James River to Deep Bottom; since then we have
taken part in three engagements—two of them severe ones—but
have suffered lightly—our casualties not exceeding twenty. We
hear by rumor that Genl. Wright has captured the Weldon railroad
after a severe fight, this is a great advantage gained if true. The
object of our present expedition here is inexplicable to us—but

such undoubting confidence in Grant's plans is entertained by his soldiers that we are satisfied it will come out all right.

I hope you are enjoying yourself. We are in a splendid country here—there wants but benignant Peace to render our stay delightful. I have past [*sic*] the second year of my term—what remains will glide swiftly by—and I shall be home to your hungry arms again before you know it. . . .

Your's devotedly

F.

Lockley and the Seventh New York were given little time to rest upon their return to Camp Dusty the night of August 20–21. Within two hours of their arrival, they received orders to march again—this time west instead of north. They were to assist Warren's men in destroying track along the Weldon-Petersburg Railroad near Reams Station, some ten miles south of Petersburg. Building corduroy roads along the way, their marches were desperately muddy until August 23, when the weather finally cleared, allowing Fred and his comrades a chance to admire the unravaged countryside—and forage it with abandon. Chickens, pigs, and ripening corn were all casualties.

Destroying the railway consisted of lifting the iron rails off their ties, stacking the ties in heaps, laying the rails over the ties, and then burning the whole, destroying the ties and bending the iron rails beyond usefulness. The men enjoyed themselves immensely, although Fred wondered why Lee would allow such destruction considering how important the Weldon Railroad was to his sources of supply.

Ream's Station, Va

Augt. 24th 1864

My dear Wife,

The last letter I wrote—whether to you or Emma I forget now—was addressed from Deep Bottom. From that time till now I have had no opportunity to write to you one line. We have had deluging rains—saturating everything I carried—the roads became impassable—and the open lots so marshy—that numbers of cavalry horses have been lost mired to the neck.[13] Yesterday and today have been lovely, the air fresh and balm—but the sun is murderously hot. We returned from the north bank of the James on Saturday last (the 20th) reaching our former camping ground about 8 the next morning. Here we halted two hours and then went on a circuitous march until we struck the Weldon Railroad.[14] We have a large force of cavalry with us—who ride on ahead and drive the enemy while we advance the demolition of the railroad track. We have already destroyed about eleven miles of it—and I am ignorant how much farther we shall advance. We are in an abundant country—hitherto unvisited with the ravages of war—the green corn is just filled—and we pass thousands of acres of it every march—the way the men fill themselves with this delicious succulent vegetable is a caution. As we follow pretty closely upon the exit of the scared inhabitants, we have good chances for foraging—and sheep, pigs, chickens—and sich fall in our way pretty generally. This raid we consider quite an offset for Early's raid in Maryland. But for the blazing sun we should enjoy ourselves hugely. The impression is that Lee's forces must be weak or he never would allow us to destroy so completely this main and important avenue to the south. We are willing to submit to any privations and endure any hardships if we can only advance the termination of the war. This is an important step in that direction and we are encouraged to renewed exertion. A sicker set of sinners than we bronzed and hardy soldiers are of this desolating conflict, mortal eyes never beheld.

I was half sick on Monday—had a sort of cold with severe pains in my limbs—couldn't grub any—and wanted to hang in the rear. In the afternoon it rained heavily—wetting me to the skin— the regiment moved after dark—but I spread my blankets on the track between two blazing piles of ties hoping to dry out thro' the night.[15] But it rained all night—and I arose wetter than I lay down. It cleared off that morning—and with the rain my feeling of sickness went also—I am sound as ever at this present writing. Good bye—excuse a short letter.

Your's

F

[P.S.] I cannot write often until we settle down. Will you please send me one of my razors by mail. I am greatly distressed for one. It will cost you about 30 cents.

Frederic was correct to worry about Lee. Lockley's generals, especially George Gordon Meade, should have worried more. Meade was not without caution. He knew Hancock and his men were vulnerable to attack as they destroyed several miles of the Weldon line. And he promised to send reinforcements, but they never came. Thus, on Thursday, August 25, the Seventh New Yorkers and other Second Corps men had no sooner begun their work that morning than Southern cavalry, infantry, and artillery under Confederate Gens. Henry Heth and A. P. Hill showed up in force. Three times that afternoon, the Confederates launched attacks on the Union positions to the east along the Weldon tracks. Repulsed with heavy losses twice, they succeeded in breaking through on their third assault late in the afternoon. As Frederic wrote to Elizabeth in a letter on September 17, he was not on hand for the first two assaults but did witness the third, a devastating charge coupled with enfilading fire that broke the Union line and sent many of the Federals in disorganized retreat.

His August 27 letter to Lizzie details much of the action. Writing so immediately after the fight, Frederic got some of the details wrong, but he made corrections in his memoir years later (nine Federal cannons captured rather than eight, for example, and ninety-six Seventh Regiment casualties rather than one hundred). His memoir also enhanced the portrayal he had given Lizzie, such as how the storming Confederates were "led by a gallant officer who placed his cap on the point of his sabre to wave them on" and, most important, how his Seventh comrades had had to fall back when other units gave way and how they lost one of his personal heroes, Maj. Edward Springsteed, who commanded the regiment during all three assaults. "The gunners at the field pieces," he wrote years later,

> were nearly all disabled, and every horse shot down. Our breastwork thrown up hastily and composed largely of fence rails, splintered about our ears at every shell that struck, and officers and men were catching it badly. Suddenly an enfilading fire was

poured on us from the left, and a hasty stampede was made for the rear. We passed Maj Springsteed in our flight, lying on the ground, Co A's cook holding the dying officer's head on his knee. "Come, Terry," one of the fugitives called to him; "you'll be gobbled." "I'll stay wid the ma-ajor," he replied; and allowed himself to be taken in with his commander.[16]

Altogether, Union losses were more than twenty-seven hundred men, most taken prisoner. Many of them would die in Confederate captivity. Southern losses were more than eight hundred. Hancock, who had tried exasperatedly to rally his men when they began to flee during the third assault, never got over the defeat. Coupled with lingering wounds from Gettysburg, the Union rout at Reams Station led him to give up field command for more administrative duties in late November.[17]

Northern newspapers downplayed the defeat, while Southern newspapers trumpeted a great victory. The view from Grant and Meade's headquarters was more sanguine than Hancock's, although hardly joyous, and the events at Reams Station did boost Southern morale for a time. Union forces still held part of the Weldon-Petersburg Railroad, however, forcing Lee to adopt more cumbersome means of transporting supplies. From his viewpoint in the thick of it at the time, Lockley assessed the battle as succinctly as anyone: "The rebels will claim a brilliant victory—but such another one would ruin them."[18]

Camp near Petersburgh. Va.
August 27th 1864

Ma tres chére Femme,

We have returned near our old camping ground—and shall probably go into camp and remain quiet until our muster and pay-rolls are made out. We had a good time tearing up the Weldon railroad with a rich and abundant country to forage in, but the general in chief seeming to take umbrage at some of our proceedings, sent an armed force to expel us [from] the premises, and the result was quite a serious collision on the 25th inst. It was the most desperate and furious battle I have ever seen waged. Our force was quite inadequate to contend against the numbers hurled upon us, our position proved indefensible—and our artillery (an exceptional case) acted very indifferently. The result was we were driven from our breastworks—losing eight guns [officially nine]—and perhaps 2000 prisoners. Our regiment in killed, wounded and missing lost fully a hundred.[19]

It had been impressed upon the minds of all the men that Gen[l] Lee would make a titanic effort to recover possession of the roads; and as we were merely out on a raiding scrape, with but two divisions of cavalry and two of infantry, we recognized the imminence of our danger should Lee attack us in force. Still I felt every confidence in our comd[g]. generals never for once supposing they would allow themselves to be surprised. On the morning of the Battle the 2[d] division of our corps had started along the charred and smoking line of railroad to extend their work of demolition, when their progress was arrested by a sudden dash of rebel cavalry—and a splattering of musketry from the fringing pine woods. They about faced—and the whole force was placed in position for battle. Two of the reg[t]. were bro[t]. in wounded from the skirmish line and we then learned that we had Wade Hampton's legion of cavalry—and A.P. Hill's corps in front of us. Our brigade was placed behind a miserably constructed breastwork—and very soon got into action. An open corn field lay in front of them—in the rear of this wood—and from there the rebel line of battle emerged intent upon storming our rifle pits and carrying them. This was the first time our regt. has ever had the opportunity of fighting behind breastworks afforded them; and their conduct was singularly good. They stood cool and determined—their deadly rifles levelled, the finger on the trigger awaiting the command to fire—the rebels approaching them in extended line and yelling like demons. Suddenly their pieces belch flames—the whole line repeats the eruption—a battery planted on the right belches canister right into the rebel bosoms—and they fall in multitudes—half the line seem to fall. They recoil and return to the cover of the woods. This desperate and murderous charging into hellfire was kept up at intervals thro' the whole day—until we were flanked on both sides by overwhelming numbers—our breastworks battered down—and our ranks left without defence[,] continuity—or object. A hasty flight was made for the rear—and numbers were shot or intercepted in their retreat.

Our officers lost—are Maj. Springsteed—mortally wounded & captured; Capt. Kennedy severely wounded and captured; Adj^t. O'Brien wounded and captured—Capt. Wright[20] (promoted from lieutenant the day before) killed—and two lieutenants missing (captured beyond doubt). As we ran the rebels swarmed into our works—and at this precise moment a division of the 9th Corps arrived to cover our retreat—and the rebel commander not knowing the strength of our reinforcements—hastily swept up whatever spoils were laying around—and then retreated in hot haste towards Petersburgh. The rebels will claim a brilliant victory—but such another one would ruin them. Their losses are immense—while ours are quite severe.

We are having lovely weather lots of rain and thunder—a letter containing $1^{oo} reached me to-day. Glad you enjoyed your country trip—Love to all—I am writing this under a tree as I have no tent up yet.

Your's

F.

The fight at Reams Station was the last battle for the Seventh, although the soldiers did not know it at the time, and death in the ranks would continue for another six months during the Petersburg siege. As the regiment's chronicler would observe more than a century later, since first arriving at Spotsylvania on May 25, exactly one hundred days before, the Seventh New York, for all intents and purposes, "had been destroyed."[21]

Fred felt the carnage. "Such constant losses of Officers and men seem to deprive us of every familiar face," he wrote to Elizabeth at the end of August. "We started from Albany one thousand strong and since then have received fourteen hundred recruits; now all we have present with the Regiment are eight officers and two hundred and two men." The action had been so constant and the losses of manpower so great that Frederic was now overwhelmed with paperwork to catalogue it all. In hopes the regiment might be paid the following month, he said, "Our few remaining Officers are making desperate efforts to get pay rolls made out," which in turn made him think of Lizzie's finances. "How many months' rent do you owe?" he asked. "How do you possibly manage to live without receiving a cent from me?"[22]

He only had time enough to write short letters, but if he had had more time, he might have told her of the growing problem of desertion, especially among the most recent recruits—"bounty men," they were often called—and the army's increasingly severe response: summary executions. One such was performed with the entire First Division as witness on September 2.[23]

Frederic would refer to the increasing number of executions for desertion in subsequent letters, but for now, the flies and monthly returns received most of his attention—along with his fascination at having slept in a downpour with no apparent harm.

Near Petersburg, Va. Sept. 4 / 64

Ma chére Petite Femme,

It lacks about ten minutes of dusk and I am undertaking to write you a letter this evening. Our whole regiment is out on fatigue—I have been busy with the monthly return. There are no Sundays in the army, vous savez.[24] My office is a linen fly—that is, the sheet of canvas that is stretched over the slope of a wall tent, so I am open at both ends—and exposed to the weather from the sides. To obviate this[,] I have had a frame work of poles put up around and these are filled in with pine branches—which affords partial protection from the sun's rays—but none from the flies. The annoyance we suffer from these pestiferous animals no pen can describe. The very air seems thick with them—they have the pertinacity of a Dublin mendicant—and the savage voracity of a sharpened meat axe. Hand[,] head and face are kept in a continual state of irritation with them. They are a very small species—not more than half the size of a common house fly—very light in color—and armed with a proboscis capable of killing a man.

I was expressing my surprise to the Surgeon of the Reg^(t)[25] at man's capacity of endurance—and illustrated my views by citing the exposure of a soldier's life. He remarked that man is made to live out of doors—that when you exposed him to the sun's rays, and the chill of night airs—and the all-penetrating rain, you but placed him in a position he was intended for—but one which enervating Civilization has removed him from. Take a man from his home— and give him an out-door life for three years—granting that he starts with a sound constitution—you at once place him without his tendency to be affected by climatic changes—and he assumes the meteorological imperviousness of the inhabitants of the forest.

We are having lovely weather. The Richmond papers are making great calculations on bilious and malarious fevers prostrating this army more effectually than rebel bullets during this present month. The Government is taking every precaution against it. The men are ordered to draw woolen blankets—and are required to sleep under tents—the food is varied—and a good proportion of fresh vegetables is furnished us. We are very healthy at present, our location seems a wholesome one. We have been largely indebted to the Christian & Sanitary Commissions for their liberal contributions this Summer. Health good as usual. Razor arrived safe—much obliged. Excuse a hurried letter . . .

Thine

F

Unknown to either of them, Fred and Lizzie wrote to each other next on the same day—September 8, a Thursday. They were on the move again, Frederic said, although in reserve. "I used to have a notion that this was an enviable duty. I thought those in the front did the marching and the fighting. . . . But we find <u>Necessity</u> is always calling us—keeping us on the <u>qui vive</u> early and late— marching—building breastworks—throwing up redans—and either fighting or menacing us with fighting every spare interval." As a consequence, "We are derisively called Genl Hancock's boot cavalry." They were gaining in numbers, however, with more recruits arriving each day.[26]

Just returned to Albany, Elizabeth found two letters from him. "I dreaded to come home lest I should hear bad news or no news from you. . . . You still live I pray unceasingly that you may be spared." Noting how the fall of Atlanta on September 2 "must be a staggering blow to the rebels," she hoped the hard fighting was over. She had spent a week in New York City with her father, who paid all expenses. While there, she met Liz Hill, the mother of Frederic's first wife, for the first time. As for finances, she urged him not to feel uneasy. "We shall not suffer."[27] But three days later, she detailed her debts: thirty-six dollars for nine months' rent, eight dollars for the previous winter's coal, a small bill to Dr. Becket[t], and thirteen dollars to Emma—altogether the equivalent of about $1,000 today. "If all goes well I will go down tomorrow to see about getting coal" for the coming winter, she added. "We can get through all right," she assured him. "I owe no grocery bills."[28]

Often in low spirits since returning to the Petersburg lines, Frederic rebounded with cooler weather. "I again feel life pulsing through my veins—an interest in my country again animates me," he declared. He wanted to see Lincoln reelected, an end to the war, and then peace. "We want success to still the clamors of this traitorous peace party," he said referring to Northern Democrats. "The army wants peace—I crave for Peace . . . but it is only out of this nettle Danger that we can pluck the flower of Safety." His voice was still for war, "severe but short—and then a beating of our swords into ploughshares."[29]

In a longer letter September 17, he said they still feared attack. The task of completing their payrolls—which must be done before he could send money home—discouraged him. Some of the company papers were lost a Reams Station, he admitted, when he convinced the quartermaster sergeant to go with him to watch the fight. Left behind, the papers were forgotten in the headlong flight to escape capture.

Hd Qrs. 7th N.Y.V. Art[y]
Near Petersburg Va. Sept. 17th / 64

Ma chére petite Femme,

I have received letters from you three days in succession. On Wednesday evening after I had retired for the night, the mail carrier presented himself at my tent with a handful of mail matter for the Commanding Officer and two letters for the serg[t]. major. I had no candle—but there was a brilliant moon light. I arose and stepped outside the tent to read the letters. One was from Capt. Treadwell, and his characters being large and course, I read the letter without difficulty. But your writing being petite and delicate (like the fair writer) I could not read it till the morning. . . .

. . .

Our regiment is out watching the rebel movements. They—the regiment—occupy a strong work on our left flanker—surmounted with an impregnable redoubt. Gen.[1] Lee is on the <u>qui vive</u>—and evidently contemplates a dash somewhere—but he has a lynx watch upon him—and any collision that he courts will be bloodily repulsed. The weather is lovely—and our men have opportunity of rest. I remain behind—and am having quiet times. The cooks and the few sick are all that remain. We had a drove of cattle about seven hundred incautiously pastured two or three miles beyond our lines—the rebels stole over and captured them. A seasonable supply to them.[30]

I am becoming discouraged about our pay-rolls. Seven companies have their's completed—the other five are not started upon. Capt. Shannon is loafing at home—and takes no thought for his company. At the battle of Ream's Station—when the rebels made their third charge upon our lines—I invited the Q.M. Serg[t]. of Comp[y]. I to accompany me to witness the encounter. He left his knapsack, containing all the company papers in charge of a cook (an enlisted man); with orders to remain under cover of a frame church. When the musketry opened—and the rebel shells began to drop about promiscuously, this fellow took fright and ran off for dear life—abandoning the knapsack which was lost. The rebel advance through the open field led by a daring officer who gracefully waved his sword around his head. He was so conspicuous that our artillerymen training their pieces upon him—several of our men declare they made him their mark—still he brought his men gallantly on—until within one hundred paces of our breastwork—when such a deadly volley was poured into their faces that they fell in win[d]rows. The line halted—some faced about and fled—others disarmed and made for our lines—but our men were so full of fight that they knocked them over as [they] climbed the breastwork to give themselves up.

Our regiment has just returned—and are full of exciting stories. Our cavalry have been scouting through the country— and have returned with a crowd of adult negroes—and several

August–September 1864

wagon loads of fat staring little piccaninnies. The horses becoming frightened (for they were captured too) at the mass of soldiers who surrounded them—refused to stir and our men propelled horses and wagons along the road, hilariously calling upon their comrades to come and see Abe Lincoln's family. No enemy is to be seen for miles.

. . .

Yours in haste

F.

Elizabeth delighted at receiving his letters and asked a favor of him for her grandmother, whose Southern grandson was in Federal prison in Ohio. She, too, hoped for Lincoln's reelection.

Albany N.Y.

Sept 15th 1864

My dear dear Husband,

Another welcome letter from you yesterday. You do well to write as often as possible for I am an intolerable grumbler write[,] write letters no matter what they are written on, or how they are written as long as I can decipher them it[']s well. but do not as you value my peace and comfort neglect writing. I give you credit Fred you are deserving of it for writing so constantly. I do not really see how you [do] amid such confusion[,] discomfort and frequent changes. Oh! Fred I fairly count the weeks and days 11 months and 3 days only.[31] I do most fondly hope before next summer the fighting will be over.

Your letter to Lieut-Col Hastings has been published in the Knickerbocker a portion of it was copied in the morning express but I have not seen the whole of it. I mean to send down to Mrs. Bull's for the paper today.[32]

. . .

Grandma has sent me a note asking you to write to her son E.H. Metcalf. I will enclose it but doubt whether you will be able to read it it is written so confusedly. She wants you to write to her son. Address this E.H. Metcalf Montgomery, Alabama and tell him that his son William has been in prison in Columbus, Ohio since

January 1st. Give his father his address. Wm. H.J. Metcalf. Prison
No. 1—Camp Chase Columbus, Ohio. He is not willing to take the
oath of allegiance and although I am sorry for him, I feel that he is
a rebel and as such deserves to suffer some[;] perhaps it will be the
means of bringing him to his senses. If it is possible Fred write to
E.H.M. for Grandma's sake, she has a suspicion that a letter from
you will reach him more readily than one written by her.

Devotedly Yours

E.M.L.

Albany N.Y.

Sept 18th 1864

My own dear Husband,

You are faithful and constant, you know what I value most is kind
loving letters from you. I had the delight of receiving quite a long
(very long compared to what you have been able to send for some
time past) cheerful letter on Thursday evening, we were all on a
visit to Mrs. Duncan when Mr D brought it in. I like Mrs D better
than any other woman in Albany.

The general excitement here is in regard to the election. I
think Lincon will be reelected. I trust so, for I think he has shown
that [he] will do what is for the best interests of our country. I
fear McClellan is to[o] easily led. Has not stability or punctuality
enough for the position, tis said that Lincon is not dignified
enough, that may be so, but we will gladly put up with his lack of
dignity if he will only guide our bark safely through these troblous
times. The prevailing opinion here is that the fighting will be
finished this fall. The Democrats are going to have peace whether
or no when they get the power all in their own hand. We shall
see these poor craven peace Democrats come to grief ere long. I
think you were in better spirits when you last wrote than you have
been in for some time, not that your letters are ever discouraging.
I speak in regard to the war[;] as regards other matters you have
ever written cheerfully, and given me encouragement and hope.
Had you ever treated me with neglect in not writing as often as you

should I know not what I should have done. Only 11 months Fred, I say only because it seems short compared to 3 years.

. . . I sent a handkerchief yesterday. It is an old one but I hope you may get it. I got your letter published in the Knickerbocker shall send it to Grandma to read think it was firstrate. I send you the Journal with this. The weather continues cool. The wind blows a perfect hurricane tonight. I fear if it blows so with you it will blow your house over. You have high winds sometimes I believe.

Let me stop here ere I tire you quite out. God Bless and keep you darling

Yours most devotedly but sleepily
Lizzie M.L.

Settling in along the Petersburg siege lines, Frederic, like so many around him, were content with their situation. He did well with his commanding officers, but he regretted having lost Major Springsteed.

Headquarters 7th N.Y. Art[y].
Near Petersburgh Va. Sept. 21 / 64

My dear Wife,

Don't you think Gen[l]. Hancock is treating his pet lambs of the Second Corps very tenderly? We have laid here since the 10th and things are assuming a really comfortable air. It is astonishing what an accumulive proclivity a soldier acquires. We knock cracker boxes to pieces and with the boards thereof manufacture tables—washstands—pantries—seats—as the case may be. They are rude but serviceable. And the accumulation of pots and kettles which insensibly gather in every encampment is surpassing wonder. . . .

I have not had so happy and contented a feeling—and have not enjoyed myself so unreservedly since I have been in the army as I do at this present. I am very fortunate in my relations with the regimental Commanding officers. I have never yet received an unpleasant word from any one of them—but have uniformly been treated with kindness, consideration, and confidence. Maj. Murphy[33] our present commander is a rough hurly-burly sort of man, but within he has a kindly heart, and is one of the most genial and whole souled fellows in the world. I have never yet proved the limits of my influence with him.

Major Springsteed's father[34] is here with the vain hope of recovering the body of his son. Having to abandon the ground so hastily, we do not even know where he is buried. Grief has furrowed deep lines in his aged cheeks; his appears to be the poignant grief of blank despair. It is grievous—terrible sacrifices of this war. . . .

Capt. Anable wounded on the 16th of June, has just rejoined us—it is really a treat to see a familiar face return. He and Capt. Shannon—who is in hospital at Annapolis are the only two Captains remaining of our original ten. I cannot write to Mr. Metcalf until I get a ten cent silver coin to enclose—this cannot be procured in the regiment can you send me one? . . . .

Your's lovingly
F.E.L.

[P.S.] Did Josie receive my long letter?

17

Fighting Is Almost Incessant
September–October 1864

The Seventh New Yorkers soon moved to Fort Morton, very near the front in the siege of Petersburg and just east of the site of the disastrous Crater assault of July 30. Frederic and his comrades also found themselves near where they lost so severely in their charge on Petersburg defenses on June 16. As he related, they felt bitter and defeated then. Now, "we feel ourselves victors."

Head Quar's 7th N.Y.V. Art[y].[1]

Sept[r] 25th 1864

My dear Spouse,

We have moved again—the 10th Corps has been relieved, and we occupy their place in the first line of breastworks. We are three miles nearer to Petersburgh—the fortifications here are of a powerful character—the woods have been cleared—the camp policed—and the men are all much pleased with the place—it is probable that we shall stay here a month. Until we get to rights—I am staying in the major's quarters—an almost impregnable bomb-proof. This is likely to be a warm place here—as the enemy are in close proximity to our lines. We are within a few rods of the ravine into which we retired after the fatal charge of June 16th. The place is full of interest to us, altho' greatly altered in appearance; as we reconnoître around we recognize many familiar localities. Here is where the battery stood that enfiladed in from the right; and here is where the line of rifle pits run that arrested our advance. Our loss was 600 men and officers on that fateful evening—and what made the loss more bitter was the conviction that we had accomplished no good. How different our feelings now from those that possessed us then. At that time we were jaded out—discouraged with our severe losses—and hopeless of suppressing the rebellion. Wherever we assailed the enemy after our horrible forced marches—he was always there in force to repel us—and to us it appeared as if our expenditure of energy and life was fruitless.

Now we feel ourselves victors. The labors of campaigning no longer oppress us—we have become used to their vicissitudes—and we believe our foe to be already nearly beaten. We no longer dread encountering him; he is manifestly weak and cautious—altho' any day he may be driven to take desperate chances—but we place implicit trust in the skill of our general—and the strength and morale of the army are all that can be wished. The hardest work of the campaign is over.

The news from Sheridan is glorious. Two brilliant victories with large spoils—and a routed foe flying confusedly before him.[2] These are the peace negotiations the country needs. Genl. Grant, before a great while, will open another series of peace negotiations—and the results of these diplomatic enterprises will be so satisfactory to the loyal masses of the country—that the great Pacificator, Abraham Lincoln—will be reelected as the choice of the people.

Your enclosure reached me this morning. Much obliged. I owe Col. Hastings five dollars—and have felt annoyed at my inability to pay it. Having things so pleasant here—the Officers will be able to finish their muster and payrolls—and then we shall be promptly paid. You owe nearly one hundred dollars, I learn from you, I have $139 due me to Aug. 31st and shall be able to send you enough to pay all your debts and buy a few groceries besides. Will that content you? We shall get thro' like a fiddle. Only do not work too hard and overtask your strength. I am in a most tranquil state of mind. I suppose the country is in an awful state and my domestic affairs in confusion and ruin; I suppose I have inveigled into this abolition war, and am the victim of a despotic administration—still, I am nearly happy. I never past my time more pleasantly—the future appears bright to me—and all goes along swimmingly. I shall have the Adjutant's desk here to-morrow—that with the regimental records are sent to the rear when we move—and then I shall scribble off a few more memoranda. I may use them when

I get home—I think I can gather materials together to produce
a readable salable book. Don't mention this to anybody except
Emma. . . .

Devotedly

F.E. Lockley

Although settled into a siege, they continued to move about, as
Frederic made clear in his next letter. At times, they were but 150
paces from the Confederate lines and in constant danger, although
Fred insisted, "We are perfectly safe."

Nearer Petersburgh, Va. 28 / 9/ 64

My dear Wife,

I write because it is Wednesday—not because I have anything to
say. We have been moved again—once or twice. Directly after I had
mailed my last letter on Saturday—orders were brought us from
Corps headquarters to pack up quietly and move off at dark. The 10th
Corps had been moving to our left (southward) and we were to take
their places. We marched probably three miles to the right bringing
us within 1½ miles of Petersburgh—and we took our position
behind a strong line of breastworks, and were giving [given] to
understand we should make a considerable stay here. The position
was a pleasant one—and we were much pleased with our lot.
Notwithstanding it was Sunday—a heavy detail was made from the
regiment to build bomb-proof quarters for the Officers—and indeed
we all went to work fitting up and arranging things to our minds.
Towards 7 p.m. another order came ordering us to pack up again.
At nine we moved filing thro' a narrow excavation in single line
with a high breastwork thrown up to protect us from rebel bullets.
They whizzed over our heads pretty closely—but we were perfectly
safe. We have become veteran soldiers—and can tell as it were by
instinct where we are safe and where we are in danger—the whiz of
bullets six inches from our ear does not affect us in the least if we are
satisfied they can come no nearer. Here we are perfectly safe. After
defiling thro' extraordinary works—a narrow pit—high breastwork
on one side—and deep excavations on the other side where the
troops retired when the enemy commences shelling. These they

call gopherholes—and the only way you can get at the occupants is to stand at the pit's mouth and fling missiles in at them. Finally we were halted—a few men thrown out as videttes—fifty of the regiment divided into three reliefs—so as to have one third of the regiment always in arms and vigilant. We remained in these trenches 24 hours—and then were relieved by another brigade. Our line runs within 150 paces of the Johnny's line—and our work is covered with sand bags with loopholes, to look and fire thro. The least exposure of your person is dangerous. Our men acted with great judgment[;] not a man was hurt during the whole day. A vigorous shelling was opened in the afternoon and we had a few casualties in the rear. This close neighborhood with Johnny Reb was quite a novelty to us, and we all derived much interest from it. I stood for hours watching their movements thro' the loopholes—they were evidently busied upon their works—the end of a plank would be seen bobbing along as it was carried on a man's shoulder—then we would [see] a beam raised and dropped incessantly as if they were driving something into the earth [as tho' they were laying down a platform for a heavy cannon.][3] But few ventured to show themselves—and those were dressed in blue. Our men wished to open a conference with them and exchange newspapers—for this purpose they raised white handkerchiefs tied to staffs—but the rebels would not respond. I should have much liked to have been able to take a peep at their inside doings. The weather is very warm—I have taken off my chemise. I do not like this encampment. The shells burst all around you—and the bomb proofs thrown up for protection terribly mar the appearance of the scene.

. . .

Devotedly

F.

Lizzie wrote to him that same day. When she walked past a Union rally underway at Albany's Tweddle Hall,[4] she hesitated to go in alone, but she would push such fears aside in coming days, wooed by intensifying interest in the coming election. Insisting they would keep up with current expenses, she sent the ten-cent piece Fred said he needed to afford sending a letter south on behalf of her grandma.

Albany N.Y.
Sept 28th 1864

My dear dear Husband,

Letters are coming thick and fast let them come the more the
better. I do not know that you have written more than the usual
number but they are sometimes a day or two late, and two reach
me the same day[.] it happened so last week and yesterday. Emma
received a letter in the morning and I one in the afternoon
although mine had been written two days previous to her's, and
this evening another has been handed to me. I have not been very
well today and, have had the blues but your letter is so cheerful
that I feel almost well. It seems a perfect marvel to me that you
can be in such good spirits when in so much danger. Truly our
successes are enough to make us feel jubilant. Yes these are the
only true peace negotiations, the country is looking forward with
hope and faith for the end and I think a few more such peace
negotiations as Sheridan has offered the enemy[5] will bring about
the desired result most speedily.

. . .

Your letter to the Lt Col Hastings appeared in yesterday[']s
paper,[6] I send it herewith or rather Mrs Bull sends it for she gave it
to me and insisted upon giving me the stamp for it. I tried to get it
at the newsrooms today but could not. I like to save them perhaps
I may steal one somewhere, all the letters that appear in the papers
are eagerly read by those who have friends there. I don't think I shall
flatter you by telling you what I think of it. Mrs Bull who is always
imaginative wishes me to ask you if you know what kind of character
Michael Galonby[7] (I know I have not spelt it right but the name is
so outlandish that I forget how) bore in the Regt also wants to know
what pay is owing to him and if you think Capt Moore[8] would have
kept $100 that was given by his company to send his body home, you
recollect my asking about him before. Mrs. Bull would not make
these inquires but she is at swords points with the Aunt of the above
mentioned[.] she lives in the same house with her.

Pardon me Fred for my negligence but I have been so busy that
I did not look for the spelling book it being in the book box, I will
tomorrow find it.

Your letters are such a comfort to us. I know not what I should do if deprived of them. But I send you but a poor return for your interesting ones. I could not write on Sunday. I had half a mind to tear it up after I had written it but thought you would be disappointed if you see no letter. You will find a ten cent piece enclosed also a few postage stamps. I should have sent you stamps before, but I have been very short. I have had to borrow of E to the amount of $20 and shall have to still further. If I could only get work enough to keep up current expenses it would be all right but I have very little work this summer; but for all that I have never felt discouraged I know we shall come out all right; likely I shall have some this fall. The speculators are coming to grief[.] the prices of provisions and merchandise are falling, may they continue to fall till they are once more sold at reasonable prices. Dr Springsteed's case is a sad one. I saw a queer item in this morning[']s paper I will send it. The idea of promoting a person supposed to be dead. Excuse this jumbled up and confused letter. The blessed babes are well. They and Emma send love to you. With most earnest prayers for your safety.

Your Wife
E.M.L.

Fred would not be able to answer this letter for more than a week but instead hurriedly penned a short letter to Lizzie on September 30 to say they might be marching to Deep Bottom again and to let her know he had finally been paid. He could not send the total sum ($139) all at once, however, for fear of having it stolen in the mail. Tending an ailing Major Murphy behind the lines did increase his security, although he maintained, as he always would, that the front was the safer place.

H^d Q^{rs} 7th N.Y. Art^y
Septr 30th 1864

My dear Wife,

I have time to write you but two or three lines. We are all packed to move—and are living out of doors. The camp is broken up—and our regiment occupies the 2^d line of the rifle pits. The whole army appears to be on the move—Birney with the 10th Corps gained a distinguished success yesterday and is following the retreating rebels Richmondward.[9] We are expecting that Grant will move after Birney—if so we have another wholesome little trip to Deep bottom before us. Good news pours in from every quarter—we are ready to take a hand in finishing up the work. Sixty thousand recruits and convalescents have joined the army during the last seventeen days. We expected a fight last night. Lee filled up his works in front of us—and about 8 o'clock opened a heavy mortar fire upon us. But no charge was made—our casualties were two— fore-arm in both cases fractured. The Major is sick—and I am staying in the rear with him—but here as every where else—the front is the safer place. Last night I was disturbed frequently by pieces of shell whizzing about—and once I was awakened by a minie ball thudding into the ground a few feet from my head. I am willing to take my chances when awake—and trust to my good luck in dodging their murderous missiles but this peppering a fellow while he is asleep I am decidedly opposed to.

Six companies of the regim^t. were paid yesterday—the field officers and non-commissioned staff also. I don't know how to send my money—the express agent is so busy at City Point receiving money packages—that he cannot give receipts. I am afraid to trust a large amount by mail—so will send ten dollars in every letter until I find a better means of sending it. I enclose ten herewith— your Grandma's money I will transmit by and bye.

I must close for want of more time. Love to all—Weather lovely—health good.

Yours as ever

F.

The Seventh did not march to Deep Bottom, but they continued to see action amid the rain and mud in the Petersburg trenches, which were quickly resembling those in France fifty years hence during World War I. Nevertheless, he was not "perfectly safe" there. He did not relate having had another close call to Elizabeth at the time, but he described it years later in his memoirs. On his way to picket duty, he had preferred a more exposed route and almost paid for it dearly. As he explained,

I chose the covered way as affording protection from hostile bullets. But a recent heavy shower had flooded the lower ground, so to avoid wading thro' water, I leapt up to the open plain trusting to speed to escape danger. But hardly had I appeared in view than half a score bullets whizzed in dangerous proximity to my ears. I immediately descended to the lower level, preferring water to hot lead. Within half an hour of this faux pas, a sergeant in Co. G, taking the same risk, was shot dead as he ran.

Making the incident sadder still was that the Company G sergeant had just been married while on furlough. "Such mischances are constantly happening in war. What determines them?" he asked. Pondering fate versus divine intervention, he concluded, "The Lord takes no part in human strife."[10]

Near Petersburgh 1/10/64 [October 1, 1864]

My dear Wife

I enclose ten dollars again—I suppose you receive them safely. We are lying here still—having an occasional fight where there is an immense expenditure of lead and iron but very little damage done. We occupy the first line of works, and are charged by the division commander to hold them at all costs. A commanding officer abandoning his position without proper orders is threatened with a court martial.

I am interrupted—and shall have to send this as it is. I hope you pay Mr Duncan the postage on my unpaid letters. Insist on his taking it.

Octr. 2^d

We have been having heavy rains lately our trenches are flooded—we have to wade thro thirty inches of water to get in or out. Our regiment has been four days in this muddy hole and the men are wet thro' and plastered from head to foot. I have a softer thing of it—staying at headquarters with Col Murphy.[11] His commission as Lt. Col. arrived yesterday. You wonder at the promotion of Maj Springsteed: you will understand that altho' there is no doubt of his death—he being left gasping and insensible in the pit when we retired—still his death has not been officially announced.

We are in the midst of active operations—fighting is almost incessant on some part of our line. The impression with us is that things are progressing favorably—but we can get no reliable news. This weather rather impedes operations but to-day it looks like clearing up. I hope our regiment will be relieved to-day for staying so long in these muddy trenches is enough to kill every mother's son of them

Excuse a miserable letter. I will write more fully next time. I will write to Mr Metcalf forthwith.

Adieu

F.

While Fred coped with muddy trenches and whizzing minié balls, Lizzie contended with an insistent seven-year-old and then reaffirmed her faith in Lincoln.

Albany N.Y.

Oct 2nd 1864

[no salutation]

Mama Mama aint you going to get up and write to Papa. There commenced a series of anoyances most disagreeable to an individual who is half asleep such as tickling my neck, kissing me, pulling my hair, sticking pins in my bosom to see if there was any cotton there, all such pranks your daughter Gertrude played upon her sleepy Mama. This afternoon I was half inclined to be vexed for I had a chill headache but she was so cunning withal about it that I could not scold, but got up determined to write as well as she would let me for she is still fidgeting me. Emma has written you quite a long letter and Jossie commenced one also before going to church, so you see you are not neglected by your female friends.

This is a dull rainy day[.] it poured this morning and I alone ventured to church, but I was fully repaid for my wet walk by hearing a most excellent sermon. Presume you hear very few good sermons; you never mention your worthy chaplain what has become of him?

What does ail me. I cannot write all is confusion within. do you not feel sometimes as if it were utterly impossible to give language or words to your thoughts?

On to Richmond is the cry. The army is again in motion, but Grant's movements are all veiled in mystery.[12] The newspaper correspondents set forth various theories and plans but are all undecided as to what his present movement means, time will develop all. the greatest confidence is reposed in him by all parties. I think the coming election will be one of the most exciting the country has ever witnessed. The copperhead democrats are perfectly rampant and the republicans determined to stick to their text through thick and thin. please take note of major Gunther's letter in the Albany Journal. My cousin Wm Richardson in New York writes in the Mayor[']s office, he despises the man.[13] when the news of McClellan's nomination was received he ordered the City Hall decorated with Flags but when Atlanta fell[14] no flag was raised. that was enough to show what sort of man he was. I feel almost certain that Lincon will be reelected.

. . .

E.M.L.

[P.S.] Emma wishes me to ask you if you should be allowed to wear a Lincoln badge. if you would like it she will send you one.

As Frederic and his Seventh comrades continued to occupy the muddy trenches, firefights broke out daily. But they all perceived the enemy's weakness and noted the growing number of Confederate deserters.

Very near Petersburgh Oct. 5 / 64

Ma chére Petite,

Things still remain status quo with us: everything packed up ready for immediate orders to move. The reg[t]. still occupy the trenches— this is their seventh day there—they have no opportunity to come out to wash themselves and stretch their le—excuse me—I mean elongate their bifurcated extremities. Lt. Col. Murphy is convalescent—altho' still unfit for duty. I remain at headquarters with him: have a tolerably comfortable time but spend an hour or two with the boys daily.

. . .

The army is busy at all points. We hear fighting to the right and left of us almost daily—and we manage to kick up a muss every other day. Last night about nine we had quite a sharp fire; musketry and our mortar batteries with a few long range guns from the Appomattox making all the din of a full sized battle. The rebels responded with one mortar (!) the belief is that they have removed their artillery—and I should not wonder if we are ordered to carry their works by assault—unless Grant can take them from them at a less cost. We cannot help feeling the war is about used up. The evidences of weakness and exhaustion are evident in the movements of the foe—and Grant has got him in such a position that unless he can stretch his lines from extreme left to right he is sure to be penetrated. I think this fall will see the last of the fighting.

Night before last three rebel deserters came in. They stated that over twenty of their comrades were desirous to follow them, and that they only waited a signal gun to assure them of the safety of these to start them over. But Capt. Anable (in command of the reg^t. during Col. Murphy's sickness) a nervous unmilitary man—thought he could see some perfidy in the arrangement—and would not have the gun fired. The consequence was the others did not come over. The Col. gave him a severe talking to—but the opportunity was lost.

I must close—I have plenty of work awaiting me—I enclose a ten dollar bill—this is the third—I suppose they reach you in safety. I have written to Mr Metcalf. I will get you to return your Grandma's loan—I have lots of money to send you. Pay up all your debts—every cent. "Owe no man anything." S^t. Paul.

Good bye and best love to all

Your devotedly

<u>F.E.L.</u>

In Albany, Lizzie stayed atop current events and thought Southern reaction to a friend taken prisoner reprehensible.

Albany N.Y.
Oct 6th 1864

My dear Husband,

Your last letter was written a week ago yesterday. I shall look with
hope for one today. I do not expect letters now as regularly as when
you were stationed in Washington. Then I knew just when to look
for one but now I hope for them at any time. I do wonder where
you will take up your winter quarters somewhere in the vicinity of
Richmond if not within its devoted walls. I do not see your corps
mentioned as having taken part in these last engagements.[15] We
hope and pray that Richmond may fall without so much bloodshed
as people predict[.] it is only nature to suppose that they will offer
all the resistance in their power. Great consternation prevails in
Richmond at Buttler's[16] near approach they fear he will retalliate
for all the evil things they have said of him the inhabitants are
leaving as speedily as possible. the wealthy will turn their faces
Europe-ward. Jeff Davis will speedily follow I think. Stephen
Corliss[17] who was in the Libby Prison Hospital is now home on
parole. He says when they left Richmond instead of conveying
them immediately to the transports which lay only a short distance
from the hospital, they paraded them through the principal streets
in order to gratify their brutality and the curiosity of the ladies who
thronged the streets and doorsteps to see them and make all sorts
of rude remarks to them such as "hell Yanks how do you like it, aint
you had most enough.["] How wicked and cruel to jolt these poor
sick and wounded men about in such a manner, they certainly will
receive their punishment. I will send you this morning[']s and
yesterday[']s papers.

I should not care about being in such a close proximity to
the Rebs tis most astonishing to me how men can become so
accustomed to the whiz of bullets. I should not make a good
solider. There has been a good many female soldiers engaged in
this war.[18] I do not see how they can endure the hardships and
exposure incident to a soldier's life. I noticed a case of a western
girl who has taken part in 12 battles has been wounded a number
of times, when discovered, she was only 19 years of age and
declares her intention of again seeing if she gets well.

. . .

Just 6 months yesterday since you came home. the children are all well and my health is very good this fall. . . . God bless and preserve you my darling Husband.

Lovingly
Lizzie

"I have no opportunity of writing to you to day," Frederic said in a short note dated October 8. He had good reason. His tent had gone up in flames. "I had just finished a long letter to you yesterday and was in the act of addressing the envelope when our roof of dry pine brush caught fire and enveloped us instantly." Others rushed in to save the desks and company records, he said, but much of his clothing and his $100 linen wall tent were gone. Nonetheless, he saved his letter, and finished it the next day.[19]

Near Petersburgh, Va. Oct. 9 / 64

Ma chére Petite,

I commenced a letter to you two days ago but have been so dreadfully busy that I have not had time to complete it. We have been for nine days under marching orders—that is, Office books and Officers' luggage packed up and in the wagon away to the rear, and we enlisted men with haversacks full and all snug and ready to fall in at the first call. The third quarter of the year has expired and every kind of report is wanted. Yesterday the books were ordered up—and now I am up to my ears in business. You must again excuse a short letter—I scribble this off while the mail carrier goes thro' camp to collect the letters. The regt. was withdrawn from the picket line last night after having spent ten days in the pits. There seems to be lots of fighting at some portion of the line the whole time—but no decisive results are obtained. We fare exceedingly well during these stirring times—we have been under the rebel fire for 10 days—and had six casualties. At the slaughter-house—Coal harbor—we lost 10 a day while occupying the same position.

Rebel deserters are continually coming in. A North Carolinian came in the other night, who had been six months without paymt.

He states that no quartermaster stores are issued to the army now—that the force is greatly disaffected—and that the principal rations they have received lately were derived from the 2500 cattle they stole from us at City Point.[20] He was an intelligent man—a wagon maker—intended going north to work at his business—and being well treated and cordially received by all hands—was the happiest man in Virginia.

I enclose an editorial clipped from the Herald.[21] The remarks are salient and no doubt in the main true. I have not time to enquire about Private Galouly's affairs to gratify Mrs Bull's love of scandal—I am overwhelmed with applications of a similar nature—such information can only be derived from the Company Commanders, to whom all such enquiries are referred. I forgot to thank Emma for her kind offer to send me an electioneering badge—je ne m'en sers de si chose.[22] She has forgotten her usual good taste. I shall vote for Lincoln—but do not propose to serve as his town crier.

I do not wear my heart upon my sleeve
For daws to pick at.

I have owed Lt. Col. Hastings $5^{00} for quite a while. Will you be pleased to learn his address (I think in Division S^t.) enclose this in an envelope—with a line expressing my thanks for the accommodation—and leave or send the note to this house. I have sent you thirty dollars and Emma $20—has it all arrived safely? I will transmit your Grandma's loan anon. when I learn of the save [safe] arrival of my previous remittances I will send you $50 more—I have lots of money yet.

Your's very fondly
Fred E. Lockley

PS I find I have no five—so I sent you a twenty. I presume it will go safely.

Lizzie assured him she was receiving the money he sent and paying debts as fast as she could.

Albany N.Y.
Oct 12th 1864

My dear Husband,

About 2 hrs ago Mr Drydale[23] gave me your letter of the 9th it
is now 10 P.M. good time to begin writing a letter. . . . All the
remittances have been received $20 dollars in the last, and $20
Emma received last night in all you have sent $70. glad you have so
much money. I can give it away as fast as you send it. I understood
you to say that you wished me to pay Grandma so I sent her the
third ten I received from you.

   I shall feel quite relieved when I am out of debt. Although your
allowance is so liberal to me it will not pay all[,] but what is left
over there will be no urgency about. I can meet them by degrees. I
met Mr Davis the other day and told him why I had not been able
to pay him[24] he said he knew all about it, that he was in no hurry.
I could pay him when I chose. we shall get through like a fiddle.
do not deprive yourself for the sake of sending so much to us. you
have been so long without money that you must need some now.
Dr Becket[t][25] is a staunch republican and says he will be most
happy to deposit your vote in the ballot box for you. He is the
Dr who attended me. I paid him last night his charge was a very
reasonable $6.00

   I will send the $5 as you desire to Lt Col Hasting's.

   I am just scribbling this of[f] in haste to assure you of the safety
of the money sent.

   I sent Jossey[']s letter presume it has reached you ere this. The
babes are well, and ful of frolic as ever.

   Good night pet. I am awfully sleepy and somewhat tired.

Very affec your wife
Lizzie

18

Which Ticket Are You Going to Vote?
October–November 1864

As Fred tried to recover from his tent fire, he played host to some
election commissioners from Albany County, in camp to take the
soldiers' vote, which surprisingly, he said, went for Lincoln. The
soldier vote throughout the Union Army went overwhelming for
Lincoln despite the president's Democratic opponent being George
B. McClellan, the army's former commander. In fact, Lincoln's
soldier vote majority would eclipse that of the civilian vote, which
he also won.[1]

Camp in the Field, Va.
October 13th 1864[2]

Ma plus chére Femme,

I have been so busy to-day, that I have had no time to prepare
a letter for you in time for the mail. We have two Republican
Election Commissioners here from Albany Co, New York, to take
the soldiers' votes. They have established their Rendezvous at our
headquarters—and my interest in the cause is sufficient to prompt
me to vacate my crude office accommodations in their behalf. I
have told you that I am head over ears in business and this turning
myself out of doors, with my hundreds of documents strewn loosely
about—and the din of political discussion ringing incessantly
in my ears, have so bewildered me, that I feel quite incapable
and disinclined for labor. Some time since Lt. Col. Murphy sent
in a recommendation to Gov' Seymour for my promotion to a
lieutenancy—Nothing has been heard from it at present; the
probability is that the gubernatorial office is so full of politics that

they cannot attend to any army business. I enclosed a letter to the County clerk (Mʳ Smith Waterman) in a communication to Mʳ Duncan. I used to be on familiar terms with him and he is a jolly good fellow withal. I asked of him the favor to step into the Adjutant Genˡˢ office—have a blank commission filled out—and sent on to me. The Col. also wrote to his intimate friend William G. Weed to interest himself in the matter—but we hear nothing of it at present. Still the Col. is confident that it will come—and as the duties of a Sergeant major are of a somewhat difficult nature, he thought it advisable to break some non-commissioned Officer in in advance, and selected the Actᵍ Regᵗ. Comˢʳʸ Sergᵗ. as my successor. So determining to go to work this morning—I detailed a force of men some to go to the wagon and bring up my wall tent—others to cut crotches and poles for a bed and pine brush for a carpet and this being done to pitch the tent, build my bunk, and carpet the floor—and now as a reward for my energy I can sit comfortably at my desk in a sweet-scented apartment, and hear the rain beat upon my canvas tenement away from the crowd—the noise and the bother. The Serᵍᵗ. a tip-top fellow—(Sergᵗ. Wood of Co. C)³ and I have been busily at work all day—and I expect with his assistance to get straightened out in a few days.

I intended to write you a long letter this evening, but I am interrupted so much to assist these election gentry that I must delay the completion of it till to-morrow. Capt. Filkins⁴ is one of the Canvassers—of the 177ᵗʰ N.Y. Regt. He is a splendid fellow—and well deserves the high reputation he gained in the service.

October 13ᵗʰ 1864

It is noon—the polls are about closing—and the harvest has been indeed plentiful. The 7ᵗʰ is notoriously a democratic regt. And in our estimates of the election, we have always conceded a ¾ vote for McClellan. But the result of the voting shows a decided majority for Lincoln voters. This is a marvellous triumph—and augurs well for the safety of the State. You seem to be growing quite a politician. Which ticket are you going to vote? . . . We are having things very quiet here. Now and then a sharp mortar practice and always a lively picket fire—but field fighting we are entirely away from—and are at a loss to conceive what Grant is doing. Please send me some stamps—also a neat little memorandum book—I cannot get such an article here. Don't pay more than 2/—or 3/ for it. Wrap it with both ends open—the postage is 2 cents per oz. I will detain you no more. Adio. Love to all.

F.

[P.S.] Josey's letter reached me—a very pleasant—unstudied effusion. She is an exemplary little dame—I am proud of her success in study.

In his next, Fred took Lizzie on an imaginary tour of their works, rather nonchalantly referring to the dangers of manning the Petersburg siege lines. After two years of army life, and some close calls the past five months, he was still thankful to be out of the book business.

Head Quars. 7th N.Y. V. Art.
Near Petersburgh Va. Octr 15, 64

Ma chére petite Femme,

. . .

You say you wonder what we are doing—and what sort of place we are in. The regiment is fully employed with Picket and Fatigue. Picket duty consists of occupying the advanced line—in our case within a hundred yards of the enemy—and either blazing away at any object your eye may single out—animate or inanimate—or lying lazily in the sun, smoking—dozing, or gambling. Some of our men expend sixty rounds of cartridge in a day—and most probably are innocent of rebel blood. Fatigue is labor spent upon fortifications; and as this is generally performed within range of the enemy's rifles, the work has to be performed at night. Building breastworks, excavating pits—throwing up redoubts for field artillery—mining the enemy's works—are the principal labors performed. Frequently the enemy will hear our men at work and open fire upon them; if they are not covered from their missiles, they generally desist—as the Engineer officers who have the direction of the work—as a general rule—are not great fire-eaters.

The country around here is a fearful wreck. A stranger to travel over it would suppose it inhabited by digger Indians or some other subterranean species. As our camp is directly within the plane of the enemy's fire—and that fire occasionally is pretty vigorous— security against their exploding shells is the first requisite. Accordingly we first dig a big hole—then build a stockade of massive logs—roofing it with timbers eighteen inches thro', and then instead of digging another hole to put the dirt in, we throw that on the roof and west side of our log houses—until we have a covering of earth eight feet in depth. This is considered a bomb-proof—the name given to our habitations—and when the hostile artillerymen engage in their mortar practice, which occurs nearly every evening—we stand outside to admire the curved lines of fire which their deadly projectiles describe thro' the heavens— and when a "Johnny shell," as we call the rebel projectiles, comes roaring too near our position—we skedaddle into the bomb proof to await its explosion—and get out of the way of its scattering fragments.

A walk to the picket line would interest you. Your ears must first become accustomed to the sharp whizz of the minié bullet—or that hasty messenger tracking your footsteps wherever you tend— might disturb your enjoyment of the walk. I piloted two canvassing commissioners yesterday to the front work—one a Maj Gridley[5] late of the 18th an old and esteemed friend of mine in Schenectady— the other a civilian. We will suppose you [are] in the party. We walk through our camp, and turn to the right along a plank road—At every few paces we pass a pile of gathered missiles—rusty solid shot—fragments of shell—and quite a number of unexploded shell with wooden plugs. This testifies that the rebels are short of ammunition—and fire their shells as solid shot—for want of the explosive filling. A sharp cut across a chaotic field (its bosom rent with many a furious storm of shot and shell[)] and we arrive at the covered way leading to our trenches. This consists of a narrow cut with the earth embanked upon the right—and this constitutes a wall about the height of a man—covering him from the fire of the enemy. The recent heavy rains have partially washed down this embankment in places—and these spots are keenly watched by the rebel sharp-shooters. I cautioned our civilian friend of the danger when we approached these places—and he hesitated to pass them. You can bend as you pass them—thus keeping yourself from view—or you can pass them as the soldiers do, on a run— just "to give the Johnnies a show." You draw their fire—but there is slight chance of their hitting you. When we reached the advanced work where if you expose the top of your head it would be blown off you—our friend became nervous—and a man discharging his rifle a few yards behind him so electrified him that he threw himself down and declared he was certain he should be shot. "The hand of little employment hath the daintier sense";[6] we consider ourselves perfectly safe here. I enclose you $50—you can make your fortune off the interest that will accrue upon it, if you keep it long enough. You acknowledge the receipt of all I have previously sent you. Acknowledge this on coming to hand. I have cast my vote—thro' the medium of these Albany gentry. Much obliged to your friend Dr Beckett. How does friend Duncan progress with the dye business? I shall congratulate him when he safely escapes from the Book trade. He has taken less desperate means than I did to deliver himself.

Warmest love to all. I hope you have left that amount with Col. Hastings—If you have not—do it immediately. I have reasons for urging it.

Yours in the flesh and the spirit.

F.

The following Sunday, Frederic walked some distance from camp, climbed a hill overlooking Petersburg, and observed the city's church steeples "towering toward heaven," though "sadly dilapidated" from Union shelling. "Those eloquent bells ringing out their holy summons, the fitful thunder of our cannon bursting in at intervals like a spirit of Evil," he thought, created a curious admixture of moral opposites. As he contemplated the scene, a member of his regiment, gathering mushrooms, happened by. "Sergeant Major, those church bells sound human." Frederic agreed. His fellow soldier "had roughly expressed the sentiment."[7]

That same day, Union Gen. Phil Sheridan turned defeat into resounding victory against Jubal Early in the Shenandoah Valley by making his famous ride on his horse Rienzi to further rally

Union morale and support for Lincoln's reelection. Lizzie was ecstatic, fired up all the more by having attended four Union rallies at Albany's Tweddle Hall.

Albany N.Y.

October 20th 1864

My dear Husband,

I have shamefully neglected you, but it really was not my fault. You know how it is when there is company. I posted your memorandum book this afternoon, and wrote a short note to enclose therein not knowing that it was against the rules but the man asked me if there was any writing in it and I told him yes he told me without the writing it would be only 2 cents with it it would cost 22 cents so I took it out.

News of a splendid victory reached us yesterday. Sheridan or little Phil, as they call him[,] seems determined to follow the rebs up and whip them at every meeting.[8] These are the true peace demonstrations and the only ones that will end the war. I have been to four Union meetings at Tweddle Hall two this week. I would not stay away on any account Gov Andrews[9] of Mass made one of the best speeches that I have heard on Monday evening. He denounced traitors and Copperheads in the strongest language, but there was not the least tinge of coarseness in any portion of his address. It was sound[,] statesman-like, and elegant in the fullest sense of the word. he read and explained the Chicago platform and to show the contrast read the resolutions adopted by the Baltimore convention.[10] I feel as if I had learned much hearing so many sound and instructive lectures or speeches. I feel almost like voting myself.

. . . I am glad to hear the 7th is going to maintain her honor by giving her vote for the saving of our Republic Col Hawkins of the Hawkins Zouaves[11] spoke here Wednesday evening. He made a full expose of McClellan's character and showed most conclusive evidence that little Mac was a traitor and a humbug. He read several articles taken from the southern papers while McClellan was commander in chief showing that he had more than once offered in the commencement of the war his services to the enemy.

To think of such a man having the entire control of Millitary affairs for nearly 2 years, it is only strange that the rebels did not gain more than they did.[12]

I never was so excited before about anything as I am about the coming election. I can scarce think of anything else. I fancy you will think something is the matter when I have so neglected you. Think not that you are forgotten No! No! ever uppermost when listening to the outpouring of patriotic and noble mens['] minds my thoughts reach forth to you and I would fain draw you to my side that you too might listen to the words that make me forgetful of all else, so deeply am I interested. God preserve and sustain our glorious republic.

. . .

[no valedictory]

It would be fully a week before Frederic wrote again, but he and his regiment had been busy. "We are on the wing again," he explained on October 27, anticipating they would join Hancock and Warren's forces in their attacks on the South Side Railroad, which came to be known as the Battle of Boydton Plank Road. As was his wont, he was wildly optimistic, hoping to spend the winter in Richmond because of the action, which he thought could not fail. He and his unit did not march, however, but instead remained in position at Fort Morton and saw action, some of which he details in a letter the next day.

Hd Qrs—7th N.Y.V. Art[y].
Fort Morton—Va—Oct 27th 1864

My chére Femme,

Your letter containing Miss Gertie's first effort, is just to hand.[13] You have received $120 in all—$10 of which is owing to your Grandma and $5[oo] to Col. Hastings. We expect to be paid again in two or three weeks—I do not think I will send you any more at present—if you can make shift till next pay. I have just $20 left. . . .

. . .

We are on the wing again. A general collision along the line is expected at any moment night or day. Our baggage is all sent to

City Point—every man is provided with a week[']s rations, and we are just in trim for a fight. We have an immense force to our left (I forget how many million men of all arms) and it is expected that the collision will be initiated by Grant moving this left wing upon the enemy's railroad communications—the South side road—and the Weldon road. Our forces are so preponderating that Success is certain—It is possible that the enemy may seek to penetrate our lines in the centre—we are just here to assist him in that effort. The impregnability of our position gives us such confidence— that we are all impatient for the ball to open. We could lay Ream's Station upon them again with such effect—and avenge the bloody days of June 3^{d} and 16th (Coal Harbor and Petersburgh). We have been in this state of vigilant preparedness for two days— and cannot help wondering [what] keeps these opposite electric currents apart.

We expect this will be the closing battle of the campaign. I see some reg^{ts} are building winter quars. But this is undoubtedly premature—I hope to winter in Richmond. We are having lovely weather and are acting as infantry support to a battery. 2/3 of our regt. Are on picket—a zig-zag line dug by Burnside's darkies—the opposing lines are within a hundred paces of each other (in some places) and the Feds and Confeds are on the most amicable terms. I have nothing to write about that will interest you. We are up at 4 o'clock every morning—and I declare such early rising dulls my faculties all day.

How nearly out of debt are you? Col. Murphy promises to obtain my commish for me—if he does, I can make a more liberal provision for you. . . .

Take care of yourself, old woman. I will close for want of matter. Good bye—Love to all

Devotedly

F.

[P.S.] Your memorandum arrived safe—just the thing I wanted—I sent a dollar to pay for that and the stamps.

Fort Morton—Va
Oct[r] 28th 1864

Ma Femme–

I have forgotten to make known my requirements in my last two
or three letters. I want a small piece of comb also a pipe—I had a
nice one presented to me by Maj. Murphy—which was burnt up
together with all my little miscellanea in the conflagration of last
Sunday. I enclose a dollar[,] don't pay more for it—a small briar
wood pipe—pack it in a little cardboard box—the postage will be
about 12¢/. Get M[r] Duncan or some gentleman friend to buy it for
you. I don't want tobacco[;] I have plenty.

   We had the liveliest kind of time last night. During the
afternoon it was whispered around among the Officers that we
were going to charge the enemy's works at dusk. We had supposed
this murderous work was over—and there were a few long faces at
the announcement. Towards five 100 of the 148 Penna. Vols. armed
with Spencer rifles (8 shooters) stormed and carried a small fort,
capturing 4 officers (1 colonel,) and twenty men. The rebels rallied
and drove our men out, killing the officer who led the charge
(Lieut. Price 66th N.Y. Vols). Immediately the fort was captured
an aide was sent to the Post commander (Lt. Col. Mincer)[14] for
re-inforcements. It was now dark—and it was raining heavily. A
hundred of our reg[t]. were promptly sent forward as a support—
and seven or eight detachments of fifty each—were gathered up
and sent forward at short intervals. During the delay of sending
for re-inforcements—Col. Mulholland[15] comdg our brigade—
directed Capt. Niles,[16] a promising young officer of our reg[t]. to
gather up ab[t]. 30 of our picket—and skedaddle over to the fort—
and hold it till reinforcements arrived. He did as directed—but
on reaching the enemy's abattis [sic]—he found he was followed
by but one Serg[t]. and 6 men. Here the enemy's fire became so
hot—that he and his little party had to lie down. He lay there 15
or 20 minutes pelted by the rain and the enemy's bullets—until he
found an opportunity to return to our lines as wet as a rag.[17] From
the captured rebels we learnt that their line was drawn out to a fine
point—their men being placed three ft. apart, from our front to
the Appomattox—and their artillery all moved to their right. The

best part of the fun is we are playing the same game of bluff. All our fighting men are away to the left where they have driven Lee's right seven miles—capturing the South side railroad—and all we have here are teamsters, cooks—musicians—dead beats and the refuse and riff-raff of the corps. We make a big display of tents, and our drum corps perambulate the woods beating the calls in half a dozen places—During the night we were aroused twice by an alarm from the left. Our fort opened with ten-in. mortars and long-range batteries to the right and left kept a constant stream of missiles in the air—and the racket from so many pieces was perfectly deafening. After our demonstration upon their lines the Johnnies rec.[d] prompt re-inforcements—and the way they showered their bullets over our works was a marvel. Our regiment fired 15,000 rounds during the night—and their consumption of ammunition must have been as great.

As a reconnaissance our movement was eminently successful—it developed the weakness of the enemy's lines—and satisfied him that the reception we were prepared to give him was decidedly too warm to be agreeable. In our reg[t]. we had one killed and three wounded—our total loss about forty. You will think I have been preparing a newspaper account. But I have 0 else to write about. We think we have a soft thing here—The Bulk of the fighting will be to our right and left.

Your's truly

F.

Lizzie was not getting his letters regularly and had only just received his of October 8 saying that fire had destroyed his tent. But she monitored involvement of Second Corps in its attempt to cut the South Side Railroad and wondered if he was involved. Attending communion prompted her sense of unworthiness. "I enjoyed the services so much, still a shaddow rested upon my heart. I am not as faithful as I should be. . . . Pray for me dear Fred."[18]

Fred sent a short note on November 2 to inform her of his promotion to first lieutenant—without having to extend his term in the army.[19] When he wrote at greater length three days later, he said he hoped to take command of Battery I in coming days and would make significantly more money now. She should therefore live more liberally and demand nothing more of Emma. Meanwhile, he had no patience with her self-reproach.[20]

Novr 5th 1864

My dear Wife

I am still so constantly employed with Reg^t returns that I cannot find half an hour to devote to you. I expect to get clear of the Adjutant's office in a few days and take command of my company—then I expect to have a little leisure. It is blowing a perfect gale of wind as I write—the Adjut's office consists of an old condemned wall tent—in consequence of the destruction of our other tent by fire and its ill-secured sides flutter so tremendously in the wind, that my desk is in a perfect "joggle"—and I write with the utmost difficulty.

I spoke to you in my last about living more liberally—this do. My salary is now $110 per mo. but I shall not immediately realize the benefit of it. As an officer I draw neither clothing nor rations from the government—everything is seriously dear here. I paid (or rather was trusted by the Sutler[)] $30 for a blouse and $27 for a sword and belt. I want sundry other articles to complete my outfit, which will absorb considerable of my pay. Rather than go into debt out of doors—I would advise you to borrow enough of Emma for household expenses for the next three months—by that time I shall [be] able to recover myself and I can then discharge your obligations. Of course—you will allow Emma to pay board no longer.

I received your very interesting letter yesterday. I do wish you would cease your self-accusations of unrighteousness. I shall not pray for you—you do not need it. You are just as pure and free from taint as God intended his creatures to be, or rendered them (d—m this desk) capable of being—all your repeated self-complainings are unnecessary and in my sight foolish. If you are guilty of faults—correct them; if you have no faults do not accuse yourself of them. But for our dear Almighty Father's sake do not continue in that pitiable, imbecile hopeless—impractical—monastic state of mind which leaves you to be ever complaining of sin—and at the same time hinders you from self reformation. My nature is much crasser than yours—and <u>Earthiness</u> partakes

October–November 1864

more largely of my composition—but I do not regard myself as a reprobate[,] as an outcast. I perform my duties—I am surpassed by no man in reverent devotion to my benign Maker—and I do not regard myself as unworthy of his goodness.[21]

While I write this, I am maintaining a conversation with two or three officers—and I do not know what I am saying. Excuse me. It is blowing a small hurricane. I must get out side, or the whole thing will come down on the top of me. The reg^t is away to take part in a division review.

Bye-bye! I am building myself a comfortable house—and shall tent with a Lieut Knickerbocker[22] of Co. M.

Love to all

F.

Elizabeth had not received these admonishments when she wrote next, but she commented on those she had received and then, imbued with the political stakes in question, quickly turned to the election. "I can think of naught else."

Albany N.Y.

Nov. 6th 1864

My very dear Husband,

Would that I could spend this lovely Sabbath day with you, but such wishes are vain and should not I suppose be indulged in. No letters from you since Monday when I rec two, one dated the 27th the other the 28th. I shall hope and look eagerly for one tomorrow. I hope my letters now reach you as usual. As you may suppose nothing is thought of or talked of but the election. The people are in a fever of excitement and suspense[,] not but that all seem confidently to look forward to Lincon's reelection[23] but the astounding revelations that have come to light within the last three weeks, of fraud, and murderous plots, and conspiracies make even the stout-hearted ones of the land pause and tremble to think what the result might have been had not all this wickedness come to light in time to crush it. O! the wickedness of the heart . . . I can think of naught else . . . I feel as if I had grown very much older during the last month or two.

I went last evening in company with Dr Becket[t]'s sister in
law to the last Union meeting that will be held it was the closing
scene[.] these meetings which are held at Tweddle Hall have ever
been largely attended by the most respectable class of citizens both
men and women. The inteligent[,] the noble and the patriotic.
I firmly and truly believe that our nation[']s destiny rests not in
the hands of men but a higher power controls it. God reigns we
have naught to fear. Our republic shall live, we shall come out of
this furnace of affliction and trial; refined and purified a nobler
and truer people, our country shall indeed be one of liberty and
freedom, with the blighting stain and curse of slavery forever
removed from it. too long ah too long has this incubus, this crying
sin rested upon the bosom of this fair land. . . . There must be
an intense anxiety in the army. the soldiers having the power to
vote and being defrauded of it or attempting to do so must make
them feel desperate. What is the meaning of Col Murphy's arrest
in Washington. is it possible that he to[o] has been dabbling in
the most despicable fraud voting. is he a republican or democrat?
Some people predict a terrible row here election day. Gov
Seymour[24] says I believe that there shall be no militia at the poles
[*sic*] but perfect order shall be enforced. Should they begin to riot
I presume he thinks to stop them by his bland palaver calling them
his friends[.] another week and the great question in regard to the
nation[']s welfare will be settled. All will be well. I fear not.

. . .

Do tell me Fred if you suffer from cold or if you have proper
shelter. I pity you having to rise so early. I can not see how they
would employ them at such an early hour. Have you rec your
pipe yet?

. . .

The children are light headed and happy as usual. You are
often the subject of their thoughts and conversation. They love
their Papa.

Monday morning 8 O'clock

. . . I see by this morning[']s paper that Lt Col Murphy has been
honorably discharged as having had no part in the fraud voting. I
am glad to hear of this for I do not want such a stain to rest upon

your regt. I see Adjt D.J. O'Brien[25] has arrived home, he is slowly recovering from his wounds rec the 25th Aug.

. . .

Very aff your wife
Lizzie

Like many of his comrades, Frederic knew winter weather would bring an end to active campaigning, which in turn meant indefinite consignment to the Petersburg trenches, an unwelcome outlook. "The only mode of fighting now remaining is pounding each other at a distance with artillery—picket firing, which causes a considerable waste of life or limb, or in a sudden dash upon the enemy's lines," he explained. Such a life, he added, was "insufferably dull . . . as bad as a fireman's." Still, he looked forward to Lincoln's reelection.[26]

November 7th 1864

Petite Femme,

It is raining—we have just moved here; we have head quarters tent up—and it is crowded with Officers who are glad to crawl out of the rain. I had my comfortable quarters built at our last encampment—and did not have the satisfaction of sleeping in them. Our army have built habitations enough during this campaign to furnish house room to all the good people of this State. We are anxious now to go into winter quarters—the weather is getting too inclement for active operations. On Saturday night we broke up—and went to the front line to resist an attack—The enemy seized our picket line—and drove our men from a position of our front line—which they held till morning. But we succeeded in driving them back—capturing sixty prisoners.

Your useful little package reached me yesterday—your letter and paper came to hand to-day. Much obliged for your provident care—the pipe is just the thing.

We have been greatly exercised by the trouble that has fallen upon Col. Murphy. An aide called at these headquarters to arrest him—he being in Albany at the time—a telegram was sent to arrest him there. We see in the Washington Chronicle of Friday last—that he was apprehended and committed to the Old Capitol prison in that city. [His] name is mentioned in the public prints in connection with these Donahue frauds,[27] but as he warmly espouses the election of Lincoln—of course his name has been fraudulently used.[28] We are anxious for his return—he went home on sick leave and he writes that his committal to the prison has so affected his health that he will have to get an extension.

I have been buoying my spirits up with the conviction that this campaign would finish the war in Virginia. But here we are in the month of November—and Petersburgh gates are still closed upon us. The election to take place to-morrow will no doubt result in the re-election of President Lincoln—that may have a determining effect—otherwise I see nothing before us than for each party to gather his forces together during the coming winter—and renew these scenes of slaughter and mutilation next summer. A merciful heaven avert such a national calamity.

I merely write to let you know that I am safe—not because I have anything to say—I have not assumed command of my company yet—Capt. Anable (in temporary command of the reg^t.) cannot bear the idea of my leaving the Adj^{ts} office till the monthly returns are completed. I shall have to get some money soon, I have not a cent left. Do not send me any—I can borrow what I want here.

When I get some permanent quarters and my mind at ease—I will write to you more satisfactorily—At present you will please to accept these hasty scribbles.

Good bye—all is well

<u>F.</u>

Like so many Union regiments, the Seventh voted for Lincoln better than two-to-one, and the total Northern soldier vote helped Lincoln win reelection to another four-year term.[29] For his part, Frederic applied for leave to go first to Washington DC and then to Albany—to Washington in hope of locating the records he needed to get his company paid and to Albany to purchase an officer's outfit in keeping with his promotion to first lieutenant. As he stated in his November 5 leave application, the company books "were left behind at Belle Plain, and the documentary records were lost at Ream's Station." As a result, his muster rolls could not be made out, "and my company has not been paid for eight months." He was granted fifteen days' leave, but he did not return to camp until November 30.[30]

19

Johnnies Deserting by Wholesale
December 1864–January 1865

After more than two weeks on leave, Frederic returned to the Petersburg siege lines on November 30. He was relieved to find that his regiment had moved to a new location and more comfortable quarters, from which the soldiers observed the Confederate entrenchments only 150 yards distant. Still, Union Fort Gregg, eight miles west of Fort Morton and one of three forts forming a crescent on the far left of the Union's Petersburg siege line, afforded them some greater safety than they had enjoyed previously, although they were still subject to mortar and artillery fire.[1] Both sides watched each other warily but with little conflict.

Before Petersburgh, Va Decr 1–64

Ma chére Femme,

I arrived in camp last evening safely. I had to stay a day in Washington as I reached there too late to take the boat to City Point. The regiment, in fact, the whole corps has moved about 8 miles to the left—that is[,] further south of Petersburgh. We have changed places with the Fifth Corps—and they had built quite comfortable winter quarters. We step in and avail ourselves of their labors. It is the best streak of luck that has befallen us yet. We are on the best of terms with our Johnny neighbors. I took a walk out to the picket line to-day—which is in plain view of the rebel pickets—an open field separates our pits from their's—we are distant from them about one hundred and fifty yards. You would have been charmed with the quiet of the scene. Officers and men of the rebel force were walking about without the least reserve; the officers visiting the picket posts and the men carrying wood—fetching water and such like necessary errands. I formed one of a group of five officers who sate down on the sward—the rebel pickets gathered and pointed us out to each other—one, more demonstrative, waved his hat to us. We sate and watched the movements of those men with the intensest interest. Not a shot was to be heard along the whole line. Each side was vigilant—but the dire alarums of war are pretermitted.

An unpleasant affair occurred last night—sixteen men belonging to the Sixty-first New York deserted to the rebels. These are recent recruits—big bounty men. Regrets are universally expressed that their dastardy was not perceived in time—as a thirty days furlough is granted to that man who shoots down any traitor escaping to the rebels.

I am quartering with Capt. Niles and Lieut. Kirk[2]—two very agreeable tent-mates. I mess with Lieuts. Berry[3] and Kreps.[4] It is not expected that there will be any fighting on our part of the line this winter. "Going to the Front" has a sound that would chill many a peaceful citizen—but on reaching here he would find his ideas of the place widely astray. My mind is far from settled down yet—Lt. Kreps I believe is willing to accept the Adjutancy—it lay between him and me—so I am in command of my company. I don't know but it is a preferable duty—at least, it affords much more leisure. I enclosed you a dollar bill—which has no currency here.

Hope the babes are reconciled to my leaving. Col. Murphy has not returned yet. Best love to all

Faithfully yours
F.E.L.

Excuse a short letter—my ideas are too confused for prolixity at present.

Two days later, he announced to Lizzie, "I am an officer of the line," and then apologized for his letters having "degenerated into a mere military journal. I have no doubt they are wearisome to you." The weather, he said, was favorable, and their quarters comfortable. He had received two letters from her, neither of which survive. Captain Shannon was under guard and being escorted from Rock Island, Illinois, for court martial, charged with "gross indifference to the interests of his command." He added hopefully, "We may succeed in getting rid of him yet."[5]

Their comfortable quarters did not last long, pulled down soon after Fred's return to make way for maneuvering artillery to meet a feared attack. He regretted not having written for a week, but he had been on picket duty, and the weather had made writing impossible. In answer to her query, no one had asked about his overstaying his leave.

Before Petersburgh, Va Decr 11th / 64

Ma chére Petite,

You will, I know, hold me guilty of the unpardonable sin—a week has elapsed since I last wrote to you. Let me explain. I generally write on Wednesday and Sunday. Last Wednesday I commenced a letter to you—but it was raining at the time—and the rain beat thro' in such a manner that I was unable to achieve my task. The next morning I was detailed for picket—and as I heard that we were likely to be out three or four days, I took writing materials along. But it was impossible to write, my dear honey. Snow and rain and cold freezing blasts rendered writing so difficult a matter—that I had to forego the undertaking. We remained three days—and were relieved yesterday at noon. The night before we left camp (Wednesday) we were called up at midnight to pull down our houses as an attack from Genl. A.P. Hill's corps (recently returned from the valley)[6] was expected, and room within the breastwork was required for the manoeuvering of artillery. The men set to work—packed up their personal effects—and tore their comfortable log houses down—and then spread their blankets and slept for the night. When we returned after our three days severe exposure—we came to a desolate camp, and the poor worn out fellows had to go to work and reconstruct their quarters before they could find a hole to lay their heads. Last night it froze intensely—and the wind blew a hurricane—I feared our slight canvas roof would blow away—but I slept warm and soundly—three heavy wet blankets kept my

December 1864–January 1865

bedfellow (Capt Niles) and myself in a perfect steam. At reveillé my tent mate was unable to get up from rheumatism in the knees—but I sprang forth to vigilance and watchfulness like a giant refreshed. We are in expectation of an attack upon our lines from the rebel Hill's corps, but he has difficulties enough of his own—without seeking more. While on picket—I would watch the Rebels relieving their posts—they were not more than 75 or 80 yds distant—so that I was enabled to distinguish their features—A detachment of about 120 men led by an officer would halt in front of a pit, 6 or 8 men would be detached from the right—and those relieved would fall in on the left. Such a motley looking set of heathens you never saw outside of a wild animal show. There were but three overcoats amongst the whole party—and two of them were blue—some wore citizens' clothes—some red or white shirts—others rusty red uniforms—and a few their dull grey. Some wore a blanket wrapped round their loins—but the majority had to face the keen blasts of the driving sleet. Nine rebel deserters came in last night—and they report the utmost destitution prevailing. A man from the 40th N.C. reg. said his whole reg were waiting an opportunity to come over. We lose severely by desertions. During the three days I was out— 27 men from our Brig. went over. Nary [a] man from the Seventh. That gallant reg is "trustie and trew." All these renegade poltroons are big bounty men—1 year men—new recruits. They steal over in a dark night—and the satisfaction of shooting them with the reward of thirty days' furlough is denied our men. I had no trouble in find[ing] the Reg. on my way to camp—I met an orderly with the col's horse going to meet him—he conducted me to the reg. Not a word was said about my overstaying. Maj Pruyn reported to the reg. to-day—He is senior officer present—but declines taking command—he will go [to] the hospital—Soldiering here is too rough for him. Did I tell you that Capt. Shannon is here under arrest to take his trial for neglecting the interest of his comp? It is likely he will be dismissed.

Goodbye—love to Emma and the babes

F.

Having just returned from picket duty, he wrote sleepily a few days later of a "perfect quiet" prevailing between the lines. "We are distinctly in sight of each other—field officers ride along the lines—but a hostile shot from either side is never fired. Still this induces no relaxation . . . our present understanding is merely tacit." As an officer, he must keep on the "qui vive." Governor Seymour, meanwhile, was handing out commissions "beyond count"—at least twenty issued since Frederic had been home in mid-November.[7]

No communications from Elizabeth survive intact between mid-November 1864 and early March 1865, although torn pieces of a few letters from February 1865 do. What is preserved alludes to domestic concerns predominantly and at one point to Frederic's suggestion they consider moving to Minnesota after the war.[8] Fred's letters indicate no interruption in receiving letters from home, however. In them, he inquired about her health, their finances, and other domestic affairs. His letters, meanwhile, provided detailed views of camp life.

When Fred began his letter of December 18, for example, he was interrupted by the arrival of a clothing requisition, which required his attention, but not before he thought the war news was so positive he would soon have to find a new way to make a living. "The indications of the day unmistakably point to a speedy suppression of the Rebellion. Vexing, isn't it? Now I have attained a comfortable posish—to be menaced with the probability of being turned adrift." Viewpoint was everything. To Lizzie, a chance for him to be "turned adrift" meant he would come home, after which they would make their way ahead together.[9]

Fred's promotion to first lieutenant was expensive. He had to provide his own board, and the cost of food was high. "I shall have to apply to Mr Duncan for a loan of $10⁰⁰," he said. "Having to supply my own commissariat—prices are so extreme here—that it exhausts one's funds rapidly." To go into debt to the sutler, he added, "is to pay one hundred per cent interest for the accommodation."[10] The next day he deliberately missed drill to write to her again and tell of action along the picket line.

Before Petersburgh, Va.
Monday Dec 18th

My chére Femme,

. . .

Monday Decr 19th

The regiment is out on Battalion drill—I had set myself so much
work to do, that I thought I could not spare the time to drill—so
I incontinently stayed away. In some regiments this offence would
subject an Officer to trial by court martial—but in our regiment a
more cordial and democratic feeling exists amongst the Officers—
and venial offences are overlooked. Last night there was a little
excitement on Picket.[11] The night being very dark, a small part of
the enemy crept cautiously thro' the woods with the intention of
surprising the pickets and capturing three or four officers who had
made their hd qrs. in a barn. The rebs crawled up to our vidette
posts—then raised up, uttered a yell—and the line in their rear
fired a volley. This sudden outburst so electrified our line that
eleven new recruits flung down their arms and ran precipitately
to the rear. Our line promptly returned the fire, and the raiders
finding that their surprise had not emptied our pits—made the
best of their way back—We lost one killed—one wounded and
three missing—the rebels have six wounded.[12] . . . A letter from
you last night. A merry Christmas t'ye. The next one we will try and
spend thegeither.

F.E. Lockley

The weather was bitter, made more insufferable by having to
live in tents. "I am almost frozen up," Fred wrote on December
22, "and my faculty of conception is congealed." "We do not build
permanent quarters—as we expect to winter in Petersburg or Richmond. This sounds farcical, I know; but is there any conceivable
reason, why we should not?"[13]

With the wind blowing a "dreary dirge" through his canvass tent,
he noted, "It is but a small difference whether one is within or
without doors." To keep warm, he said, "I burn about half a cord
of wood a day." Amusing himself playing with the fire and chant-

ing the church liturgy, he thought of home. "There is inconceivable elasticity in my feelings tonight—superinduced, I suppose[,] by the keen bracing air." He urged her to enjoy the holidays. "Eat a mince pie for me."[14]

His mood was not quite so festive when he wrote again on Christmas Day, but he continued hopeful the war would end soon. Even as he envisioned a "prodigal gathering" for the holiday, he reported more Union desertions from "big bounty men" and consequent hangings of those apprehended.

Christmas 1864—

Thank God, this is the last Christmas I shall spend in the army! As the months wane, my impatience increases. I don't know that I have any particular reason for this—any more than the general truth that man never is, but always to be blest. The weather has moderated and is again lovely—everything remains quiet, and we manage to live along with tolerable comfort. But this season of festivity sends the thoughts coursing homewards—shut your eyes to the vision resolutely as you will—still the various groupings of this immemorial holiday will obtrude. The prodigal gathering of the rude comestibles—then the finished product in the shape of savory turkey—rich flavored mince pie, and that omnivarium of the earth's fruitfulness—the royal English plum pudding. The visionary streets are fully of happy parties on their way to merry and hospitable hearths, and an undefined jingle of ubiquitous sleigh-bells diffuses mirth and music in the air wherever I turn. I suppose I ought to be getting sober now—and these seasons of mirth and enjoyments have less influence upon my feelings. But having a young thing of a wife, and a bevy of romping girls with all the rich promise of a glad life before them, I cannot lose interest in these holiday times—I am still amongst you, and participate so unreservedly with you in feeling, that youth and buoyancy and rapt anticipation, are potent with me as ever.

It is miserably dull here. We have cheering news every day—it is evident the confederacy is rapidly falling to pieces—and I begin to believe that Uncle Sam will not want me after May 1st, but the interval drags along so slowly. Last night there was considerable firing in the rebel camp—and we supposed that they had gotten up a fight among themselves—but towards 2 o'clock a.m. five deserters came in—and they informed us that the rebels were only ushering in Christmas with salvos of musketry. We are informed by Genl. Grant that there are but five days rations in Richmond—still a number of misguided men will persist in deserting to them. The night before last two from the 69th N.Y. left us; last night again two from the 5th New Hampshire went over. These are all big bounty men—substitutes generally. Three more renegade soldiers were hung before the division on Friday—as they disgrace the name of soldier by their dastardy and perfidy, no sympathy is felt for them.

No orders for Winter quarters yet. It is evident that Genl. Grant has no idea of wintering here. With our numerous armies in the rear of Lee all rapidly using up the several forces opposed to them, it is demonstrable that a combined effort will be made very soon to drive Lee out of Richmond. With the present disposition of our forces the thing can be easily enough done. Gen^ls. Stoneman[15] and Burbridge[16] are rapidly advancing towards Lynchburgh; that place once attained the destruction of Lee['s] communications will be entirely destroyed. Or that failing, Genl Butler[17] can capture Wilmington and disembarking his land forces—send them to the rear of Lee—which will immediately bring that general to the study of his means of retreat. Before many days look out for stirring news from this quarter. We begin to think the fight is well nigh ended; Lee's army is the only fighting element the rebels now have to look to—and our rapidly concentr[at]ing armies outnumber it three to one. It is the scene of Napoleon and the Allies in 1812 re-enacted.

Enjoy yourselves—it will all come right yet. Spring will restore Peace to the country—then we will bind our bruised limbs with victorious wreaths—and our war desolated plains shall again bud and blossom as the rose. A bientôt. I expect a letter to-night. From your ardent admirer.

F.E. Fiddlefaddle.

A few days later, Frederic wished Elizabeth a happy new year. His mood contrasted markedly with the previous year's low, although he noted that of the seven Seventh New Yorkers who went with him to Albany in November 1863 to vote, he and only one other survived. Some of the seven were taken captive, and "we are learning of the deaths of a large number of our men in southern prisons," he said. "I drop seventeen this month from the rolls of Comp[y] I. Comp[y] C drops twenty-six."[18]

New Year's Day was dull and uncomfortable, and, for lack of wood, especially cold. He even had to burn his pillow. Col. Lewis O. Morris, the man who raised the regiment originally and who was killed at Cold Harbor on June 4, was sorely missed, especially compared to his present commanding officers, Lieutenant Colonel Murphy[19] and Major Anable, both "unprincipled" in his estimation. Worse, Captain Shannon had returned and put Lockley under arrest when Frederic refused Shannon's demand that he surrender the company papers to him. Lockley had gone to too much trouble to retrieve them from Rockville, Illinois, where Shannon had taken them. Morale, both his and the regiment's, he admitted, was low.

> Jan[y] 1st 1865
> Camp near Petersburgh Va

My dear Wife,

This is the dullest and most uncomfortable New Year's day I ever remember to have spent. The weather is cold, a keen freezing wind is blowing, and we have no wood in camp. We are a mile and a half away from timber, and as we have but two wagons to haul it— we are but very insufficiently supplied with fuel. Yesterday being muster day, when every man is required to be in the ranks we had no wood brought—and we suffer a dearth to-day in consequence. I have just chopped up and burnt my pillow—to keep a fire up I suppose I shall have to burn my bed next. I am like my friend Mr. Lemm, whom Emma so often talks about—he was reduced to the necessity of burning up several useful articles, in a similar straight, and his greatest perplexity was what article he should fall foul of next.

Our regiment is going to the dogs fast for want of a capable head—Col. Morris' loss is felt more and more every day. Lt. Col. Murphy and Major Anable are both of them scheming unprincipled politicians—the colonel is brave while the major's bravery is more than doubted—but the latter has a gentlemanly deportment (an indispensable qualification in a regimental commander) and the colonel is a primary election rowdy, a drunken loafer. I have tried to respect this man in virtue of his being my commanding officer, but my sober judgment spews him out—and like Caliban,[20] I am tempted to berate myself for my false devotion.

What a thrice double ass was I, To take this drunkard for a god, and worship This dull fool![21]

The evening of the Colonel's return, he called Major Anable into his quarters, and abused and insulted him in unmeasured billings-gate. The major has preferred charges against him and he is now under arrest. That same evening Capt. Shannon came to my quarters, and in a very imperious way demanded his company papers—he having been assigned to duty with the regiment. I refused to deliver them on the ground that I had not been officially informed of his release from arrest. "I inform you now," Said he, "as your commanding officer. Do you doubt my word?" I replied: "Most assuredly I do." "Consider yourself under arrest," was his rejoinder. He then demanded my sword, but I plainly instructed him that if he was a better man than I was—he could take it. I was released to-day—and assigned to the command of Battery F., Lieut Berry being absent on leave. The arrest was not a legal one—and therefore not binding, but as the recognition of it saved me from all duty—I was satisfied—and was quite reluctant to be released. The morale of the reg^t. has fallen thus low. The truth is the war has lasted quite long enough—both sides are sick of it. Our officers are tendering their resignations—overstaying their leave for the purpose of dismissal—and every one is busy planning some method to get out. The Johnnies are deserting by wholesale, no less than thirteen hundred came over last week. I shall try and stick it out this month and next—if things don't improve by that time—I shall exercise my ingenuity to get out. The men are insufficiently fed—and irregularly clad—and their duties are so constant that they suffer greatly—a great many are giving up sick. This statement would not do to publish—it would not tend to encourage enlistments—but it is an o're true tale.

How do you like this style of thought to open the New Year with? I count myself extremely happy from the knowledge that I have a blessed haven of rest whenever our paternal Uncle shall give me his benediction and his discharge. The discharge I more particularly want—the benediction is not so essential. Enjoy yourselves, womankind! I am with you in spirit though not in flesh. If I were I should make your mince pies suffer. Excuse a miserable letter—I will do better next time. A happy New Year to all.

Your's as ever

F.

PS My hands are cold and the ink is frozen—so excuse illegible writing.

Frederic was little happier a few days later. "To-day there was an execution[,] the Division being present." Meanwhile, the men's winter quarters remained unfinished, and clothing and rations were inadequate. Still, there was some room for mirth, and his youngest daughter provided it. If he seemed "the impersonation of dullness," Gertie, his seven-year-old, offered sparkle. "That misunderstanding of Miss Gertie's when she thought Aesop's fables in verse—was Eat up fables and burst" had provided a needed laugh in camp.[22]

In his next, he told her of camaraderie between the lines, of enemy deserters being welcomed, and of exhibition hangings of their own defectors. The war had become paradoxical.

Camp 7th N.Y. V. Art.^y

Before Petersburgh, VA. Jan 9–1865

My dear Wife,

I am too late for the mail to-night—but I avail myself of a few minutes' leisure—that you may not be without one to-morrow. I received a letter from you last evening, wherein you speak of being sick—I trust it is nothing serious. I am anxious to hear from you again—that I may learn of your being in an improved condition. Your letters are a week on the way! I believe the water in the Potomac is low—and the Mail boats do not make their trips regularly. So long an interval elapses between my writing to you—and your answer arriving—that I forget what is the subject under discussion. I sometimes think some of my letters cannot reach you. The children will please excuse my delay in answering their pleasant letters—I am not quite through the muster rolls yet.

To-day I am detailed as Brigade Officer of the day. The duties are light. Merely to see the Camps are well policed, (that is, cleaned up) and to visit the Picket two or three times. To invest the Office with dignity—a horse is furnished. To-day as I rode along the line of pits—I saw a cluster of Johnnies—and reined in to see what they were doing. They pointed me out to one another—and then waved their hats. These fellows are becoming quite friendly. Almost every man who comes in brings his gun with him—as a small oblation—a free will offering to the strength of our cause. Every man who comes in reiterates that the whole line in front of us are anxious to come over. To-day one of our men shouted to the group of butternuts—"Say! Any of yez coming in to-night?" One of them answered—"The night's too bright." So they take the day for desertion. Two ran over this afternoon—and three came in on Saturday morning. We very rarely lose any. There was an arranged plan with the Rebel recruiting Officers in Canada. They would enlist men for their service—and then instruct them to enlist in our army—take the large bounties offered—$1000 to $1500—and then desert to their lines. The Fifth New Hampshire—and the 7th N.Y. Inf^y in the 1st & 3^d. Brigades of our division have been rendered infamous by the operations of these worthies. We are treated to a hanging exhibition every Friday—and the men have grown to enjoy the spectacle. We lose all human feeling towards such dastards and traitors. A Johnny we can respect—and regard as a brother soldier.

Lt. Parker is out of the service.

No news—I am annoyed that Ham. Berry did not stay a while with you. But he is a strange being. He went off so suddenly I had no time to write one line to enclose in the parcel I sent you. Write constantly—your letters are a necessity to my existence. Weather pleasant. Love to all. I don't know when I shall find time to write to your Grandma. Send my dutiful love to her when you write.

Addio

F.

On January 12, the Seventh New York got a new commander: Col. Richard C. Duryea, a West Point graduate transferred from the First U.S. Artillery. He would attempt to instill regular army discipline and busy the men with drill, parade, and other duties, but the New Yorkers, what few of them were left, may have seen too much to revert to stern military order with much elan.

Also in mid-January, Fred was appointed acting adjutant, replacing Lt. Frazier Kreps, whose irritability had displeased almost everyone. He acknowledged accepting a heavy workload with the appointment, "but it is only for seven months." Besides, he said, "I prefer the Official work of the regiment to military duties."[23] Still, he needed to borrow Lizzie's watch. His was broken, and if details from his regiment were late to fatigue and picket duty, he would be blamed. He stayed busy keeping records in order, but disaffection came easily. "We are here to await the slow progress of the disintegration of the rebel armies," he said. "This does seem so dismally tedious a business—that my patience flags and I become homesick and unhappy." He never received the $10 he requested from Duncan, but perhaps the letter containing it went astray. "How do you fare for funds?" he asked Lizzie. "Poorly, I know." Company payrolls—except Shannon's—were all in, and the regiment should have been paid soon. He expected to have money to send her before long, so "don't starve yourselves to death."[24] He thanked her for her "long, interesting letters." They helped fortify his perseverance.[25]

Meanwhile, several men from the Seventh New York had escaped imprisonment in Columbia, South Carolina, but only one had made it to General Sherman's forces in Georgia. The others were recaptured. Confederate deserters "still come into our lines," he wrote, and "a rebel Captain came over yesterday—with four privates," but "desertion from our side seems to have ceased."[26] Three days later, he reported "sixteen Johnnies" having come in the night before and reported "great destitution" in Petersburg. "They say the women and children there are starving."[27]

Camp Near Petersburg Va
Jany 27th 1865

My dear Wife,

You will begin to think me a regular nuisance. Always drivelling
about want of time. I despise a man who is always hurried. Our
beloved who is a West Point graduate, and is creating a favorable
impression, finds the regiment in a somewhat demoralized state—
and in his efforts to bring it up to a good standing, he imposes
rather a severe strain upon us.[28] The Adjutant's Office had grown
terribly demoralized in consequence of the disaffection and
fretfulness of my predecessor. Being Adjutant—having inferior
help the Serg^t major has been absent from the reg^t over three
weeks[;] my office is so cold that it is with effort I keep myself to
my desk—and having increased indoor and out of door business
to attend to, I declare I am kept in a whirl the whole time. When
Napoleon the 1st contemplated an invasion of England he gathered
an army together at Boulogne—and drilled them early and late in
order to bring them to a high state of efficiency. Marshal Soult[29]
who was in command of the Post complained to the emperor that
such incessant labors would break down the morale of the troops.
Napoleon replied, "Those who are unable to bear these labors will
serve to garrison posts; and those who can endure them are fit to
conquer the world."

I fortify myself by remembering this sentiment: except at that
murderous spot Cold Harbor, when for about ten days I was
half sick and wholly dejected, I have kept up my ambition and
my spirits. I possess my soul in patience; do not let my business
drive me, and find that I am becoming equal to the onerous task
imposed upon me. but I want a good sergeant major badly.

. . .

It still keeps jolly cold. We have a great dearth of wood—and are
unable to build winter quarters. I think this must be an unusually
cold winter. We had no such continuance of cold weather as this
last winter—three hundred miles north of here.[30] Then I had all
the luxuries of garrison life. A commodious office—comfortable
well furnished quarters—and liberal food. But variety is charming
and we have plenty of change (not <u>loose change</u>) in a soldier's life.

I write my letters so entirely a l'improviste,[31] that I am sure they must make disjointed reading. Tell Miss Gertrude she must not think I am neglecting her; on the contrary, I am reserving my best efforts for her. She is my young sweetheart—my charming chére amie—and I must not address any hurried every day scrawl to her.

. . .

Good bye pet—love to all

Your's devotedly

F.E.L.

[P.S.] Capt. Shannon and I are on best of terms. I cannot hold resentment and he knows I am in a position now where he would play a losing game to run counter to me.

20

The Fighting Is Nearly Over
February–March 1865

The regiment's new commander, Col. Richard Duryea, was good to his word for military regimen. "Not a moment's leisure is afforded any one man in the command," Frederic told Elizabeth. Heavy details for guard, picket, and fatigue absorbed the strength of the regiment, and drills and parades kept the few remaining in camp plenty busy.[1] Fred, too, felt overtasked, and he had little quality help. His assistants, a sergeant major and a clerk, were "so dumb" that he had yet to distinguish any common sense in them, and the regiment's officers "are nearly all new" and thus inexperienced in official duties. A few were downright illiterate. "I have but little rest [but] I keep cool over it," he told her. Still, "any person who supposes an Officer's life in the field is an easy one had better come try it."[2]

Except for that week at Cold Harbor, his health had been remarkably resilient, but now he had caught a cold, perhaps the flu. He was not alone. He estimated that two-thirds of the command was in the same condition, thanks to unthinking commanders. The first week in February he was so hoarse he could only speak in a whisper and finally won a day to recuperate, although his colonel suspected him of shirking. The cause was a division review on the coldest day of the year. "I really thought I should freeze stiff in my saddle." They had awaited inspection for an hour in summer attire to be reviewed by a variety of officers, including Maj. Gen. Andrew Humphreys and other officers, all of whom were "well booted, cloaked and furred to the ears."[3]

By February 8, he was feeling better but reported heavy fighting on both sides of their line for two days. "On Sunday night [February 5] we pulled up stakes and marched out" to man the front but returned the following morning. They did similarly the next night, but had "escaped" being involved in the struggle.[4] The action encompassed three days of fighting at Hatcher's Run and constituted Grant's renewed efforts to cut Lee's sources of supply from the South.[5] The effect on the regiment, other than a man slightly wounded in the hand in what would be the last of the Seventh New York's 1,485 casualties, was to require them to move camp again after finally completing their winter quarters.[6]

Hd Q^{rs} 7th N.Y.V. Art^y
Feby 10th 1865

Ma chére Femme,

We have just moved camp—everything is in confusion. We have driven the rebels about two miles and have advanced our line. After incredible labor we had nearly finished our former camp the labor being so greatly increased by the prevailing scarcity of timber, and the constant duties of our men. A good soldier is never discouraged—he knows that war causes all kinds of sudden derangements, and he is prepared for them all. If he rests but a night in a place—it is his business to make himself comfortable there. Ergo; I am the opposite of a good soldier. After unavoidable delays of nearly two months I had at length succeeded in getting an Adj$^{ts'}$ Office built—and the very day after I had moved in, the order came to git up and git.

A conviction weighs upon our minds that we shall not stay here long. Still we are busy at work preparing timber for quarters—and shall endeavor to make ourselves comfortable while we stay here. Serg^t. Major Wood[7] returned to the regt. to-day. I have quite recovered from the effects of my cold—and feel a little like work again. The weather is lovely but the nights are severely cold—Last night we put up a tent, five of us crowded in for the purpose of using our blankets advantageously (ten in all); and we went to bed with a huge log fire blazing in front. We slept warm—but we lay close to do it.

. . .

I am writing in the chill winter air—and I have considerable difficulty in keeping warmth in my fingers sufficient to guide my pen. You really must excuse short letters until I can assume a cast of mind and have opportunity afforded me to become more communicative. But that you are my dear, loving, constant little wifie following me through all vicissitudes with your ever welcome messages—I should consider it an impossibility to write to any one.

We are about two miles from Hatcher's run—we expect in less than two weeks to clean the rebels out of there. But we want more troops—I don't see any of "three hundred thousand more" coming forward. . . .

Yours lovingly

<u>F.</u>

Valentine's Day recognized the world's desire for love, but there was none in camp. A hundred men assigned to fatigue duty had loudly protested short rations within earshot of the commander, who had not been pleased. The sutler was cheating the men, and Fred knew it, but his having declined to punish the men more demonstrably than calling on them to quiet down would be his undoing with Colonel Duryea.[8]

Camp 7th N.Y.V. art[y]

Feby 14th 1865

Ma trés chére Femme,

. . .

We had an unpleasant affair this morning—which caused two of our officers to be placed under arrest—and charges will be preferred against them. It happened in this wise. These two officers, Lieuts Hawes[9] and Maher,[10] were detailed from these headquarters to take charge of a Fatigue detail of 106 men—to report at Brigade headquarters for instructions. The men were assembled, counted off, and by me turned over to the senior lieutenant. He received them of me—and assuming the command proceeded to march them off. Just as they faced by the flank, and before leaving regimental headquars. they set up a howl of "hard tack"; and the more I tried to still the noise—the louder they yelled. It is dis-graceful in me to acknowledge the fact, but I sympathized with the men. Two thirds of them had not broken their fast—and they were leaving camp for a day's work—without a morsel in their haversacs. This recurs every second day. The men receive every alternate day food enough for four moderate meals—two meals they are deprived off [*sic*]. As the two officers led the shouting mob past division head quars. The maj. gen[l]. comdg conceived himself insulted. The idea of hungry men shouting for their breakfast as they passed the gen[ls] sumptuous quarters disturbing his pleasant anticipations of a well prepared meal, was truly outrageous—He felt it as such. The officers leading them as I said were put under arrest, and the men are threatened with all sorts of severe treatment, except increase of rations. Aint' you getting tired of this oft repeated refrain—"Short rations!" It causes quite a discussion here—I hope to see the evil soon remedied. Your delicious love messages come frequently. They are ever welcome. My appetite grows by what it feeds on. . . .

Whoop, jug! I love thee

F.E.L.

Fred continued effusively in his next letter two days later. The division band was playing "Listen to the Mocking Bird" and making him think of her. "At such a moment one would ask a fair form to commune with, and leisure and opportunity to give way to feeling." Believing that she shared with him "the love of <u>Bizarrerie</u>— nonsense—extravagance," he gave way, exuberantly and suggestively.

"<u>Love</u>! He is the only earthly deity I recognize—and when he chose thee for his minister, my worship of him became apotheosized and spiritual. No! that is a mistake! Although pure and hymnical there is yet earthiness in my devotion—to cause me to long for a rude soldier's clasp of your yielding waist—a delirium of kisses—a Good bye—I shall commit myself. Wait till I get home—Thrillingly— longingly—lovingly your's."[11] Lizzie answered this in kind in the surviving part of a letter otherwise torn in half. She had a mind to "give you a good scolding for your sauciness and flattery. If you dare to presume to lay it on so thickly again I'll do desperate things. I'll do all in my power to charm the first soldier you may chance to send this way," she added teasingly. "See if I don't" and then with uncharacteristic intimacy signed off, "Good night darling."[12]

February–March 1865

Down to earth in his next, Fred said he had been dismissed as acting adjutant because of the men's protests of short rations. He confessed to having mixed emotions about it, but while still in the adjutant's office—and in the colonel's absence—he had contrived to transfer himself out of Company I and away from Captain Shannon.

Camp in the Field, Va.
February 21st 1865

My dearest Wife,

Lt. James A. Harris[13] of Batt.y I will deliver this to you. He has been kind enough to express a desire to call upon you—so to render his visit the more acceptable, I make him the bearer of this. . . .

The camp is in confusion to-night. A dispatch is being read to the various regiments announcing the fall of Winchboro',[14] Augusta, Columbia, and the occupation of Charleston with two hundred guns. The death of Gen¹. Beauregard is also announced.[15] This afternoon we again advance our picket line without a struggle. Good news actually rains upon us.

This morning I was gratified with seeing my well-meaning and faithful little friend Frank Butt.[16] I thought he would have kissed me in his delight at meeting with me. He looks well and hearty; but gives a melancholy record of deaths in Batt.y I. Half of the 400 men whom we bear on our records as prisoners of war are undoubtedly dead.

I have been relieved from my position as Act.g Adj.t Col. Duryea has never seemed to place confidence in me—and failed to treat me with that courtesy and intimacy which are due a regular army Officer, and he appears to have very poor opinion of the Officers of the Regiment. He has appointed as my successor a newly commissioned Lieut. (a German Jew) who served as a private in his command in the 1st United States artillery. This Officer is a good and brave soldier but utterly unqualified for the position he is appointed to. The Officers one and all are kind enough to express their regrets at my displacement. It is annoying to me simply because I have been treated so generously—and entrusted so largely with the confidence of all our previous regimental commanders. Otherwise I am much pleased with the change. It will afford me leisure—and now that we are at length established in comfortable quarters—I propose to use it to my great advantage. Thinking that such a change might occur, I had the forethought to avail myself of my position to transfer myself from battery I to F. I am now doing duty in my friend Lieut. Berry's company, and my relations are of the pleasantest kind.

The paymasters have arrived—our regiment will be paid in a day or two. I have but two months' pay coming as we shall be paid upon the December roll—and my bill with the sutler is rather steep for clothing and food. . . .

You minx! I shall be home in a few weeks—the war is coming to an end so fast—and then I will eat you out of house and home! God bless the butcher! Three cheers for the devil! You will have small cause to rejoice at my change in <u>posish</u>—for I have grown so into the habit of scribbling that from sheer necessity of employment, I shall bear you down with frivolous communications.

Your's benevolently
F.E. Lockley

Whatever leisure his transfer from Company I had afforded him, it did not last. Within days, Fred's regiment was broken up and ordered to various locations in and around Baltimore. Traveling first to Fort McHenry and then embarking thirty miles south to Annapolis, he arrived as senior officer in charge of more than one hundred Seventh New Yorkers. They were there to assist in managing thousands of former Union prisoners now paroled from Confederate captivity. Among them were some old Seventh New York comrades.

Camp Parole,[17] Annapolis Md
February 27th 1865

My dear Wife,

I wrote to you in great haste at Fort M°Henry two days ago—and having a little leisure this evening I shall devote it to giving you a few details of our late experiences. Last Tuesday (the 21st inst) our regiment lay in its old camp near Hatcher's Run.[18] I was detailed as Officer of the Picket to report at 9 a.m. the next day. I retired to bed as usual—and was awakened early the next morning by a general noisy hilarity among the Officers. At length one burst into our quarters (I have told you that Lt. Berry & myself quartered together) and from his exaggerated gesticulations—and more particularly from his extraordinary revelations I thought he had been drinking. The regiment had been ordered to Baltimore to relieve the 91st N.Y. Vet. Vols stationed there—and that we were to strike tents—pack up and be ready to march to Patrick's Station as soon as our pickets were relieved.[19] He removed our incredulity by his asseverations of truth—so we jumped up—ate breakfast—packed up—and were ready for the march in a short time. We reached City Point in due time—where we embarked for Baltimore—and arrived there after a pleasant voyage of three days. I wrote to you from Fort McHenry last Saturday—informing you how the regiment had been distributed around the department. We now belong to the Eighth Corps.[20] At the time I wrote I was actg. adjt to the detachment at Fort McHenry—but when the two companies marched to embark for this post—as the detachment was short of Officers, the Colonel ordered me to proceed with them[.] Being senior officer I took command. My force numbered ninety-four men and three officers beside myself—Lt. Berry was with it. Arrived at the wharf—we embarked on transport— and steamed thirty-two miles down the Chesapeake Bay until we reached the historic city of Annapolis. A three miles march along the rail-road track brought us to this far-famed camp. We relieved two companies of the 91st N.Y. who had orders to proceed to their regt headquarters on the arrival of troops to relieve them. That regt., 1700 strong, is ordered to the front to take our place. On our march through Annapolis and on our arrival here—any number of our lost members, men captured at Coal harbor and Petersburgh— and now paroled, rushed forward to greet us with enthusiasm. The idea of their old friends of the Seventh being sent as garrison to this post—seemed like a divine interposition.

This is a very extensive institution. At present there are about 6000 paroled prisoners here—and 20,000 more are expected daily. The men are well-behaved—and give no trouble but they are without organization—all regiments and all branches of the service being heterogeniously mixed up. A few disorderly ones occasionally introduce liquor into camp—and a disturbance is generally the consequence. My little force constitutes the sole garrison of the place.

Soldiering here is a slight change from soldiering at the front. Here we have comfortable commodious quarters—board at an excellent table—can keep clean, dress well, and partake of some of the comforts of civilization. I think we are likely to stay here some little time—perhaps for the rest of our term of service. I directed you to address your letters to Fort McHenry. Don't do it. Address them as follows. 1st Lieut, detachment 7th N.Y.H. Art[y] Camp Parole, Annapolis, Md. I have received no letter from you since we left Peter his burgh—and shall soon die of hymeneal inanition.[21] I hope to have a few forwarded me from the Reg[l]. headquarters in a day or two.

Mar 1st

I commenced this letter the evening before last—and have had no chance to resume it until now. I am up to my eyes in business. The men have to encamp out to make room for this expected influx of P.P.[22] I have been busy drawing lumber—making requisitions for Quartermaster's stores—ordnance stores—making arrangements for their rations being cooked—in addition this, yesterday the men were mustered for pay—and monthly returns and muster and pay rolls have to be made out with as little delay as possible. I am really driven with work.

Capt. Knickerbocker[23]—comp[y]. M—has just reached here— This relieves me of the command—and with it the labor and responsibility. We are very deficient in officers. Lt. Berry is superintending building the camp—Lt. Le Roy[24] is Officer of the day—Lt. Duncan[25] is away with a hundred exchanged prisoners— taking them to Camp Distribution Alexandria. I am busy with muster rolls. This keeps us all on duty. The addition of Capt. K–to our force is quite a relief. He is an excellent Officer beside. I am filling this letter with all sorts of loose gossip—which can possess no possible interest to you. I am told the Paymaster will be here tomorrow. Perhaps that will be more interesting to you.

I am anxious to hear how Emma progresses—Has she removed to Schuylerville yet? Do you think of breaking up house-keeping for the Summer? Has your sister reported yet?[26] Write directly you receive this—as I am quite ignorant of what you are doing.

I find this so soft a thing—that I believe I shall take another hack at Soldiering for three years longer. If I keep you sufficiently supplied with money you cannot possibly object. If I come home I relieve you of command—and you know as well as any one that it is better to reign than to serve. The fighting is nearly over now—I have had the downs of a military life—now I am willing to try the ups for a while. Eh! Wifie! how say you.

. . . A whole ocean of prostrate devotion to my cherry-cheeked empress.

Thine

F.

Even as Fred detailed the changes in his military life, Lizzie remained largely in the dark, thanks to irregular mail service. She was aware of his move to Baltimore but of little else. In her first letter to survive intact since November, she focused mostly on domestic matters but with an eye to national events.

Albany N.Y.
March 5th

My very dear Husband,

I can scarce restrain myself, I am so eager and impatient to hear from you. I do not wish you to be so delighted with your change of location as to forget to write to me. If I don't hear from you pretty soon I'll make a trip to Baltimore. Your letters written the day you arrived, and enclosed with one you had designed sending by Lt Harris I received Monday the 27th Feb. I have had no letter since then. I must have one tomorrow. I charge you write regularly if you expect to have peace of mind.

I had a letter from Pa two days ago, he is quite well. He cannot yet tell whether he is to come to New York State or no, he has not had an answer to his letter, as soon as he hears I shall know. Pa was so certain in regard to the matter that he took Amelia[27] from the Normal School in Montreal and took her to Perth in order that she might visit with sister Olivia before coming here. . . . Amelia would be great company for me when Emma goes.[28] . . .

The President has again entered upon another 4 years term; may it prove a less trying and troublous term than the one that has just expired. Yesterday was to have been a day of rejoicing in New York they were to have a grand celebration, but if the weather was as unfavourable there as it was here it must have put a stop to all their preparations. . . .

. . .

Monday morning. I am writing this letter by snatches. A letter from you just arrived this morning. You are in Annapolis now. . . . I do not think it will be wise to break up housekeeping this summer. 3 or 4 weeks in the country and then have your own house to come to is the best thing. Children are best at home, no where are they so free and happy as at home. I will write more on this subject bye and bye. . . .

Yours in haste and devotion
Lizzie M.L.

With Fred's remove from Petersburg and thus from harm's way, his and Lizzie's future was less troublous, but it was hardly untroubled. As Lizzie's letter reflected, money matters and an unknown future dominated their worries now. Even as they contemplated arrangements for the coming summer Elizabeth wondered if she should visit him in camp in the meantime, now that he was safely away from the front. What their letters meant to each other and the anticipation of being together again grew more urgent as Fred seemed more assured of surviving the war.[29]

Lizzie admitted to being in debt, "more I know than you think," even though "we practice the strictest economy" and "spend no money foolishly."[30] A week later, on the same day she told of borrowing $150 from Emma. Having finally been paid, Fred received $205, $75 of which he would send in small amounts. The rest he needed for his own debts. It was not enough, he knew, so he encouraged her to ask her grandma for help, which Elizabeth had already done.[31] Later that month, after being paid again, he would send $85 by express, and further on, he would ask for an accounting of her debts—and learn they would owe more than $200, about $3,500 in today's dollars, when he returned home.[32]

In his letter of March 5, Fred minced financial matters further and then lamented the despair betrayed in her previous letter, explaining more explicitly than ever before how much her letters meant to him. He then waxed poetic with what they both called "nonsense."

Camp Parole Annapolis M[d]

March 5th 1865

My dearest Wife,

Since I last wrote, I have had the happiness to receive three delightful letters from you: two addressed to Petersburgh, and one to Fort McHenry, Md. More are still due as the one you allude to in your last as containing an exposition of your financial affairs, has not yet reached me. The Paymaster came yesterday and paid me for 1 month & 28 days—to Dec[r] 31st $205.50. Of this amount I cannot possibly spare you more than $75. . . .

What was the matter with you when you wrote that you had lost all interest in household affairs—that a lethargy had settled upon you which rendered all exertion a burden—and shrouded the future with darkest hues? I know it was but the expression of a morbid feeling—which had most probably purged off your mind before the characters which conveyed it came to hand. But it produced an unpleasant effect upon my feelings. Instead of the buoyant elasticity of youth; the ever-confident love for me, and the interest in the children, which attributes in my mind you are ever undoubtingly invested with, I had a picture <u>incised</u> into me of marital gloom, exhaustion—and <u>désepoir</u>.[33] Perhaps you do not fairly estimate the power your sentiments exercise upon me. My being here is dull—the tireless monotony of a military life in the trenches would weary any one; but when I abandon myself to home recollections—where the pure beings there concentred are transfigured with feelings of purest devotion—and whom time and distance have hallowed until they assume an air of sacredness: then to have the central and chiefest character of this magic grouping utter such doleful and inharmonious strains—it destroys the whole allusion—as Ophelia says—"it is like sweet bells jangled out of tune and harsh."[34] You young Uzzite! (Job came from Uz,[35] you know), if you indulge in any more such sentimental Wertherisms,[36] I will commence a legal process for the recovery of the $5 I paid for you—and send you back to your relatives for medical treatment.

Your Aunt Maria is with you again? She will want to see this letter. You cannot show it to her. I cannot bring myself down to the level of talking common-sense to you. I wooed you with my facile extravagances, and with a girl's guilelessness and warmth of passion, you generously accepted my uncurbed metaphors as a faithful express of the love I avowed. My fugitive destiny has allowed me so little hum-drum domestic intercourse with you since you have graced my hearth as a Bride—that the passionate yearning of a lover towards you has never been weaned from my breast. Still to me you are my Bird of Paradise—my queen of Song—my loved one in whom are many delights. When you shall become staid and matronly—and I assume slippers—an arm-chair and that "large volume" you talk about; then I will try to address you in well-chosen terms—and my discourse shall be mature and weighty with good sense. But ere that unwelcome time we yet have an interval measuring how long? Fifteen years? ten years? No matter. The day is not yet upon us. It is nature with us all to prefer amusement to instruction, so I yet arrogate the right to play the antic with my pen when I choose it. I do not address a staid wife—with a frilled coiffure, and an overwhelming sense of propriety: but rather a mischievous young malapert, an April embodiment, whose tormenting raillery and unfathomable sobriety are responsive to inscrutable influences. How now, Audrey, do my features send you? To teach you—to have you scold and love, and see you tax your unmathematical brain to compound a pudding for your husband's dinner; to know you innocent and trust and feel the rich possession of such worth with a claim whose genuineness is undisputable. Psha! I am writing another billet doux—does your appetite for this style of composition remain? What about going to board this summer? I still advocate it. I suppose this recall of our regiment will defeat our Minnesota project. It is rather far away and I fear the Winter's are severe. But for a single matter of culinary abundance—we might sit up o' nights to feed. Love to Emma and the young imps.

Thine with decaying imperceptible affection

F.

Lizzie waited a week to respond to this effusion, and when she did, her letter was fairly well all business until the end, when she commented: "Your last was quite a billet doux, it suits me well some times, my appetite for nonsense is unabated. ought I to be ashamed to say so?"

Before receiving this letter, Fred had written again, this time providing a rare glimpse into life among newly released and unruly Union prisoners of war at Camp Parole, Annapolis.[37]

Camp Parole Annapolis Md

March 7th

Ma plus chére <u>Femme</u>—

Another welcome letter from you to-day—dated Mar 1st. You seem like myself full of business. I have just finished my muster rolls— after a solid week's work upon them. I received a great compliment from the Paymaster last Saturday. He pronounced my last rolls for batt[y] F (made out while Ham. Berry[38] was home) the neatest—the clearest—and the best finished rolls that had ever passed through his Office. I tell you I am getting red tape through me to some effect. I am Officer of the day aujourd'hui[39]—I wear a red silk sash over my Shoulder and round my waist—carry my sword all day— and perform the duties of chief constable. Yesterday there was fun in camp, and today we had a reckoning. The sutler advanced his prices—apples he sells for 15¢ each and cigars the same. In reprisal the boys determined to go thro' him. We have about six thousand paroled prisoners here—without organization or discipline—and they could raise quite a tumultuous mob if they were allowed the least heading. The Officer commanding this post Lt Col. Chamberlain[40]—an old and scarred soldier learned of their intentions, and had Lt. Berry—Officer of the day—and his guard paraded to resist the onset. Berry, grim as death—just the man for the occasion—deployed his force along the railway track—giving them instructions to aim low and not fire till they received the command. On came a strong body—seven or eight hundred—a reconnaissance in force—the Col. met them ordered them back to their quarters—and snatched one Serg^t bald-headed (as the phrase is) who ventured to give him some talk back. The determination of this Officer—and the proximity of the bright muskets daunted them. They slunk off one by one—and the threatened raid was squelched. This morning at Guard mounting when I reported for instructions—I was ordered to have my guard in line at 10 o'clock. At the given hour the whole of the paroled prisoners were formed on the parade ground—in three Battalions four deep—and the Col. made a speech. It was a fine specimen of military oratory. Said he, "While I recognize in these ranks some excellent soldiers—I also declare there is a large infusion of d—d mean dogs. The influence of these men is pernicious and I warn every soldier who has any self-respect—any regard for the cause in which he took arms, to beware of it. These men were not taken in honorable conflict. I have not served 11 years in the army without knowing something [about] how these things work. They are skulkers—stragglers—coffee-coolers—dead beats. They do not go near a fight. They straggle on the march and are picked up. In the event of confusion in our lines these men will take no chances to escape—their first impulse is to throw away their guns unbuckle their belts and surrender." The old fellow harangued them in this strain for awhile—and then demanded of all those who carried concealed weapons to deliver them up to the Officer of the day— who would deposit them with the Adj^t for transmission to their homes. At this point I marched up my guard—deployed them as a thin skirmish line around the entire mass—and taking the Serg^t and a man with me had them file past me—that I might detect those who carried weapons. The search resulted in the capture of three revolvers. The affair passed off quietly and quiet is again restored.

. . .

February–March 1865

I am now employed reading Sir Walter Scott's <u>Abbott</u>[41]—it is one of his most successful compositions. Do the children get much reading matter? I should like Josie to spend at least an hour a day in reading. If she has access to books do not attempt to control her taste. Given a healthy intellect and a pure mind—there is nothing that can sully its whiteness—it is self-preserving—it is so skillful an alchemy that it will deduce sustaining nutriment from utter poison. God controls these things; we can leave results to the governance of his infallible laws. I must tire you with my long letters—shall I abbreviate them? If I recover the faculty of writing—I shall overwhelm you with my verbosity. However I suppose you will survive the infliction. Good bye chick—I'll bite a piece off your cheek the first chance as a token of love.

F.E.L.

21

The Little Mischief
March–April 1865

Rarely was Camp Parole not plagued by meagre supervision and an insufficiency of guards, and the problem grew particularly severe when Grant recruited as many able-bodied men as possible to strengthen his final push against Richmond and Petersburg that March. Thus, the guard contingent at Camp Parole was stripped to a skeleton force. Inadequate to the task, Lockley and his ninety or so Seventh New Yorkers would be replaced.[1]

Camp Parole Annapolis Md
March 12th 1865

My dear wife

I supposed we should be stationed here for some time to come and had made myself comfortable for a long sojourn. But to-day we received an order to proceed to Baltimore on the arrival of other troops to relieve us, what our destination will be there we have yet to learn. Lt. Mather and the rest of the Paroled officers of our reg[t] remain here until they receive their leaves which are hourly expected. . . . I wrote a hasty letter to you yesterday and have not time to write to you much in detail to-day—as I am busy packing up—and shall probably march to-day. I am not sorry to leave here—our guard is miserably insufficient for the duties of this post—and the Co. Comdg here is quite apprehensive of an outbreak amongst the men held here awaiting exchange. Satan finds some mischief still for the idle hands to do—and the enforced idleness and military restraint in which these men are held here, prompt them to all kinds of excesses. Yesterday I was officer of the day and the men getting whiskey freely amongst themselves became drunken and riotous—and I was busy half the night preserving the peace of the camp and arresting the most noisy ones. At this moment several hundred <u>fresh fish</u>, as they call them have arrived—and every addition aids to swell the current of mischief which forever flows in our midst. I suppose the Col. has procured a larger force—which is greatly needed.

. . .

Au revoir—Sweetheart—you are almost uppermost and most welcome to my thoughts.

F.

Having arrived at Fort Federal Hill in Baltimore, Fred and others commenced building quarters for themselves, but no sooner had they gotten underway than they were ordered to Fort McHenry to guard Confederate prisoners. "At this post, there is a large number of rebel prisoners held—military and political—together with a thick sprinkling of deserters and bounty jumpers," he wrote upon reporting for duty. Going from a bad situation to something worse, he and his comrades disliked the change. "Everything is crude and uncomfortable."[2]

He would remain at Fort McHenry for the rest of his service, which, unknown to him and his comrades at the time, would end in June. For all they knew, they would have to serve their full three-year enlistments—that is, until mid-August.

On the positive side of settling in, exchange of correspondence became more regular and with it, Fred sent Lizzie badly needed funds.

Albany March 15th 65

My very (not) dear Husband,

A perfect shower of letters today, not less than four and three of them from you. . . .

But in regard to your letters Fred one was dated the 11th not quite so long as some of your letters but cheerful and conversational, in it $10 dollars was enclosed, you mentioned having sent me two $25's beside the $22 enclosed in Emma's. This announcement made me feel quite uneasy for the second $25 had not come to hand, I feared it was forever lost but my mind was set at rest this afternoon by the arrival of the truant letter. I wonder what could have detained it. You had written me two, and E one since you sent that. The third letter announced the fact that you had orders to pack and march to Baltimore. I do most fervently trust and pray that you will not be sent back to the front again.

I hope the change will prove a pleasant one; I was sorry when you wrote that you had been sent to Camp Parole, for I felt sure that an unruly set were there you could scarcely expect it to be otherwise, among such a mixed multitude. I shall await with anxiety your next letter. Would you like to return to <u>Fort Reno</u>?

I very much fear that you are stinting yourself Fred in sending me so much money. I have received $82 altogether that is what you sent is it not? But I would not send any more this way Fred, it seems somewhat risky, would it not be better to send it by express or if possible send a check?

I had the <u>exquisite pleasure</u> of seeing Aunt Maria safely on board the cars for Mechanicsville yesterday. She has made herself very useful indeed assisting me in repairing and lengthening the childrens dresses and other articles of clothing. She is very industrious and persevering, she worked incessantly and made me work too, not even allowing me time to write to you at the usual times. I gave way for the sake of peace knowing it was to be of short duration. I am sorry to say that there is material dislike between Mrs M and Emma. You know how rough and abrupt Aunt M is, when I think she goes to[o] far I come down upon her, give her a piece of my mind and am done with it. I do not allow her to impose upon me. But there are many unpleasant things which I pass over, because she is my visitor. E having a positive dislike to her would not pass over little things and the consequence was that they had a spat nearly every evening. She [Emma] may be glad to rec a little assistance from Aunt M while she stays in Schuylerville at least it would be more pleasant to be upon good terms.

. . .

. . . I am glad you approve of my decision not to break up house keeping. . . . You ask me if I wish you to abreviate your letters. No not exactly. Your letters are a great source of comfort. No! no! I could not endure it if I was deprived of your frequent loving and cheerful words. . . .

. . . I wish I could see into your quarters tonight and know where you are and what you are doing. Good night undisturbed repose and pleasant dreams of home.

Most lovingly, Lizzie

While at Fort McHenry, Fred labored at a variety of tasks, all largely desk work but challenging and time-consuming—from service as judge advocate for court martials, to reconstituting his regimental and company records, to working as commissary general of prisoners on the brigade staff. He lamented particularly the difficulty in reconstituting records:

All the men who have been killed in action—who have died in hospital—who have been done to death in rebel prisons—who have been transferred—or discharged—or have deserted—all these men require to have their final statements rendered to the war department giving an accurate statement of their account with the government; the amount of U.S. bounty paid and yet due; the length of time yet to be paid for; the amount of clothing drawn together with full particulars of their military history.

To accomplish that, "I have the most confused company books and the most imperfect records you can well imagine. Accordingly," he said, "I have procured new books from the quartermaster—and have undertaken to write the records all afresh."[3]

Lizzie in the meantime had kept him informed of affairs at home, including her father's move to New York to take a position with the *New York Tribune*, her receipt of various amounts of money from him—"I only write to acknowledge the receipt of the money by express namely $85 dollars, money, money. Soon I shall be out of debt"[4]—his sister Emma's preparations for opening her millinery shop in Schuylerville, and her Aunt Maria's visit to Albany.

Fred's comrades also visited her on occasion. "Lt Mather called on Friday in company with his Father . . . he called so early that he found me looking like <u>Sam Hill</u>," she admitted, adding, "I am always sure to be in costume when any of your soldier friends chance to call." Mather had offered to take a small package to Fred when he returned to camp. "Perhaps he would convey me," she wrote suggestively. "I would not make such a very large parcel."[5]

For Fred, proximity to Baltimore was an ongoing temptation, but work and faithfulness kept him moored. Fort McHenry proved a notable contrast with what he had seen at Annapolis.

Fort McHenry Md Mar 24 1865

My dear little Chick

Your letters come more regularly now. I receive on an average two a week. One charming missive reached me this morning—and one earlier in the week. I don't know how I am going to find time to write to you, though. I'll be hanged if I haven't got a busier job than any I have yet had. I am kept driving early and late. I steal a few moments to address you but I must make up for it by working later this evening. I suppose when I get more familiar with my duties I shall find the performance of them less irksome. There are two classes of Officers in this Regiment—the ornamental and the useful. I suppose I must class myself with the latter from the fact that whenever a laborious task presents itself it is sure to be put upon "Lockley." I do want a little leisure badly. I have been promising myself to do a little writing on my own account, but small show has there been for this same so far. Would you believe that I have not read more than sixty or seventy pages in Charles O'Malley?[6]

Well, I suppose you are getting tired of this subject. We are getting comfortable here—have good roomy quarters. I and three other Officers have started a mess—we have bought a cooking stove, and necessary culinary utensils—and have a sort of cook and enjoy tolerably good fare. Our proximity to so opulent and fashionable a city as Baltimore affords quite a relief to the tedium and monotony of garrison life; still I cannot help comparing my fate with that of Tantalus. He was doomed, you remember, to have water forever babbling near his lips, but when he stooped to drink, it fled from his reach. I am reminded by my occasional mingling with

That sex which is the type

Of all we know or dream of beautiful,[7]

of the rich and varied joys which await me at home; but a blue uniform[,] a piece of parchment and "an oath—an oath! I have an oath in heaven!" keep me as effectually sundered, as if the sluggish impassive Styx flowed between me and civilization.

Things are looking healthy, tho! Gold down to 150 and our generals having it all their own way. Not many days can lapse before the decisive blow will be struck. Then won't we have a glorification!

Five hundred rebel prisoners embarked from here to-day to be sent to Wilmington to be exchanged. They presented rather a different appearance from our poor union devils whom I saw disembark at Annapolis after being delivered from the tender mercies of the Rebels. These men were rugged and hearty, fit to take up arms and do lusty battle in support of their failing cause. Among those landed at Annapolis was a Serg[t] Morgan[8] (Chief of police Morgan's son of Albany.) He was captured at Ream's Station because he was afraid to take his chances in running across a corn field which the rebels had an artillery and musket fire upon. The way those devils peppered us was alarming to weak nerves. An officer a few yards from me was blown literally to pieces with a shell which exploded as it struck him. This Serg[t] Morgan was carried ashore in a stretcher and died six hours after he landed. Another serg[t] (Sullivan)[9] who remained in the pit with him died in the rebels['] hands. The choice was a hard one—but I prefer running for it.

I cannot fill this Sheet so fill three sides. I throw an old shoe after Emma. She ought to put up with your Aunt's angularities— for she has a heart—with a touch of Nature on it. Good bye—how long now till the day of Ascension.

My watch is not worth a d—.

Frederic E. Lockley

Lieut Judge Advocate

Thus did Frederic find little sympathy for Confederate prisoners, as he related in a telling incident in camp.

My dear Wife,

We have a captain appointed to Comp F. which of course relieves me of the command. I have had two days of studious leisure. Being so near to Baltimore the officers are all crazy to spend their leisure in that city. but my stay at home habits still cling to me here—I can find amusement enough in my own quarters to detain me. I have been writing—you will find more memoranda enclosed—do you read these jottings from memory? do you like them? . . .

We have five hundred rebel officers confined here. The prisoners['] barracks are so full—that these men are confined in the open grounds. The weather is pleasant—though chilly— but they must have a tedious time of it. Most of them are Marylanders—and they have quite an intelligent look. Yesterday four ladies—an old gentleman—and little child drove into the gate in a carriage—friends of one of the prisoners. They are surrounded with a guard—and are allowed intercourse with no one. So all the satisfaction these friends had was to station themselves outside the guard—and gaze at their captive friend. In the party were the rebel officer's father, mother, wife and child. He wanted the young one to advance and kiss him—but the child would not venture from its mother. A corporal forgetting his duty and prompted by kind feelings carried the child to its father— who fondly embraced him. I, with one or two other bystanders condemned the action of the corporal—and the sergeant censured him and ordered the child back to its mother and her away. This seems rough—it is trampling upon the most sacred instincts of our nature—but it is War. They are rebels—traitors—they have caused all the desolation which afflicts our country—they are the authors of their own woes. I have heard enough of their inhuman treatment of our poor fellows captive in their hands to stifle in my breast all feelings of humanity towards them. With whatsoever measure ye mete it shall be meted unto you.

. . .

Do not let your employm[ts]. prevent you from writing regularly— You are a good girl in that respect and deserve a sugar plum. Love to Emma and the womankind. Accept a kiss and a patronizing pat. Good-bye hussy!

F.E.L.

She did not respond to this letter for two weeks because she had not received it, although she posted other letters in the interim. When it did come to hand, she would answer it with similar playfulness.

In truth, with the end of the war in sight, their separation grew unbearable. They were genuinely infatuated, and he wanted to see and be with her as much as she did with him. For several weeks they deliberated the idea of her coming to camp on visit. It would never happen, but their desires to see each other were palpable. In fact, he could not tolerate the least indication that she was less eager than he. When Lizzie had said, innocently enough, that his effusions of March 5 had been "quite a billet doux" and that his nonsense suited her well "sometimes," he took offense. His effusions suited her only *sometimes?* Protesting vehemently, he confessed, "I think of you until I am unable to contain myself." He likened her response to an anecdote involving Emma. When a gentleman extended his hand to his sister while she was sewing, she had forgotten the needle still in her fingers and pricked him with it when she took his hand. "Your reciprocation is about as cordial."[10]

Feathers still ruffled, he admitted the following later in the same letter:

> I have lucid intervals—there are times when I can transact official business as punctiliously as another man—but when I sit down to address you—and abandon my feelings to the magnetism of your influence—all sense of staid decorum immediately departs from me—and I become mutable—love-lorn and rattle-brained. Then when you undertake to play Madame Prim—and affectedly tell me that when you are indulgent you can receive a little nonsense Lord! I want to get at you![11]

He need not have worried. In her next, Lizzie was quite reassuring. The children were not home from school yet, and her responses to his fretfulness became mixed with other concerns, such as receipt of more of his memoranda on the war and his sister's move to Schuylerville, there to sell bonnets she made by hand. Lizzie would go to Schuylerville to help Emma get established. Still composing her letter when the girls arrived home from school, she had to complete it with seven-year-old Gertie, now able to read, peering over her shoulder.[12]

Albany March 28th 1865

My very dear Husband,

I wait not for my usual writing day but as I have a little leisure, and the house quite to myself I will devote an hour to you. . . .

. . .

A letter from you just received tis dated the 27th how very quickly it has come because it brings good news I suppose; I should be perfectly delighted could I have the joy of spending a week with you my heart beats fast to think of so much happiness but I mean not to think too much about it, lest by some unforeseen accident I might be prevented from going. I shall not speak of it at present, not even to Emma I think.

What a tide of glorious war news flows in upon us from all sides we are having it all our own way most decidedly. Tis selfish I know but we are all more or less selfish where the safety of the dearest one on earth to us is concerned. I felt so thoughtful when I read the particulars of the engagement before Petersburgh to know that you were not in the conflict.[13] I see your old corps the 2nd were engaged in the contest. May you be allowed to smoke your pipes in safety and quiet for the rest part of your term. Is your Col a fighting man? Or does he enjoy the quieter mode of life in garrison?

I always take the liberty of reading the memoranda you send tis always fraught with interest to me. I know not how to give compliments or I should try my skill upon you. My love for you blinds me to any faults you may have. I fear sometimes that it amounts almost to idolatry but you are worthy [of] all the love I can bestow. . . . The children will be home from school in a few minutes then adieu to quiet. They are full of animal spirits and seem not to have a thought for anything. I wish their childhood to be free and joyous; a bright and lovely oasis to look back upon. They are very dear to me.

Emma has been away since morning buying goods and constructing bonnets (not breastworks). She begins to dread the time coming when she must leave the time set is a week from to day. I do not want to stay longer than a week at Schuylerville. I would take one of the children but I think Auntie[14] is so unsettled that she might perhaps be in the way.

As you say I must write regularly while away. I will strive to do so. Tutie is trying to read my letter the little mischief and she succeeds admirably; a little while ago I did not care how much she overlooked me but now the rogue can read writing. I must look out for her.

Adieu darling

Most truely your Wife

Lizzie

Then came the fall of Richmond.[15] Fred was jubilant. The end of the war was inevitable. For her part, Lizzie was embarking for Schuylerville with Emma to help with the new millinery shop. Fred was eager to help, but his thoughts were on Richmond.

Fort McHenry Md. Apl 5, 1865

Wife

I have sent Emma a flaming advertisement, extolling her wares to the Seventh heaven. If she can get it extensively published through her county—in the Bungtown Annihilator and such like—it will be the making of her. By the bye, I want you to keep your eyes open—learn all the mysteries of shirring, framing and piling up the magnificent mountain of indescribable conglomerables which raises beauteous woman so many chipekcs[16] above her natural attitude. There is a story current here that when our troops entered Richmond, two of the men who entered President Davis's house were seized with symptoms of delirium tremens. It was afterwards proved that these trembling spasms were not induced by an immoderate use of intoxicating spirits, but that Mrs Davis's last darling of a bonnet which in the confused state of her household she had forgotten to put away, met their eyes as they entered her chamber, and their apprehensive imaginations immediately construed it into a horrid explosive device intended to blow them and the whole habitation into minutest particles.

I hope things <u>is</u> prospering. Everybody is delirious here over the capture of the Rebel capital. Baltimore has been gloriously hilariously and patriotically drunk ever since the news first arrived. Tonight we are to have a general illumination, bonfires, free liquors, music and buncombe. I don't know but I shall make one of the fools. The rebel prisoners here don't like the present aspect of affairs at all. They believe the evacuation of Richmond to be another blessing in disguise, and think that Lee has abandoned the rebel capital in order to get Grant just where he wants him. I spoke to some of them to-day whom I saw working under guard. "What do you Johnnies intend to do," I asked, "now the Confederacy has gone up? Come over to Uncle Sam again—and be good boys?" "The Confederacy hasn't exactly gone up yet, you'll find," one of them answered. "There will be an awful sight of powder burnt yet before old Lee or Davis either will give up whipped." "Tut, man!" said I, "They have given up already. Your president has left his wife in Genl. Grant's hands—and Lee is hurrying the remnants of his troops away in perfect rout. Why, they cant fight another battle." They gazed at me incredulously. "Things ain't all as you gentlemen represent it," one of them replied.

The little Angel (that's the name they gave Maj. Hobbs) with two officers and about forty men are cruzing in the bay in the hope of picking up Jeff. Davis. It would be a huge thing if they could succeed in capturing him. Write often—or I will engage your grandma to box your ears for me. Love and best respects and warm congratulations to your respected female relatives. Goodbye, Duck

F.

Once arrived in Schuylerville, Lizzie wrote infrequently, and Fred complained of not hearing from her. On April 9, two days before he wrote his next letter, Gen. Robert E. Lee agreed to Gen. Ulysses S. Grant's surrender terms at Appomattox Court House. The war was all but over, pending final surrender of other Confederate forces, yet none of these events warranted mention in their correspondence, which otherwise was full of domestic news and scenes immediate to hand.[17]

Fort McHenry, Md.

April 11th 1865

Ma chére Femme,

You are abusing me shamefully—not a word except a few pencilled lines for more than a week. I can't live on such insufficient aliment. I shall be found some morning a clayey corpse in my bed. When I took you to task for putting me off with brief, cursory, hastily written messages—I am not aware that I expressed myself in any such manner as would justify you in the inference that I would rather have none than such. I urge you to think more of my wants—and minister more liberally to their satisfaction. Transcendent military successes will do, the termination of the war is not unacceptable; beer, national salutes and patriotic blather are all well enough. But these are public affairs. The old person over there with the fruit stand is as much interested in these matters as I am. I want love assurances from my wife—pleasant talk about home events—and now and then a little wifely adulation, which falls more sweetly upon my ears than the music of the spheres.

. . .

Admiral Farragut[18]—landed at Baltimore to-day—our regiment acted as escort.[19] Everything pleasant except the mud, and that we had a prodigal plenty. The Court Martial is still in session—it keeps me fully employed. Capt. Courtney[20] my Comp[y] commander has gone, together with thirty men, in an armed steamer to Indian Creek—to gather up the remains of the Harriet DeFord[21] a steamer which the guerrillas seized and burnt. If he can come across any of the men his instructions are to catch them or kill them. I have no news to write. I address this to Albany—as there is a doubt in my mind whether it would reach Schuylerville in time to meet you. . . .

It's quite chilly—I must have a fire lighted. Good bye! Negligent hussy!

F.

Lizzie had just returned to Albany worn out, but she felt compelled to answer his pleas for a letter anyway. Delighted that he might still arrange for her to visit him in camp, she nevertheless remained skeptical.

Albany
Apr 14th 1865

My very dear Husband,

I am home again once more; came last evening but as the house
was in a happy state of confusion, I left the babies at Mrs D[']s, and
went over to Smallwood's to sleep. I had a long and rather tedious
journey home, left Schuylerville at 10 ½ A.M. and reached Albany 7
P.M. The roads were very bad but we did not happen to stick fast in
the mud, as we did on our way up.

I am perfectly worn out, if it were not that you plead so
anxiously for a letter, I would certainly put you off. I wrote twice
to you while in S—, on my arrival last evening I found a letter with
memoranda enclosed, also two coppies of the military Register of
Company F. You must have a little patience with me Fred, and not
blame me to[o] seriously for writing with lead pencil. I thought
it would be better than no letters. I rec two letters from you at
S—one enclosed in a letter to Emma, the other addressed to
myself. You have not I see given up the idea of my visiting you; and
you wish me to bring Gertrude with me. I have no doubt she will be
highly delighted to accompany me. I shall not speak of it however
till it is settled when we shall go. I almost wish you had said Dollie
on account of her puny looks, but it shall be just as you say. I have
no preference, only I thought a trip might be of benefit to her.
She is not sick only delicate looking as she always has been. Mrs D
gave a pretty favorable report of the Lockley Corps, only one thing
you erred in appointing Jossie / Sergt. Mrs. D says it should have
been Dollie as she was the most orderly of all. The children gave
me a hearty welcome. You would have thought I had been absent a
month instead of a week it is a cause of great gratification to me to
know that they miss me, and long for my return when absent from
them for a short time. Emma I think felt a little lonely when I left
her yesterday, she has laughingly called me Mother since I have
been there because I gave orders to the woman who cleaned for
her and was general business woman. Emma was still staying at Mrs.
Mair's when I came away[,] her house not being in readiness she
will write to you soon and give you particulars. Excuse this scrawl. I
will write on Sunday if all is well.

. . . The babes are well and desire kindest and best love to their dear Papa. Lovingly your negligent

Hussey

E.M.L.

Not having received this letter yet and still eager to hear from her, Fred toyed with the idea of rejoining the army. Many of his buddies were considering duty in Mexico, where they might help Liberal forces under Benito Juárez resist the imperial designs of the French and the Hapsburg archduke, Maximilian. Then again, he thought not. Instead, he read letters written by the Confederate prisoners in their charge—and bore them little pity.

Fort McHenry Md. April 14 [1865]

You continue your complaints of not receiving letters from me—I have written regularly twice a week—one letter I sent to Schuylerville—and one to Mr Duncan—presume by this time they have both come to hand. I have been writing since 6 this morning[;] it is now noon—and I am wearied hand and brain. Col McCaulay[22] our Brigade Commander promises to dissolve the court to-morrow—then I shall have a little leisure again. I shall then be detailed as Commissary General of Prisoners on the Brigade staff—a responsible office and a very respectable position.

The war being over our men are all full of going to Mexico to relieve Emperor Maximilian of his troubles there—Col. Duryea is about to make application to be counted in on that service in the event of any difficulty arising. If it were not for the old lady and kids I should much like to participate—but under present circumstances I shall respectfully decline. I have serious thoughts of tendering my resignation early in June—I am getting very restless and there will be no difficulty in getting out of the service.

We have been having a grand time. Our Brigade acted as escort to Admiral Farragut on his visit to Baltimore—and the next day he visited this Fort—accompanied with the principal men of the city.

This is rather different from soldiering at the front. The weather is lovely—Excuse a short letter—I will do better next time. I am sorry Duncan is going to leave Albany—has he engaged or is the thing only talked about? Would you like to take his house—what rent does he pay—I suppose he has a lease and could transfer it.

5–15 P.M. I went to dinner, some friends visited us—there are three of us mess together—Lts. Pettit,[23] Wilsey[24] & myself—after dinner I strolled into the Fort with them—dropped into Brig. HdQrs—and there found the Col's aide up to his eyes in Confederate literature. He had at least half a bushel of letters to read written by the rebel prisoners to their friends. At his invitation I sat down and read about a hundred. It is rather a painful exercise reading these effusions. Yearnings for home—complaints of ill-treatment—bitterness at the defeat—of their army and the ruin of their cause—no generous acceptance of the arbitration of war. Of the large number I read not three were fairly written and correctly spelt. Those that are illegible are destroyed—I tore up several in disgust. These people four years ago to-day made it their boast that they had humbled the American Flag—that flag is the emblem of national greatness—free institutions—and general virtue and intelligence. In its place what have they attempted to substitute? It has cost rivers of blood to vindicate the case of right—and now let us legislate that Right shall remain in the ascendant. I believe in some of these traitors paying with their lives or property the price of their sins. Enow

Thine

22

A Soul Struggling to Be Free

April–May 1865

However focused Fred and Lizzie were on their immediate cares, national events finally intruded. The stunning news of Lincoln's assassination at Ford's Theater the night of April 14 and his death in the early morning of April 15 pulled them up short, as it did the rest of the nation. Neither Frederic nor Elizabeth ever mentioned remembering where they were or what they were doing the moment they learned of the president's assassination, but both would comment feelingly about it soon afterward.[1] Having attended church on the morning of April 16, Easter Sunday, Frederic returned to camp to collect his thoughts in a letter home.

Fort McHenry, Md. April 16–1865

Ma chére petite femme,

Your letters are somewhat interrupted but I suppose you will settle down soon and resume your customary habit. You must tell me how you left Emma—how she likes the appearance of things— and what her business prospects are. the young ones are glad to have you back again, I have no doubt.[2] I presume they grew just as homesick as you did. How much do you or I—for I suppose it is all the same—owe Emma now? I wish you would give me a correct list of your debts including <u>everything</u>. Are Mr. Davis and Mr. Faker paid yet. I shall receive pay again in about twenty days then I will send you enough to discharge all your debts, if they are not too large. Do not neglect to give me a list of all your indebtedness.

This fearful trajedy has found plenty of work for our detachment. One officer (Lt. Weed) and twenty-five men are patrolling the river with two field pieces to prevent any vessels leaving Baltimore—two companies are under command of the provost marshal who has them picketed along the railroad to prevent any egress from the city by that way. So far the diabolical villians [*sic*] are not caught, but the police authorities feel confident of their arrest before long. And the remainder of our forces are under arms ready at a moment's notice for service. The embargo upon the railroads I see by this morning's paper, is removed, and the fears of any outbreak in the city are now quieted down.

I could not believe that the death of a public character could have afflicted the individual mind with so poignant a feeling of grief as "this sudden taking off" of our national chief has produced. Men grieve for him as for the loss of a parent. He has carried us through the maelstrom of civil war with so undaunted and skillful a hand; he has shown such an impassibility to any human infirmity of temper, rising like a demigod above all the angry and senseless invective with which his name and character have been assailed. The amiable Stephen who asked forgiveness of the Almighty for the act of his assassins, "Father, forgive them! they know not what they do!" does not shine forth more prominently as one impersonation of the Christian spirit of meekness and forbearance, than the martyred Statesman has uniformly evinced during all his dealings with this foul rebellion which has sought to hurl him from his seat—which has dis-quieted his days—and tortured him until his health gave way. Four years of provocation have failed to rankle his breast to any feeling of resentment. And when the time had at length arrived wherein his enemies ceased to oppose his government, and he had ceased to fight them, his kindly spirit at once prompted him to extend forgiveness to all. The golden opinions he has won hallow his memory, and the affections concentre around him as one of our own household.

Then his death creates such a gap in all our plans for our political future. For four years of political convulsion his name has been upon our lips so constantly that he has become identified with the age and the events which are to grow out of it. We cannot dissociate his name from our purview; with him away it seems as if our history had come to a sudden collapse.

April–May 1865

I attended church this morning. The exercises were painful. Sitting there with Meditation for your counsellor, as I listened to the preacher's powerful contrast between the exuberant feeling which brightened every face as we gathered together at our last Sabbath worship to render God thanks for our signal victories, and to sing poeans at our delivery from the dark wilderness of desolation, and our feelings <u>now</u>. A great nation humbled in the dust, a great man fallen this day in Israel. Dr. Johnson says that the talk of the public heart being afflicted at the death of a public character, is mere exaggeration—people grieve but for their own friends. Until today I would have sworn by that scripture. But this even disproves the doctor's saying. I could not keep my countenance composed—I could not restrain my tears—and I noticed there were but few dry eyes in church. The president does not seem a stranger to us. Common danger and common affliction have knitted the people's heart to his—he has been with us in every moment of reverse and humiliation—the destiny of the country was in his hand—and every man knew that if human wisdom and the patriot's integrity could preserve our honor unsullied—the foresight and the truth were in that leader's brain and heart to go through triumphantly with us. Particularly was he the soldier's friend. During this fearful carnival of blood when the enraged passions of man were lashed into a tempest—and statesmanship was thrust aside until the shock of encountering armies one side or the other was borne to the ground, we all knew and felt that in the President we possessed a friend who was ready to every appeal—who watched the struggle in silent awe, and whose hand was extended to avert the strife the moment it could be done without compromising our national honor.

This Easter Sunday, the Christian church from time immemorial has adopted this as a season of festivity and thanksgiving. This lovely April day is as pure and as radiant as the stainless soul which this day rose from the earth to redeem us. But our national grief so numbs the breast that all feelings of gladness are swallowed up in present gloom. When Byron rode over the fatal field of Waterloo and the grave of a buried friend was pointed out to him he gave expression to verses which will depict our present condition

There have been tears and breaking hearts for thee
And mine were nothing—had I such to give;
But when I stood beneath the fresh green tree
Which living waves where thou didst cease to live,
And saw around me the wide field revive
With fruits and fertile promise, and the Spring
Come forth her work of gladness to contrive,
With all her reckless birds upon the wing
I turned from all she brought to those she could not bring.[3]

   This is a perfect jeremiad—I will sing you a comic song
in my next. Don't give way to gloomy thoughts they spoil the
countenance. Young people should be merry. What are national
troubles to you? Love to the babes—a rapturous kiss—ah—nice!

F.

As Frederic composed his letter to Elizabeth that Sunday, she
wrote to him. While in Schuylerville, her house in Albany had
been broken into and various items stolen. She quickly identified the culprit as the son of her next-door neighbor. Prepared to
confront the family, the boy's mother approached Lizzie first and
together they confronted the boy, who confessed and led them
to the missing items—silver coins, jewelry and rings belonging to
the children, money, and other things. "I will tell you all about
it when I see you." She then turned to the national tragedy with
both sadness and anger.

Albany N.Y.

Apr 16th 1865

My own dear Husband,

   . . .

   O! Fred how dreadful is the stroke which has taken from the
nation its head, and plunged the land in the deepest mourning
possible at such a time as this when the end of the long and fierce
struggle seemed at hand[,] when light seems ready to break
forth, and the blessings of peace once more be restored to our
beloved land. I can not think of his sad end without shuddering

and turning sick. I was so shocked when I heard it that I felt faint. I could not believe it. What a diabolical and fiendish plot to strive to take the lives of the most useful men in the land. Tis too horid to dwell upon. F Seward[4] is reported dead also, tis too be hoped W. Seward may recover. All the public buildings and the greater part of the private dwellings are draped in mourning. Dr Sprague delivered a most impressive sermon with trembling voice and heartfelt emotion he prayed that the family and nation might be supported under this deep affliction. The church was densely crowded, all seeming to feel that a great sorrow had fallen upon them.

I hope to hear from you soon again, write me good long letters . . . God be with you.

Your devoted Wife,
Lizzie M.L.

Frederic began his next letter irritated with what appeared to be irregular mail delivery and with Emma's prickliness. "Sometimes I am a little forbearing myself—but it greatly annoys me to hear your occasional mild complaint of her unreasonableness and ill-temper." Expressions of grief for the assassinated president were ongoing in camp.[5] Many people turned to religious guidance for understanding, Frederic among them.[6] He attempted to interpret the unthinkable through parallels with Moses denied entry to the promised land and quotations from John Milton's *Paradise Lost* and Shakespeare's *The Merchant of Venice*.[7] He believed, as many did at the time, that Andrew Johnson's elevation to the presidency was fortunate. To counter all his seriousness, he added an endearing anecdote relating to his young friend, Jimmy Van Benthuysen.

Fort McHenry Md Apl 19th / 65

My dear Wife,

. . .

This is like Sunday. We had religious services this morning at which the whole garrison was present. The buildings within the fort are heavily draped—a salute of 13 guns was fired this morning at daybreak—a gun is fired every half hour—and at sunset another salute of 35 guns will be fired.

The idea I am about to express does not show any abatement of affectionate respect for our late amiable and exalted chief magistrate nor does it in any way mitigate our detestation of the perfidious wretch who dealt the assassin blow. But as loyal citizens of a great and indestructible republic the reflection affords consolation. I mean the character of the newly elected President. While President Lincoln combined incorruptible honesty, firmness, elevation of purpose and statesmanlike sagacity which have raised him to a level with the majestic Washington as well on the page of history as in the hearts of his countrymen, he still lacked that Jacksonian sternness of character which is alone the fitting one to deal with the broken remnants of this unparalleled treason, and trample out the smouldering remains of that incendiary spirit which came so near destroying the whole country. Perhaps the great Lincoln had fulfilled his mission. Concentrating in his unswerving integrity the confidence of the entire loyal people, and leading us through an uncharted country—a howling wilderness beset with danger and uncertainty—he finally brought us to another Mount Pis-gah whence we could perceive the promised land of peace and re-union spread out in sunshine before us. But like his great antitype—the Jewish Deliverer—this pleasant country he is not permitted to enter. Our Joshua arises in the person of Andrew Johnson.

> The only faithful among faithless found.[8]
> Since <u>Treason</u> is the highest crime known to the constitution, I urge dealing with it as such. What an emollient to our outraged feelings it is, to know Justice will be meted to traitors!
> For, as thou urgest Justice, be assured
> Thou shalt have justice—more than thou desir'st[9]

This statesman is ripe in experience, of unflinching moral courage, which he has evinced through an ordeal as terrible as that of the Prophet Daniel; and he brings to the work an intimate knowledge of the deadly bane of Secessia, which in his mind is intensified to keenest hatred by the afflictions and persecution which it has visited upon his head. I give the Rebels joy of their choice.

Dear me! I appear to forget that I am writing a love-letter—and not a newspaper article. Talking of love-letters—I must introduce my little friend, Jimmy Van Benthuysen again. He has been corresponding with an unknown Fair in Boston—whose dainty <u>billets-doux</u> he has shown me with great unction. The subject of interchanging photographs has been diplomatically touched upon in several communications—and I had become quite interested in the matter myself. If he had <u>too choice</u> a prize, I was going to be jealous myself. (Eh!) Well—yesterday a counterfeit presentment of their fair lady arrived. <u>Be chesm</u>! (That's a Persian oath[10] of gentility and means "my eyes!" When you wish to indulge your feelings—or give point to your expressions, always swear in a foreign tongue— because that's the thing!) What a falling off was there my countrymen! She was at least double his age—not prepossessing and not at all stylish. Never mind, youthful Jimmy, try again!

Your's for a given period.

F.

Even as Frederic wondered about his sister, Lizzie wrote to tell him of Emma's relocation to Schuylerville. Reluctantly, she also tallies her debts, as he requested.

Albany Apr 19th 1865

My very dear Husband,

I had the exquisite pleasure of rec two letters from you yesterday. . . . Had a letter from Emma yesterday she enclosed one for you which I will send herewith. You wish me to tell you concerning Emma. I think her prospect for business is good, and she has a good many warm friends there who will assist her all in their power. Her rooms are airy and pleasant, and I think she may be very happy there. She has probably moved to her own establishment by this time as she was only waiting for the paint to dry on her store floor. She will need to come down here quite frequently to buy goods, which she will I have no doubt look forward to with pleasure. I miss Emma I knew I should, but upon the whole I think I shall be happier alone. E says Grandma is not well, and the startling and dreadful news of the President[']s death quite overwhelmed and unnerved her. Grandma fails gradually, but she seems so delighted to get back to the old house once more she grew quite [tired] of being at Mrs Collins's it is so out of the way, so difficult to get the mail matter, and see agreeable friends.

You want a list of all my indebtedness Fred. I am almost afraid to tell you, it will be quite out of your power to pay all at this time. I will however at your request, give you a list of my debt. I paid Mrs Fake, her debt was $21.75. I also gave Grandma $50 from the last money you sent me towards paying up the $140 I borrowed to pay Emma.

Mrs Metcalf [Grandma] $90.00
Emma 23.29
Mr Davis, rent 30.00
Mr Cumming[11] [ditto] 25.00 to 1st May

I also owe Dr Becket, but I do not think his bill will be very large. Mrs Duncan too I have not paid for the children[']s board. This seems a good deal to one Fred; but you know quite as well as I can tell you that none of it has been incurred through extravagance, merely for the necessaries of life. . . .

You have had the honor of an introduction to Admiral Farragut he with other brave and tried men might well be styled conquering heroes. The account given of his visit and reception at Fort McHenry is very interesting. . . . Do you think seriously of resigning Fred? Good night

Most lovingly your wife
Lizzie

When Lizzie wrote of her house being broken into by a neighbor's son, she had said her heart sank, not at the loss of possessions or even for the violation of her property but rather "for the grief his mother would feel when she was made acquainted with the fact."[12] Still feeling Lincoln's death acutely, Fred took his cue from Lizzie's reasoning to deliberate further on how such things as a president's assassination could, as the sermonizers were saying, reflect God's will. He wasn't convinced it did. But he was thankful for Lizzie's convictions just the same.

Fort McHenry Md
April 21st 1865

My dear Wife,

Your letter reached me yesterday—elaborate—pleasing—and very much to your credit. It struck a note in my breast which I thought was mute to such influences. I have been painfully affected by the President's death—I have listened to and read a large number of sermons upon the subject. The theory of the preacher is that God permits these horrible scenes of bloodshed and assassination for a wise and inscrutable purpose. It has always been a cardinal point in my religious faith not to mix the name of the Almighty with sources of human violence. I can with glowing devotion trace his hand in the odor and tint of the flower, in the divine symphony of song, in the balmy evening zephyr, and the gorgeous pageantry of the setting sun. In these exhibitions of his divine artistry I love to trace the Almighty rule. Dear Mother Nature is another name for God. But when we descend to human passion and misrule, I have been accustomed to regard these universal evidences of human imperfection as resulting just as naturally from man's unfinished moral condition, as the rusting of iron when exposed to moisture. In losing Abraham Lincoln we lose a ruler endeared to us by the exercise of the most exalted qualities of human nature, but it is possible that "the deep damnation of his taking off," may have been wisely ordained. This is a subject which affords unceasing exercise for my thoughts.

What led me into this strain was the admirable Christian linc in which you speak of the depredations committed upon you by the little vagabond neighbor. I am not a Christian myself—but I thank the Almighty he has given me one in my wife. Give me a prayerful home—a pious mother—and an influence is implanted in the child of which he can never divest himself.

There! Now don't' give me any sermons . . .

. . .

I shall want you and Tute about the middle of next month—To stay one week mind you.

Your's lovingly F.

In his next, Fred said he was "dreadfully homesick." "These last sands of military service run out very tediously," but "for pecuniary reasons," he thought it best not to resign just yet. Better to wait until mid-June. It would prove a wise choice, and one in character. He had always promised Lizzie—and himself—to see things through to the end of his service. Besides, he had come too far to quit now, and he had plenty to do as he immersed himself in judge advocate duties. "I don't know but I am qualifying myself for the position of Attorney General," he quipped.[13]

Otherwise, he was, as was his wont, excessively optimistic with the emancipation from slavery in Maryland.[14] Henceforth, he believed, Maryland's young "are to be instructed in such virtues as chastity— love of truth and piety; and in the practice of sobriety and the exercise of benevolence. . . . Oh, thank God! All the delusions— and deceits and hollow shams of this counterfeit state of society, are all swept away with the reverberating cannon." Old prejudices died hard, however, and emancipation and Reconstruction would not resolve deep-seated social problems nor dispel racism. But for now, he rejoiced. "We have paid a fearful price for the goodly land we have redeemed and disenthralled," he said, echoing the hopes for redemption others embraced as well. He was correct, however, in believing history would judge the sacrifice justified.[15]

Writing on the same day, Lizzie's thoughts were more down-to-earth, relating primarily to having heard from "cousin Jack," who said he was now serving in Company H of the Eleventh Maine Volunteers under an assumed name. "This unregenerate and ungrateful boy occupies a place in my heart. I will not despair of him." Otherwise, she was elated to think she would see Fred soon. "Your constant letters come like so many pure gems. . . . Am I ready to see you in the course of three weeks? I can not think about it, it sets me wild with joy." As for visiting him at Fort McHenry with Gertrude, she said, "You have restricted Tutie and myself in regard to the time we shall spend with you we don't intend to quarrel about it now; we will come and when we get there you will find it so agreeable to have us that you will want us to prolong our stay."[16]

Such hopes would be frustrated, as they had been so many times before when one thing or another interceded. In this case, it was the lack of accommodations. He lived in a barracks, so he would

April–May 1865

have to find room for her elsewhere. The chaplain demurred their staying with his family—there was no room—and a hotel in Baltimore would cost prohibitively—$8 a night. A private family lived in a brick house outside the gate, he said. Perhaps that would be an option. He warned her also of taking board. "You will have to grub with us. . . . Our table is rather crude," but he and his comrades "will be delighted to have a lady grace the table." Still, she would need to bring tablecloths and silver spoons "to civilize our ménage a little."[17]

That was on Wednesday. By the following Tuesday, their plans were dashed. The company had moved to Fort Federal Hill. "I stay behind for a week" to finish judge advocate business, he wrote, but "this will rather upset my arrangements." He would check around Fort Federal Hill for suitable accommodations, but he expected to be home in a month, so the effort might be unjustified.[18]

Meanwhile, he found his living accommodations—more specifically, his roommate—disagreeable, but with one exception—an opportunity to teach Blacks to read and write.

Fort McHenry Md

May 3^d 1865

My dear Wife—

It is not good for man to be alone—this truth I certify to by present experience. My room-mate and commanding Officer, Capt Courtney[19] who left me yesterday is an empty headed rattle brained fellow, but he is good company, where you merely want noise and frivolity. He has a negro servant—an honest, quiet, excellent fellow. I used to give him lessons in spelling and reading—and he conceived quite a liking for me. It is really interesting to see how these ignorant darkeys take to study now the opportunity is afforded them. Of an evening when the Captain was in town and I perhaps in some other officer's quarters two or three of these sons of Night would cluster round my desk their whole souls absorbed in mastering some simple piece of dissyllabic composition. I have been so much accustomed to our apt northern children, with their bright clear eyes, and fair skins and blue veins, and quick conceptions—that now I have adopted these sable and homely pupils I can hardly accustom myself to the difference. They are attentive[,] diligent, and tolerably quick, but when you look at their yellow eyes, their thick lips and their coarse dusky features, and perceive thro' this rough exterior the scintillations of a soul struggling to be free,[20] it leads the thoughts to metaphysical inquisitions. But with the exodus of my roommate these scholastic exercises are over—and I am left to my natural habit of quiet studious retirement. Thank God the hour of my restoration to home and connubial and parental enjoyments is rapidly approaching.

. . .

F.E. Lockley

Otherwise, Fred struggled with a recalcitrant watch. It would stop a dozen times a week until he got it repaired while in Baltimore. It had gone "excellently since," he said, until this day. "I put a dozen eggs into the saucepan to boil—and consulted my watch so as to accurately time their boiling—and would you believe that after running well for six weeks the d—d thing stopped while the eggs were boiling! What would you do with such a watch?"[21]

In a more serious vein, he took exception to her saying he was fulsome in his praise of her and her letters. "'There is a touch of Irish in your composition,'" he quotes her as saying.[22] "This, I take it, is synonymous with saying that I prate without sincerity—that my devotion is mere bombastic exaggeration. It may be so. I never knew it though. . . . I am constitutionally phlegmatic, and am painfully prone to cynical reflections." It may also have been the Irish comparison that roused his ire. Whatever the case, he added, "I'll pay you for this, madam! I wish I had you here I'd stick my pen in you—it's fit for nothing else."[23]

"You saucebox," Lizzie retorted upon receiving this letter. "I have a mind not to write to you for three days. You need not be so offended at me dear Fred for saying I thought there was a touch of Irish in your composition. I know tis not blather & meaningless flattery on your part. I know you to[o] well to think that. Tis because I feel ashamed that I do not deserve all the credit you ascribe to me that I speak thus. I shall never more offend in this way tell I am an angel and I will believe it (if I can)."[24]

Delaying her visit to his camp, meanwhile, made her all the more eager to see him. "I can scarce restrain myself," she wrote. Ever since the war began, she had longed to see "a little of military life." But, "I will give it up if you think best [but] you do not know what a struggle it costs me to say so." Whatever the case, "I have finally resolved that whether there be war or peace you shall never leave us again." Would that she could have it so. Much of his subsequent thirty-year career as a newspaper journalist in the American West would be spent moving from one place to another or on assignment away from home.[25]

But that was in the future. For now, with time on his hands, Fred wrote more frequently to his three daughters, and they responded in kind.[26]

23

I Share with You in This Impatience
Early to Mid-May 1865

Lizzie said she let the girls write what they would and then she would point out what errors she found "to make them more watchful," little realizing she would precipitate a spat by relaying what seemed well-meaning enough. Dollie was on her way to Schuylerville and regretted leaving school. "If it were not that I thought it would be conducive to her bodily health . . . I would not consent to her going," Lizzie admitted, but she thought the girl would catch up quickly upon her return. Still, "I shall miss the affectionate little minx most dreadfully."[1]

While Lizzie's thoughts centered on the children, Fred's gravitated to his experiences in camp, including a visit to his commander to summarize his work as judge advocate, which prompted comments on class status that said as much about himself as it did about the general and his family. Toward the end of the letter, he commented a bit too derisively on her instructing the children. Realizing immediately that he had erred, he pled forgiveness, but he sent the letter anyway.

Fort McHenry Md
May 9th 1865

Ma chére Femme,

I have been halting between <u>three</u> opinions: whether to take a walk to Fort Federal hill, or to play a game of Cribbage with Friend Wilsey,[2] or to write a letter to the <u>old 'oman</u>. I determined not to go to the fort as it is muddy walking; I abominate cards, it seems— such a waste of time, and I hesitate to write to you for my mind and body are so stagnated, that I have no ideas to fill a letter with. So I sate down and read the New York papers. Letters from you and kids! Your letters come very irregularly—sometimes they go to Fort Federal hill—I hope your letter containing the ten dollars is there—how did you get the money—borrow it of Mrs Duncan? I remove to Federal Hill to-morrow! I do not see why you indulge in so much pathos about your disappointment in visiting me—there is still a possibility—altho' things are very uncertain. If we get paid soon—and Amelia[3] relieves you of the command you shall certainly come—if we get dis-charged while you are with us I will look after quarters—and if it is possible you shall certainly come.

I paid a visit to the Old Gen'l[4] this evening. He is very unpopular here—his manners are disagreeable—and he is suspected of Secesh proclivities. He is a superannuated old fogey to say the least. The Court Martial adjourned <u>sine die</u> yesterday, preparatory to the General issuing his order dissolving it—and I went to give an account of my Stewardship. I had a very pleasant interview with the old gentleman. His daughter, a young lady of eighteen (sweet eighteen, you know! if we could for ever retain that age!) he introduced me to her.[5] I found her a girl of superior culture—we had quite a lively conversation upon Shakspere and the musical glasses[6]—but when she ascended into aesthetics—and entertained me with her views of Egyptian antiquities, and society at West Point, and the miniature species of roses that Pa' has in his garden, and Meyerbeer's operas[7] I had to be exceedingly cautious in what I said for fear of exposing my ignorance.

You know, I believe in that mode of life where you rub closely up against society—where you take an interest in learning at which establishment you can purchase groceries for the least cost, and where the wits are sharpened in a close encounter with your fellow man. This has a tendency to knock all <u>dilettante</u>, namby-pamby mock-sentimentalism out of you. It is education for the moral feelings—and the soul expands and brightens with the contact.

But it is nice to be removed from all care of the world. To have your elegant home furnished by government, your liberal salary punctually paid—no matter whether trade is good or bad, and your society of the choicest and most elite. The nation may reek with fratricidal blood—and the victims of war may flee homeless over the barren land; you have your well-selected library—your accomplished teachers—your cultivated friends—and your luxurious home. Living in such an element the mind acquires an elegance, your carriage becomes reserved and graceful, and your air and conversation exhale a flavor of good breeding which we <u>working bugs</u> can never successfully counterfeit. It takes all kinds to make a world. Your upper-tendom may devote their energies to floriculture, upholstery, and <u>de tels arts élégants</u>—we have a more real life to live—and our thoughts must be devoted to matters of more practical import.

I am much pleased with the children's letters—they are naïves—prettily written—and eminently characteristic. But I think Josie (why do you persist in spelling her name with two s's) Your talking of pointing out their errors for their future avoidance and spelling your own words badly reminds me of Mr Pickwick trying to look stern with three large tears rolling down his waistcoat.[8]

Excuse me, ma'am! I didn't go to do it! It came out before I meant it. You spell your words all correctly you are an angel—and you have a sweet heavenly face—and there is no wonder that I married it. Tute says—"I hope I will not be disappointed about going to see you—I want to go and see you very badly." If it is possible she shall not be disappointed. . . .

. . .

good bye missus—love to the kids.

F.

Having not received this letter yet, Lizzie wrote happily of having him home soon. And he should let those who wished it continue their service in Mexico.

Albany N.Y.
May 10th 1865

My very dear Husband,

I do verily believe we shall have you in our midst very soon. The Knickerbocker yesterday morning stated that it was reported and generally believed that the 7th would be discharged this week. I don't believe that to be so. you can not depend upon that paper at all times. A letter from you yesterday. I am so greedy I would like one every day. The box sent by express arrived to day. I felt a little disappointed that there was no letter inclosed, presume you had not time to write. This is the third letter I have written today, one to Pa[9] and one to Emma. Had a letter from Emma this morning she inclosed one to you which I will send with this.

Now bend down while I whisper a few words in your ear. Emma has got a beau an Englishman a widower without children. She wrote me very little concerning him so I can tell you nothing more. I expect her down next week to buy goods. The gentleman a Mr Watson by name is going to drive her down to Mechanicsville in time to take the early train. he wants to come all the way with her but she says she does not know whether she will let him. I told her by all means to do so if she wished; in my heart Fred I believe this will be a match. E seems in something of a twitter an affection of the heart not an incurable disease[;] for her own sake I hope he may prove to be the right one. if matters go on favorably she will probably tell you all about it but for the present say nothing. . . .
. . .

My mind is in such a tumult I can not write. I wish you were here write to me the moment you know that you are to be discharged. and when you expect to be home, let those who like the service go to Mexico. . . . The children have come in from School and are noisy as usual. I showed them your cape and asked them if they could guess how it came here they thought at first that you were home and went screaming through the house in search of you. . . .

Adieu darling
Most truely your wife
Lizzie

When his letter of May 9 came to hand, Lizzie was not pleased with his reproof for her instructing the children, but she did not let it dominate the letter entirely. Besides, she knew where she stood with the children, and she subtly let him know it.

Albany N.Y.
May 14, 1865

My very dear Husband,

I have half a mind to give up writing to you, none of my letters of
late seem to please you. Had I given an immediate answer to your
last, I fear you would have been still more displeased. I was not
in a pleasant frame of mind when your letter was handed to me,
and when you gently hinted that I ought to write my own letters
correctly, before I attempted to correct the children's, I knew
full well that you did not intend to hurt my feelings still I could
not help feeling annoyed for the moment; but it is all over now;
I see my weakness. annother thing I am annoyed with myself for
[and] that is expressing so much regret at the thought of being
disappointed in going to you. I look for you home very soon; and
that for <u>good</u> as the children say. so that will be 10 times 10 times
better than going to you for one short week. . . .

The babes are all asleep. I went with them this evening to their
Sabbath School concert. it was a perfect struggle all the way home
who should walk next to me, I told them I wished I had three
sides that they could all walk with me. Tutie who always seems to
consider herself still the baby looks out for her interests pretty
closely. we are all happy in each other[']s society, it only wants your
prescence, and loving heart to make our happiness complete and
we fondly trust we shall soon have it.

. . .

I look for Emma down [from Schuylerville] this week. I wonder
whether she will bring her beau for my inspection. I am all anxiety
to see him. I hope for Emma's sake he will prove to be the one she
has so long waited for she would be so much happier if she were
only married. . . . Good night Fred

Lovingly Lizzie

That same day, Fred wrote of moving back to Fort McHenry to
assist with yet another court martial, which actually pleased him,
although he was growing as dissatisfied with the army as ever.

Fort Federal Hill Md
May 14th 1865

Ma chére Femme,

This letter is addressed as above, but to-morrow I return to Ft McHenry. The Court Martial of which I was appointed Judge Adv. was dissolved by Order of Genl Morris—he expecting I should be detailed as mustering out Officer. But as soon as he learned that my detail was not issued he immediately convened another Court, and this requires me back to the other Fort. Nothing could suit me better, for I should weary to death here. The more I see of the army the more I am convinced that it is a false institution. Like all relics of feudal times, it is a rude mixture of barbarism and splendor. We live here isolated from society, surrounded with fortified walls set up on a hill—and our whole lives are spent in a mere routine of military exercises. We have admission to no respectable civilian houses—so the amusement of the Officers is confined to visiting haunts of ill-repute—or running from one drinking house to another. These employments, my domestic relations as well as my tastes, prevent me from engaging in. I do not make pretension to much style—but I claim to have sound tastes and a becoming regard for decency. Then the fastidiousness of these gentry. After we have wallowed in the mud at Coal Harbor and picked the lice (saving your presence) off our bodies at Petersburgh, and been glad of a brief interval of security and rest, to cook a meal[,] wash a shirt and mend our stockings—now we have grown so <u>picked</u>[10] (the adjective is Shakspere's) that we are incapable of serving ourselves. It is dis-graceful [to] brush a coat or to empty a wash-basin. When I contemplate the profitless lives these young Officers lead—not one of them ever looks into a book—or gives expression to a rational thought, and reflect upon their vicious amusements and extravagant habits[,] I feel perfectly wearied of my companionship with them. Thank heaven! Very soon we shall soon all be sent home, and then it is to be hoped we shall amend our ways—and adapt ourselves to a more rational estimate of our position.[11]

The Knickerbocker was premature in saying that our Regiment was to be discharged immediately. There is no doubt we shall soon go, however[, but] . . . this, certainly, does not look promising for your visit here. All our paroled Officers are dis-charged—and no more are to be mustered in—From one cause or another our Reg^t has lost sixteen Officers within the last two weeks.

Excuse the dullest kind of letter. . . . Your remittance came safely through—very greatly obliged. . . . How do you manage to get along without money? I hope to be able to send you some before long.

You are the very spirit of mis-chief. I declare I will tell Emma every word you say about her. Were you never troubled with "an affection of the heart?" And did it prove curable in your case? Good bye—pet. I could somewhat enjoy an evening in your company. By-and-bye. Au revoir

F.

Two days later, with her letter of May 14 voicing annoyance in hand, he apologized. "I owe you—not a thousand apologies—but one sincere apology which I respectfully beg to tender." He promised to not indulge in levity at her expense in the future. "You show a becoming spirit in taking exception to such epistolary license, and I promise to offend no more." He had received $50 in extra pay for serving as judge advocate and would send her $20 of it. Washington newspapers meanwhile hinted at his regiment's speedy discharge, "but we hear nothing authentic."[12]

He did not mail this letter until he could accompany it with another two days later, admitting then that he had not received the $50 but would seek it yet again from the quartermaster. Still somewhat contrite—"I don't know whether you hate me or not"—he promised, "I am really going to be a good boy when I get home. I will swear only a very little. I will forbear using all intoxicating liquors—I will dis-continue all vulgar camp habits—I will attend church once every Sunday (when the weather is fine) and I will remove you from Albany. Then if I dress decently, and keep my hair cut short, people won't know but that I am a decent personage yet." The important promise here was to leave Albany and begin life anew somewhere else. Like Adam and Eve, he said, "The world is before us. . . . I hope we shall have a pleasanter time than they had."[13]

That same day, Lizzie wrote of much family news and asked what he thought of Jefferson Davis's capture.

Albany May 18th 1865

My dear dear Husband,

I am a day late in writing, I was so thoroughly tired last night that I retired to rest shortly after the children. Dear little Dollie Dumpling has gone to Schuylerville; our family seems so small only three of us now. Hurry home. Monday morning just before dinner Aunt Maria, and Emma, presented themselves. Mrs M came to purchase furniture and Emma to buy goods. by the way I think Emma has been very successful so far, she has taken $90 dollars in just three weeks and her stock very slightly decreased as this has been for work altering bonnets & co. She is in excellent spirits. I dare you to tell Emma what I said concerning "an affection of the heart." You are coming home soon to make it safe to do so. you know full well I would box your ears if you did. almost the first question she asked me was if I had told you. I told her yes, that as we were one I did not call that telling. She seems interested but does not mean to commit herself till she learns more of him. he has not been very long in Mr Comstock[']s employ has no relations in this country he has been 14 years in the country, but is not as thoroughly Americanized as she could wish. he has no children living. one son fell in this war. E is very anxious we should both see him. she thinks some that she will come down with him the 29th of this month. I hope for her sake that he will prove to be all she hopes or expects. Aunt Maria says she must not have him, for he is poor and homely too. Money is very well in its place but I would not let that be any objection if he is worthy. but I will say no more of him before long you will probably see him. Dear little Dollie how we all miss her when they came home from School, I was on the point of asking why Dollie did not come. Tutie will I think miss her more than Josie. she seemed reluctant to go and clung to me most affectionately asking me if I would not come up soon to see her. I do hope she will not be lonely. I will write frequently to her and she will find playmates, and be pretty happy, and grow strong and fleshy.

Our guests [Aunt Maria and Emma] did not make a very long stay. They came Monday noon and left early Wednesday morning.

What think you Fred of the capture of Jeff Davis in peticoats, the grand finale of the southern chivalry. O! dear O! dear, what a craven coward if he had sought to defend himselff and lost his life by the means, we would have given him credit at least for devotion to his failing cause. I wonder what disposition will be made of him.

. . .

I am not in the humor to write I can think of nothing but your coming home. . . .

Devotedly your Wife

Lizzie.

A day later, she had received his apology and said: "I grant you full pardon." She missed Dollie, "a doz times a day." "I see plainly that you are impatient to get into active employment, you have no settled plans in view have you?" He did not, but his work history as a butcher and then as an editor would shape his future in ways neither of them could have foreseen.[14] Three days later, Gertie awoke with a toothache that Lizzie hoped she could make go away. By the next evening, they had been to the doctor, who had extracted two infected teeth. "How the dear child did scream." Schuylerville seemed to agree with Emma, "especially if she finds M George W to be a congenial spirit, one with whom she can spend her life happily. You think me a great tease I know, I found a sure and lasting remedy for the heart disease as you know, and Emma will perhaps."[15]

At Fort Federal Hill, Frederic grew depressed. Likening himself to the character Jacques in Shakespeare's play As You Like It or, worse, to Hamlet, he had sat outside his quarters the previous Sunday afternoon "feeling more lonely and wretched than I ever remember." "I felt as Hamlet did [but] I have no copy of Shakspere—so I cannot quote his gloomy musings."[16] He then related the circumstances of how a letter from her with $10 enclosed had been lost under suspicious circumstances and asked if she was still angry with him.

After receiving her letter of May 18, he said he was pleased to learn of Emma's business success. Having sent his sister a letter that morning, he noted, "I did not mention her little <u>affaire de Coeur</u>, she has been so unfortunate in her previous experiences in the court of Cupid—that I thought I would not be premature in my allusion to this new attachment."[17]

Meanwhile, "the panorama of war is rapidly dissolving," but his sick roommate intensified his bitterness toward the South. Lt. Franklin Pettit[18] "was captured at Petersburgh, and was subject to the kind treatment of the rebels for six months—exposure to all the vicissitudes of the weather has ruined his constitution—he will never be a man again." In addition to all those killed in action, "as many more have broken down in health so that their lives are no pleasure to them. These crimes should be taken into account in dealing with the arch-traitors now in our hands. I advocate a short shrift and a sure cord for a good share of them."[19]

That same day, Lizzie wrote to say Gertie was doing better after her tooth extractions, but she warned that Dollie did not care for Emma's suitor.

Albany May 24[th] 1865

My dear dear Husband

Your letter of the 22[nd] with Josie's enclosed was gladly received this morning; what a grab Jo made at it when I held it up and she saw it was for her. we were just sit[t]ing down to breakfast when we heard the postman's knock. I almost fancy each letter I receive that it will be the last, that before you have time to indite another you will be in our midst. You did not of course take part in the grand review[20] at Washington yesterday. The bronzed heroes were greeted with heartfelt joy, they all richly deserve all the praise that is lavished upon them; it must have been a splendid sight certainly.

Your letters never are insufferably dull Fred next to seeing you they are the greatest blessings I could have[,] but in comparison to your presence Ah! well I fail to express the idea. You are growing restless and impatient to come home. I share with you in this impatience. You do not wish to be examined with a view of remaining like many of your brother Officers; it will be unmarried men who will remain in the army those who have families will gladly return as soon as the chance is offered them. I wonder if Jack will return. . . .

Our dear baby Gertie (I call her so for fun sometimes) is almost well again but she has had quite a trying time she has not been to school this week, but I think she will go tomorrow. I had a letter from Dumpling yesterday, she seems very homesick at present perhaps it will wear off, it would not do to have her remain long if she continued to be homesick. Emma wrote that she thought she did not like the stranger[21] he is very kind to her[,] brings her candies and tries to coax her but she will not touch the candies nor make friends with him at all. that is a strange freak for she is not generally shy with strangers. I wish I could feel the child's arms around my neck at this moment. A letter from you will tickle her to death. I wrote to her on Monday.

How awfully vexatious to think you never rec the $10 dollars I sent to you it is quite enveloped in mystery you will never see or hear more of that letter you may rest assured.

You speak of not hearing regularly from me of late. I have not neglected you dear Fred far be it from me to do that. I have written regularly, & will continue to do so as long as it is necessary to write at all; but I hope that will be but a short time now.

I left this unfinished intending to add a few last words this morn but the mail will be collected in a few minutes so I will send it as it is.

> Most impatiently
> Your wife E.M.L.

24

My Last Letter!!
Late May–June 1865

"I am not home yet—am I?" Frederic commenced a two-part letter on Saturday, May 27. Detailing all the bureaucratic steps a man must take to muster out, he yet again contemplated resigning to get out sooner. "I find it so insufferably dull here." He wrote to Dollie in hopes of cheering her up, promising to visit her once he got home.[1]

On Sunday he spoke about how truly fortunate they were in having survived the war. His words contrasted so starkly with those he wrote in December 1862, when he extolled heroic war and belittled domesticated home life, that he may have had that previous correspondence in mind. Whatever the case, he felt quite differently now.

Fort McHenry Md
[May 28th 1865]

Ma tres chére Femme,

. . .

    This is Sunday, and I should not be happy if I did not write to you—I sate down without having a word to say to you—and I have filled my sheet with the dullest kind of details. Never mind! It is not for long. You are pleased to assure me that notwithstanding my letters are always welcome, the physical presence of the man will afford you an incalculable enhancement of delight. The day is coming. I thrill at the anticipation. Three years separation have not been submitted to without profit Woman! I think I can appreciate the heaven of a leal and loving wife—obedient children and a happy smiling home. Providence has benignly protected me and mine through the past fearful ordeal. While unnumbered thousands have fallen—and an equal number return home mutilated and scarred, and again multitudes are broken down in health, usefulness—ambition and energy—I return to your enfolding arms, whole and unscarred—with the hue of health undimmed—and the native ardor of my breast fervent as of yore. My wife too has borne the pang of separation uncomplainingly and heroically—some women have fallen moral wrecks by the way-side—some it has pleased God to take away—and the sacred flame of domestic hearth is extinct. But to me and mine—Life—and affection—and youth and health have been preserved. I return after the storm that desolated the land has past away—and the reward of the nation's heroic efforts it is mine to participate.

For the wars are over
The Spring has come;

. . .

Good bye! It is time for church—God bless you—my loved one

<u>F.</u>

That same day, Lizzie confessed her impatience for him to be home. Dollie, she said, was more content with her stay in Schuy-lerville, but Emma's romantic status remained unsure. She eagerly followed the ongoing investigation and trial of Lincoln's assassins and made light ridicule of the supposed circumstances of Jefferson Davis's capture.

But it was the children who "talk incessantly about your com-ing" that dominated her letter. Children had been much on her mind also when she had had what was for her an uncharacteris-tic confrontation with Mr. Duncan, the Albany businessman who had done much for the Lockley family the past three years. Confi-dent of her own view of raising children, she had dared contest his.

My very dear Husband,

I too feel as if it were quite impossible to write a connected rational
letter. . . . O! I am so impatient for your return, I eagerly scan the
papers to see which regts are to be sent home first. I see all the
troops are to be mustered out in their own respective states so
as soon as the hour of release arrives all you will have to do will
be to strap on your Knapsack and come home. The children talk
incessantly about your coming[;] every letter that comes from you
they say didn't Papa say when he was coming. . . .

    We have had another letter from Dollie she seems more
contented. She wrote to her sisters, and Emma enclosed a few
lines to me, they had not yet rec your letters. Emma said that she
expected to be here tomorrow for an hour or two, but would
probably come alone. I don't know what to make of it when she was
here she thought of coming with Mr Watson. I shall know all about
it tomorrow. I long to hear from Emma's own lips how Dollie is. . . .
I am so glad you wrote to her.

    Tutie and Josie were both very much pleased with their letters,
and wish me to say that they hope you will be home before you
can write many more letters to any of us. . . . Duncan is getting
along very well in the way of business I guess he has sold out all
his interest in the dye works. I am glad I am not his wife. He is a
perfect lord in his own house all the care of the children mentally
and physically devolves upon her [Mrs. Duncan] he does not know
anything about their studies. They had an argument the other
evening when I was there he maintained that it was the Mother[']
s business to have entire care of the children. I told him plainly
but politely that I differed with him. O! yes I had better darn
their hose, I told him that was not necessary, but he would have
his own way so I gave up. he ought never to have had children.
I never meet him at home without drawing comparisons in my
own mind between him and another Father I know who feels an
interest in all that concerns his children. Mr D does not actually
know what books George[2] studies nor what progress he makes I tell
you there is a vein of selfishness in the man but I had better hush

I do not well to judge my neighbors Mrs D has always treated me very kindly[.] the peticoat hero is at present the great sensation. I see the ladies think of calling the peticoats Jeffcoats hereafter and discarding hoops entirely. Does it not seem very remarkable that the confederacy after struggling so long should colapse so suddenly, one disaster after another followed in such quick succession that you can scarce take note of them all it would have been unsatisfactory if the arch traitor the leader of the rebellion had escaped. let justice have full sway with these miserable wretches who have entailed so much misery and woe upon our fair lands. This assassination trial is developing new facts concerning their barbarities to our prisoners. We know enough already. O! how much they will have to answer for[.] God help them they are to be pitied.

Your youthful major[3] is handsome, tis well you constrained me or I might have kissed his picture. I think though it would be more satisfactory to kiss the original.

. . . I did hope you would be home to spend my birthday [May 29] with me but alas and Alas it comes upon the morrow so it can not be but I shall spend it far more happily than my last I trust. Then you were in the field facing the foe fighting and marching weary and dispirited with fatigue. I do not wonder that you contrast your present comfort with your past discomforts and congratulate yourselves upon the change. . . .

Most devotedly Your wife

E.M.L

[P.S.] I had inclosed a picture of a friend of yours[4] in the parcel F Mather was to take but as it did not go I will enclose it herewith.

Frederic welcomed receiving her photograph, the equivalent, he said, of "a conjugal embrace." But it didn't do her justice. "The features are not brought well out—they lie flat like Lely's paintings of Queen Elizabeth."[5] But he was happy to have it, though photographs could be dangerous. "Do you know that an instance occurred in our Regt. of a woman's ambrotype killing one of our best and bravest soldiers," he asked. A Corporal Russell,[6] "a stout, robust, herculean fellow" captured at Petersburg and "consigned to the slaughter pen at Andersonville," the infamous Confederate prisoner-of-war camp in Georgia, had become transfixed by the picture of his girl. "He was incessantly contemplating it. He would sit for whole days in moody dejection. His comrades would endeavor to arouse him to life and activity—but the gaze of his lady love had frozen the marrow in his bones—he became dropsical, scurvied—the lice ate holes in his body and he died." Notwithstanding such exceptional stories, he hoped to get pictures of many of his comrades, perhaps even a group picture.

Otherwise, he was pleased to learn Dollie was adjusting to Schuylerville, and then observed, "You don't like the Scotch style of husbands, then?" Her estimate of friend Duncan "is far from flattering. But I think he is a model of a husband compared with some. Amelia Hill's father—for instance—was an unadulterated specimen. His wife must black his boots and rise the middle of the night to fill his pipe." As for Hill's daughters—who, besides Amelia, included Frederic's first wife, Agnes Jeannette—"he always treated as he would sailors upon a ship's forecastle." As for himself, "I suppose I spoil my wife." Perhaps he even risked having her "turn round some day and astonish me." But for now, "she is so full of endearments . . . I abandon myself to her blandishments and forego all defensive vigilance."[7]

In response, Lizzie confessed in one of her next letters that "a holiday feeling" had taken possession of her. "No wonder I am impatient. How can I help it, words are wholly inadequate to express my joy. . . . You have spoilt me entirely Mister," but it was too late to "draw the reins tighter." "<u>You will never be able to make a Scotch wife of me now</u>; catch me getting up in the night to fill my Husband['s] pipe. You will always find me willing to obey all reasonable demands; but you know if you were exacting I would be very wilful."

So, "you do not like my picture," she added. She did not like it either and hesitated to send it. "I do not take a good picture."[8]

A day earlier, she had been able to report more fully on Dollie. Emma's "affair of the heart," meanwhile, seemed to be mellowing his sister.

Albany N.Y.
June 1ˢᵗ 1865

My very dear Husband,

. . . Emma came down [to Albany] Monday morning to buy more
goods. She had determined to return in the evening but the day
being stormy she was unable to accomplish her business so she
remained till Tuesday afternoon. She reports Dollie as being far
more reconciled and thinks she will be quite happy there for a few
weeks. She makes her home with Emma but goes up every day to
Aunt Maria's[;] she is perfectly charmed with the kids. They are so
tame." . . .

Your letter of Sunday was cheering in the extreme. I have
been told by quite a number that those Artillery Regts now doing
garrison duty would probably remain till the expiration of their
terms; but you are not going to wait. We shall have the joy of
welcoming you perhaps before we know it minutes seem hours
and hours weeks almost[,] so impatient am I for your return. I do
realize dear Fred how very much reason we have for thanksgiving
that we have all been spared an unbroken family. This long and
painful separation has not been without its effect but God grant
such a separation may never be necessary during our lives again.

Emma has made rapid strides in the 'court of Cupid' or I should
perhaps say her love had, for he has already drawn from her a
promise of her hand and heart. He would like her to consent to
their marriage as early as the 4ᵗʰ of July, but this she will not do. He
will have to restrain his impatience a little she has already seen him
more times during their 5 weeks accquaintance than you and I saw
each other during our 6 months courtship. I do teaze her, it does
one good; and does not seem to displease her in the least. What
a marvelous change love makes sometimes; I know E wants you to
know of her progress in this delicate affair but has not the courage
to write it herself, she would tell you if you were here. Mr Watson is
the gentleman's name. E says he is a regular John Bull and that she
would much rather he was an American. I am anxious to see the
gentleman he has the assurance to tell Emma that he knows I shall
like him good cheek eh?

. . .

Weather warm and pleasant. All days will be pleasant when you are home again.

Faithfully E.M.L.

In his next, Frederic reported jubilantly that a sizable portion of his regiment had been ordered for discharge, and he would surely be in it. He hoped to be home in a week.

Fort McHenry Md. June 4 / 65

Ma plus chére Femme,

This probably is not the last letter I shall write to you from this place—but it is among the <u>last</u>. Our regiment has been ordered for discharge, and the Officers are busy upon their muster out rolls. It is most likely that we shall be mustered out this week—but there is no certainty about this, as there is such a pressure of business upon the departments, that a delay in the examination and acceptance of our various returns may take place. I will inform you, however, when the muster out takes place, so that you may be prepared to receive me into your arms. Only a portion of the regiment will return—those who belonged to the Original 113th—probably two hundred fifty men. It is expected we shall return as a regiment with arms, music and banners—and I suppose the old Capitol city will give us a reception. The intervening days seem insufferably tedious—I hope this week will finish my military career.

. . .

I am pleased that Emma is progressing so favorably with her tender affair—she does have the most comical beaux that ever woman was visited withal. You say it is astonishing how the influence of Love alters a woman's character. Upon your own experience? Or upon any marked change in Emma's conduct? A woman was made for marriage—her more delicate nervous organization as well as her position in society, render the support of a strong arm and loving breast necessary to her. Deprived of this with an uncertain and unpromising future before her, is it but natural that she should become fretful, irritable and unhappy. If this worser half and helpmete will have the effect of relieving Emma's mind of her fretfulness and irritability, God consummate their union, and bless their bed with fertility! I grant you the profundity of your aphorism. I do agonize its philosophical verity.

. . . You will excuse a short letter—I will soon be present in the flesh—and my ready tongue shall tell you in five minutes more than my unready pen could communicate in an hour. Have a nice bouquet in your room—the perfume of a bed of roses which adorns the Genl's Garden fills my chamber and wafts my thoughts to heaven. . . .

I cannot write—my thoughts are home—I can already taste the nectar of your sweet pouting lips. Did I ever tell you they were just made for kissing—I will not bid you, good-bye! The French salutation is more appropriate <u>Au revoir</u>! Till then!

Oh so ardently and impatiently thine

F.E.L.

Still awaiting discharge, Frederic wrote in disgust of raucous celebrations among other units. He had taken a pleasant boat ride with "fellow idlers," but he had grown dissatisfied and home-sick. Impatient as a schoolboy for want of action and adventure, he would do anything now to get home, but he still had no word of when his discharge would come.

Four days later, it was much the same. "No order for our discharge yet." One of his regiment's officers visited headquarters the day before and was told the orders for immediate mustering out of 381 men and 7 officers was being printed. "I presume I am one of the seven," he said. "The papers to-day give a sickening account of a soldier riot in Washington a few days since."—what he described as "an unprovoked attack upon the negro quarter."[9] Slavery was abolished but not racism and violence. Otherwise, he said, "I have nothing to do," and he signed his letter, "Your's perdurably."[10]

Then on June 14 came his final letter. He could report they were making out muster rolls and preparing to leave for New York. He was ecstatic.

Fort McHenry Md.
June 14–1865

Ma plus chére Femme,

Your letter received—I am much pleased to hear that your Father has visited you at last, bringing your long-expected Sister with him. He comes very opportunely. The long-delayed Order to muster our Reg^{t}. out was received at Reg^{t}. Head Quars yesterday—and we are just as busy as bees making out muster out rolls. Eight Copies require to be made—clothing accounts balanced, discharges for the men filled out—public property turned over—and the Reg^{t}. is required to be in New York this week. I don't see how it can be done—still we shall work night and day—and you may expect us about Sunday. Try and prevail upon your Father to stay till I return—I should be disappointed to find him gone. You must have liberal housekeeping—I suppose you have not a cent. Stick it out a few days longer—I shall return as rich as Croesus.[11] Excuse brevity—I have not a minute to spare. That you may not be disappointed—I enclose some love letters written by an English Lord—they beat my style hollow.

The war is over, wife—our long and painful separation is accomplished—and I impatiently wait the moment to throw myself into your arms.

Excellent wretch!
Perdition catch my soul, but I do love thee!
-S-sh! Ain't I ashamed? Best love and cordial greetings to all!
Cock-a-doodle-doo!
Thine—le—vôtre
F.
20 Officers and 381 men return home
My last letter!!

Epilogue

As Frederic wrote his last letter, pandemonium swept the camp at Fort McHenry. Word had come that the Seventh Regiment was mustering out. They were going home, although the list did not include everyone. Only those who were part of the original enlistments in July and August 1862—381 men and officers—would return to Albany just then. Those who enlisted after October 1, 1862—another 322 men—would remain in service until the end of July.[1]

Frederic was part of the first group, but to get the men mustered out required paperwork, and as the regiment's principal clerk, he was at the center of that storm. He worked furiously, but men eager to get on with their lives were understandably impatient. Actual mustering out did not begin until June 15, with the last man not accounted for until the morning of June 16.[2] That night, the lucky 381 boarded a train for Albany, Fred Lockley among them. They arrived in Philadelphia the next morning for breakfast. From there, they traveled by train to Perth Amboy, New Jersey, and then by ferry to New York City, where they spent two nights. Finally, they took the transport *City of Norwich* to Albany. Having traveled all night, they arrived at the city's docks at 5 a.m. on June 20. Despite the early hour, a cannon salute and thousands of boisterous family, friends, and well-wishers greeted them.[3]

Joyous reunions and celebrations erupted everywhere along the quay, but it would be a sickly Fred Lockley who came down the gangplank that morning. "We steamed from Baltimore to New York in a transport," he recalled, "and the weather being hot and the vessel crowded, we all suffered from thirst. The only beverage supplied was ice water, of which I drank freely, knowing at the time it was injurious, but I could not restrain myself."[4] In New York, they had been housed in a market house, with officers assigned to sleeping quarters upstairs. For men accustomed to rougher camp life and inured to sleeping outdoors, the confined quarters were insufferable. "With one accord we all descended to the open market place," he said, where they could breathe fresh air and sleep on the lawn. By then, Fred was reeling from the effects of the ice water, and as soon as they arrived in Albany, he bid leave from his commanding colonel and hurried home.[5]

For others in his regiment, the festivities continued. Crowds thronged the streets and sidewalks, cheering them as loudly as when they trooped through town on their way to war in August 1862. They were treated to speeches and accolades and a sumptuous fare in the ornate dining room of Albany's Stanwix Hall. Then, after marching to the New York governor's residence where Reuben Fenton gave an address from his front steps, they settled into a banquet at Tweddle Hall. After that, they were assembled one last time on Broadway Street and given their final command: "dismissed!"[6] Some men yelled, "Hurrah!" Others quickly escaped to family, some even sang hymns, and others stood in awe, unsure what to do. Jubilation and despair mixed strongly as the weight of the past three years settled in. "The Seventh returned with band tooting and colors flying," Frederic observed, but "it had fearfully shrunk in its fair proportions; my company, as a specimen— mustered 31 men in line out of 150." And he missed it all. "It was seriously disappointing to me, after having served my full term without one day's sickness," he wrote later, to "be laid helpless on my bed and deprived of this ovation."[7]

Fred's doctor diagnosed his ailment as "congestion of the liver."[8] Whatever the case, he recovered quickly. Just exactly what he and Elizabeth and the girls did in the next few weeks remains a mystery; they were not writing letters anymore. They had talked of country camping and long family picnics. "I think when you return we must pack up knapsack haversack tent and blanket and take a couple of weeks holiday," Lizzie had urged just two weeks earlier.[9] They probably did just that. Undoubtedly also, they traveled to Schuylerville to see Fred's sister Emma, her new millinery shop, and, intriguingly, Emma's husband-to-be, George Watson. Too, Fred had promised Dollie they would come to see her, and Lizzie would want to see her Aunt Maria Mair and Grandma Metcalf as well as other friends and relatives there. Frederic's memoirs are silent on these days and weeks, and the sudden absence of correspondence renders their exact whereabouts and undertakings unknown, as it does their discussions of future hopes, dreams, and plans.

Yet it was a resumption of correspondence two months later that brings their lives back into view. "I like Cleveland much, and think of staying here," Fred wrote to Lizzie in late August. He had considered seeking public employment in Albany, the state capital, but friends had warned him away from it. Others recently mustered out presented too much competition for too few jobs, and soldiers were in bad odor generally for lack of qualifications.[10] "I could see no other way open to my emprise than to go farther a-field," he explained later. As he said, he would "follow Horace Greeley's advice once more and 'Go West!'" He had been as far west as Chicago and had lived there, so he headed that way. He purchased a lay-over ticket so that he might stop at cities along the route to seek employment. Beyond Buffalo, Cleveland was the first stop.[11]

He was in Cleveland but a few days before he landed a job as proofreader on one of the city's major newspapers—the *Cleveland Herald*. He would make $20 a week. Paying $1 a day for an inconvenient room at Cleveland's City Hotel, he was already looking for a house and writing to Lizzie to pack up the children and household goods and join him as soon as she could. As always, his instructions on how to accomplish the move were detailed, but ten days after his arrival, he remained ecstatic. "I calculate to make this city my resting place for the remainder of my days."[12]

Lizzie obediently answered the call to move west. "I was to pack up our household goods and join him," she recalled years later, adding with characteristic understatement, "That was the first, but not the last, that duty devolved on me."[13] They indeed did make Cleveland their home—for a while. Within a year of arriving there, they had their first child together—another girl, whom they named Maud—the first of five, three of whom, including Maud, that would survive infancy.[14] Fred soon changed jobs and went to work for the *Cleveland Leader*. Then, with two partners, he started a paper of his own, but when that effort failed, he went back to work for the *Leader*. He was dissatisfied, however, and after three years in Cleveland, he ventured west again.[15]

From Cleveland he went to Kansas and became a roving newspaper correspondent based in Leavenworth. He filed long reports on affairs in Indian Territory for New York, Chicago, and Leavenworth newspapers. While in Leavenworth, he and Lizzie had their only son, whom they named Fred, after his father. After two years in Leavenworth, Frederic joined two other Leavenworth newspapermen and moved to Salt Lake City, Utah, to own and operate the *Salt Lake Tribune*. Frederic and his partners would turn the *Tribune* into a major urban daily and a resolute opponent of Mormonism. Fred Lockley battled Mormon theocracy for seven years in Salt Lake before tiring of the fight, selling out his *Tribune* interests, and moving to Walla Walla, Washington, there to try farming. Lizzie loved it. Finally, they would enjoy permanence and country living.

But Frederic, whose entire background was urban, quickly grew restless. The pastoral life didn't suit him. He was in southeastern Washington less than a year before he accepted a lucrative offer to become editor-in-chief of a new Republican newspaper, the *Inter Mountain*, in Butte, Montana, one of the West's most urban places. He was in Butte four years, covering the city's riotous transition from gold and silver camp to copper metropolis. Powered by copper taken from "the richest hill on earth," Butte became the Pittsburgh of the West, an industrial behemoth. But permanency eluded the Lockleys there too. Returning to Kansas in 1885, Fred tried owning and editing a small-town weekly newspaper, the Arkansas City *Traveler*. Eventually, that plan, too, foundered, although the *Traveler* survived and publishes to this day.

From Kansas, Fred Lockley finally completed his cross-continental search for stability by settling in the Pacific Northwest. His daughter Josie, the oldest of the three girls Lizzie had taken as her own during the Civil War, had met her husband James Shepard[16] while they both worked in the *Salt Lake Tribune* production department in the 1870s. By the 1880s Josie and James had relocated to manage a cherry farm outside Salem, Oregon, and Fred and Lizzie followed them there. Frederic bought into part ownership of a new paper, the *Capital Journal*, but he soon drew out and spent his final years in semi-retirement. Lizzie was with him every step of the way (although Butte and the death of her fourth child in infancy there precipitated a short-lived marital crisis). In 1899 Fred suffered a stroke that paralyzed his left arm. He was left-handed but had learned to write with his right hand when a boy, and, at the urging of his now-adult son, Fred Lockley Jr., he began writing what would become a twelve-hundred-page memoir, more than a third of which detailed his Civil War experiences. He completed his memoir and, with extensive family papers, turned it over to his son, Fred, who became a rare book dealer and secured its preservation. Frederic died on December 19, 1905, in the upstairs bedroom of his daughter Maud's home in Missoula, Montana, Lizzie at his bedside. Elizabeth herself outlived her husband by twenty-four years, passing at age eighty-six in Portland, Oregon, on October 25, 1929.

Thus, Fred and Lizzie had followed Greeley's advice, and then some—certainly beyond anything they could have imagined as they dutifully wrote their letters twice a week during the nation's ordeal of Civil War.

In mid-May 1865, one newspaperman wrote, while observing the Grand Review of Grant's and Sherman's soldiers in Washington DC, that those tens of thousands of men on review, bayonets glistening in the sun, would soon disperse, and as they did, the army would melt back "into the heart of the people whence it came."[17] As it did so, men like Fred Lockley would, as Margaret Leech wrote, "take up the threads of small ambitions."[18] Such ambitions were not small to the men who tried to fulfill them, nor was their connection with the Civil War forgotten. No matter how diverse and sometimes dramatic his experiences in a thirty-year newspaper career, Fred Lockley would, like hundreds of thousands of others, always see his Civil War service as the high point of his life. To Frederic and certainly to Elizabeth, family came first in the affections, but supporting the home life to sustain those affections required finding work in Gilded Age America and working hard. Fred Lockley would do both with a mix of results, even if it meant ricocheting across the North American continent in pursuit of the next best chance. He was forty years old when he returned to Albany in June 1865, and he would live to be eighty-one. Half his life was still before him, and what a life it would be. But in June 1865, for him as for so many others, his life's most unforgettable experience had just ended.[19]

Appendix 1

Frederic's Letter to Elizabeth, January 11, 1863

Fort De Russey D.C. Jan 11th
1863

My small pet,

If music be the food of Love, play on; give me excess of it! How delicious was your last letter! Music to the ears; balm to the mind; Elysium to the affections! Now thou art mine own true wife again. Never mind if potatoes are dear, and coffee renchére;[1] let us forget these domestic affections, occassionally, and only remember that to love is a luxury which we can universally enjoy despite the alarming rise in the price of commodities. If you know how sacred is every object which has been hallowed with your touch; how every word that you utter is dearer than holy writ; you would not grudge, when you design to bless me with your charming epistles, to rise above the atmosphere of mutton and house-rent, and indulge my craving for Love—exhaustless Love. I feel like a schoolboy who has escaped a whipping to-day. My wife has again vouchsafed to indulge her husband's absurd taste, and to send him a delicious letter, dropping myrrh and frankincense, and filled with love costly as the chariots of Solomon. Because to me age has not brought wisdom; because I cannot unceasingly upine[2] at our financial derangement, I don't know that it would be improving the matter any to have my wife's ruby lips curt in disdain at my folly, and to have her administer perpetual raps on my knuckles because I do not sober down to dulness amid the troubles which surround us. Oh, I canna [cannot] be fashed![3] The doleful is not my temperament. I am insensible to the gravity of my troubles, and

355

when I tell[4] over all the wealth I possess in the pure affections of my wife, and the docility and promise of my priceless young ones I want to burst out in an epithalamium[5] of connubial ecstacy and to dance with my unmentionables on even tho' I should be despised as the censorious Michal—Saul's daughter despised the saltatory[6] sans-culottic[7] performances of the triumphant David.[8] Your loving letter has filled me with such joy—that for two hours this morning I lay in a tumult of happiness reading Solomon's passionate love song and applying every syllable of those delicious Oriental love utterances to this my love, my dove, my spouse, my sister, my undefiled! Stay me with flagons,[9] comfort me with apples: for I am sick of love.

Hence tho' the country is in an awful condition, and the safety of your butter is precarious, and you suffer that greatest of all earthly ills, the inflammation[10] of your weekly bills; still do not ask me to grow gray and ghastly over it. I will apply certain seasons to deploring these troubles. I will stint my diet that so much may be saved for the general use but allow me at intervals to be nonsensical. At times I will be good and counsel with you discreetly: but when passionate Love runs riot thro' my veins— where I would give all the substance of my house for love, when my love is as strong as death, and many waters cannot quench its prevailing influence, oh, then let the gladness of my heart speak forth, let me worship thy countenance and drink the inspiration of thy voice; for sweet is the voice of my beloved, and thy cheeks are comely without rows of jewels.

Here this blessed Sabbath eve, with the stillness of death reigning in the camp, I abstract my thoughts from all present cares and enjoyments and invoice like freight my soul with the treasure of a virtuous woman. My soul doth safely trust in her, so that it shall have no need of spoil. Her children arise up and call her blessed; her husband also praiseth her. Many daughters have done virtuously, but thou excellest them all!

There I have done. I feel better. I shall not venture to read this string of extravagance. "He hath not loved," says the Prophet Shakspere, "whose love hath not betrayed him into every absurdity." With advancing years I sought to gain sense, and leave those lines to school boys. But I cannot! You tempt me, you young

Appendix 1

jade, with your over the hills and far away wantoning; and like a spark applied to tow, I am infected with the witchery of your invocation, and my thoughts run dallying in the chambers of delight. Away! I shut my eyes and anticipate the joys of return— and acknowledge that all the happiness which is placed for me in reservation, is cheaply purchased by the three year's absence which enhances so immeasurably the <u>délicat</u>[11] of my wife's society.

Now then—take this aside. Forget all domestic cares—read these words of unexaggerated devotion. Your eyes will swim— your pulse will quicken, your breathing will come and go— these are the symptoms of unrestrained uncalculating Love! The immortal Sappho,[12] whose life of burning passion is crystallized in two or three love verses—can only describe these effects. For the Promethean spark burns alike in all, and he who most directly expresses its sensations appeals with the greatest force to every human lover.

By night on my bed I sought whom my soul loveth: I sought her, but found her not. Ha! I tho't you said you were done. Adieu. <u>Serez heuseusse</u>.[13]

Your husband and father.

<u>F</u>

Appendix 2

Frederic's Letter to Elizabeth, August 7, 1864

Portions were altered in Fred Lockley Memoirs (misdated as August 4 in FLM, 337–42). Here, reproduced, is the original letter of August 7, 1864.

Camp near Petersburgh, Va.

August 7th 1864

Ma chére Femme,

I am going to try to write you a letter. If I succeed it will be under serious difficulties—the flies are tormenting—ready to devour me alive; the heat is intense, and I am subject to continual interruptions. This is Sabbath morning—the camp is alive with business: two days' rations are being delivered to the men—and the Quartermaster is making a large issue of clothing. We have fallen into the routine of camp life—guard mounting—drill-inspections, dress parade—and fatigue details—and are about as monotonous as when in garrison life at Fort ~~Reno~~. We hear the almost incessant firing of the pickets—at intervals of ~~every few~~ minutes ~~a heavy cannon from our lines~~ gives tongue and belches a shell right into the ~~enemy's midst~~. This sometimes provokes a retort—and occasionally a brisk artillery duel will ensue—but each party is so effectually covered—that little damage can be done. On Friday ~~evening~~ the enemy attempted to spring a mine—they failed—~~but the attempt~~ was followed by a charge ~~upon~~ on our lines. A ~~hasty~~ order was sent to our headquarters for the division to take a hand in—they ~~marched at~~ double quick ~~to the scene of~~

~~action~~ but ~~by the time they reached there the attack had been repulsed and the fight was over.~~

The newspapers are blathering about the <u>esprit du corps</u> of the ~~army~~ of the Potomac; how. ~~How~~ that Genl. Grant is confident of success and the men devoted to the cause and impatient to be hurled against the enemy. Springes to catch woodcocks! A sicker set of ~~wretches~~ you never ~~saw~~. A feeling of discouragement has become infectious. Our immense ~~army~~ has been wasted in ~~battles and horrible~~ and forced marches until it is now too weak to work with; Petersburgh seems impregnably fortified, and our efforts to disconnect Richmond from the south have ~~been unsuccessful~~. I am unable to see that anything has been accomplished by this campaign, from which so much was expected, it is not visible to the naked eye. Meantime, every day spent here is an epoch of endurance—intolerable heat—scarcity of water and ~~no shade~~. The country is ~~drifting rapidly in bankruptcy—and~~ the "promised end" disappearing ~~in the~~ dim and visionary ~~distance~~. When newspaper correspondents ~~prate~~ about the élan and enthusiasm of ~~the soldiers you must understand that the 4 Brig. is excluded.~~

~~Your letters all arrive—I grieve that your health is so poor—I trust that two weeks in the country will invigorate you.~~ I arose early this morning—started two men away into infinite space in pursuit of water—who returned with a camp kettle full. I washed all my dirty clothes—cooked breakfast (we live well here) attended Guard mounting (9 o'clock) and ~~then intended to devote to private writing.~~

But my fortitude is not equal to the task. The glare of the sun distresses and the flies are so pestiferous that my hands and face are literally covered with them. Do you know those little devils are in the confederate service. To write calmly—philosophically and wisely under such circumstances ~~passes my powers~~. I should much like to write to your rebel cousin in Cincinnati[,] but you do not tell me his regiment—do you know that he is there still? I have intended to repay Mr. Owen's visit—but his corps is away in Maryland. My health is excellent—and notwithstanding the hot weather I eat enough to make a horse ill. As I write our tattered and blood stained flag flouts the hot breeze that fans these headquarters—and Jimmie Van Benthuysen treads his silent beat as sentry over the sacred presence of our commander. I think I have told you that Maj Springsteed had resumed command of the reg^t. After the futile interregnum which has ensued since Col. Morris' death on the 4th of June it is quite a relief to have the familiar and much respected Major amongst us again. He is an excellent officer and very popular with the men. Some boisterous friends of Major Murphy's have just arrived—so I will adjourn. Love to all–

Your's devotedly
F.

Appendix 3

Timeline of Key Events

1821   **March 9**: Emma Lockley born in London, England.

1822   **ca. September**: Mary Anne Lockley born in London, England.

1824   **December 31**: Frederic E. Lockley born in London, England. Two brothers born subsequently died young.

1832   **ca. 1832**: Agnes Jeannette Hill born.

1843   **May 29**: Elizabeth Metcalf Campbell born in Fonda, Montgomery County, New York.

1848   **August 24**: Frederic Lockley arrives in New York City from England on board the *Delta*.

1850   **June**: Frederic's father, Samuel, dies. Frederic returns to London to run the family butcher business but gives it up, puts his mother in a home for widows, and returns to the United States with his sister Emma.

1852   **August 17**: Fredcric marries Agnes Jeannette Hill in New York City (hereafter NYC).

1853   **June 10**: Josephine (Josie), first daughter to Fred and Agnes, born, NYC.

1855   **February 19**: Emma Louise (Dollie), second daughter to Fred and Agnes, born, NYC.

1857   **July 6**: Gertrude (Gertie), third daughter to Fred and Agnes, born, NYC.

1859   **March 24**: Frederic becomes a naturalized American citizen.

1860   **March 4:** Agnes Jeannette dies of a spinal tumor in Troy, New York.

   September 16: Fred's first love letter written to Elizabeth Metcalf Campbell.

1861   **February 28:** Frederic and Elizabeth marry at Elizabeth's Aunt Maria Mair's house in Schuylerville, New York.

1862   **August 11:** Frederic enlists for three-year term in regiment recruited by Col. Lewis O. Morris.

   August 18: Frederic is promoted to corporal in Company I.

   August 19: Morris's regiment is designated as the 113th New York Volunteer Infantry.

   September 5: Frederic and his regiment are stationed at Fort DeRussy north of Washington DC.

   December 10: 113th New York Infantry is converted to artillery regiment.

   December 19: 113th New York is redesignated as Seventh New York Volunteer Heavy Artillery Regiment.

1863   **February:** Frederic's regiment is attached to Second Brigade, Haskin's Division, Twenty-Second Corps.

   October 4: Frederic is detailed as a clerk in regimental adjutant's office at Fort Reno.

   October 17: Frederic is promoted to quartermaster sergeant of Company I, Seventh New York, and reassigned to Fort DeRussy, thanks to machinations of Capt. William Shannon, who wanted him back.

   November 1: Frederic begins first two-week furlough home.

1864   **February 1:** Frederic is promoted to sergeant major, Company I, Seventh New York.

   May 14: Frederic and the Seventh New York are ordered to join Ulysses S. Grant's Overland Campaign in Virginia.

   May 18: Seventh New York arrives on fringe of Spotsylvania Court House battlefield; is assigned to Gen. Robert O. Tyler's Artillery Division, Second Corps, Army of the Potomac.

May 19: Seventh New York is involved in its first fight at the Battle of Harris Farm.

May 23–27: Seventh New York is involved in the Battle of North Anna River.

May 27: Frederic assists color guard, who is killed, in retreat from North Anna River.

May 29: Tyler's division is broken up with the Seventh New York reassigned to Fourth Brigade, First Division, Second Corps, commanded by Gen. Francis C. Barlow.

May 30: Seventh New York is involved in the Battle of Totopotomoy Creek.

June 1–12: Seventh New York is involved in the Battle of Cold Harbor.

June 3: Seventh New York is in assault at Cold Harbor, immortalized in sketch by Alfred R. Waud. Total Seventh New York casualties are 422. The Seventh New York, as with the rest of Grant's line, settles into trench warfare until wheeling south and east to cross the James River at midnight on June 14.

June 16: Seventh New York is in assault on Petersburg defenses. Seventh New York casualties are estimated at 425, including half the regiment's thirty-three officers.

June 22: Seventh New York is involved in the Battle of Weldon-Petersburg Railroad, during which, in the so-called Barlow Skedaddle, the regiment's position is overrun, and forty-nine men are counted as casualties. Seventh New York subsequently is assigned to a bivouac it called Camp Dusty, east of Petersburg and behind forward Union lines.

July 26–30: Seventh New York is involved in the First Battle of Deep Bottom.

August 14–20: Seventh New York is involved in Second Battle of Deep Bottom.

August 25: Seventh New York takes part in the Battle of Reams Station; regiment sustains 107 casualties.

September 24: Seventh New York is moved forward to occupy trenches near Fort Morton opposite Confederate siege lines east of Petersburg and near site of the Battle of the Crater.

October 10: Frederic is commissioned as a first lieutenant, Company I, Seventh New York.

November 5: Frederic applies for leave to acquire an officer's uniform in Albany and retrieve company records in Washington that were lost at Belle Plain in May.

November 26: Seventh New York is transferred to Fort Gregg, six miles southwest of Petersburg and more removed from front lines.

1865 February 22: Seventh New York is ordered to Fort McHenry near Baltimore with Lockley's company assigned to Camp Parole near Annapolis, Maryland, to guard newly paroled Union prisoners of war, but only for about two weeks.

February 25: Seventh New York is officially attached to Second Separate Brigade, Eighth Corps at Baltimore, Maryland.

March 12: Frederic writes to Elizabeth on March 12 that he has been reassigned to regimental headquarters at Fort Federal Hill, but he is there only a day before being transferred to Fort McHenry to guard Confederate prisoners about to be paroled.

June 16: Frederic's official discharge papers are signed.

June 20: Frederic is among 381 Seventh New Yorkers to arrive in Albany, New York.

August 24: Frederic writes to Elizabeth from City Hotel, Cleveland, Ohio, where he is looking for work. On September 3, 1865, he states, "I calculate to make this city my resting place for the remainder of my days." It was not to be. He and the family would move frequently during the next thirty years, including to Leavenworth, Kansas, in 1869; Salt Lake City in 1873; Walla Walla, Washington, in 1880; Butte, Montana, in 1881; Arkansas City, Kansas, in 1885; and Salem, Oregon, in 1889.

Notes

All Frederic and Elizabeth Lockley letters not cited otherwise are from the Frederic Lockley Papers at the Huntington Library. These 405 letters are gathered in packets by date in three of the collection's more than twenty boxes. To assist the reader, the following listing for letter packets and boxes reflects their location:

Box 2: Letters from Frederic to Elizabeth Lockley
    Packet 1, December 3, 1860–December 13, 1861
    Packet 2, January 21–August 13, 1862
    Packet 3, August 24–December 31, 1862
    Packet 4, January 8–June 26, 1863
    Packet 5, July 1–December 29, 1863

Box 3: Letters from Frederic to Elizabeth Lockley
    Packet 1, January 1–May 14, 1864
    Packet 2, June 10–August 30, 1864
    Packet 3, September 4–December 28, 1864
    Packet 4, January 1–March 29, 1865
    Packet 5, April 5–June 14, 1865
    Packet 6, August 24–September 3, 1865

Box 5: Letters from Elizabeth to Frederic Lockley
    Packet 3, May 13–December 27, 1863 (and one letter from Emma
        Lockley dated June 7)
    Packet 4, January 13–November 6, 1864
    Packet 5, January 10–December 17, 1865 (and one letter from
        Josephine Lockley dated April 2)

Abbreviations

FELM: Frederic E. Lockley Memoirs

EMLM: Elizabeth M. Lockley Memoirs

HL: Huntington Library, San Marino, California

Preface

1. Few similar collections offer such continuity. Exceptions include Peirce and Peirce, *Dear Catharine, Dear Taylor*; Bird and Bird, *Granite Farm Letters*; Bowler and Bowler, *Go If You Think It Your Duty*; Engs and Brooks, *Their Patriotic Duty*; Poe and Poe, *My Dear Nelly*; Hager, *I Remain Yours*. See also Rhoades and Bailey, *Wanted—Correspondence*, and Roberts, "This Infernal War."

2. Elizabeth seems to have deliberately destroyed part of one letter at a later time because she thought it too personal, which is seemingly ironic because so many of the letters are quite personal. Frederic E. Lockley (hereafter FEL) to Elizabeth Metcalf Lockley (hereafter EML), January 11, 1864, box 3, Frederic E. Lockley Papers, The Huntington Library, San Marino, California (hereafter HL).

3. Although son Fred Lockley donated family documents and materials to other institutions as well, he gave the bulk of the family collection, including all of Fred and Lizzie's Civil War letters, to the Huntington Library.

4. It is a commonplace in studies of Civil War soldier letters that it was easier for the wife, mother, sister, or sweetheart left behind to save the letters a soldier sent home than it was for a soldier, especially one in the field, to save the letters he received from home. Friends and family had greater opportunity to keep letters safe; soldiers had little or no opportunity to store letters from home, certainly not in any quantity. More typically, soldiers kept one to three letters that seemed precious or, thanks to circumstance, sent them home or saved them by some other means. See, for example, Engs and Brooks, *Their Patriotic Duty*, xvi. As one historian has noted also, women's letters from home have not been preserved as well because, until recent years, they were not considered as important. Hager, *I Remain Yours*, 107–9, 295–96; Bowler and Bowler, *Go If You Think It Your Duty*, 13; Nelson, "Writing during Wartime," 48n160, 61.

5. See, for example, FEL to EML, May 8, 1864. Only an estimated one in five soldiers in the Army of the Potomac had children, which makes the Lockley letters an uncommon opportunity to assess the roles and influence of children on a Civil War family. Glatthaar, "Tale of Two Armies," 317; Sizer, "Mapping the Spaces," 542.

6. As he wrote in 1862 to his middle daughter, Dollie, then seven years old, "Because I have delayed writing to you till last, you are not to suppose that I love you least. To make amends for the delay I will try and write you the nicest letter," FEL to Emma Louise "Dollie" Lockley, September 9, 1862, folder 20, box 79, Sherburne Collection. On children in the Civil War, see especially Marten, *Children's Civil War*.

7. Unlike in subsequent wars, Civil War soldier letters were uncensored.

8. The most prominent use of the Lockley Civil War letters has been Pomfret, "Letters of Fred Lockley." See also McPherson, *For Cause & Comrades*, chapter 3, note 7, which quotes from FEL's letter of June 1, 1863, and chapter 12, note 9, quoting FEL's letter of August 7, 1864; Keating, *Carnival of Blood*. Keating's title, *Carnival of Blood*, is taken from FEL to EML, April 16, 1865, which Pomfret included in his 1952 *Huntington Library Quarterly* article.

9. See, for example, Adams and Adams, *My Dearest Friend*, versus Adams and Adams, *Adams Family Correspondence*.

10. What is considered essential has changed with the times. When John Pomfret attempted to have a selection of Lockley Civil War letters published, he chose 113 of Frederic's letters and none of Elizabeth's and had them typed, compiled, and sent in two notebooks to New York publisher Alfred A. Knopf for consideration. Knopf returned the notebooks to Pomfret. In the upper-right corner of the first page of the first notebook, Pomfret wrote, "A.K. turned this mss. down. Not enough 'battle action.'" Box 4, Lockley Papers, HL. In the early 1950s, as collections of Civil War soldier letters and diaries were reaching publication in a post–World War II rebirth of interest in the common soldier's experiences, battle action was a key consideration for publishers. Wiley, *Life of Billy Yank*, 439–41; Hager, *I Remain Yours*, 52; Delahanty, *Soldiers' Letters and Diaries*, 5–6. Jason Phillips calls the predisposition the "heroic view." Phillips, "Battling Stereotypes," 1408–9.

11. Phillips, "Battling Stereotypes," 1419–20.

12. Berry, *All That Makes a Man*, 11.

13. Carmichael, *War for the Common Soldier*, 11, 13.

Prologue

1. Frederic Lockley, "The Virginia Campaign," *Albany Evening Journal*, December 19, 1884. Literacy among Union soldiers has been estimated at 90 percent and that among the Army of the Potomac alone, soldiers wrote a million letters per month on average. McPherson, *For Cause & Comrades*, viii; Gallagher, *Union War*, 57–58. Almost everyone wrote, even the poorly educated. Hager, *I Remain Yours*, 56.

2. Lockley, "Virginia Campaign," *Albany Evening Journal*, December 19, 1884.

1. The Setting

1. The Campbell children were Margaret Marie, born May 10, 1841; Elizabeth Metcalf, May 29, 1843; John, April 21, 1845; Amelia Stewart, May 5, 1847; and Olivia, September 13, 1849.

2. Elizabeth M. Lockley Memoirs, 2, 6–8, folder 3, box 5, Lockley Papers, HL (hereafter EMLM). See also FELM, pt. 2, 470–71. Margaret Campbell died March 17, 1851. Elizabeth apparently arrived in Schuylerville in late December or early January 1860 and lived with her grandmother and aunt for fourteen months, ending with her marriage to Frederic on February 28, 1861. EML to FEL, August 23, 1863.

3. FEL to EML, January 21, 1862.

4. FEL to EML, April 15, 1862.

5. Keating, *Carnival of Blood*, 2–3.

6. EMLM, 29.

7. Frederic E. Lockley Memoirs, pt. 2, 481–82, box 1, Lockley Papers, HL (hereafter FELM).

8. FELM, pt. 2, 479.

9. McPherson, *Battle Cry of Freedom*, 491–93.

10. McPherson, *Battle Cry of Freedom*, 482. On soldier motivations, see Frank, *With Ballot and Bayonet*.

11. Frederic thought it a "religious duty to vote" for Lincoln. FELM, pt. 2, 465.

12. Richard Kiper, drawing from James M. McPherson and Joseph A. Frank, concluded that patriotism, fear of anarchy resulting from disunion, sense of duty, and desire for adventure were "the principal reasons" Civil War soldiers went to war. Peirce and Peirce, *Dear Catharine, Dear Taylor*, 9.

13. Certificate of naturalization as U.S. citizen, March 24, 1859, box 1, Lockley Papers. In his statistical analysis of the Army of the Potomac, Joseph T. Glatthaar found that three of eleven Union soldiers were foreign born, most from Ireland, Germany, and England, and that their immigration from places with constrained economic opportunities and fewer political freedoms motivated them to join the army as "risk-takers." Glatthaar, "Tale of Two Armies," 325–26.

14. FEL to EML, December 21, 1862.

15. On why men enlisted for many different reasons, see Flotow, *In Their Letters, in Their Words*, 20–26, 36–37.

16. For "figs in a hurricane" comment, see FEL to EML, March 1, 1863; FELM, pt. 2, 480.

17. Keating, *Carnival of Blood*, 5; FEL to EML, August 24, 1862, November 11, 1862, November 19, 1862, and December 25, 1862; McPherson, *Battle Cry of Freedom*, 491–93; Catton, *Bruce Catton's Civil War*, 228–29. Glatthaar found that most Union soldiers in the Army of the Potomac were "comparatively poor" and had no wealth, defined by real and personal property. Thus, bounties of $100 and $200 were attractive to them. Frederic Lockley fits this description. See Glatthaar, "Tale of Two Armies," 317–19, 323.

18. FEL to EML, September 13, 1862. See also Mitchell, *Civil War Soldiers*, 184–85.

19. FELM, pt. 3, 1–2.

20. FELM, pt. 2, 30, 34–35. "Card-playing I have an instinctive horror of—especially by daylight." FEL to EML, January 21, 1863.

21. FELM, pt. 2, 18–21, 27, 29, 34–35, 39–40.

22. FEL to EML, January 21, 1863; FELM, pt. 3, 51–52.

23. FEL to EML, February 25, 1863.

24. Whenever Frederic did imbibe, it was not during his regiment's raucous trip from Albany to active service in Washington DC, in August 1862. On an eight-hour train ride from Jersey City to Philadelphia, amidst a "jovial and hilarious" party of drinkers, he said he "simulated so successfully the process of imbibing" from a proffered canteen that he avoided offending his companions. "I can confidently assert that I tasted no drop of liquor from the time I left home until I arrived in Washington." "Army Reminiscences," *Albany Evening Journal*, August 30, 1884.

25. Frederic said his mother dispensed ale three times a day, even to the children. FELM, pt. 2, 87–88.

26. FELM, pt. 2, 40–42, 46.

27. FELM, pt. 2, 49–50; Cobbett, *Advice to Young Men*.

28. FELM, part 2: 37, 50–51, 85.

29. Frederic told Elizabeth he addressed her in French because "I am unwilling to let any casual observer know to whom I am writing." FEL to EML, February 10, 1863. He continued the practice after the war, however.

30. FELM, pt. 2, 50–51, 56–57, 62–63.

31. FELM, pt. 1, 62–65, 82, 207.

32. FELM, pt. 2, 116, 118–22. For Rowe's first name, see FELM, pt. 2, 141.

33. FELM, pt. 2, 176–79.

34. FEL to EML, March 18, 1864; FELM, pt. 2, 160–62.

35. FEL to EML, March 19, 1864. Frederic Lockley estimated thirty to forty copies of *Arthur Frankland* were sold. See FELM, pt. 2, 190–92, and *Literary Gazette*, February 12, 1848, in Lockley Papers.

36. FELM, pt. 2, 206–8.

37. FELM, pt. 2, 300–305.

38. His father, Samuel Lockley, died June 4, 1849. His mother had tried to continue his father's business but eventually asked Frederic to come home to help. The letter apparently took some months to reach him. FELM, pt. 2, 344–55.

39. FELM, pt. 2, 358–66.

40. A fourth daughter was married and living in Brooklyn. FELM, pt. 2, 366.

41. At least one scholar has argued that Victorian men marrying younger women had to do with their comfort level as a patriarch in the home. Whether this was the reason for the appeal of the younger Agnes Jeannette Hill (nineteen or twenty in 1852) and Elizabeth Metcalf Campbell (seventeen at the time of her marriage in 1861) to Frederic Lockley is difficult to discern. His sense of intellectual superiority is plain in both cases, but his sense of eventual partnership-as-equals is also evident in his memoirs and subsequent correspondence. Rose, *Victorian America*, 158.

42. Oddly, Frederic never mentioned Jack in his memoirs, but the boy is noted in other family papers and in the 1855 New York City census. See J. L. Sherburne reminiscence, folder 1, box 1, J. H. Sherburne Collection; and New York State Census, 1855, 48.

43. They were married August. 17, 1852, See J. L. Sherburne reminiscence, folder 1, box 1, J. H. Sherburne Collection; New York State Census, 1855; FELM, pt. 2, 370. Frederic remembered that Emma "felt seriously hurt" by his marriage to Agnes and "made no great effort to conceal" the fact. FELM, pt. 2, 368.

44. FELM, pt. 2, 427–29. See also Steele, *The Sun Shines for All*, 44.

45. See Garner, "Thomas Bangs Thorpe in the Gilded Age," 35–52; and Oswald, introduction, vii–xiii.

46. FELM, pt. 2, 421–23.

47. FELM, pt. 2, 398, 443.

48. Frederic E. Lockley to Elizabeth Metcalf Campbell courtship letters, folder 4, box 3, Fred Lockley Papers, MS 389, New York Historical Society, Albany.

49. EMLM, 22.

50. FEL to EML, September 21 and 22, 1861.

51. FEL to EML, November 1, 1861.

52. FEL to EML, November 6, 1861.

53. FELM, pt. 2, 478–82.

54. Emma Lockley was born March 9, 1821.

55. FELM, pt. 2, 376–78.

56. Telling references are sprinkled throughout her correspondence, such as when Elizabeth wrote, "I dreamt of you while taking a snooze this morning. . . . O! for one pleasant vivid dream of you[;] it is always something mixed up and unnatural. I never dream of you, but I immagine it is first yourself then Pa[.] I hate such troubled and indistinct dreams." EML to FEL, July 26, 1863.

57. Elizabeth Metcalf Lockley diary, entry for January 5, 1863, box 5, Lockley Papers, HL (hereafter EMLD). She repeated this theme in a letter to Frederic: "My life now is filled with care and anxiety[;] still I would not exchange it." EML to FEL, October 4, 1863.

58. FEL to EML, February 17, 1863.

59. EML to FEL, June 10, 1863.

60. Frederic was hardly alone in seeking stability through correspondence from home. Flotow, *In Their Letters, in Their Words*, 19; Hager, "Bonds," in *I Remain Yours*, 89–128. As another historian noted, letter-writing during the Civil War furthered the

democratization of the postal network, which in turn made affection, influence, and shared purpose portable between family members. Henkin, *Postal Age*, 11, 147.

61. FEL to EML, September 13 and 14, 1862.

62. FEL to EML, April 26, 1865.

63. EML to FEL, August 16 and 17, 1863.

64. "The correspondence of Victorian couples is filled with exchanges on children." Rose, *Victorian America*, 162.

65. Marten, *Children's Civil War*, 10–11.

66. Christopher Hager used the words "blankets of words" to describe dampening "fear's chill" among the family's children. Hager, *I Remain Yours*, 113.

67. On fathers' interest in children's upbringing, see Rose, *Victorian America*, 172.

68. Rose, *Victorian America*, 134–47.

69. Hager, *I Remain Yours*, 209; Marten, *Children's Civil War*, 70, 89.

70. Carmichael, *War for the Common Soldier*, 69, 81–82, 85, 314.

71. Charles Maguire enrolled as a captain in the Seventh New York at age twenty-two in August 1862. He would die July 4, 1864, of wounds sustained June 22 in fighting at the Weldon-Petersburg Railroad. Keating, *Carnival of Blood*, 35, 219–20, 454.

72. Frederic Lockley, "The First Battle," *Albany Evening Journal*, December 8, 1884; Keating, *Carnival of Blood*, 34–35. The fighting at Harris Farm on May 19, 1864, was part of the Battle of Spotsylvania Court House.

73. EML to FEL, June 7, 1863.

74. See, for example, FEL to EML, April 8, 1863, and February 23, 1863. See also FELM, pt. 3, 257, 261–62.

75. Carmichael, *War for the Common Soldier*, 111.

76. On what he describes as "the importance of literacy to recapturing traditional masculinity," see Michael C. Nelson, "Writing during Wartime," 65.

77. Stephen Treadwell, a fellow soldier in the regiment, would credit Fred Lockley with saving his life. FELM, pt. 3, 286–87.

78. FELM, pt. 3, 368–71.

79. FEL to EML, October 9, 1862; FEL to EML, September 30, 1863; EMLD, entry for October 1, 1863. Many soldiers brought books to camp, but as one historian noted, camp was not a congenial place for a reflective mind. See Zimm, *Wicked Rebellion*, 40.

80. By early 1865 Frederic had seen too much incomprehensible tragedy and experienced the true practicalities of the field to return to what he viewed as the arbitrary camp discipline his new commander, Col. Richard Duryea, insisted on. At first, he said, Duryea was exacting, but "I keep cool over it." But ten days later, he told Lizzie, Duryea's efforts to regenerate the regiment through camp discipline fell on himself as adjutant, and "I am too disaffected to exert myself." He admitted, "I have that indifference for his good opinion that I cannot exert myself to obtain it. It is time this war was over." FEL to EML, January 30, 1865; FEL to EML, February 8, 1865.

81. Lockley would never desert, but he did reject promotion for fear of lengthening his term. See FEL to EML, July 8, 1864, on rejecting promotion and FEL to EML, November 10, 1864, on accepting a commission because it did not extend his term of service. McPherson speculates that desertion rates were probably higher among married soldiers, especially Confederate soldiers, but that the temptation to desert was counterbalanced by soldiers' sense of honor in the service of their country. McPherson, *For Cause & Comrades*, 138–39. Christopher Hager cites another reason: shame. Hager, *I Remain Yours*, 217.

82. FEL to EML January 9, 1865. As one historian put it, the Confederacy was hemorrhaging deserters in the final year of the war. The desertion rate from the Army of Northern Virginia in the last months of the war was estimated at twelve hundred men every ten days. Glatthaar, "Tale of Two Armies," 336. Total numbers are still contested, but desertions in the Confederate Army were said to total about 120,000 during the war and ranged from 200,000 to 280,000 for the Union Army. Mitchell and others (including Randall C. Jimerson) take their totals from Lonn, *Desertion during the Civil War*, 231, 233, although Mitchell notes Lonn revised the Union estimate downward elsewhere. Mitchell, *Civil War Soldiers*, 242n80; Jimerson, *Private Civil War*, 231. These calculations likely underestimated the number of men who went on unauthorized leave. McPherson, *For Cause & Comrades*, 177–78. Hager notes that frequent mentions of execution for desertion in soldiers' letters are out of proportion to the number of actual executions, which he estimates to have been in the hundreds. Hager, *I Remain Yours*, 224. James I. Robertson Jr. seems to concur, saying that of five hundred soldiers shot or hanged as criminals during the war, two-thirds (perhaps three hundred) were executed for desertion. Robertson estimated the odds for a deserter to escape successfully at three-to-one. Gerald Linderman's estimates for Union deserters caught and returned to the army—eighty thousand of two hundred thousand deserters (2.5-to-1 odds)—would seem to agree roughly, although his estimates (21,000 men caught and returned out of 104,000 Confederate deserters) indicate better odds for Rebel defectors (about 5-to-1). Robertson, *Soldiers Blue and Gray*, 135; Linderman, *Embattled Courage*, 176.

83. FEL to EML, January 9, 1865. On the ease of escape, both from the field and from hospitals, see Catton, *Bruce Catton's Civil War*, 280–85. On the hardening of Fred Lockley's attitudes, both toward Union deserters and later toward the Confederate prisoners he saw at Fort McHenry, see FEL to EML, March 29, 1865. Gerald Linderman termed this hardening of soldier sympathies "annealing." Linderman, *Embattled Courage*, 241.

84. Gallagher, *Union War*, 128–29; Mitchell, *Vacant Chair*, 32–34; Wiley, *Life of Billy Yank*, 286–88; McPherson, *For Cause & Comrades*, 142–44.

85. Earl J. Hess has written on soldiers' loyalty to ideas. Hess, *Liberty, Virtue, and Progress*.

86. Frederic was one of 381 Seventh New Yorkers released on June 16, 1865, and to reach Albany four days later. Keating, *Carnival of Blood*, 307–9.

87. Gallagher, *Union War*, 77; McPherson, *For Cause & Comrades*, 119; Mitchell, *Vacant Chair*, 68.

88. FELM, pt. 3, 41–42.

89. FELM, pt. 3, 42–43.

90. Frederic seems to have used the terms he did as a means, for his era, of making respectful reference, however condescending or offensive they may seem to us today.

91. FEL to EML, November 6, 1862. See, for example, Flotow, *In Their Letters, in Their Words*, 164; Zimm, *Wicked Rebellion*, 115, 128–30. Lockley may have been a little ahead of most. Gallagher notes that such opinion was held widely only by early 1864. Gallagher, *Union War*, 76. Indeed, as Hager observes, few abolitionists were among those who answered Lincoln's call for volunteers in 1862. Hager, *I Remain Yours*, 67. But with time, many soldiers found the war an opportunity to see Blacks as human beings. Zimm, *Wicked Rebellion*, 112; Glatthaar, "Tale of Two Armies," 326.

92. FELM, pt. 2, 300, 302.

93. Lystra, *Searching the Heart*, especially 75, 177, 178.

2. August–September 1862

1. Maria H. Mair was Elizabeth Lockley's aunt, her father's sister. Frederic and Elizabeth were married in Maria Mair's home in Schuylerville, New York, on February 28, 1861.

2. FELM, pt. 2, 480. Lincoln issued his call for three hundred thousand voluntary enlistments on July 2, 1862.

3. Edward A. Springsteed, age twenty-two, enrolled as captain of Company I on August 14, 1862, would be mustered in as major four days later. Wounded at Cold Harbor on June 16, he would be killed at Reams Station on August 25, 1964. Keating, *Carnival of Blood*, 503.

4. Our Lady of Victory Parish, Troy NY.

5. Emma Lockley.

6. Bob Acres, a character in Richard Brinsley Sheridan's play *The Rivals* (first performed in 1775), is commonly considered a coward.

7. "Army Reminiscences," Albany *Evening Journal*, August 30, 1884. Lockley's regiment may have been lucky to receive rifled muskets, although by mid-1862, such arms were not as scarce as they had been at the beginning of the war when some units received smoothbore muskets because rifled muskets were in short supply. Undoubtedly, his unit received Model 1861 Springfield rifle muskets, the most common infantry weapon of the Civil War. More than a million were manufactured, not including the modified 1863 Springfields. Lockley speaks little of using his musket.

8. Alexandria, Virginia, eighteen miles south of Washington DC and a port on the Potomac River, was quickly occupied by Federal forces after the firing on Fort Sumter in 1861. A major supply point, it remained under Union control throughout the war and became a major hospital center to treat the war wounded. It remains unclear why Lockley datelined his letters from Camp Alexandria. He and his regiment were never stationed there but rather near Tennallytown as soon as they arrived in Washington DC. Cooling and Owen, *Mr. Lincoln's Forts*, 6–7; Keating, *Carnival of Blood*, 10–13.

9. Of Johnson, Fry & Co.

10. Frederic's mother-in-law from his first marriage.

11. Like the Seventh New York, the Sixteenth Maine Infantry Regiment enlisted in August 1862 for three years and went first to Washington DC. Unlike the Seventh, the Sixteenth Maine saw action as soon as the Battle of Antietam in September 1862, at Fredericksburg in December, and in a heroic delaying action during the first day of the Battle of Gettysburg in July 1863. The regiment then saw action during the Overland Campaign and in the siege of Petersburg in 1864.

12. Springfield rifled muskets weighed approximately nine pounds.

13. This was likely Philadelphia's Cooper-Shop Volunteer Refreshment Saloon, located near the Wilmington & Baltimore Railroad station and established in 1861 by Mr. and Mrs. Cooper and others in the William M. Cooper & Co. cooperage. Through June 1865 the volunteer relief agency provided meals, hospital care, and washing, sleeping, and writing facilities to 826,000 soldiers, refugees, and freed people. "Not a soldier passed through that city during the entire war, but was made welcome to the bounties of those estimable ladies," Lockley wrote twenty years later. "That lunch in Philadelphia was gratefully referred to long after we had settled down into soldier life." "Army Reminiscences," *Albany Evening Journal*, August 30, 1884; "The Philadelphia Cooper-Shop," *New York Times*, June 2, 1865; M. H. Traubel, *Cooper Shop Volunteer Refreshment Saloon*, 1862, chromolithograph, Library of Congress, Washington DC, https://www.

loc.gov/resource/gdcwdl.wdl_09448/?r=0.183,1.129,0.854,0.586,0; Wiley, *Life of Billy Yank*, 35; Mark, "Union Soldiers Fondly Remembered."

14. Originally named Tennally's Town, then Tennallytown, after area tavern owner John Tennally, the name has evolved over time to become Tenleytown today.

15. Most soldiers lacked experience with cleanliness and food preparation. Frederic was the exception. Browning and Silver, *Environmental History of Civil War*, 19–20; Wiley, *Life of Billy Yank*, 245.

16. Fort Alexandria was in Virginia, not Maryland.

17. G. S. Duncan, another book agent, whose office for Johnson, Fry & Co. was located at 94½ State Street. He lived at 5 Hamilton Place. Albany City Government, *Albany City Directory for 1862* through *Albany City Directory for 1866*.

18. The Albany city directories for the war years, 1862–1865, list only one resident named Bull: John C. Bull, a cabinetmaker living at 211 Hamilton Place.

19. The Second Battle of Bull Run and Second Battle of Manassas are the same battle. Bull Run, which referred to a stream coursing through the battlefield, was preferred by the North; Manassas, which referred to a nearby town, was preferred in the South.

20. A popular crossing of the Potomac River northwest of Washington DC.

21. Second Battle of Bull Run (Second Manassas) was fought August 29–30, 1862. Union casualties totaled about fourteen thousand killed and wounded. A significant tactical Confederate victory, the outcome encouraged Robert E. Lee to launch his Maryland Campaign of 1862.

22. Stonewall Jackson no longer threatened Washington DC because he was moving north and west of the Union Capital with the rest of Robert E. Lee's Army of Northern Virginia as part of the Maryland Campaign.

23. Keating, *Carnival of Blood*, 11, 16.

24. Fort DeRussy was one of sixty-eight forts that would eventually surround the capital, connected by twenty miles of pits and thirty-two miles of military roads, and manned with ten thousand troops. The spelling should be Fort DeRussy, named for Rene Edward DeRussy, engineer and military educator responsible for constructing coastal fortifications on the East and West Coasts. Lockley misspelled the name consistently as "DeRussey." Cooling and Owen, *Mr. Lincoln's Forts*, viii, 150–55.

25. Taneytown, Maryland, not to be confused with Tennallytown.

26. Edwin Vose Sumner (1797–1863), in command of the Second Corps, and Nathanial P. Banks (1816–1894), a Union general and Massachusetts politician in command of a division, had both retreated to Washington DC with the rest of the Union Army of Virginia under Maj. Gen. John Pope after the battles of Second Bull Run (Second Manassas), August 29–30, and Chantilly, September 1.

27. These were men who had fought at Second Bull Run and Chantilly and were now streaming into the capital to reorganize and refit under a new but familiar commander, George B. McClellan, whom Lincoln had reinstated on September 2.

28. About twenty-five miles southwest of Albany NY.

29. Edmund M. Parker, a twenty-six-year-old accountant from Kinderhook NY, enlisted as a private and was immediately promoted to corporal and then to regimental quartermaster-sergeant. Promoted to second lieutenant in December 1863, he was discharged for disability in January 1865. Keating, *Carnival of Blood*, 474.

30. Joseph L. Rogers, a twenty-two-year-old teamster, became one of Frederic's best friends. Born in Broome County NY, Rogers enlisted as a private and was promoted to

corporal immediately and then to first sergeant in May 1863. He was killed in action at Cold Harbor on June 3, 1864. Keating, *Carnival of Blood*, 486.

31. He will later name this person as Jimmy Van Benthuysen.

32. From the *Aeneid*, ancient Greek for "faithful friend."

33. Fanny Fern (1811–72) was an American novelist, children's writer, humorist, and newspaper columnist from the 1850s to 1870s. She was the highest-paid columnist in the United States at the time, earning one hundred dollars a week from the *New York Ledger*.

34. Robert E. Lee's invasion of Maryland will lead to the Battle of Antietam on September 17 and Confederate Gen. Braxton Bragg's northward thrust through Tennessee and into Kentucky.

35. The letter is today preserved in an envelope addressed to Miss Lou Lockley, Walla Walla, Wash. Territory, with return address Gus Stulfauth, SLC, Utah. Stulfauth, an apparent friend of the family, sent it to Lou in March 1881, while Lou visited her parents, who were then living in Walla Walla, Washington Territory. Later, Lou lived intermittently in Browning, Montana, with her sister Gertrude, who married J. H. Sherburne. Frederic Lockley to Lou Lockley, folder 20, box 79, Sherburne Collection.

36. Samuel E. Jones, twenty-two, enlisted in August 1862 as captain of Company B. He was wounded on June 3, 1864, at Cold Harbor and wounded and captured on June 16, 1864, at Petersburg. Paroled in March 1865, he was discharged in May 1865.

3. September–November 1862

1. Psalms 133: 1–3.

2. Hamilton Harris was the Lockley family's landlord and an attorney in Albany. See Albany City Government, *Albany City Directory for 1862*, 65.

3. FELM, pt. 3, 286–87. Stephen Treadwell, listed as twenty-one-year-old merchant from Potters Hollow NY, would become one of Frederic's best friends. He had already made sergeant and would muster in as a second lieutenant in February 1864. Wounded in the left arm at Totopotomoy Creek on June 1, 1864, and discharged that September, he survived the war. Keating, *Carnival of Blood*, 514.

4. Mark Tapley, a literary character credited with an ever-jolly disposition, is from Charles Dickens's novel *Martin Chuzzlewit*.

5. FEL to EML, September 25, 1862. The maiden name of Fred Lockley's mother, Mary Lillie, was Davies. Born about 1785, she married Frederic's father, Samuel Lockley, in 1806. Samuel died in London in 1849, and Frederic put his mother in a home for widows before returning to the United States in 1851 with his sister, Emma, leaving behind in England another sister, Mary Anne, who had by then married Samuel Palmer Davenport.

6. Should be William B. Faulk, a twenty-five-year-old machinist from Preston Hollow NY. Faulk would become one of Frederic's closer comrades and would survive the war. Keating, *Carnival of Blood*, 410. Lockley consistently spelled his name incorrectly.

7. Frederick Richwine, age twenty-six at time of transfer January 1864 out of the Seventh New York for unknown reasons. Keating, *Carnival of Blood*, 537.

8. Hamilton Berry, a twenty-four-year-old railroader from Coeymans, New York, at enlistment in August 1862, was promoted through the ranks and made first lieutenant by December 1864. He was mustered out June 16, 1865. Keating, *Carnival of Blood*, 377.

9. Samuel F. Morrow of the United Presbyterian Church, Albany, New York. Albany City Government, *Albany Directory for 1863*, 204. Eventually, Elizabeth said, "I do confess that although Mr Morrow is a very good man, he is very uninteresting." EML to FEL,

October 4, 1863. She frequently mentioned William B. Sprague of the Second Presbyterian Church, Albany, as well. Albany City Government, *Albany Directory for 1862*, 200.

10. FEL to EML, October 10, 1862.

11. FEL to EML, October 17, 1862.

12. A reference to the tale of Belshazzar's feast from the Book of Daniel in which the fall of Babylon is foretold because Belshazzar has not honored God.

13. A common expression in the nineteenth century referring to Jeremey Diddler, a charlatan character taken from James Kenney's 1803 farce, *Raising the Wind*. Herman Melville discussed him in the *Confidence Man* (1857) and "diddle," meaning to swindle or cheat, may have derived from his name.

14. When he bared his deepest feelings, however fleeting, Frederic likely touched a nerve relating to the Victorian expectation that in marrying, the man would assume economic responsibility for the woman. He also exposed the woman's fearfulness in giving up that responsibility to the man. Although Emma herself took offense, Elizabeth's response, judging from Frederic's letters, which are all we have, seems to have been more muted. At first, he threatened to withdraw from being so intimate; that is, from being so honest about his true feelings. His subsequent letters show that he would not withdraw from such honesty—necessary to the intimacy of what Karen Lystra identified as "romantic love" in Victorian-era courtship. Instead, he increasingly reserved openness for Elizabeth only. As undaunted as Frederic's final sally in this last letter sounds, the episode constituted a learning experience for him. However close his relationship with his sister Emma, he could only maintain true romantic love with his wife, Elizabeth, and she seems to have sensed that his honesty, however self-indulgent at the time, reflected something deeper to which she needed to be attentive. That something was the complete honesty and unconditional acceptance necessary to the romantic love that would sustain her marriage. Lystra, *Searching the Heart*, 142.

15. Horatio Seymour (1810–86) had been defeated (1850) and then elected (1852) as governor of New York in earlier elections and was elected Democratic governor of New York again in November 1862. Both his terms as governor were tumultuous, the second more so. He was critical of President Lincoln's wartime leadership and opposed Radical Republican policies. Nominated as the Democratic candidate for president in 1868, he lost the election to Ulysses S. Grant.

16. These trousers for Lockley and other NCOs almost certainly had red stripes running along the outer seams instead of blue. Red facing signified artillery, whereas blue facing signified infantry.

17. FEL to EML, November 16, 1862. James Van Benthuysen, a nineteen-year-old printer when enlisted in August 1862 as a private in Company I, would be promoted to corporal, then sergeant before mustering out in June 1865. His brother Henry Van Benthuysen, three years older, enlisted in Company I at the same time. He was captured at Petersburg on June 16, 1864, and died in Andersonville Prison. Keating, *Carnival of Blood*, 517.

18. FEL to EML, November 19, 1862.

4. December 1862

1. FEL to EML, October 2, 1862.

2. FEL to EML, November 26, 1862. By *inconsiderate*, he seems to have meant "uninhibited."

3. FEL to EML, November 26, 1862.

4. FEL to EML, December 2, 1862.

5. FEL to EML, December 7, 1862.

6. Lockley consistently spells Shakespeare as "Shakspere," indicating he was either using English author, editor, and publisher Charles Knight's popular illustrated editions, *The Pictorial Shakspere*, or he had adopted Knight's popularized spelling of the bard's name. First offered in the early 1840s, Knight's illustrated editions of Shakespeare's works were available for decades, appearing even on the western American frontier in the 1860s and after. Gray, *Charles Knight*; Stephen and Lee, *Dictionary of National Biography*, s.v., "Charles Knight (1791–1873)"; Minton, "Shakespeare in Frontier and Territorial Montana," 28–29.

7. Frederic is paraphrasing the Scottish poet Robert Burns (1759–1796) here, specifically taking from Burns' poem, "The Cotter's Saturday Night," first published in 1786. The poem includes the lines "The mother, wi her needle and her sheers / Gars auld claes look amaist as weel's the new" to scoff at Elizabeth's picture of domestic bliss in which she might be mending old clothes to make them look almost new. Burns is said to have taken his inspiration for this poem from "The Farmer's Ingle" by Robert Fergusson (1750–74).

8. *Rob Roy* is an 1817 historical novel by Sir Walter Scott.

9. On Edmund M. Parker, see chapter 2, note 29.

10. Each Union regiment had a quartermaster sergeant, responsible for stores and supplies, and a commissary sergeant, responsible for dispensing them.

11. William Shannon, twenty-nine at the time of his enlistment as a first lieutenant in August 1862 in Company I, made captain in August 1862, stood for court martial in 1864 but was cleared, and mustered out on June 16, 1865. Lockley and the regiment had much trouble with him. Keating, *Carnival of Blood*, 25, 300-301, 493.

12. He would say in a September 9, 1863, letter that he weighed 155 pounds.

13. From *Hamlet*, act 3, scene 1.

14. FEL to EML, December 28, 1862.

15. FEL to EML, December 31, 1862.

16. Frederic described Elizabeth's father as a "Scotch temperance evangelist." FELM, pt. 2, 461.

17. FEL to EML, January 14 and 15, 1863.

5. January–May 1863

1. FEL to EML, January 14 and 15, 1863. As Bruce Catton put it, "deep religious feeling" went hand-in-hand with "rough skepticism" for the Civil War generation. Catton, *Bruce Catton's Civil War*, 326–27.

2. EMLD, entry for January 1, 1863.

3. EMLD, entry for January 1, 1863.

4. EMLD, entry for January 29, 1863.

5. FEL to EML, January 8, 1863.

6. He would often combat his loneliness with paeans of joy over receiving a letter from her, which in turn could prompt a whole letter from him of what they both called "nonsense." See his letter of January 11, 1863, in appendix 1. Such letters could lift both their spirits. When Elizabeth received the letter, she told her diary, "I rec a most delicious letter from F today (strange term to use for a letter) but it was really charming & delightful." EMLD, entry for January 15, 1863.

7. From Homer, *The Odyssey*.

8. FEL to EML, January 12, 1863.

9. Accident probably befell the lost letters. On April 19 Frederic was so offended by Elizabeth's complaints about contemptuous neighbors, he burned her letter but added, "All your others are carefully preserved." FEL to EML, April 19, 1863.

10. Noting Dollie's birthday in her dairy, for example, Lizzie recorded, "We are going to try and break off calling her Dollie and call her Louisa instead of Emma so as to distinguish her from Aunt Emma." She must have told Fred of her decision in a letter, for he responded a few days later, "You may call Dumpling by what name you please, with me she will be Dollie as long as she lives." EMLD, entry for February 19, 1863; FEL to EML, February 25, 1863.

11. FEL to EML, January 25, 1863.

12. EMLD, entry for January 23, 1863.

13. FEL to EML, February 16 and 17, 1863.

14. FEL to EML, January 23, 1863.

15. FEL to EML, January 14 and 15, and January 25, 1863.

16. Door-to-door book salesman.

17. FEL to EML March 18, 1863.

18. FEL to EML March 18, 1863.

19. EMLD, entry for January 18, 1863.

20. Union Gen. Joseph Hooker (1814–79) instituted numerous reforms. McPherson, *Battle Cry of Freedom*, 584–86, 638–39; Catton, *Bruce Catton's Civil War*, 305–14, 315–16.

21. Catton, *Bruce Catton's Civil War*, 308–9.

22. French for "worthless person, bad lot, poor specimen."

23. EMLD, entry for April 7, 1863. Despite various Union assaults, Charleston, South Carolina, did not fall to Federal forces until February 1865.

24. EMLD, entry for April 2, 1863.

25. French for "wife."

26. Apollyon is Abaddon, the destroyer. It can be both a place and an angel of the abyss in the Bible; the place is a bottomless pit signifying the realm of the dead.

27. From the gravedigger scene in *Hamlet*, act 5, scene 1. The gravedigger made a witty pun to confuse the lie he has just told Hamlet with the notion of lying in a grave.

28. Someone who empties privies.

29. His second-oldest daughter, Dollie.

30. FEL to EML, April 22, 1863; EMLD, entry for April 25, 1863.

31. April 30 to May 6, 1863.

32. Gen. Nathaniel P. Banks and his preparations for capturing Port Hudson on the Mississippi River south of Vicksburg.

33. Flag Officer Samuel F. Dupont attacked Charleston, South Carolina, with nine ironclads on April 7, 1863. His failure was highly publicized, although his contention that the city could not be taken unless a significant land assault accompanied a naval attack was proven correct when Gen. William T. Sherman captured Charleston two months before the end of the war.

34. Lockley is writing four days after conclusion of the Battle of Chancellorsville (April 30–May 6) in which Confederate Gen. Robert E. Lee's "perfect battle" tactics, combined with Union Gen. Joseph Hooker's abandoned resolve, led to Union defeat despite superior Federal forces. Lockley was incorrect, however, in believing that Gen. Samuel P. Heintzelman provided Hooker with reinforcements.

35. He refers here to his sister Emma.

36. Although he may be alluding to his sister-in-law, Maria (nee Hill) Davis, his former wife's oldest sister, he is more likely referring to his true sister, Mary Davenport, still living in England. See his sister Emma's letter of June 7, 1863, asking how he responded to Mary's "precious copperhead epistle."

37. Lockley is wrong here. Gen. George Stoneman's cavalry raid south, intended to go to Hanover Junction, a key rail junction and supply depot, and surprise Lee from the rear, faltered completely when Stoneman failed to get his cavalry across the Rappahannock River expeditiously and Stoneman, once across, split his command and did widespread but relatively inconsequential damage to transportation facilities. Longacre, *Lincoln's Cavalrymen*, 139–45; Catton, *Bruce Catton's Civil War*, 315–19, 347.

38. To take advantage of Robert E. Lee's thrust north, Maj. Gen. Henry W. Halleck ordered Maj. Gen. John Adams Dix, who then directed Maj. Gen. John J. Peck, to cut Lee's lines of communication and attack an underdefended Richmond. The plan had great promise but few results. Longacre, "Inspired Blundering," 23–43.

6. May–June 1863

1. EMLD, entry for May 13, 1863.

2. FEL to EML, May 12, 1863.

3. EMLD, entry for May 12, 1863.

4. Elizabeth said Emma's walk to work was "fully a mile." What she did not relate to Fred but did record in her diary was the loneliness she felt because of Emma's absence. "I have been so lonely and lowspirited (am alone much of the time)." EMLD, entries for May 16 and May 14, 1863.

5. Thomas Jonathan "Stonewall" Jackson (1824–1863) was buried at Oak Grove Cemetery, Lexington VA, on May 15, 1863. Shot accidentally by his own men on May 2 during the Battle of Chancellorsville, he died on May 10, eight days later. He received his famous nickname, Stonewall, during the First Battle of Bull Run (First Manassas) and went on to establish a reputation as a gifted commander. Like his Civil War leadership, his piety, which no doubt appealed to Elizabeth, was legendary and contributed to his virtual apotheosis during and after the war. Foote, *Fredericksburg to Meridian*, 316–19; Faust, *This Republic of Suffering*, 154–56; McPherson, *Battle Cry of Freedom*, 460; Linderman, *Embattled Courage*, 178–79. See also Hettle, *Inventing Stonewall Jackson*.

6. Likely FEL to EML, April 28, May 5, and May 8, 1863.

7. EMLD, entry for May 14, 1863.

8. FEL to EML, May 12, 1863.

9. FEL to EML, May 12, 1863.

10. From Charles Dickens, *The Pickwick Papers*, in which Peter Lowten introduces Pickwick to some seedy, unkept law clerks who tell him stories from Cray's Inn about contorted justice.

11. EMLD, entry for May 25, 1863.

12. Robert Frost, a thirty-one-year-old Englishman, had served in the Crimean War. Wounded at Petersburg in September 1864 when a shell fragment required amputation of his left arm, he was discharged in February 1865 for disability. Keating, *Carnival of Blood*, 417.

13. The episode apparently did not prove harmful to Kirk's career. As Lockley notes, Joseph W. Kirk was the son of an Albany merchant. Enlisted at twenty-two in August 1862 as a private in Company I, he was promoted subsequently to corporal and ulti-

mately mustered in as a second lieutenant in October 1864. He survived the war and was mustered out in May 1865. Keating, *Carnival of Blood*, 443.

14. EMLD, entry for May 25, 1863.

15. Brig. Gen. William Farquhar Barry (1818–79), a graduate of West Point and an artillery commander during the Mexican-American War, coauthored *Instruction for Field Artillery* (1860). After serving with McClellan in the Peninsula Campaign, he supervised forts and ordnance in the defenses of Washington DC before campaigning with Sherman in Tennessee, Georgia, and the Carolinas.

16. *Jesse*, now an obsolete idiom, meant "to punish."

17. Possibly William J. Williams, age forty-three, discharged July 23, 1863. Keating, *Carnival of Blood*, 538.

18. Her hopes, and no doubt Frederic's, that he might come home on leave were heightened when General Hooker, after taking command of the Army of the Potomac in January, reinstituted the possibility of soldiers getting ten-day furloughs. EMLD, entry for April 8, 1863; McPherson, *Battle Cry of Freedom*, 585; Catton, *Bruce Catton's Civil War*, 309.

19. Cousin Jack appears to have been Agnes Hill's son, John, by her first marriage or perhaps a son of one of her sisters. He was listed as six years old in the Lockley household in the 1855 New York State Census, which would have made him age fifteen at most when this letter was written. See also J. L. Sherburne reminiscence, box 1, Sherburne Papers.

20. "You may expect a visit from Jack before long," Frederic warned her. He added, "Jack's military service has been far from creditable to him. I am anxious to know whether he comes home with his evil habits confirmed—or better qualities developed." Less than two weeks later, he answered his own question: "I should not distress myself about Jack," Frederic advised. "Let him go for what he will fetch. He seems past redemption." FEL to EML, May 12; FEL to EML, May 24, 1863.

21. Elizabeth recorded on May 28 that Emma had sprained her foot and would stay with Mrs. Owens where she worked for a couple of days. She stayed a week. Lizzie noted, "I feel very lonely going to bed without her." EMLD, entry for May 28, 1863.

22. The Twenty-Second New York Infantry Regiment, also known as the Second Troy Regiment, was formed with eight hundred men in 1861 and was combined with other units, which together became known as the Iron Brigade of the East (not to be confused with the Iron Brigade of the West, the Black Hat Brigade). They served at Second Bull Run, South Mountain, Antietam, Fredericksburg, and Chancellorsville. Most of the regiment had two-year enlistments and were mustered out on June 19, 1863.

7. Mid-June–Mid-July 1863

1. Lockley no doubt means *comment ça se fait*, French for "How come?" or "How is that?"

2. French for "naive grace." Frederic likely meant innocent gracefulness.

3. Frederic refers here to the wreck of the HMS *Birkenhead* on February 26, 1852, off the western cape of Africa, eighty-seven miles from Cape Town. Of the estimated 643 soldiers, Royal Marines, seamen, men, women, and children onboard, 193 survived. An iron-hulled ship built for the Royal Navy and launched as a troop ship in December 1845, the *Birkenhead* hit a submerged rock three miles off the coast and went down in twenty minutes. Many of the soldiers and sailors stood silently at attention as the ship went down, for which Rudyard Kipling wrote a tribute, "Soldier an' Sailor Too,"

in 1893. The *Birkenhead* sinking standardized the heroic procedure of "women and children first"—the *Birkenhead* drill—for evacuation of sinking ships.

4. *Copperhead* was a pejorative term applied to Peace Democrats by prowar Republicans. Opposed to both the war and emancipation, Peace Democrats sought a return to status quo antebellum. The term referred initially to the venomous copperhead snake and later to the badges made from the image of Liberty taken from Liberty Head large cent coins. Varon, *Armies of Deliverance*, 8, 12.

5. The Second Battle of Winchester was fought June 13–15 between Confederate forces under Lt. Gen. Richard S. Ewell and Union Maj. Gen. Robert H. Milroy. Ordered to retreat, Milroy instead held his ground and was routed, losing thirty-five hundred Union soldiers captured and hundreds more in killed and injured. Foote, *Fredericksburg to Meridian*, 439–40; McPherson, *Battle Cry of Freedom*, 648.

6. Clement L. Vallandigham, leader of the Peace Democrats and candidate for governor of Ohio, had been arrested for treason in May 1863 for a speech that purposely defied Gen. Ambrose Burnside's Order Number 38 against declaring sympathy for the enemy. President Lincoln, attempting to defuse "the most celebrated civil liberties case of the war," commuted Vallandigham's sentence of imprisonment for the rest of the war to banishment to Confederate lines. Vallandigham ultimately fled to Canada. McPherson, *Battle Cry of Freedom*, 594–98; Catton, *Bruce Catton's Civil War*, 358–61; Nevins, *Organized War, 1863–1864*, 168–72.

7. Lockley refers to Fernando Wood and his brother Benjamin Wood. Fernando Wood was a three-nonconsecutive-term mayor of New York City. Sympathetic to the Confederacy and known for outspoken opposition to President Lincoln, he advocated in early 1861 that New York City should declare itself an independent city-state (in effect, secede) so that it might continue the profitable cotton trade with the South. He continued to be an outspoken peace advocate and political operative throughout the war. His brother, Benjamin, was editor and publisher of the New York *Daily News*, which he purchased in 1860 and which, along with four other New York City newspapers, was put on notice for encouraging pro-Confederate sentiment. Having referred to "the dictatorship" of Lincoln's "Bloody Administration" and likening Lincoln to Henry VIII, the *Daily News* was effectively shut down when the city postmaster refused to mail its papers. When the *Daily News* tried to ship editions independently, they were confiscated. Holzer, *Lincoln and Power of the Press*, 303, 343–48, 391; McPherson, *Battle Cry of Freedom*, 247; Burrows and Wallace, *Gotham*, 831–41, 862, 865–68, 886–87; Varon, *Armies of Deliverance*, 243–44.

8. Horatio Seymour, elected governor of New York twice, 1853–1854 and 1863–1864, but who narrowly lost reelection in November 1864, was a Democrat, opposed emancipation, and was a "vigorous critic of the administration but no Copperhead." Donald, *Lincoln*, 422; McPherson, *Battle Cry of Freedom*, 560, 592. See also Catton, *Bruce Catton's Civil War*, 292–93, 302–3; Burrows and Wallace, *Gotham*, 886, 888; Holzer, *Lincoln and Power of the Press*, 411, 442; Nevins, *Organized War, 1863–1864*, 125–26, 170, 174.

9. George B. McClellan (1826–1885), former general of the Union Army and well-known for his Southern sympathies, including noninterference with slavery, was linked politically to Fernando Wood and other Peace Democrats. McPherson, *Battle Cry of Freedom*, 504–5; Slotkin, *Long Road to Antietam*, 15–16, 27, 48–49, 176; Sears, *George B. McClellan*, 355, 448n9.

10. A newspaper publishing error (when the dash was dropped from copy labeled "Fighting—Joe Hooker" and became a separate headline) resulted in the famed moniker "Fighting Joe Hooker." Foote, *Fredericksburg to Meridian*, 234.

11. In his letter of June 21, Frederic said he was sending "a nasty lot of money" but suggested she might not want to build "a brown stone house" just yet. FEL to EML, June 21, 1863.

12. Gertrude turned six years old on July 6. Josie had turned ten on June 10.

13. FEL to EML, June 23, 1863.

14. EML to FEL, June 28, 1863.

15. FEL to EML, June 26, 1863.

16. President Lincoln and Gen.-in-Chief Henry W. Halleck accepted Hooker's impetuous resignation and replaced him with Maj. Gen. George Gordon Meade on June 28, 1863, three days before the Battle of Gettysburg commenced.

17. Port Hudson, twenty miles northwest of Baton Rouge, Louisiana, was the site of the longest siege of the Civil War to that time (forty-eight days) and the last Confederate stronghold on the Mississippi River to fall to Union arms. Despite Union assaults in May and June, the outnumbered Confederates held out until learning on July 4 of the fall of Vicksburg. Deeming further resistance hopeless, Confederate Maj. Gen. Franklin Gardner surrendered the garrison on July 9, 1863.

18. EMLD, entry for July 7, 1863.

8. July–September 1863

1. EML to FEL, July 12, 1863.

2. More than one hundred people, many of them African Americans, lost their lives July 13–16, 1863, in the New York City draft riots, one of the most racially charged incidents of violence in American history. The riots began as a working-class protest against new draft laws passed by Congress and the ability of wealthier men to escape the draft by paying $300 or hiring a substitute. Federal troops did not reach the city until the second day of the riot, by which time homes, businesses, and public buildings had been ransacked or destroyed. McPherson, *Battle Cry of Freedom*, 609–11; Burrows and Wallace, *Gotham*, 883–99; Bernstein, *New York City Draft Riots*.

3. EML to FEL, July 17, 1863.

4. EML to FEL, July 26, 1863.

5. EML to FEL, July 29, 1863.

6. Emma to FEL, July 29, 1863.

7. EML to FEL, August 23, 1863.

8. James O'Hair, twenty-six, enrolled as second lieutenant in Co. I in August 1862, was quickly promoted to first lieutenant. Wounded and captured June 16, 1864, at Petersburg, he would be paroled on March 1, 1865. Keating, *Carnival of Blood*, 472.

9. He said he had lost hearing from swimming, FEL to EML, August 9, 1863.

10. Frederick W. Mather, a twenty-nine-year-old railroad man from Greenbush, New York, enlisted as a private in August 1862, was quickly promoted to sergeant, and then mustered in as a second lieutenant four days after Frederic wrote this letter to Elizabeth. Mather, who became one of Lockley's closest friends in the Seventh New York, was captured at Petersburg June 16, 1864, paroled the following March, and mustered out of the service in May 1865. Keating, *Carnival of Blood*, 456. Mather returned to Albany and became a recognized writer and editor on fishing topics. He died in 1900.

11. FEL to EML, September 9, 1863.

12. Rosa Bonheur (1822–99), considered the most famous female painter of the nineteenth century, was a French painter, mostly of animals.

13. An ungracious description. A *grass feeder* was someone bovine-like, considered at the bottom of the food chain, of low intelligence, and not a hunter, with eyes wide apart.

14. *Eclats de vire,* literally French for "shards of life."

15. Clarence Tuthill, eighteen, a farmer when enlisted as a private in August 1862, survived the war and was mustered out in June 1865. Keating, *Carnival of Blood,* 515.

16. George Shipley, a forty-year-old weaver and private in Co. I, died of disease July 12, 1864, on board transport from City Point to New York City. Keating, *Carnival of Blood,* 495.

17. Constructed as Fort Lyman in 1755 and renamed Fort Edward in 1756, the post was established at a customary portage around the falls of the Hudson River. The distance from Fort Edward to Schuylerville is about twelve miles.

18. Likely Jane Van Olinda, a widow listed on Hamilton Street, *Albany City Directory 1863,* 146. Elizabeth hoped to get work as a copyist in Washington DC, but she never did.

19. Lockley almost always accented *chére* but in this case did not.

20. The U.S. Sanitary Commission, although derided at first, nonetheless received grudging federal authorization as a private relief agency in summer 1861. Proving essential to the Union war effort, it provided an estimated $25 million in aid to Union armies during the war, some $15 million of which was distributed as food and other aid directly to Federal troops and prisoners in Confederate prison camps. Women played crucial roles throughout the commission's operations, including the estimated fifteen thousand women volunteers who worked in hospitals during the war. Giesberg, *Civil War Sisterhood.*

21. Freeman Gauther (also Gauthier and Gunther), a twenty-year-old baker from Canada, enlisted in July 1862 as a private. Captured on June 19, 1864, at Petersburg, he was sent to Andersonville Prison but escaped from there almost a year later and was mustered out of the regiment on June 16, 1865. Keating, *Carnival of Blood,* 419.

22. EML to FEL September 27, 1863.

23. Aeolus, mentioned in Homer's *Odyssey,* is the divine keeper of winds, releasing them only at the command of the greatest gods to wreak devastation upon the world.

9. October 1863

1. Fort Reno had been constructed by the 119th Pennsylvania Regiment in winter 1861 and named Fort Pennsylvania. Located on Washington's north side at the highest elevation in the city, it was renamed Fort Reno in 1863 after Maj. Gen. Jesse Lee Reno (1823–62), who died from wounds suffered at the Battle of South Mountain in September 1862. A small post at first, Fort Reno eventually became the largest defensive installation at the capital.

2. Daniel O'Brien, a twenty-two-year-old clerk from Manchester, England, enlisted as a private in August 1862, made sergeant-major by November 1862, and was mustered in as a second lieutenant in July 1863. Advanced to first lieutenant in January 1864, he was wounded and captured at Reams Station on August 25, 1864. Released from Libby Prison a month later, he was advanced to captain before being discharged for disability in February 1865. Keating, *Carnival of Blood,* 471.

3. Rowland S. Norton, a twenty-five-year-old merchant from Granville, New York, enlisted as a private in August 1862 and was promoted to sergeant major in August 1863. Mustered in as a second lieutenant, then first lieutenant, and then captain in 1864, he was mustered out in June 1865. Keating, *Carnival of Blood,* 470.

4. Routine housework supposedly kept a woman busy more than forty hours a week, and women typically dreaded washing the most because of the toil involved. In addi-

tion to the physical labor of scrubbing, rinsing, and hanging clothes to dry, handling the amount of water—estimated at fifty gallons—that had to be carried in and used, and then disposed of, was arduous. Gordon, *Rise and Fall of American Growth*, 57, 275.

5. This was likely the fight precipitated at Bristoe Station during Meade's retreat to the Manassas area.

6. A friend of Lizzie's who Lizzie had hoped could get her a copyist job in Washington DC.

7. EMLD, entry for November 9, 1863.

10. November 1863–January 1, 1864

1. EMLD, entry for November 9, 1863.

2. EMLD, entry for November 15, 1863.

3. FEL to EML, November 18, 1863.

4. Lizzie and Emma slept together in the same bed.

5. All three girls would mature and marry happily; two, Josie and Gertie, would have many children of their own.

6. Frederick E. Scripture was a twenty-one-year-old clerk from Hartford, Connecticut, when he enlisted as a private in August 1862. Promoted first to commissary sergeant and then to quartermaster sergeant, he was mustered in as a first lieutenant when appointed regimental quartermaster in January 1863. Scripture would be captured by John S. Mosby's Confederate raiders in May 1864, paroled in March 1865, and discharged in May 1865. Keating, *Carnival of Blood*, 492.

7. FEL to EML, December 2, 1863. Today, the National Park Service commemorates Fort DeRussy as a historic Civil War site. The fort, now part of Rock Creek Park in northcentral Washington DC, was one of several Civil War posts built atop the highest elevations surrounding the city. Today, trails leading to the outline of earth mounds and parapets are densely forested.

8. Designed by the American sculptor Thomas Crawford, the almost twenty-foot statue weighed almost fifteen thousand pounds. It had been cast in five sections at Clark Mills's bronze foundry just outside the city. Architect of the Capitol, "History of U.S. Capitol Building" https://www.aoc.gov/explore-capitol-campus/buildings-grounds/capitol-building/history; FEL to EML, December 2, 1863.

9. FEL to EML, December 6, 1863.

10. The two men were Samuel E. Jones and Joseph M. Murphy, ages twenty-two and twenty-seven, respectively, at the time of their enlistments in August 1862. The incident apparently had no detrimental effects on their military careers. Samuel E. Jones (see chapter 2 note 36, for background) would be discharged as a captain in May 1865. Murphy, promoted to major in January 1864 and to lieutenant colonel in October 1864, would be mustered out in July 1865. Keating, *Carnival of Blood*, 439, 468. Precise statistics for incidents of rape and sexual abuse are difficult to compute for Yankee soldiers and impossible for Rebel soldiers because most Confederate records were destroyed, but the Civil War is commonly considered a low-rape war. Historians have generally depended on Union court-martial records to document such crimes, and those total fewer than 450 cases of rape or attempted rape. Thomas P. Lowry reported surveying less than 5 percent of court-martial records in the National Archives and finding more than thirty trials for rape, but it was not until after April 1863 that soldiers could be prosecuted for such crimes under the Lieber Code. Low numbers of documentable cases have generally led historians to conclude that incidents of rape during the war

were relatively rare. "The Civil War was remarkable in how little rape took place," wrote Reid Mitchell in 1993, crediting a Victorian "code of manly restraint" as the reason. "How much rape did take place," he added, "remains something not known and perhaps not knowable." More recent scholars have argued differently, especially in light of the more than 180,000 documented cases of venereal disease among Union soldiers (again, Confederate statistics are unavailable) and given the customary unwillingness of victims to report abuse or rape. Although often severely punished when proven, rape was rarely reported and infrequently prosecuted when white women were involved, and rarely reported and almost never prosecuted when black women were involved. Mitchell, *Vacant Chair*, 109; Lowry, *Story Soldiers Wouldn't Tell*, 31–32, 123–31; Feimster, "Rape and Justice in Civil War"; Beck, "Gender, Race, and Rape During Civil War." See also Murphy, *I Had Rather Die*; Feimster, *Southern Horrors*. On Confederate records retrieved at Richmond in April 1865, see Guarneri, *Lincoln's Informer*, 352–53, 465n10.

11. FEL to EML, December 8, 1863.

12. EML to FEL, December 7, 1863.

13. EML to FEL, December 13, 1863.

14. FEL to EML, December 21, 1863.

15. EML to FEL, December 24, 1863.

16. As noted in chapter 3, note 12, Belshazzar's Feast, or the story of the writing on the wall, is told in the biblical book of Daniel. In the story, considered historical fiction, Belshazzar rewards Daniel for his interpretation of the writing on the wall, itself a message from God of Belshazzar's demise.

17. Charles M. Niles, twenty-one, merchant, enlisted as a private on August 12, 1862, and promoted subsequently to sergeant, was mustered in as second lieutenant, Company I, August 10, 1863, first lieutenant in April 1864, and captain in October 1864. He was mustered out on June 16, 1865. Keating, *Carnival of Blood*, 470.

18. From *Don Juan*, canto 1, stanza 220.

11. January–March 1864

1. Whether this "surprise" was her pregnancy or his efforts to have her come live near camp and cook for the officers remains unclear.

2. This is the only evidence of intentional self-censoring in Frederic and Elizabeth's Civil War correspondence, and it may have occurred when Elizabeth reread the correspondence in late January and early February 1913. Elizabeth wrote, apparently to her son, Fred Jr., to whom she was sending the family papers, "This finishes Fred's letters from the Army. I have read them all during the last week February 4th 1913," in Lockley Papers, box 2. Less likely, the censoring may have occurred ten years earlier. In a 1903 letter to his son, Frederic wrote, "For the last score of years your mother has been hoarding every family letter that came into her hands; until she now has such an accumulation that they have become burdensome. She has concluded the best thing to do with them is to destroy them; so thro' the long winter evenings now drawing to a close, she has been reading over the correspondence of one member of the family after another, indulging in reminiscences suggested by what she read, and then unwillingly passing each missive to its doom." FEL to Fred Lockley Jr., March 6, 1903, box 6, Lockley Collection, HL.

3. EML to FEL, January 17, 1864.

4. The expression relates to Lake Serbonis in Egypt. Described by Herodotus as a bog blown over to make it appear as solid ground, it can be used metaphorically to represent a situation from which extrication is difficult.

5. Rowland S. Norton. See chapter 9, note 3.

6. Fort Kearny, located near Tennellytown, filled a gap between forts DeRussy and Reno, north of Washington DC. Like the Nebraska fort of the same name, it was named after Maj. Gen. Philip Kearny, killed at the Battle of Chantilly, September 1, 1862.

7. From Shakespeare, *Troilus and Cressida*, act 3, part 2.

8. EML to FEL, January 18, 1864; FEL to EML, January 20, 1864.

9. EML to FEL, January 21; EML to FEL, January 24, 1864.

10. FEL to EML, January 28, 1864.

11. The U.S. Sanitary Commission struggled constantly for funding, even with strong support from multiple sources, including the mining centers of the Far West. In response, two women, Mary Livermore and Jane Hoge, conceived the "grand Northwestern fair," held in Chicago in September 1863. The extravaganza (Abraham Lincoln even donated an original copy of the Emancipation Proclamation, which auctioned for $3,000) was such a success that other Northern cities duplicated the effort on large and small scale, including this bazaar in Albany.

12. EML to FEL, January 28, 1864.

13. EML to FEL, January 31, 1864.

14. FEL to EML, February 4; FEL to EML, February 26, 1864.

15. EML to FEL, February 7; EML to FEL, February 12, 1864.

16. FEL to EML, February 26, 1864.

17. FEL to EML, February 14, 1864.

18. Frederic relates this story also in "Army Reminiscences," *Albany Evening Journal*, November 7, 1884.

19. *Wie geht's* is a cant German expression, meaning "How are you?" or "How goes it?"

20. EML to FEL, March 6, 1864.

21. EML to FEL, March 10, 1864.

22. FEL to EML, March 13; FEL to EML, March 16, 1864.

23. FEL to EML, March 19, 1864.

24. FEL to EML, March 19, 1864.

25. He told Elizabeth in a letter written that morning that Sgt. William B. Faulk would be home on leave and visit her Monday or Tuesday, March 21 or 22. Keating spells the name "Faulk" in *Carnival of Blood*, 410.

26. Philip Jenkins had been reduced in the ranks previously since enlisting in August 1862. He would be captured at Petersburg in June and die in Andersonville Prison in October. Keating, *Carnival of Blood*, 438.

27. From *Hamlet*, act 3, scene 1.

12. March–April 1864

1. FEL to EML, March 25, 1864. Oscar Bigelow, an eighteen-year-old student from Troy, had enlisted as a private less than three months earlier. He was killed while on picket duty at Cold Harbor on June 4, 1864. Keating, *Carnival of Blood*, 377.

2. Roswell B. Corliss (Lockley misspells his first name as Rosswell), an eighteen-year-old painter from Albany, New York, enlisted January 22, 1864, as private in Company G. He was captured June 16, 1864, at Petersburg, died of diarrhea August 24, 1864, at Andersonville, Georgia, and is buried there. Keating, *Carnival of Blood*, 394.

3. *Dejeuner* is French for "lunch."

4. *Ungaurt d'heure* is French for "unguarded hour."

5. *A la bonne heure* is French for "approval," as in "that's the spirit" or "apropos," "at the right time."

6. EML to FEL, March 27, 1864.

7. Francis Pruyn was age forty-five when enrolled in August 1862 as a captain in Company G. Mustered in as a major in January 1864, he was captured June 16, 1864, at Petersburg, and exchanged in October 1864. He resigned his commission December 30, 1864. Keating, *Carnival of Blood*, 478.

8. Samuel E. Jones, twenty-two, enrolled as a captain in Company B August 1862, was wounded at Cold Harbor on June 3, 1864, and wounded again and captured at Petersburg on June 16, 1864. Paroled in March 1865, he was discharged in May 1865. Keating, *Carnival of Blood*, 439.

9. Robert H. Bell, thirty-four, enrolled in August 1862 as a captain in Company F, was wounded in May 1864 at Spotsylvania and died of amputation of his left leg in a Washington DC hospital in June 1864. Keating, *Carnival of Blood*, 376.

10. FEL to EML March 31, 1864.

11. Her letter of March 30 and 31, 1864.

12. Charles W. Hobbs, twenty, enlisted as a second lieutenant and later made first lieutenant. He was wounded June 3, 1864, at Cold Harbor, made captain in November 1864, and major on March 22, 1865. Mustered out on July 3, 1865, Hobbs would continue in a military career, achieving the rank of brigadier general. "Gen Hobbs Died at Waverly Home," Washington DC, *Evening Star*, December 22, 1929; Keating, *Carnival of Blood*, 432.

13. From *Hamlet*, act 2, scene 2, in which Hamlet comments on an actor's emotional identification to Hecuba when Hecuba means nothing to him. Hecuba was the wife of King Priam of Troy and mother to nineteen children, including Hector, Paris, and Cassandra.

14. EML to FEL, March 27, 1864.

15. FEL to EML, March 25, 1864, in which he describes Sgt. Joe Rogers as being severely ill with the measles.

16. Son of Mr. and Mrs. G. S. Duncan. She said in her April 17, 1864, letter that he was deathly sick.

17. EML to FEL, April 25, 1864.

18. EML to FEL, April 28, 1864.

19. FEL to EML, May 2, 1864.

20. FEL to EML, May 5, 1864.

21. FEL to EML, May 8 and 9, 1864.

22. FEL to EML, May 5, 1864.

13. May–June 1864

1. Frederic refers to Union Maj. Gen. Benjamin Franklin Butler's Bermuda Hundred campaign, launched May 5 as one part of Grant's overall plan to attack Southern forces on several fronts. Butler's immediate objective was to cut the Richmond and Petersburg Railroad, although he could threaten Richmond itself, but Confederate Gen. P. G. T. Beauregard constructed the Howlett Line across the neck of the peninsula and effectively bottled up Butler and his army. Known for his lack of military skill, Butler was a highly successful trial lawyer and Democratic politician whose loyalty was especially important

to Lincoln in the election year of 1864. Butler was despised in the South. He became a hero to abolitionists when, in 1861, he was first to declare that escaped slaves could not be returned to their owners because they were contraband of war, a policy soon adopted by the Union Army generally. As military governor of New Orleans in 1862, he drew Southern wrath for a variety of harsh and insulting actions, especially toward Southern womanhood. After one summary execution, Confederate President Jefferson Davis declared Butler a felon who, if captured, could be executed. Butler never ventured anywhere without a large security force as a result. As a Northern war Democrat, he remained in high command (second only to Grant) until after Lincoln's reelection and was relieved of command in January 1865 after leading an incompetent assault in the First Battle of Fort Fischer at Wilmington, North Carolina. Bruce Catton labeled him "the archetype of the fixer," a man about whom "a tremendous scandal was always on the edge of breaking, but the break never quite came." Catton, *Bruce Catton's Civil War*, 581–82. See also McPherson, *Battle Cry of Freedom*, 354–56, 820; Catton, *Grant Takes Command*, 205–6, 401–3.

2. Battle of the Wilderness, May 5–7, 1864.

3. Grant's Army of the Potomac was engaged at Spotsylvania Court House as Frederic wrote this letter. Grant had sustained more than seventeen thousand casualties in the Wilderness, May 5–7, and the Spotsylvania battles May 9–21 would be the costliest of the war with another eighteen thousand casualties on the Union side and more than thirty thousand casualties on both sides. The three generals he mentions died within four days of each other. Maj. Gen. John Sedgwick (1813–64), a graduate of West Point, was wounded three times at the Battle of Antietam and killed May 9, 1864, when shot by a sharpshooter at the Battle of Spotsylvania Court House. Brig. Gen. Alexander Hays, a graduate of West Point with a long record of courageous leadership, including in the Seven Days Battles, Second Battle of Bull Run, and Gettysburg, was killed when struck in the head with a minié ball during the Battle of the Wilderness on May 5, 1864. James S. Wadsworth (1807–64), a political general who had been a Republican presidential elector in 1860, was commissioned a major general in the New York state militia in 1861. He served at the First Battle of Bull Run and oversaw Washington DC defenses briefly while Lockley was posted there. He went on to serve at the Battles of Chancellorsville and Gettysburg. The oldest divisional commander for Grant at the Battle of the Wilderness, he was shot off his horse in the Wilderness and then captured on May 6 and died in a Confederate field hospital on May 8.

4. The arrest seems to have been negated when the Seventh New York was ordered to march south to join Grant in Virginia two days later. Mather would be captured in an assault on Petersburg on June 16.

5. French for "cute" or "lovely."

6. Frederic is using the alternate spelling of Belle Plains, Virginia, here. Located on the Potomac River a dozen miles northeast of Fredericksburg, the landing became a major Union supply point during the Overland Campaign.

7. Lockley used the nineteenth-century spelling for what is today Spotsylvania.

8. Soldiers often misspelled Fredericksburg in their letters.

9. Winfield Scott Hancock (1824–86), a graduate of West Point in 1844 and from an aristocratic family whose loyalties were with the Democratic Party, served in the Mexican-American War with his namesake, Winfield Scott, and afterward in Minnesota, Florida, Kansas, Utah, and California before the Civil War. He was wounded at Antietam and Chancellorsville, after which he assumed command of Second Corps. Hancock performed well at Gettysburg in summer 1863 but was severely wounded and did

not rejoin active field duty until Grant's Overland Campaign, in which he led Second Corps, which by then included Lockley's Seventh New York. Hancock supervised the execution of the Lincoln assassination conspirators in July 1865 and, after a brief assignment in the West, was transferred to Reconstruction duty in Texas and Louisiana, where his General Order Number 40 restoring civil government and ensuring white property rights proved popular with the local population. His actions in Texas contributed to his Democratic Party nomination for president twice, in 1868 against U. S. Grant, and again in 1880 against James A. Garfield. He lost both times. He served in command of the Division of the Atlantic until his death, a year after he presided over Grant's funeral.

10. This is the Ni (or Ny) branch of the Mattaponi River.

11. Including encounters at Harris Farm on May 19, Milford Station on May 20, and several clashes along the North Anna River, May 23–26.

12. John Morris, twenty-six when enrolled August 9, 1862, was killed by a shot to the head on May 19, 1864, at Spotsylvania. Keating, *Carnival of Blood*, 465.

13. "Letters from the Seventh Artillery," *Albany Knickerbocker*, June 5, 1864. See also Wynkoop Hallenbeck Crawford Company, *Annual Report of the Adjutant-General*.

14. Regimental physician James Edwin Pomfret attended Morris, who suffered a bullet to the spine, until early morning the next day. "The moment I saw him I knew it was a fatal case. . . . I so told him. . . . He took my hand which he kept in his own until he died." James Pomfret to his wife, Almeda Pomfret, June 5, 1864, Albany Medical College Archives.

15. Keating, *Carnival of Blood*, 127.

16. None of these letters has survived.

17. Lewis Owen Morris, thirty-eight, was killed by a sharpshooter on June 4, 1864, at Cold Harbor. Keating, *Carnival of Blood*, 365.

18. On Joseph Rogers, see chapter 2, note 30.

19. Alexander Swinton, a painter from London, England, enlisted as a private in July 1862 and was promoted to corporal in early 1863. Wounded in the right shoulder on June 3, 1864, at Cold Harbor, he was discharged from a Washington DC hospital for disability in January 1865. Keating, *Carnival of Blood*, 509.

20. On Stephen Treadwell, see chapter 1, note 77, and *Carnival of Blood*, 514.

21. Sgt. Maj. Lockley oversaw the regimental records, which were best not kept on the front lines.

22. Josie, born June 10, 1853, was eleven.

23. Keating, *Carnival of Blood*, 173.

24. Keating, *Carnival of Blood*, 197–98, 207–11. See also Bearss, *Eastern Front Battles: June–August 1864*, 86–92; Trudeau, *Last Citadel*, 42–46.

25. Assault on Petersburg line, June 16, 1864. See Keating, "Another Cold Harbor," chap. 10 in *Carnival of Blood*, 170–98. Battle casualties were variously estimated later at 444 and 425. Keating, *Carnival of Blood*, 197.

26. Keating, *Carnival of Blood*, 211. Francis C. Barlow, who entered the war as a private and achieved the rank of brevet major general, was twenty-nine at the time of this clash.

27. Frederic was not alone in criticizing newspaper correspondents for "heroic vocabularies" and "goading the soldiers forward." See Linderman, *Embattled Courage*, 217.

28. Either Frederic misdated this letter or wrote it before 8:00 a.m. June 21, when, according to Keating, he and his regiment were ordered to form up for march. They halted briefly before they resumed the march, which would take them close to ten miles to the Jerusalem Plank Road. Keating, *Carnival of Blood*, 212–13; FELM, pt. 3, 301.

The men had received "a heavy backlog of accumulated mail" the evening before on June 20, which jibes with this letter in which Frederic said they received "a heavy mail yesterday." Keating, *Carnival of Blood*, 211.

29. A fateful assault on rebel lines east of Petersburg on June 16 in which 425 Seventh New York men were killed, wounded, or captured. Keating, *Carnival of Blood*, 197.

30. On Mather, see chapter 8, note 10.

31. Fellow officers credited Barlow with fighting courageously during engagements at Seven Pines and Malvern Hill and later at Antietam, but he was not revered by his men, especially the mostly German Eleventh Corps Brigade. That brigade was victimized by Stonewall Jackson's flank attack at Chancellorsville and then was posted too far forward, forcing it to flee during initial engagements northeast of Gettysburg on July 1, 1863. Warner, *Generals in Blue*, 18–19; Creighton, *Colors of Courage*, 89–94. See also Tagg, *Generals of Gettysburg*; Brown, *Meade at Gettysburg*, 147–49.

32. On Oscar Bigelow, see chapter 12, note 1.

33. Battle of Second Cold Harbor. Lockley consistently referred to the place as Coal Harbor. As Earl B. McElfresh notes, the battle site of Cold Harbor went by many names, including Cool Arbor, Coal Harbor, Burned Cold Harbor, New Cold Harbor, and Old Cold Harbor. McElfresh, "Maps and the Civil War." The name itself is a misnomer, for Cold Harbor, Virginia, is neither cold nor a harbor. Instead, *harbor* may mean "a place of shelter" as when one harbors a fugitive, which then evolved into a term for *inn*. *Cold* may refer to the food being served cold at the Old Cold Harbor Inn. See American Battlefield Trust, "10 Facts: Cold Harbor."

34. Perhaps a friend of Jack, the son or nephew of Frederic's first wife. Keating, in *Carnival of Blood*, lists no George Swan having served in the Seventh New York.

14. June–July 1864

1. FELM, pt. 3, 257, 261–62.

2. FELM, pt. 3, 257, 261–62.

3. FELM, pt. 3, 233; Keating, *Carnival of Blood*, 45.

4. In reality, there was little difference in the capabilities of the Springfield and Enfield rifle muskets.

5. Lockley did not note whether the musket was of Confederate or Union origin.

6. Samuel L. Anable, age forty-one at enlistment on August 15, 1862, had been enrolled immediately as captain. A farmer by trade, he would be wounded in the right shoulder near Petersburg on June 16, 1864. Mustered in as a major later that summer, he was mustered out on June 16, 1865. Keating, *Carnival of Blood*, 369.

7. FELM, pt. 3, 237–38.

8. The man killed was David H. Crawford, a twenty-seven-year-old teacher when enlisted in August 1862. Crawford, listed as killed in action on May 27, 1864, had been promoted to corporal just a month earlier. Keating, *Carnival of Blood*, 88, 396. Color bearers were special targets under almost any circumstance, especially during charges. See, for example, Robertson, *Soldiers Blue and Gray*, 223.

9. FELM, pt. 3, 259–60.

10. Elizabeth would write at least fourteen letters to her husband during the period covered in this chapter—May 19 to August 7—judging from references in Frederic's letters to her. Her letters were most probably lost while he was on campaign.

11. Sgt. Joe Rogers was killed at Cold Harbor on June 3, 1864. Keating, *Carnival of Blood*, 162–63.

12. Frederick W. Mather, who Lockley had said was hospitalized, returned to the regiment in time to be captured June 16, 1864, during the Seventh regiment's assault on Petersburg defenses. Just before capture, he tried to bury his sword on the battlefield and was almost robbed of it by a trophy-hunting civilian until a Confederate officer interceded. Mather, a lieutenant, then presented it to the Confederate officer willingly. Keating, *Carnival of Blood*, 192.

13. Hancock had been wounded severely on the third day of Gettysburg during Pickett's charge when a bullet had struck the pommel of his saddle and entered his right thigh along with wood fragments and a large nail. He had not recovered well since and had taken leave periodically, including June 17, just before the Battle of Weldon Road. He gave up field command permanently the next November. Walker, *History of Second Army Corps*, 539.

14. Five of Frederic's letters since leaving Washington DC, beginning with May 19, survive.

15. Quoting this letter in his memoirs, Frederic added to this sentence: "during the night, however, if left undisturbed, it [the water] will clarify." FELM, pt. 3, 308.

16. In his memoirs, Frederic added, "We also lack vegetable acids; bacon, hardtack and coffee constitute our dietary." FELM, pt. 3, 309.

17. On Fernando Wood see chapter 7, note 7.

18. The phrase refers to Humphrey, Duke of Gloucester (1390–1447), sometimes praised as the patron of learning and benefactor of Oxford University. The expression was common in Elizabethan literature and meant to go without dinner by referring to the story of a man who visited the tomb of Duke Humphrey of Gloucester, got locked in the abbey, and missed dinner. Shakespeare portrayed Duke Humphrey positively in *Henry VI*, parts 1 and 2.

19. Heliogabalus, a boy emperor also known as Elagabalus or Antoninus (204–222 CE) was known for decadence and eccentricity; Edward Gibbon, in *Decline and Fall of the Roman Empire*, chapter 6, said he "abandoned himself to the grossest pleasures with ungoverned fury."

20. Few if any soldiers North or South escaped the exasperation of lice, and few sources on the common soldier fail to mention it. See, for example, Miller, "Historical Natural History," 235–37; Billings, *Hardtack and Coffee*, 80–82; Browning and Silver, *Environmental History of the Civil War*, 25–26; Robertson, *Soldiers Blue and Gray*, 153–54; Rhea, *On to Petersburg*, 87.

21. May 19, 1864.

22. FELM, pt. 3, 315.

23. Frederic repeated the word *painful* in the original letters.

24. In his memoir, he added, "Imagine a column of men extended seven miles, all jostling and heavy laden, marching for hours encompassed with a suffocating cloud of dust, yet encountering no stream. At last some vile stagnant pool of warm water presents itself; the men break tumultuously to drink of it; their officers cannot restrain them. It is nothing that the water is pestilential—poisonous, drink they will if they die for it." FELM, pt. 3, 315.

25. FELM, pt. 3, 315–16.

26. Keating, *Carnival of Blood*, 274, 289.

27. Frederic elaborated in his memoir on the ecstasy of receiving fresh fruit such as a lemon. "I happened into the division hospital a few days ago to procure information, and the steward (my friend Sergt Gooch) gave me a lemon. It was too precious to eat selfishly

and alone: I wanted to diffuse the enjoyment, so I carried it to camp. Would you believe a small group of officers gathered about me, feasting their eyes on the luxury? And then we fell to discussing citrous fruits. After awhile, at my request, one of the group divided the delicacy into five slices, and we each luxuriated on a slice." FELM, pt. 3, 309–10.

28. He refers to the Battle of Jerusalem Plank Road, also known as the First Battle of the Weldon Railroad or, more derisively, Barlow's Skedaddle. While part of an operation to cut one of the railroad lines supplying Lee and the Confederates in Petersburg, the Seventh Regiment and other units under Hancock fell victim to a surprise attack by a Confederate division under Gen. William Malone. Union casualties numbered more than 2,900, 49 of them members of the Seventh Regiment, many of them taken prisoner. Frederic Lockley, "Letter from the 7th N.Y.V Artillery," Albany *Knickerbocker*, September 19, 1864; Keating, *Carnival of Blood*, 215–16, 350; FELM, pt. 3, 302.

29. Grant sent Sixth Corps troops in two groups, the first of about thirty-three hundred men on July 6 and then, realizing Early's raid was more serious, some ten thousand more on July 9. Guarneri, *Lincoln's Informer*, 290; Catton, *Bruce Catton's Civil War*, 613–14; Leech, *Reveille in Washington*, 338–39; Rhodes, *All for the Union*, 168–71.

30. Rhodes, *All for the Union*, 171.

31. Chernow, *Grant*, 426.

32. Lockley and the Seventh New York were experiencing the same extended hot spell that influenced the Battle of Fort Stevens a few days later.

33. Jubal Early's raid on Washington DC, part of a larger effort to clear the Shenandoah Valley for the Confederates and to relieve Union pressure on Petersburg, occurred on July 11–12.

34. Frederic was correct. General Lee sent Lt. Gen. Jubal Early north to clear the Shenandoah Valley of Union forces and to threaten Washington DC, hoping to relieve the pressure that U. S. Grant's forces exerted on Richmond.

35. Frederic referred to Maj. Gen. Darius N. Couch and Maj. Gen. Franz Sigel, who fought Jubal Early at Harpers Ferry.

36. Elizabeth's letter urging him to decline a commission is apparently lost.

37. Frederic's refusal to obtain a commission at this point may have saved his life. When he finally did accept a commission as a first lieutenant in spring 1865, he was immediately put in command of a company. With the growing paucity of officers in the Seventh New York after Cold Harbor, he probably would have been given such a command in July and consequently would have been in harm's way far more often—including the Confederate attack at Reams Station on August 25.

15. Mid-July–Mid-August 1864

1. FELM, pt. 3, 279–80.

2. From the pamphlet *The Lockleys*, provided to the author by Jerry Shepard, Zena, Oregon.

3. FEL to EML, July 10, 1864.

4. These were in fact two railroads: the Weldon-Petersburg and the Richmond and Danville. In a campaign to disrupt one of Lee's southern supply lines, Frederic's regiment engaged in one of its bloodiest engagements—at Reams Station.

5. Frederic is referring to his regiment's charge on the Petersburg lines on June 16, 1864.

6. Robert Blair (1699–1746), Scottish poet famous for the poem *The Grave*, illustrated by William Blake in a later edition.

7. Lethean, usually capitalized, can be used as an adjective to mean causing oblivion or forgetfulness of the past; it is derived from one of the five rivers of Hades—the Lethe, river of forgetfulness—in Greek mythology.

8. A word is missing from his original letter; he could have meant *place* or *waste* or simply *shadelessness.*

9. Keating, *Carnival of Blood*, 162–63.

10. Francis M. Kelso, Forty-Fourth Tennessee Infantry Regiment, commanded Company B at the time. Along with the capture of many of Springsteed's men, Kelso's men, which he said numbered seventeen, also obtained the Seventh Regiment's silk banner, which was not returned until 1898. When the New York state historian reported the flag's return in his annual report, he included two letters from Kelso, then a Tennessee legislator, detailing his capture of the Seventh New Yorkers and others on June 16, 1864. The report also noted that the large, heavily fringed flag, originally presented to the 113th New York Infantry by New York Governor Edwin D. Morgan, had been taken upon capture to the offices of the *Richmond Examiner*, which reported the following in its July 20, 1864, edition: "Either face of the banner bears a painting illustrative of battle scenes in the Revolutionary war with the figure of General Washington in the foreground. It is the largest and most superb regimental flag we ever saw. The silken folds are rent in several places by bullet and shell, and the top of the staff is shattered by a minie-ball. Splashes of blood here and there upon the torn silk suggest a hand-to-hand conflict." State of New York, *Third Annual Report*, 89–96. See also Keating, *Carnival of Blood*, 182, 187–92.

11. Keating, *Carnival of Blood*, 192.

12. FELM, pt. 3, 297–98; Keating, *Carnival of Blood*, 189–92; "Letter from Major Springsteed," *Albany Morning Express*, June 17, 1864.

13. Joseph L. Rogers would have been about twenty-four at the time he was listed as killed in action at Cold Harbor on June 3, 1864. On Rogers and the search for his body, see Keating, *Carnival of Blood*, 162–63, 486.

14. Frances Butt, a London-born carpenter, was a private about thirty years old when captured in the Petersburg assault of June 16. Exchanged in December 1864, he was mustered out a year later in June 1865. Keating, *Carnival of Blood*, 385.

15. Keating is not so critical of Springsteed. Keating, *Carnival of Blood*, 189–92.

16. FEL to EML, July 24, 1864.

17. FELM, pt. 3, 334–35. What Frederic may have been witnessing was, combined with the heat, the final, deadly reaction to extreme thirst. Browning and Silver, *Environmental History of Civil War*, 16.

18. Fort Darling (or Drewry's Fort on Drewry's Bluff) was a Confederate military installation overlooking a bend in the James River south of Richmond. It protected the approach to the city until April 2, 1865.

19. Several eighteenth-century plantation houses were nearby. Other soldiers had commented on the beauty and richness of the James River plantations when Union forces crossed the river on June 14. Rhea, *On to Petersburg*, 226–29, 233.

20. The events surrounding the Battle of the Crater were as controversial almost immediately afterward as they are today, and the literature is legion. See, for example, Hess, *Into the Crater*; Slotkin, *No Quarter*; Trudeau, *Last Citadel.*

21. Frederic added to and polished this letter for use in his memoirs; this is a composite based on his refinements. See FELM, part 3: 337–42. Original letter reproduced in appendix 2.

22. French for "My dearest wife."

23. K. Oscar Broady (1832–1922), born Knut Oscar Brundin in Sweden, succeeded Lt. Col. John Hastings in late July 1864 to become the seventh commander of the Fourth Brigade since June 3. Broady had raised a volunteer company that became the Sixty-First New York Volunteer Infantry Regiment in 1861. Promoted to lieutenant colonel in summer 1864, he left command a month later when wounded at the Second Battle of Reams Station on August 25. Keating, *Carnival of Blood*, 230, 428.

24. The New York Sixty-Ninth Infantry Regiment, known famously as the Irish Brigade, was disbanded in June 1864 due to casualties but was reconstituted late that summer as the First Regiment of the Second Irish Brigade.

25. The Middle Department, a military district created in spring 1862, was renamed Eighth Corps that summer but continued to be referred to popularly by its original designation.

26. Battle of the Crater, July 30, 1864.

27. French for "respectfully."

16. August–September 1864

1. Trudeau, *Last Citadel*, 167–73; Keating, *Carnival of Blood*, 243–50. Gouverneur K. Warren (1830–1882), West Point graduate and engineer by training, had, with his Fifth Corps, secured part of the Weldon-Petersburg Railroad line in the Battle of Globe Tavern a week before, August 18–21, 1864. Dissatisfied with Warren's too-careful defensive tactics, Grant had ordered Hancock's Second Corps, including Lockley's Seventh New Yorkers, south from Deep Bottom to wreak further destruction on the railroad, precipitating the Second Battle of Reams Station on August 25.

2. FELM, pt. 3, 346.

3. Keating, *Carnival of Blood*, 244–46.

4. They thought they might be going to Washington DC to bolster defenses there or fight Jubal Early's Confederates directly in the Shenandoah Valley. FELM, pt. 3, 346.

5. In his memoirs, Frederic amended this number to "several," although Keating says surviving official reports indicate no losses that day. FELM, pt. 3, 346; Keating, *Carnival of Blood*, 242.

6. On the north bank of the James River.

7. Frederic tallied six killed, twelve wounded, and three missing in his memoirs; Keating says four killed outright, one who died later of a head wound, and ten others wounded. FELM, pt. 3, 347; Keating, *Carnival of Blood*, 245.

8. He means during the Battle of Cold Harbor.

9. Fredereic references writing and sending what he terms *memoranda* to Elizabeth several times, and he refers to using them to write his memoirs, but none of these notes apparently survive.

10. EML to FEL, August 19, 1865.

11. Keating, *Carnival of Blood*, 247–48.

12. Keating, *Carnival of Blood*, 249.

13. He corrects this exaggeration to read "to the belly" in his memoirs. FELM, pt. 3, 354.

14. On the Weldon-Petersburg Railroad south and west of the Federal line.

15. "I found my bed had been in two or three inches of water. The fires were still burning, and I stayed to dry out," FELM, pt. 3, 354.

16. FELM, pt. 3, 360; Keating, *Carnival of Blood*, 266, 270–72. See also Walker, *History of Second Army Corps*, 581–612. Springsteed died that day, and Keating says the

Company A cook who Keating identifies as Patrick Fowler, a forty-three-year-old Irish farmer, died in Salisbury Prison in North Carolina three months later. Walker, *History of Second Army Corps*, 266, 415.

17. Walker, *History of Second Army Corps*, 598; Trudeau, *Last Citadel*, 187, 252; Bearss, *Eastern Front Battles*, 399–400.

18. For a detailed description of the battle, see Bearss, "The Second Battle of Ream's Station," chap. 6 in *Eastern Front Battles*, 321–407.

19. Frederic corrected this to ninety-six. FELM, pt. 3, 358.

20. Lockley was incorrect. Nathaniel Wright, twenty-eight when enrolled as a first lieutenant in August 1862, did not die on the field at Reams Station but instead was captured and died in Confederate captivity at Salisbury Prison, North Carolina, in February 1865. Keating, *Carnival of Blood*, 530.

21. Of the Seventh New Yorkers who left Belle Plain fifteen weeks earlier, less than 5 percent remained in the ranks fit for duty. Keating, *Carnival of Blood*, 273.

22. FEL to EML, August 30, 1864.

23. Keating, *Carnival of Blood*, 295–96

24. French for "you know."

25. Dr. George H. Newcomb. FELM, pt. 3, 356-57; Keating, *Carnival of Blood*, 469.

26. FEL to EML, September 8, 1864.

27. EML to FEL, September 8, 1864.

28. EML to FEL, September 11, 1864.

29. FEL to EML September 12, 1864.

30. This is the so-called Beefsteak Raid by Confederate cavalry commander Maj. Gen. Wade Hampton, September 14–17, 1864. Trudeau, *Last Citadel*, 193–200.

31. That is, until Frederic will have completed his three-year term of enlistment.

32. Frederic's letter appeared in the *Albany Knickerbocker* on September 12, 1864.

33. Joseph M. Murphy, twenty-seven when enlisted as a captain in August 1862, was promoted to major in January 1864 and to lieutenant colonel on October 1. Dismissed on April 16, 1865, he was reinstated in June and mustered out in July 1865. Keating, *Carnival of Blood*, 468.

34. Dr. David Springsteed. Albany City Government, *Albany Directory for 1864, 132.*

17. September–October 1864

1. See *Federal Works from Jerusalem Plank Road to Weldon and Petersburg Railroad, August 22–September 28, 1864* [map] in Hess, *In the Trenches at Petersburg*, 143; Trudeau, *Last Citadel*, 249; Petersburg Project, "Fort Morton."

2. Lockley refers to the Third Battle of Winchester in which Gen. Philip Sheridan routed Jubal Early's Army of the (Shenandoah) Valley on September 19, 1864, and again at the Battle of Fisher's Hill on September 21–22.

3. Added from FELM, pt. 3, 384.

4. Tweddle Hall, on the corner of State and North Pearl Streets in downtown Albany, was completed in late 1860 at a cost of $100,000 and could seat one thousand people. Built by banker and malt merchant John Tweddle, the hall was the preeminent concert venue in Albany and played host to state political party conventions, speeches, and performances until fire destroyed most of the building in 1883. Johnson, "Tweddle Hall."

5. Philip Sheridan's raids in the Shenandoah Valley in September.

6. Frederic's letter of September 19, 1864, addressed to Col. John Hastings, appeared in the *Albany Knickerbocker* on September 27, 1864.

7. The man is likely Michael Gilhooly, who died apparently from illness or accident on February 6, 1864, at age twenty-six. Keating lists him among those Seventh New Yorkers who never joined the Army of the Potomac in the Overland Campaign. Keating, *Carnival of Blood*, 533.

8. Norman H. Moore, twenty-one, enrolled as a captain in August 1862. Captured at Petersburg on June 16, 1864, and confined at Macon, Georgia, he was paroled in March 1865 and discharged on May 15, 1865. Keating, *Carnival of Blood*, 464.

9. The Battle of Chaffin's Farm and New Market Heights, September 29–30, 1864, resulted in the Union capture of Fort Harrison. Trudeau, *Last Citadel*, 204–13. Grant had given David Bell Birney (1825–October 1864), a political general and southerner born to an abolitionist family, command of Tenth Corps in July. Birney died of illness, probably typhoid fever, after being taken home to Philadelphia.

10. FELM, pt. 3, 374–75.

11. Joseph M. Murphy had just been promoted to lieutenant colonel on October 1. Keating, *Carnival of Blood*, 468.

12. Battle of Peeble's Farm, September 30 to October 2, 1864. Trudeau, *Last Citadel*, 212–16; Bearss, "The Battle of Peebles' Farm," chap. 1 in *Western Front Battles*, 1–81.

13. Charles Godfrey Gunther, Democrat, served as New York City Mayor from 1864 to 1866.

14. Atlanta fell to Union Gen. William Tecumseh Sherman on September 2, 1864.

15. Battle of Peebles's Farm, starting September 30, 1864.

16. Maj. Gen. Benjamin F. Butler.

17. Stephen P. Corliss, listed with the Eleventh Battery, was apparently the brother of Roswell B. Corliss, an eighteen-year-old painter at the time of his enlistment as a private in January 1864. They were both listed at the same address in Albany. Captured June 16, 1864, at Petersburg, Roswell Corliss died of diarrhea two months later at Andersonville Prison, Georgia. Albany City Government, *Albany Directory for 1864*, 35; Keating, *Carnival of Blood*, 394.

18. See Blanton and Cook, *They Fought Like Demons*; Hall, "Women in Battle."

19. FEL to EML, October 8, 1864.

20. The so-called Beefsteak Raid.

21. *New York Herald*.

22. French for "I don't use it for anything."

23. Elizabeth likely dropped a letter here and the name should be Drysdale. There were two men named Drysdale in Albany in 1864 (Alexander and Archibald, the latter a bank note engraver), but we cannot say for certain which she may have been referring to. Albany City Government, *Albany Directory for 1864*, 45.

24. She owed him rent.

25. Thomas Beckett, physician. Albany City Government, *Albany Directory for 1864*, 17.

18. October–November 1864

1. In the twelve states, including New York, that allowed absentee voting, which made tabulating of the soldier vote possible, Lincoln received 119,754 soldier ballots to McClellan's 34,291. McPherson, *Battle Cry of Freedom*, 804. While the soldier vote was 78 percent for Lincoln, the president only won 53 percent of the civilian vote. McPherson, *For Cause & Comrades*, 176.

2. The date was written as October 12 but the 2 has been overwritten with a 3.

3. Likely William G. Wood, thirty-two at enlistment in August 1862 as a private in Company C, was promoted to sergeant August 4, 1864, sergeant major December 13, 1864, and second lieutenant in Company H, May 25, 1865. Keating, *Carnival of Blood*, 530.

4. Morgan L. Filkins, age thirty-six, 177th New York Infantry Regiment.

5. William Seward Gridley, twenty-two, of the Eighteenth New York Infantry Regiment.

6. *Hamlet*, act 5, scenes 1, 4.

7. FEL to EML, October 19, 1864.

8. Union Gen. Philip H. Sheridan's victory over Confederate Gen. Jubal Early at Cedar Creek in the Shenandoah Valley on October 19, 1864. He acquired his nickname "Little Phil" while a cadet at the U.S. Military Academy at West Point because of his height, five feet five inches.

9. John Albion Andrew, twenty-fifth governor of Massachusetts, served from 1861 to 1866. He helped support creation of United States Colored Troop (USCT) units for the Union Army during the war.

10. A bitterly split Democrat Party held its convention in Chicago, August 29–31, 1864, and nominated George B. McClellan for president. The Republican Party, meeting in Baltimore June 7–8, 1864, nominated Abraham Lincoln for reelection and Andrew Johnson as his vice-presidential running mate. The party renamed itself the National Union Party to attract War Democrats.

11. Rush Christopher Hawkins helped raise the 9th New York Infantry, a Zouave-styled regiment, in 1861. The unit was known as Hawkins' Zouaves or New York Zouaves. Patterned after the French Zouaves who served in North Africa, American Zouave units were first popularized by Elmer Ephraim Ellsworth in 1859. Known for their intense drill and especially for their distinctive dress, including baggy trousers, sashes, and short, open jackets, they were credited also for their esprit and quick, agile fighting style. Zouave regiments numbered about seventy in the Union Army and perhaps twenty-five in the Confederate Army.

12. While commanding general of the United States Army, George B. McClellan made little secret of his Southern sympathies and his contempt for the Union high command and for President Lincoln. He supported restoration of the Union through defeat of Southern armies, opposed emancipation, held conservative views on slavery, and was criticized for not prosecuting the war vigorously enough while commanding the Union army. Some thought him in league with Southern secessionists. In addition, Elizabeth was writing this letter two weeks before the 1864 presidential election with its increasingly heated rhetoric, and she may have been aware of commentary in the *New York Herald* that used the word *traitor* to describe McClellan as the Democratic candidate. McPherson, *Battle Cry of Freedom*, 502, 504, 506; Goodwin, *Team of Rivals*, 425; Sears, *George B. McClellan*, 378–79; Holzer, *Lincoln and Power of the Press*, 535–36.

13. Gertie (Gertrude) was seven years old.

14. William Mintzer, a lieutenant colonel of Fifty-Third Pennsylvania Volunteer Infantry at the time.

15. Col. St. Clair Augustine Mulholland, commander, Fourth Brigade.

16. Charles M. Niles. See chapter 10, note 17.

17. This action is detailed in Keating, *Carnival of Blood*, 299–300. See also Trudeau, *Last Citadel*, 249.

18. EML to FEL, October 30, 1864.

19. Reiterating that his commission did not extend his term of service, Frederic told Lizzie, "My commission—I should tell you, holds me but for the unexpired term

of my service. Had it been for three years I would not have accepted it." FEL to EML, November 10, 1864.

20. FEL to EML, November 2, 1864.

21. This paragraph has an *X* through it, although it is unclear when it was marked.

22. Henry M. Knickerbocker, twenty-one when enlisted August 1862, made second lieutenant in October 1863 and first lieutenant in May 1864 and was wounded by buck and ball on June 16, 1864. He made captain in Company M in December 1864. Keating, *Carnival of Blood*, 444.

23. Tuesday, November 8, 1864, was election day.

24. New York Governor Horatio Seymour narrowly lost reelection in November 1864.

25. On Daniel J. O'Brien, see chapter 9, note 2.

26. FEL to EML, November 10, 1864.

27. The Donahue frauds involved Moses J. Ferry and Edward Donahue Jr., two commissioners appointed by Governor Horatio Seymour and stationed in Baltimore to collect and forward New York soldier ballots from the Army of the Potomac. Both were convicted of falsifying ballots on behalf of Democratic presidential candidate George B. McClellan. Winther, "Soldier Vote," 449–52.

28. "The Election Frauds: The Proceedings at Baltimore," *New York Times*, October 29, 1864.

29. Winther, "Soldier Vote," 454–56. See also Sears, *George B. McClellan*, 379, 383–86.

30. FELM, pt. 3, 400; leave application dated November 5, 1864, Frederic E. Lockley Veteran's Records, National Archives; Commission granted October 10, 1864, box 2, Lockley Papers.

19. December 1864–January 1865

1. Their new location was Fort Gregg, six miles southwest of Petersburg and two miles west of the Weldon-Petersburg Railroad. Having moved there on November 25, the Seventh New York had far fewer casualties at Fort Gregg than at Fort Morton, where six of their number had been killed and more than twenty wounded. Keating, *Carnival of Blood*, 300. See also Trudeau, *Last Citadel*, 288, and *Petersburg: Forts and Lines, 1865* [map], 289. Union Fort Gregg is not to be confused with Confederate Fort Gregg, located almost due north along the southern Petersburg siege line and scene of desperate fighting on April 2, 1865, as the Confederate defense of Petersburg collapsed under Union assault. Trudeau, *Last Citadel*, 386–93; Bearss, "The VI Corps Scores a Breakthrough," chap. 8 in *Western Front Battles*, 515–48.

2. Joseph W. Kirk, a merchant who was twenty-two when he enlisted in August 1862 as private, was promoted to corporal and then mustered in as second lieutenant October 25, 1864. He was mustered out May 1, 1865. Keating, *Carnival of Blood*, 443.

3. On Hamilton Berry, see chapter 3, note 8.

4. Frazier Kreps, a thirty-three-year-old bookkeeper from New York City who enlisted in October 1862. Promoted through the ranks, he was mustered in as a second lieutenant in March 1864 and as a first lieutenant that November. Keating, *Carnival of Blood*, 445.

5. FEL to EML, December 3 and 4, 1864.

6. Frederic is mistaken here. It was Jubal Early's Confederates who had left the valley in mid-November 1864.

7. FEL to EML, December 15, 1864.

8. Torn pieces of Elizabeth's letters of February 22 and 26, 1865, are preserved.

9. FEL to EML, December 18, 1864.

10. FEL to EML, December 18, 1864.

11. Lockley added significant detail in his memoir: "When the picket started out about two p.m. yesterday, several officers went along as visitors. Snug quarters had been built on the picket line, and they tho't to have a night's enjoyment. They made no concealment of themselves, and so unusual a display of 'shoulder straps' must have caught the attention of the vigilant foe." FELM, pt. 3, 409–10.

12. As a consequence of the action, "the pacific feeling that has existed lately is now at an end." FELM, pt. 3, 411.

13. FEL to EML, December 22, 1864.

14. FEL to EML, December 22, 1864.

15. George Stoneman, Union general, then conducting cavalry raids from east Tennessee into southwestern Virginia.

16. Stephen G. Burbridge, controversial Union general in command of Kentucky at the time.

17. Union Gen. Benjamin F. Butler.

18. FEL to EML, December 28, 1864.

19. This is the same Joseph Murphy who Lockley said had committed rape. See FEL to EML, December 8, 1863.

20. A character in Shakespeare's play, *The Tempest.*

21. Shakespeare, *The Tempest,* act 5, scene 1.

22. FEL to EML, January 6, 1865.

23. FEL to EML, January 6, 1865; Keating, *Carnival of Blood,* 445.

24. FEL to EML, January 15, 1865.

25. FEL to EML, January 22, 1865.

26. FEL to EML, January 22, 1865.

27. FEL to EML, January 18, 1865.

28. Their new commander was Richard C. Duryea, thirty-eight and an 1853 graduate of West Point. He had served previously as captain of Battery F, First U.S. Artillery, and was now enrolled as colonel to be the regiment's eighth commander in seven months. He would lead the Seventh from January 12 to March 15, 1865, and be mustered out the following July. Keating, *Carnival of Blood,* 302, 405.

29. Marshal Gen. Jean-de-Dieu Soult, first Duke of Dalmatia, a French general and statesman who fought with Napoleon and is credited with creation of the French Foreign Legion.

30. Lockley is either overestimating the distance or exaggerating for effect. The distance from Washington DC to Petersburg VA is closer to 130 miles.

31. French for "unexpectedly."

20. February–March 1865

1. FEL to EML, February 3, 1865.

2. FEL to EML, January 30, 1865.

3. FEL to EML, February 3, 1865. Maj. Gen. Andrew A. Humphreys, previously chief of staff to the Army of the Potomac, had assumed command of Second Corps with Winfield Scott Hancock's transfer the previous November. Nicknamed "Old Goggle Eyes" for his eyeglasses, he has been described as a grim taskmaster and martinet but a capable Union officer. Catton, *Bruce Catton's Civil War,* 231–32, 256, 377.

4. FEL to EML, February 8, 1865.

5. Battle of Hatcher's Run, February 5–7, also called Dabney's Mill, was fought west of Fort Gregg. Trudeau, *Last Citadel*, 315–27; Bearss, "The Battle of Hatcher's Run, February 5–7, 1865," chap. 3 in *Western Front Battles*, 165–240.

6. Keating, *Carnival of Blood*, 303; Trudeau, *Last Citadel*, 321–27.

7. William G. Wood, thirty-two, a molder by trade, enlisted in August 1862 and was promoted through the ranks to sergeant major in December 1864. He made second lieutenant in May 1865 and was mustered out in August 1865. Keating, *Carnival of Blood*, 530.

8. FELM, pt. 3, 430–38. Corrupt officers and sutlers cheating soldiers in procurement was not unusual. See, for example, Wiley, *Life of Billy Yank*, 230–31.

9. George Hawes, twenty-two when enlisted in July 1862, was promoted through the ranks to second lieutenant in November 1864 and resigned April 29, 1865. Keating, *Carnival of Blood*, 428.

10. John Maher, age thirty-one at enlistment in August 1862, was promoted through the ranks to second lieutenant in November 1864 and mustered out in July 1865. Keating, *Carnival of Blood*, 454.

11. FEL to EML, February 16, 1865. He also noted his watch would run by twenty-two hours.

12. EML to FEL, February 26, 1865.

13. James A. Harris of Schenectady, New York, was a printer, age thirty upon enlistment as a private in August 1862. Mustered in as a second lieutenant in Company I in January 1865, he was made first lieutenant on April 16 and was mustered out the following June. Keating, *Carnival of Blood*, 427.

14. Winnsboro (or Winnsborough) SC.

15. Lockley is incorrect here. Confederate Gen. P. G. T. Beauregard survived the war and lived until 1893.

16. Frances Butt—see chapter 15, note 14.

17. In the earliest days of the war, Annapolis was a staging area for Union troops en route to the defense of Washington DC, and when the U.S. Naval Academy was transferred to Newport, Rhode Island, the academy grounds were soon used for Federal prisoners of war recently paroled by the South. Only if formally exchanged for Confederate POWs could Union parolees return to service. Thus, they waited in Annapolis for due process to take its course. As the fighting escalated and the number of POWs increased, the Annapolis facilities were expanded, relocated, and almost constantly overwhelmed, especially after Ulysses S. Grant ordered all prisoner exchanges discontinued in April 1864. Tens of thousands of Union parolees were processed through what, by August 1862, was commonly known as Camp Parole. By the time Fred Lockley arrived in February 1865, the camp had been moved three times and was under the command of Col. F. D. Sewall. Morris, *Low, Dirty Place*.

18. Hatcher's Run, scene of much fighting, was about ten miles southwest of Petersburg.

19. Patrick's Station, named after Union General Marsena R. Patrick, was the terminus of the U.S. Military Railroad at Petersburg. Like the Seventh New York, the Ninety-First New York Infantry Regiment had been recruited in the Albany area. Organized in December 1861, it had seen action primarily in the Gulf states of Florida and Louisiana. Transferred to Baltimore in October 1864, it would now replace the Seventh New York along the siege line at Petersburg and, as part of the Army of the Potomac, would see action through the Appomattox campaign. It was mustered out in July 1865. The Ninety-First New York was victimized by mail-in ballot fraud relating to the presidential

election of 1864. Winther, "Soldier Vote," 449–51; Dustin Waters, "Mail-In Ballots Were Part of a Plot to Deny Lincoln Reelection in 1864," *Washington Post*, August 22, 2020.

20. By 1864 and into 1865, the primary duty of the Eighth Corps was the defense of Washington DC and of the Baltimore and Ohio Railroad. Gen. William W. Morris was Eighth Corps commander at the time Lockley arrived but was replaced in mid-April by Gen. Lew Wallace.

21. Frederic means "concerning marriage" in a literary sense with his use of the word *hymeneal*. By *inanition* he is threatening to mirror her inattention.

22. Paroled prisoners.

23. On Henry Knickerbocker, see chapter 18, note 22.

24. Edward LeRoy, twenty-three, butcher, enlisted January 1864 and was wounded May 30, 1864, at Totopotomoy Creek. He made second lieutenant of Company M in December 1864 and resigned April 29, 1865. Keating, *Carnival of Blood*, 450.

25. Richard Duncan, born in Holland, enlisted at eighteen as a private in July 1862. Mustered in as a second lieutenant in January 1865, he was discharged the following May. Keating, *Carnival of Blood*, 404.

26. Fred's sister Emma, who had come to Albany in 1862 to help Lizzie with maintaining the household, was moving to Schuylerville to open a millinery shop, and Lizzie's younger sister Amelia was to come to Albany to take her place.

27. Amelia was then seventeen.

28. Elizabeth's father, John Campbell, had applied for and heard positively about employment with the *New-York Tribune*. EML to FEL, March 12, 1865.

29. Some of the surviving Lockley correspondence is damaged. Torn material accompanies Frederic's letter of January 12, 1865, and Elizabeth's letter of February 22, 1865, was so torn as to preserve only half pages and interrupted sentences. Still, enough of Lizzie's letter survives to indicate they contemplated moving to Minnesota after the war. EML to FEL, February 22, 1865.

30. EML to FEL, February 26, 1865.

31. EML to FEL, March 5, 1865; FEL to EML, March 5, 1865.

32. FEL to EML, March 22, 1865, April 16, 1865.

33. French for "despair."

34. From Shakespeare's *Hamlet*, act 3, scene 1.

35. Job 1:1.

36. Morbid sentimentality, characteristic of Werther, hero of Goethe's romance *Die Leiden des jungen Werthers* (1774).

37. Lax discipline, drunkenness, disruption, violence, gambling, and disorder plagued Camp Parole chronically. Men who had taken an oath not to take up arms against the enemy until properly exchanged often had little to do and grew bored, demoralized, insubordinate, and rebellious. In the later stages of the war, Camp Parole was particularly affected by "hard cases"—usually defined as "deserters, substitutes, and stragglers." See Morris, *Low, Dirty Place*, especially 26–27, 49, 55, and 67.

38. On Hamilton Berry, see chapter 3, note 8.

39. French for "today."

40. Brig. Gen. Samuel Emery Chamberlain (1829–1908), commander of Camp Parole at the time..

41. One of Sir Walter Scott's Waverly series, *The Abbot* is an 1820 historical novel concerning mid-sixteenth-century England.

21. March–April 1865

1. Morris, *Low, Dirty Place*, 67.
2. FEL to EML, March 15, 1865.
3. FEL to EML, March 18, 1865.
4. EML to FEL, March 24, 1865.
5. EML to FEL, March 19, 1865.
6. *Charles O'Malley, The Irish Dragoon* is a comic military novel by Charles Lever published in Dublin in 1841.
7. From Lord Byron, *The Deformed Transformed; A Drama*, published in 1824.
8. This is likely James H. Morgan, a twenty-six-year-old clerk when enlisted as a sergeant in Company M in January 1864. Wounded at Cold Harbor on June 3, 1864, he was captured two months later at Reams Station on August 25. He is listed as dying at Salisbury NC, on January 20, 1865. Keating, *Carnival of Blood*, 465.
9. Michael S. Sullivan, twenty-two, a peddler from Pittsburgh, enlisted as a private in August 1862. Promoted to sergeant in February 1864, he was captured at Reams Station on August 25, 1864, paroled on February 27, 1865, and listed as having died of disease on March 12, 1865, in an Annapolis hospital. Keating, *Carnival of Blood*, 508.
10. EML to FEL, March 12, 1865; FEL to EML, March, undated [probably 20 or 21], 1865.
11. EML to FEL, March 12, 1865; FEL to EML, March, undated [probably 20 or 21], 1865.
12. Lizzie often had company when writing to Fred. Two days earlier, she had begun, "With one little girl on each side endeavoring to write and asking me numberless questions, there seems very little prospect of my writing a connected or interesting letter." EML to FEL, March 26, 1865. Yet she felt bonded to the girls completely. "Fred when I look at the children and feel how close they are to my heart, how dear to me they are, so lovingly returning my love, I am inclined to doubt the oft-repeated story that you can not love another's children as well as your own." EML to FEL, undated partial letter written sometime after February 14, 1865.
13. Battle of Fort Stedman, March 25, 1865. The Confederate attack on the far right of the Union line represented Robert E. Lee's last major attempt to break the siege line and take the offensive. Trudeau, *Last Citadel*, 334–58; Bearss, "Confederate Attack and Union Defense of Fort Stedman," chap. 4 in *Western Front Battles*, 241–309.
14. Maria Mair, her father's sister.
15. As Grant's attack broke through Confederate defenses all along the siege lines on April 2, the Confederate government fled the city of Richmond the same day. Nevins, *Organized War to Victory, 1864–1865*, 292–99; McPherson, *Battle Cry of Freedom*, 846.
16. Frederic apparently means *kopeck*, referring to a monetary unit one one-hundredth of a Russian ruble.
17. An exception was Frederic's newspaper report of Admiral David Farragut's visit to nearby Baltimore for an Albany paper (it is not noted which one) and preserved with this letter today, although it may have been added later. See newspaper clipping of April 12, 1865, box 2, Lockley Papers.
18. David Glasgow Farragut (1801–1870), who had been promoted to vice admiral of the U.S. Navy the previous December (a rank Congress created for him), was the hero of the Union's successful attack on Mobile Bay, Alabama, the South's last major Gulf Coast port, on August 5, 1864.

19. Officers of the Seventh New York Heavy Artillery Regiment, including Frederic, were among those from nearby Fort McHenry selected as military escort for Farragut's visit on April 12, 1865. Undated clipping, "Admiral Farragut's Visit," box 2, Lockley Papers; "Local Matters," *Baltimore Sun*, April 11, 1865, and "Local Matters," April 12, 1865; "Vice Admiral Farragut in Baltimore," *National Republican*, April 12, 1865.

20. William H. Courtney, enlisted at nineteen as a private in August 1862, was promoted through the ranks and had become Captain of Company F in March. Wounded in the right ankle at Cold Harbor June 3, 1864, he was mustered out in August 1865. Keating, *Carnival of Blood*, 395.

21. The *Harriet DeFord* was a steamer boarded and seized in Chesapeake Bay thirty miles below Annapolis by a party of twenty Confederate guerrillas led by Capt. T. Fitzhugh.

22. Daniel McCauley (1839–1894), after being wounded at Cedar Creek in October 1864, was detailed to the Ninth Regiment of Veteran's Reserve Corps, then garrisoning Baltimore.

23. Franklin Petitt (Lockley misspells it Pettit), thirty-four when enlisted as second lieutenant in August 1862, was captured at Petersburg on June 16, 1864, and paroled in December 1864 at Charleston SC. Keating, *Carnival of Blood*, 475.

24. Edgar H. Wilsey, a twenty-six-year-old farmer when he enlisted in August 1862, was promoted through the ranks, making first lieutenant in January 1865. He was mustered out in June 1865. Keating, *Carnival of Blood*, 528.

22. April–May 1865

1. For examples of remembering where one was upon learning of Lincoln's assassination, seen Marten, *Children's Civil War*, 208–11.

2. She had left the children with Mrs. Duncan while gone to Schuylerville.

3. Byron, "Childe Harold's Pilgrimage," *Selected Poetry of Lord Byron*, canto 3, lines 262–70, p. 79.

4. Elizabeth refers to Frederick W. Seward, Secretary of State William H. Seward's son, who was beaten with a pistol wielded by ex-Confederate Lewis Powell the night of Lincoln's assassination. Frederick was injured when Powell attempted to kill his father. Both father and son survived, although both were injured severely.

5. Grief was widespread among Union soldiers. Woodworth, *While God Is Marching On*, 266–68; Mitchell, *Civil War Soldiers*, 198–99; Rhodes, *All for the Union*, 231–32. On how soldiers, civilians, and clergy sought a religious explanation for Lincoln's death, see Rable, *God's Almost Chosen Peoples*, 376–87; Blum, "God of Wrath, God of Peace." On the nation's struggle with grief, see Faust, *This Republic of Suffering*, 156–61.

6. Some clergy, it was said, "'out-radicaled' the Radicals," while others, as did Frederic, wondered if Lincoln's death was not God's means of making way for sterner policies toward the South. Turner, "Voices from the Pulpit," chap. 6 in *Beware the People Weeping*, 77–89, especially 78, 82–83.

7. Many people turned to the Bible to help them understand the tragedy. See, for example, Flotow, *In Their Letters, in Their Words*, 215–19. In some cases, soldiers faulted themselves for having revered the president too much. Cimbala, *Veterans North and South*, 3. For a fuller range of private responses to Lincoln's assassination, see Hodes, *Mourning Lincoln*.

8. From John Milton's *Paradise Lost* (1667).

9. From Shakespeare, *The Merchant of Venice*, act 4, scene 1.

10. *Chasm* in Farsi means "eye." Lockley may be referring to an expression relating to "far be the evil eye."

11. William Cumming, grocery and grain dealer, Albany City Government, *Albany Directory*, 1865, p. 39.

12. EML to FEL, April 16, 1865. Lizzie shows her strong reliance on religious beliefs in this letter when she attributed the boy's waywardness to a deficient spiritual influence.

13. FEL to EML, April 23, 1865.

14. Lincoln's Emancipation Proclamation did not apply to Maryland, a Union border state, and the state was slow to abolish slavery. It did so, however, with ratification of a new state constitution, which prohibited slavery, in November 1864.

15. FEL to EML, April 23, 1865; Varon, *Armies of Deliverance*, 1–20; McPherson, *For Cause & Comrades*, 154–55.

16. EML to FEL, April 23 and 24, 1865.

17. FEL to EML, April 26, 1865.

18. EML to FEL, May 2, 1865.

19. William H. Courtney, Albany, enlisted as a private at nineteen in August 1862 and was promoted through the ranks to lieutenant in February 1864. Wounded in the right ankle at Cold Harbor on June 3, 1864, he made captain in Company F in March 1865 and was mustered out August 1, 1865. Keating, *Carnival of Blood*, 395..

20. This thought was typical of freedmen and their children, who readily perceived education as a means to a better life. Marten, *Children's War*, 136.

21. FEL to EML, May 3, 1865.

22. Ibid. He takes from a letter apparently written the previous Sabbath, April 30, 1865, but the letter has not been preserved.

23. May 3, 1865.

24. EML to FEL, May 7, 1865.

25. FELM, pt. 2, 479.

26. See, for example, Josie to FEL, April 2, 1865, not included here.

23. Early to Mid-May 1865

1. EML to FEL, May 7, 1865.

2. Edgar Wilsey. See chapter 21, note 24.

3. That is, when her sister, Amelia, arrives in Albany to help with housekeeping and the children.

4. Gen. William W. Morris (1801–1865) served at Fort McHenry from 1861 until his death in December 1865, principally as brigade commander in charge of the defense of Washington and Baltimore Harbor.

5. Anne Ritchie Morris (1845–1910) would marry Col. Joseph Gales Ramsay, son of Gen. George D. Ramsay.

6. Also known as the *glass harp* or *singing glasses*, musical glasses can be played by running a moistened or chalked finger around the rim of a set of wine glasses. Pitch may vary from glass to glass, or glasses may be filled with different volumes of liquid (usually water) to achieve a desired timbre. Although dating from at least fourteenth-century Persia, musical glasses were especially popular in the eighteenth century and constituted a sophisticated historical music phenomenon when Lockley wrote about them.

7. Giacomo Meyerbeer (1791–1864), a German Jewish opera composer whose works were some of the most frequently performed during the nineteenth century.

8. From *The Pickwick Papers*, chap. 41: "'Come here, sir,' said Mr. Pickwick, trying to look stern, with four large tears running down his waistcoat." Dickens, *Posthumous Papers of the Pickwick Club*.

9. Elizabeth's father, John Campbell.

10. Hamlet said to Horatio, "The age is grown so picked," from *Hamlet*, act 5, scene 1, meaning "overrefined, fastidious."

11. He amended this to "estimate of our purpose in life" in his memoirs. FELM, pt. 2, 469.

12. FEL to EML, May 16, 1865.

13. FEL to EML, May 18, 1865.

14. EML to FEL, May 19, 1865.

15. EML to FEL, May 21, 1865. "M George W" is "Mr. George Watson."

16. FEL to EML, May 22, 1865.

17. FEL to EML, May 24, 1865.

18. On Franklin Petitt, see chapter 21, note 22.

19. FEL to EML, May 24, 1865.

20. Grand Review of the Armies was a two-day procession through Washington DC, first by the Army of the Potomac under Gen. George Gordon Meade on May 23, and then, on May 24, 1865, by the Army of Tennessee and the Army of Georgia under William Tecumseh Sherman.

21. Emma's suitor, George Watson.

24. Late May–June 1865

1. FEL to EML, May 27, 1865.

2. Son of Mr. and Mrs. Duncan.

3. Charles W. Hobbs, then a major.

4. The picture is of Lizzie herself.

5. This reference is likely to Peter Lely (1618–1680), the Dutch-born portraitist who spent most of his art career painting for the court in England. Frederic's equating the flatness of Lizzie's facial features with those often seen in portraits of Queen Elizabeth I (1533–1603) may be apropos (we do not have this photograph of Lizzie to compare), but his ascribing flat portraits of the queen to Lely is probably not. Lely, who was born fifteen years after Queen Elizabeth's death, did not arrive in England until the early 1640s, and his more vigorous portraits tended to be flattering portrayals of living British royals.

6. Jonathan Russell, a twenty-six-year-old farmer from Potter's Hollow, enlisted as a private in August 1862, was captured at Petersburg on June 16, 1864, and died of diarrhea on September 15, 1864, at Andersonville, Georgia. Keating, *Carnival of Blood*, 488.

7. FEL to EML, May 31, 1865. In his memoirs, Frederic described Agnes Jeannette's father, Robert Hill, as "a crusty old Scotchman, rough as an unlicked cub, who had sailed the briny ocean as a ship's mate." FELM, pt. 3, 366.

8. EML to FEL, June 2, 1865.

9. An estimated 150 to 200 soldiers made assaults on "unoffending persons in the 7th ward" in Washington DC on June 10, attacking houses of ill repute and showing "particular animosity against colored inhabitants." "A Riot in Washington: Colored Persons Beaten and Robbed by Soldiers," *New York Times*, June 11, 1865.

10. FEL to EML, June 11, 1865.

11. Last king of Lydia, 560–546 BC, renowned for his great wealth.

25. Epilogue

1. Keating, *Carnival of Blood*, 307, 309; "Arrival of the Seventh," *Albany Evening Journal*, June 20, 1865. The second contingent of the Seventh Regiment, 322 officers and men, went home on August 4, 1865. With their discharge, the Seventh New York Heavy Artillery Regiment ceased to exist.

2. Frederic's discharge documents were signed by William E. Courtney, captain, Company F, Seventh New York, on June 16, 1865. Box 2, Lockley Papers, HL.

3. "Arrival of the Seventh," *Albany Evening Journal*; Keating, *Carnival of Blood*, 309; FELM, pt. 3, 2. Unlike Frederic Lockley's brief account, few returning Civil War veterans recorded their homecomings at the time or later. Marten, *Sing Not War*, 73.

4. FELM, pt. 3, 1.

5. FELM, pt. 3, 1–2.

6. "Arrival of the Seventh," *Albany Evening Journal*; Keating, *Carnival of Blood*, 308.

7. FELM, pt. 3, 2.

8. FELM, pt. 3, 2.

9. EML to FEL, June 1, 1865. See also FEL to EML, August 10, 1865.

10. Returning Union soldiers were stigmatized as "deceitful beggars" in the *New York Times* and elsewhere. Jordan, "Our Work Is Not Yet Finished," 493, 501n19.

11. FEL to EML, August 24, 1865; FELM, pt. 3, 7. Frederic contemplated opportunities in the oil boomtown of Titusville, Pennsylvania, but friends advised him that it was no place to take a family. "I still wish I had gone there," he wrote to Lizzie on August 27, 1865. Folder 6, box 3, Lockley Papers, HL.

12. FEL to EML, September 3, 1865. See also FEL to EML, August 27, 1865, and August 29, 1865.

13. EMLM, box 5, Lockley Collection, HL.

14. Maud, sometimes spelled Maude, was born August 26, 1866. Frederic and Elizabeth's second child together, Fred, was born in Leavenworth, Kansas, on March 19, 1871. Another daughter, Margaret Daisy, was born in Salt Lake City on April 13, 1875. An unnamed infant was born in February 1883 in Butte but died soon after. A last daughter, Edith Campbell Lockley, was born in Oregon on April 13, 1890, and died seven months later.

15. Rankin, "Sweet Delusion."

16. James's original name was Schupbach. He had it legally changed to Shepard on July 27, 1885.

17. Catton, *Grant Takes Command*, 491.

18. Leech, *Reveille in Washington*, 419.

19. The significance of Frederic Lockley's Civil War career, at least to his family, is borne out in the epitaph carved on his tombstone, which reads in part, "Frederic Lockley . . . First Lieut. Co. F. 7th NY Vol. Heavy Artillery, a Brave Soldier a Good Citizen a True Friend."

Appendix 1

1. Ranch coffee.

2. Mope.

3. Troubled.

4. Frederic uses the word "tell" here to mean count, as can be found in Genesis, 15:5: "Tell the stars if thou be able to count them."

5. Song or poem celebrating marriage.

6. Relating to dancing that proceeds by leaps rather than gradual transitions (archaic).

7. Without pants.

8. From Samuel 14:49, which describes David dancing in an undignified manner in the streets as he brought the Ark of the Covenant to Jerusalem.

9. Likely continuing the biblical context, as in a flagon of wine for the Eucharist.

10. Swelling.

11. French for "delicate" and, in late Middle English, "delightful" or "charming."

12. Sappho (630–570 BC), regarded as one of the greatest Greek lyric poets, if not the greatest.

13. French for "very happy" or "be happy."

Bibliography

When Peter S. Carmichael prepared his recent study of the common soldier, he noted that even just primary sources on the American Civil War were "oceanic" in volume, not to mention *all* sources, if monographs, biographies, and battle studies were included. Indeed, they are oceanic, and more are available each year. For that reason, it seemed best to differentiate the types of sources referenced here. Not listed are government sources such as census and marriage records, passenger lists, or military records available both in physical form and through such online sites as Ancestry.com, although the reader will find many of these cited in the endnotes.

Manuscript Collections

Albany Medical College Archives, Albany, New York
    James Emmett Pomfret Papers
Huntington Library, San Marino, California
    Fred Lockley Papers and Addenda, 1849–1958
John Frewing Papers, Portland, Oregon
Library of Congress, Washington DC
Montana Historical Society, Helena, Montana
National Archives and Records Administration, Washington DC
    Frederic E. Lockley Pension Papers
New York Historical Society, Albany, New York
    Fred Lockley Papers
New York State Library, Albany, New York
    "Army Reminiscences," Frederic E. Lockley
Oregon Historical Society, Portland, Oregon
    Fred Lockley reminiscences and letters
State of New York, Office of the State Historian
    Third Annual Report of the State Historian. Albany NY: Wynkoop, 1898.
University of Montana Special Collections, Missoula, Montana
    Joseph H. Sherburne Family Papers, 1890–1991
Washington State University Libraries Special Collections, Pullman, Washington
    Fred Lockley Papers

Newspapers

Albany Evening Journal
Albany Knickerbocker
Albany Morning Express
Baltimore Sun
National Republican
New York Times
Richmond Examiner
Salt Lake Tribune

Articles

American Battlefield Trust. "10 Facts: Cold Harbor." N.d. https://www.battlefields.org/learn/articles/10-facts-cold-harbor.

Architect of the Capitol. "History of the U.S. Capitol Building." N.d. https://www.aoc.gov/explore-capitol-campus/buildings-grounds/capitol-building/history.

Beck, Julie. "Gender, Race, and Rape During the Civil War." *Atlantic*, February 20, 2014.

Delahanty, Ian. *Soldiers' Letters and Diaries*. Essential Civil War Curriculum. June 2015. Accessed January 18, 2022. https://www.academia.edu/13219563/Soldiers_Letters_and_Diaries.

Feimster, Crystal N. "Rape and Justice in the Civil War." *New York Times*, April 25, 2013.

Frank, Joseph H., and Barbara Duteau. "Measuring the Political Articulateness of the United States Civil War Soldiers: The Wisconsin Militia." *Journal of Military History* 64 (January 2000): 53–77.

Garner, Stanton. "Thomas Bangs Thorpe in the Gilded Age: Shifty in a New Country." *Mississippi Quarterly* 36, no. 1 (Winter 1982–83): 35–52.

Glatthaar, Joseph T. "A Tale of Two Armies: The Confederate Army of Northern Virginia and the Union Army of the Potomac and Their Cultures." *Journal of the Civil War Era* 6, no. 3 (September 2016): 315–46.

Groene, Bertram H. "Civil War Letters of David Lang." *Florida Historical Quarterly* 54, no. 3 (January 1976): 340–66.

Hackemer, Kurt. "Union Veteran Migration Patterns to the Frontier." *Journal of the Civil War Era* 9, no. 1 (March 2019): 84–108.

Hall, Richard. "Women in Battle in the Civil War." *Social Education* 58, no. 2 (1994): 80–82. http://www.socialstudies.org/sites/default/files/publications/se/5802/580205.html.

Johnson, Carl. "Tweddle Hall, on the Elm Tree Corner." Hoxie! website. March 20, 2012. https://hoxsie.org/2012/03/20/tweddle_hall_on_the_elm_tree_corner/.

Jordan, Brian Matthew. "Our Work Is Not Yet Finished: Union Veterans and Their Unending Civil War, 1865–1872." *Journal of the Civil War Era* 5, no. 4 (December 2015): 484–503.

Longacre, Edward G. "Inspired Blundering: Union Operations against Richmond during the Gettysburg Campaign." *Civil War History* 32, no. 1 (March 1986): 23–43.

Mark, "Union Soldiers Fondly Remembered the Hospitality of the Cooper Shop and Union Volunteer Refreshment Saloons." *Iron Brigader* (blog). https://ironbrigader.com/2017/12/19/union-soldiers-fondly-remembered-the-hospitality-of-the-cooper-shop-and-union-volunteer-refreshment-saloons/.

McElfresh, Earl B. "Maps and the Civil War." Essential Civil War Curriculum (website). N.d. https://www.essentialcivilwarcurriculum.com/maps-and-the-civil-war.html.

Miller, Gary L. "Historical Natural History: Insects and the Civil War." *American Ento-mologist* 43, no. 4 (Winter 1997): 227–45.

Minton, Gretchen E. "Shakespeare in Frontier and Territorial Montana, 1820–1889." *Montana The Magazine of Western History* 70, no. 2 (Summer 2020): 24–43.

Nelson, Michael C. "Writing during Wartime: Gender and Literacy in the American Civil War." *Journal of American Studies* 31, no. 1 (April 1997): 43–68.

The Petersburg Project. "Fort Morton." N.d. http://www.petersburgproject.org/fort-morton.html.

Phillips, Jason. "Battling Stereotypes: A Taxonomy of Common Soldiers in Civil War History." *History Compass* 6, no. 6 (2008): 1407–25.

Pomfret, John E., ed. "Letters of Fred Lockley, Union Soldier, 1864–65." *Huntington Library Quarterly* 16, no. 1 (November 1952): 75–112.

Sizer, Lyde Cullen. "Mapping the Spaces of Women's Civil War History." *Journal of the Civil War Era* 1, no. 4 (December 2011): 536–48.

Smith, Stacey L. "Beyond North and South." *Journal of the Civil War Era* 6, no. 4 (December 2016): 566–91.

Winther, Oscar O. "The Soldier Vote in the Election of 1864." *New York History* 25, no. 4 (October 1944): 440–58.

Books

Adams, Abigail, and John Adams. *My Dearest Friend: Letters of Abigail and John Adams.* Edited by Margaret A. Hogan and C. James Taylor. Cambridge: Harvard University Press, 2007.

———. *Adams Family Correspondence.* The Adams Papers, Vols. 1–8. Cambridge: Harvard University Press, 1963–2007.

Albany City Government. *The Albany Directory for the Year 1862.* Albany NY: Adams, Sampson, 1862.

———. *The Albany Directory for the Year 1863.* Albany NY: Adams, Sampson and Joel Munsell, 1863.

———. *The Albany Directory for the Year 1864.* Albany NY: Adams, Sampson, 1864.

———. *The Albany Directory for the Year 1865.* Albany NY: Adams, Sampson, 1865.

———. *The Albany Directory for the Year 1866.* Albany NY: Sampson, Davenport, 1866.

Arenson, Adam, and Andrew R. Graybill, eds. *Civil War Wests: Testing the Limits of the United States.* Oakland: University of California Press, 2015.

Bearss, Edwin C. *The Eastern Front Battles: June–August 1864, Vol. 1 of The Petersburg Campaign.* El Dorado Hills CA: Savas Beatie, 2012.

———. *The Western Front Battles: September 1864–April 1865, Vol. 2 of The Petersburg Campaign.* El Dorado Hills CA: Savas Beatie, 2014.

Bernstein, Iver. *The New York City Draft Riots: Their Significance for American Society and Politics.* New York: Oxford University Press, 1990.

Berry, Stephen W., II. *All That Makes a Man: Love and Ambition in the Civil War South.* New York: Oxford University Press, 2003.

Billings, John D. *Hardtack and Coffee, or The Unwritten Story of Army Life.* Williamstown MA: Conner House, 1993. First published 1887 by George M. Smith (Boston).

Bird, Edgeworth, and Sallie Bird. *The Granite Farm Letters: The Civil War Correspondence of Edgeworth & Sallie Bird.* Edited by John Rozier. Athens: University of Georgia Press, 1988.

Blanton, DeAnne, and Lauren M. Cook. *They Fought Like Demons: Women Soldiers in the Civil War*. Baton Rouge: LSU Press, 2002.

Blum, Edward J. "God of Wrath, God of Peace: Popular Religion, Popular Press, and the Meaning of the Civil War during Reconstruction." In *Words at War: The Civil War and American Journalism*, edited by David B. Sachsman, S. Kittrell Rushing, and Roy Morris Jr., 363–75. West Lafayette IN: Purdue University Press, 2008.

Bonner, Robert E. *The Soldier's Pen: Firsthand Impressions of the Civil War*. New York: Hill and Wang, 2006.

Bowler, Madison, and Lizzie Bowler. *Go If You Think It Your Duty: A Minnesota Couple's Civil War Letters*. Edited by Andrea R. Foroughi. St. Paul: Minnesota Historical Society Press, 2008.

Browning, Judkin, and Timothy Silver. *An Environmental History of the Civil War*. Chapel Hill: University of North Carolina Press, 2020.

Brown, Kent Masterson. *Meade at Gettysburg: A Study in Command*. Chapel Hill: University of North Carolina Press, 2021.

Burrows, Edwin G., and Mike Wallace. *Gotham: A History of New York City to 1898*. New York: Oxford University Press, 1999.

Byron, Lord. *Selected Poetry of Lord Byron*. Edited by Leslie A. Marchand. New York: Random House Modern Library, 2001.

Carmichael, Peter S. *The War for the Common Soldier: How Men Thought, Fought, and Survived in Civil War Armies*. Chapel Hill: University of North Carolina Press, 2018.

Catton, Bruce. *Bruce Catton's Civil War: Mr. Lincoln's Army, Glory Road, A Stillness at Appomattox*. New York: Fairfax, 1984.

———. *Grant Takes Command*. 2nd ed. Boston: Little, Brown, 1994.

Chernow, Ron. *Grant*. New York: Penguin, 2017.

Cilella, Salvatore G., Jr., ed. *Till Death Do Us Part: The Letters of Emory and Emily Upton, 1868–1870*. Norman: University of Oklahoma Press, 2020.

Cimbala, Paul A. *Veterans North and South: The Transition from Soldier to Civilian after the American Civil War*. Santa Barbara CA: Praeger, 2015.

Cimbala, Paul A., and Randall M. Miller. *Union Soldiers and the Home Front: Wartime Experiences, Postwar Adjustments*. New York: Fordham University Press, 2002.

Clinton, Catherine, and Nina Silber, eds. *Divided Houses: Gender and the Civil War*. New York: Oxford University Press, 1992.

Cobbett, William. *Advice to Young Men and (Incidentally) to Young Women in the Middle and High Ranks of Life*. London: Printed by the author, 1829.

Cooling, Benjamin Franklin, III, and Walton H. Owen II. *Mr. Lincoln's Forts: A Guide to the Civil War Defenses of Washington*. Shippensburg PA: White Mane, 1988.

Crane, Stephen. *Stephen Crane: Prose and Poetry*. New York: Library of America, 1984, 1996.

Creighton, Margaret S. *The Colors of Courage: Gettysburg's Forgotten History*. New York: Basic, 2005.

Decker, William Merrill. *Epistolary Practices: Letter Writing in America before Telecommunications*. Chapel Hill: University of North Carolina Press, 1998.

Dickens, Charles. *The Posthumous Papers of the Pickwick Club*. London: Chapman & Hall, 1836.

Donald, David. *Lincoln*. New York: Simon & Schuster, 1995.

Engs, Robert F., and Corey M. Brooks. *Their Patriotic Duty: The Civil War Letters of the Evans Family of Brown County, Ohio*. New York: Fordham University Press, 2007.

Faust, Drew Gilpin. *This Republic of Suffering: Death and the American Civil War*. New York: Alfred A. Knopf, 2008.

Feimster, Crystal N. *Southern Horrors: Women and the Politics of Rape and Lynching*. Cambridge: Harvard University Press, 2005.

Flotow, Mark, ed. *In Their Letters, in Their Words: Illinois Civil War Soldiers Write Home*. Carbondale: Southern Illinois University Press, 2019.

Foote, Shelby. *Fredericksburg to Meridian*. Vol. 2 of *The Civil War: A Narrative*. New York: Random House, 1963.

Frank, Joseph Allan. *With Ballot and Bayonet: The Political Socialization of American Civil War Soldiers*. Athens: University of Georgia Press, 1998.

Gallagher, Gary W. *The Union War*. Cambridge: Harvard University Press, 2011.

Gallagher, Gary W., and Joan Waugh. *The American War: A History of the Civil War Era*. Flip Learning, 2015.

Gibbon, Edward. *The History of the Decline and Fall of the Roman Empire*. London: Strahan & Cadell, 1776–1789; reprt. New Delhi: General Press, 2021.

Giesberg, Judith. *Army at Home: Women and the Civil War on the Northern Home Front*. Chapel Hill: University of North Carolina Press, 2009.

———. *Civil War Sisterhood: The U.S. Sanitary Commission and Women's Politics in Transition*. Boston: Northeastern University Press, 2000.

———. *Sex and the Civil War: Soldiers, Pornography, and the Making of American Morality*. Chapel Hill: University of North Carolina Press, 2017.

Goodwin, Doris Kearns. *Team of Rivals: The Political Genius of Abraham Lincoln*. New York: Simon & Schuster, 2005.

Gordon, Robert J. *The Rise and Fall of American Growth: The U.S. Standard of Living Since the Civil War*. Princeton NJ: Princeton University Press, 2016.

Gray, Valerie. *Charles Knight: Educator, Publisher, Writer*. London: Routledge, 2017.

Greene, A. Wilson. *A Campaign of Giants: The Battle for Petersburg*. Volume 1. Chapel Hill: University of North Carolina Press, 2018.

Grimsley, Mark. *And Keep Moving On: The Virginia Campaign: May–June 1864*. Lincoln: University of Nebraska Press, 2002.

Guarneri, Carl J. *Lincoln's Informer: Charles A. Dana and the Inside Story of the Union War*. Lawrence: University Press of Kansas, 2019.

Hager, Christopher. *I Remain Yours: Common Lives in Civil War Letters*. Cambridge: Harvard University Press, 2018.

Henkin, David M. *The Postal Age: The Emergence of Modern Communications in Nineteenth-Century America*. Chicago: University of Chicago Press, 2006.

Hess, Earl J. *In the Trenches at Petersburg: Field Fortifications and Confederate Defeat*. Chapel Hill: University of North Carolina Press, 2009.

———. *Into the Crater: The Mine Attack at Petersburg*. Columbia: University of South Carolina Press, 2010.

———. *Liberty, Virtue, and Progress: Northerners and Their War for the Union*. New York: Fordham University Press, 1997.

Hettle, Wallace. *Inventing Stonewall Jackson: A Civil War Hero in History and Memory*. Baton Rouge: LSU Press, 2011.

Hodes, Martha. *Mourning Lincoln*. New Haven CT: Yale University Press, 2015.

Holberton, William B. *Homeward Bound: The Demobilization of the Union and Confederate Armies, 1865–1866*. Mechanicsburg PA: Stackpole, 2001.

Holzer, Harold. *Lincoln and the Power of the Press: The War for Public Opinion.* New York: Simon & Schuster, 2014.

Jimerson, Randall C. *The Private Civil War: Popular Thought during the Sectional Conflict.* Baton Rouge: LSU Press, 1988.

Keating, Robert. *Carnival of Blood: The Civil War Ordeal of the Seventh New York Heavy Artillery.* Baltimore: Butternut & Blue, 1998.

Leech, Margaret. *Reveille in Washington, 1860–1865.* New York: Harper & Brothers, 1941.

Linderman, Gerald F. *Embattled Courage: The Experience of Combat in the American Civil War.* New York: Free Press, 1987.

Longacre, Edward G. *Lincoln's Cavalrymen: A History of the Mounted Forces of the Army of the Potomac, 1861–1865.* Mechanicsburg PA: Stackpole, 2000; reprt. Norman: University of Oklahoma Press, 2012.

Lonn, Ella. *Desertion during the Civil War.* Lincoln: University of Nebraska Press, 1998. First published 1928.

Lowry, Thomas P. *The Story the Soldiers Wouldn't Tell: Sex in the Civil War.* Mechanicsburg PA: Stackpole, 1994.

Lystra, Karen. *Searching the Heart: Women, Men, and Romantic Love in Nineteenth-Century America.* New York: Oxford University Press, 1989.

Manning, Chandra. *What This Cruel War Was Over: Soldiers, Slavery, and the Civil War.* New York: Alfred A. Knopf, 2007.

Marten, James. *The Children's Civil War.* Chapel Hill: University of North Carolina Press, 1998.

———. *Sing Not War: The Lives of Union & Confederate Veterans in Gilded Age America.* Chapel Hill: University of North Carolina Press, 2011.

Massey, Mary Elizabeth. *Women in the Civil War.* Lincoln: University of Nebraska Press, 1994. First published 1966 as *Bonnet Brigades: American Women and the Civil War* by Alfred A. Knopf (New York).

McPherson, James M. *Battle Cry of Freedom: The Civil War Era.* New York: Oxford University Press, 1988.

———. *For Cause & Comrades: Why Men Fought in the Civil War.* New York: Oxford University Press, 1997.

Mitchell, Reid. *Civil War Soldiers: Their Expectations and Their Experiences.* New York: Touchstone, 1989. First published 1988 by Viking Penguin (New York).

———. *The Vacant Chair: The Northern Soldier Leaves Home.* New York: Oxford University Press, 1993.

Morris, R. Rebecca. *A Low, Dirty Place: The Parole Camps of Annapolis, MD, 1862–1865.* Linthicum MD: Ann Arrundell County Historical Society, 2012.

Murphy, Kim. *I Had Rather Die: Rape in the Civil War.* Batesville VA: Coachlight, 2013.

Nevins, Allan. *The Organized War, 1863–1864.* Vol. 3 of *The War of the Union.* New York: Charles Scribner's Sons, 1971.

———. *The Organized War to Victory, 1864–1865.* Vol. 4 of *The War of the Union.* New York: Charles Scribner's Sons, 1971.

Oswald, Delmont R. Introduction to *Life and Adventures of James Beckwourth: Mountaineer, Scout, and Pioneer and Chief of the Crow Nation of Indians* by James Beckwourth and Thomas D. Bonner, vii–viii. New York: Harper & Brothers, 1856; reprt. Lincoln: University of Nebraska Press, 1972. Page references are to the 1972 edition.

Peirce, Taylor, and Catharine Peirce. *Dear Catharine, Dear Taylor: The Civil War Letters of a Union Soldier and His Wife.* Edited by Richard L. Kiper. Lawrence: University Press of Kansas, 2002.

Poe, Orlando M., and Eleanor Poe. *My Dear Nelly: The Selected Civil War Letters of General Orlando M. Poe to His Wife Nelly.* Edited by Paul Taylor. Kent OH: Kent State University Press, 2020.

Rable, George C. *God's Almost Chosen Peoples: A Religious History of the American Civil War.* Chapel Hill: University of North Carolina Press, 2010.

Rankin, Charles E. "Sweet Delusion: The Life and Times of Frederic E. Lockley, Western Journalist." PhD diss., University of New Mexico, 1994.

Rhea. Gordon C. *Cold Harbor: Grant and Lee, May 26—June 3, 1864.* Baton Rouge: LSU Press, 2002.

———. *On to Petersburg: Grant and Lee, June 4–15, 1864.* Baton Rouge: LSU Press, 2017.

———. *To the North Anna River: Grant and Lee, May 13—25, 1864.* Baton Rouge: LSU Press, 2000.

Rhoades, Nancy L., and Lucy E. Bailey, eds. *Wanted—Correspondence: Women's Letters to a Union Soldier.* Athens: Ohio University Press.

Rhodes, Elisha Hunt. *All for the Union: The Civil War Diary and Letters of Elisha Hunt Rhodes.* Edited by Robert Hunt Rhodes. Woonsocket RI: Andrew Mowbray, 1985; reprt. New York: Orion, 1991.

Risley, Ford. *Civil War Journalism.* Santa Barbara CA: Praeger, 2012.

Roberts, Timothy Mason. *"This Infernal War": The Civil War Letters of William and Jane Standard.* Kent OH: Kent State University Press, 2018.

Robertson, James I., Jr. *Soldiers Blue and Gray.* Columbia: University of South Carolina Press, 1988.

Rose, Anne C. *Victorian America and the Civil War.* New York: Cambridge University Press, 1992.

Sears, Stephen W. *George B. McClellan: The Young Napoleon.* New York: Ticknor & Fields, 1988.

Shakespeare, William. *The Pictorial Edition of the Works of Shakspere.* Edited by Charles Knight. 8 Vols. London: Charles Knight, 1842.

Shepard, Jerry. *The Lockleys.* Self-published, 1997.

Silber, Nina. *Divided Houses: Gender and the Civil War.* New York: Oxford University Press, 1992.

———. *Daughters of the Union: Northern Women Fight the Civil War.* Cambridge: Harvard University Press, 2005.

Skilliker, Ruth L., and John W. Haley, eds. *The Rebel Yell & the Yankee Hurrah: The Civil War Journal of a Maine Volunteer.* Camden ME: Down East, 1985.

Slotkin, Richard. *No Quarter: The Battle of the Crater, 1864.* New York: Random House, 2009.

———. *The Long Road to Antietam: How the Civil War Became a Revolution.* New York: Liveright, 2012.

Steele, Janet E. *The Sun Shines for All: Journalism and Ideology in the Life of Charles A. Dana.* Syracuse NY: Syracuse University Press, 1993.

Stephen, Leslie, and Sidney Lee, eds. *Dictionary of National Biography.* 63 vols. London: Smith, Elder, 1885–1900.

Tagg, Larry. *The Generals of Gettysburg: The Leaders of America's Greatest Battle.* Campbell CA: Savas, 1998.

Trudeau, Noah Andre. *Bloody Roads South: The Wilderness to Cold Harbor, May—June 1864*. Boston: Little, Brown, 1989.

———. *The Last Citadel: Petersburg, June 1864–April 1865*. El Dorado Hills CA: Savas Beatie, 2014.

Turner, Thomas Reed. *Beware the People Weeping: Public Opinion and the Assassination of Abraham Lincoln*. Baton Rouge: LSU Press, 1982.

Varon, Elizabeth R. *Armies of Deliverance: A New History of the Civil War*. New York: Oxford University Press, 2019.

Walker, Francs A. *History of the Second Army Corps in the Army of the Potomac*. New York: Charles Scriber's Sons, 1886.

Warner, Ezra J. *Generals in Blue: Lives of Union Commanders*. Baton Rouge LA: LSU Press, 1964; reprt. 1993.

Watkins, Sam R. *Company Aytch, or A Side Show of the Big Show: A Memoir of the Civil War*. Edited by Ruth Hill Fulton McAlister. Nashville TN: Turner, 2011.

West, Elliott. *Growing Up with the Country: Childhood on the Far Western Frontier*. Albuquerque: University of New Mexico Press, 1989.

Wiley, Bell Irvin. *The Life of Johnny Reb: The Common Soldier of the Confederacy*. Indianapolis: Bobbs-Merrill, 1943; reprt. Baton Rouge: LSU Press, 1992.

———. *The Life of Billy Yank: The Common Soldier of the Union*. Indianapolis: Bobbs-Merrill, 1943; reprt. Baton Rouge: LSU Press, 1992.

Wilkeson, Frank. *Turned Inside Out: Recollections of a Private Soldier in the Army of the Potomac*. Lincoln: University of Nebraska Press, 1991. First published 1886 as *Recollections of a Private Soldier in the Army of the Potomac* by Putnam (New York).

Woodworth, Steven E. *While God Is Marching On: The Religious World of Civil War Soldiers*. Lawrence: University Press of Kansas, 2001.

Wynkoop Hallenbeck Crawford Company. *Annual Report of the Adjutant-General of the State of New York for the Year 1897: Registers of the Seventh and Eighth Artillery in the War of Rebellion*. New York: Wynkoop Hallenbeck Crawford, 1898. https://dmna.ny.gov/historic/reghist/civil/rosters/Artillery/7thArtCW_Roster.pdf.

Zimm, John, ed. *This Wicked Rebellion: Wisconsin Civil War Soldiers Write Home*. Madison: Wisconsin Historical Society Press, 2012.

Index

desertion, xvi, 22, 94, 372n81, 373n82; and bounty men, 231, 271, 273, 276, 277, 301; by Confederates, 281, 282; executions for, 22, 231, 276

Dickens, Charles, xviii, 7, 8, 11; characters from, 374n4, 380n10, 406n8; and Joe Rogers, 38

Dix, John Adams, 85, 108

Donahue, Edward, 399n27

Donahue frauds. *See* voting fraud

draft, 69, 121, 122; Elizabeth on, 113, 114, 120; Frederic's dislike of, 5, 28; and New York City riots, 113–14, 383n2

Duke Humphrey (Humphrey, Duke of Gloucester), 198, 392n18

Duncan, G. S., 32, 179, 192, 236, 255, 313–14, 375n17; and aid to Lockleys, 55, 186, 246, 255, 262, 274, 282, 329; and book trade, 258; and parenting, 340, 341–42, 343; on soldier assistance, 46, 50, 55; view of the war, 84, 107

Duncan, Mrs. G. S., 151, 192, 329; and Elizabeth, 195, 236; and Lockley children, 105, 120, 312, 322, 341–42

Duncan, Richard, 292

Duncan, Willie (son of G. S.), 176

Duncan, George (son of G. S.), 341

Dupont, Samuel F., 83, 85

Duryea, Richard C., 282, 313, 400n28; austerity of, 285, 287–88, 289, 372n80

Early, Jubal, 102, 258; at raid on Washington DC, 143, 203–4, 393nn33–35

Eighth Corps, 291

election of 1864, xiii, 5, 138, 266, 388n1, 398n10; and badges, 248, 252; and Elizabeth, 235, 236, 242, 248, 259–60, 265–66; and furlough home, 137–38; interest in, 267–68; and George B. McClellan, 249, 398n12; and Seventh New York voting, 254–55, 259, 268; support for Lincoln in, 235–36, 248; 259–60, 265, 267; and voting fraud, 268, 399n27, 399n29

Elizabeth I, 342

Eolus, 125. *See also* Aeolus (Greek god)

Ewell, Richard, 102

Fake, Isaac, 315

Fake, Mrs. Isaac, 322

Fairfax Courthouse, 35

Farragut, David Glasgow, 311, 313, 322, 404n19

Falk, William B. *See* Faulk, William B.

Faulk, William B., 136, 163, 376n6; characterization of, 117; and desertion, 173

Fenton, Reuben, 350

Fern, Fanny, 39, 376n33

Fifth Corps, 270; and Weldon-Petersburg Railroad, 223

Filkins, Morgan L., 255

First Vermont Heavy Artillery Regiment, 181

Fort Alexander, 46, 68

Fort Alexandria, 31, 32

Fort Darling, 215, 394n18

Fort De Russey. *See* Fort DeRussy

Fort DeRussy, xviii, 68, 94, 98, 143; assignment to, 36; descriptions of, 375n24, 385n7; and Jubal Early raid, 203; location of, 37; and newspaper delivery, 117; and Joe Rogers, 164, 168, 173; transfer to and from, 127, 129, 132, 135

Fort Federal Hill, 301, 325, 328–29, 336

Fort Gregg (Union), 190, 270, 399n1

Fort Kearney, 156, 387n6

Fort McHenry, 290, 291, 292, 295, 303–4, 332, 333; Confederate prisoners at, 301, 305–6; and David Glasgow Farragut, 322, 404n19; and mustering out, 349; Union deserter at, 93; Union parolees at, xii; and visiting Frederic, 324

Fort Morton, 37, 190, 239, 260, 270

Fort Reno, 126, 129, 131, 183–84, 302, 384n1; and Jubal Early raid, 203; location of, 37

Fort Stedman, Battle of, 403n13

Fort Stevens, 123, 181; and Jubal Early raid, 203, 204

Fort Sumter, 4

Forty-Fourth Tennessee Infantry Regiment, 394n10. *See also* Kelso, Francis M.

Foster, John Gary, 108

Fowler, Patrick (Terry), 228

Frank Leslie's Illustrated Newspaper, 13

Fredericksburg, Battle of, 82, 88

Fredericksburg MD, 184, 389n8

Fredericksburg Road, 2; skirmish at, 187, 200

Frost, Robert, 93

Galonby, Michael. *See* Gilhooly, Michael

Gauther, Freeman, 123

Gibbon, Edward, 11

Gilhooly, Michael, 243, 252, 397n7

Graces, Ed, 119

Grand Review, 337, 353, 406n20

Grant, Ulysses S., 185, 188, 189, 277; and Battle of the Crater, 214, 216, 220; and Camp Parole, 300; and casualties, 389n3; and Confederate surrender, 310; confidence in, 172, 181, 182, 183, 225, 240, 248, 249; and Deep Bottom, 221, 223, 245; doubts about, 191, 199, 217, 218, 256; and Grand Review, 353;

Lockley, Agnes Jeannette (wife), 13, 54, 343, 381n119; and Emma, 16, 371n43; death of, 14; marriage, 12

Lockley, Elizabeth (Lizzie); background of, 3; and Blacks, 101–2, 113, 114; and children, 57, 119–20, 128, 140, 145–46, 157, 171, 196, 308, 403n12; and children's reading, 87–88, 106, 128–29; on Copperheads, 248, 259; courtship of, 14, 45, 119, 120; on Cousin Jack, 114 141, 324, 338; on Jefferson Davis, 250, 336; debts of, 87, 160, 252, 294–95, 321–22; despondency of, 79, 94, 96, 112–13, 127–28, 153, 166, 243, 295, 380n4; and Dollie, 119, 151, 171, 312, 328, 335, 337–38; on draft riots, 113–14; on drinking, 70–71; and 1864 election, 260, 265, 394; and Emma, 16, 74–75, 83, 105, 129, 146, 158, 162, 381n21; on Emma's moodiness, 16, 114, 319; on Emma's romance, 331, 336, 338, 344; extant letters of, xiii–xiv, 74, 399n8; and father, 70–71, 232–33, 303, 371n56, 378n16; and fear of poverty, 79–81; on first furlough, 120, 127–28, 138, 139–40; and Fred Lockley Jr., 386n2, 407n14; on Frederic's enlistment, xi, 4, 28; and Gertrude, 87–88, 106, 129, 145, 309, 332, 336–37; on Ulysses S. Grant, 172; on house break-in, 318, 322; ill-health of, 150–57, 177–78, 218; and intimacy, 17, 87, 105, 114, 139, 144, 377n14; and Josephine, 88, 105, 119, 151, 177; on Lincoln assassination, 318–19, 340; and Maria Mair, 162, 177–78, 302; on George B. McClelland, 248, 259; on George Gordon Meade, 109–10; on military affairs, 108–9, 109–11, 113, 250, 308; on military discipline, 123, 147; money worries of, 53, 64–66, 70, 79–80, 157, 158–60; and New York City, xi, 232–33; non-extant letters of, 81, 369n10, 379n9, 391n10, 393n36, 405n22; and parenting, 18, 128, 308, 340–42, 403n12; picture of, 342; on rape, 145; religious faith of, 48, 72, 264, 405n12; and Sanitary Commission, 157; and second furlough, 174; on slavery, 266; on Union prisoners, 144–45, 250; on Union rallies, 242, 259–60, 266; on vaccinations, 175–76, 177–78

Lockley, Emma (sister), 88, 97, 130, 196, 248, 278; on abolition, 96, 98; and bad luck in romance, 15–16, 58, 337, 377n14; characterized, 16, 140, 154; childhood of, 8, 10; and children, 16, 46, 85, 119, 132, 407n14; on Copperheads, 98; correspondence of, xiv; on Cousin Jack, 114; devotion of, 8, 10, 13, 16, 111; and Dollie's name, 379n10; and Eliz-

abeth, 16, 74, 83 87, 89, 105, 129, 158, 162, 380n4; and Elizabeth's ill-health, 152–55, 177; emigration of, 12; financial worries of, 44, 53–54, 59, 62, 63–67, 158; dependence on, 12, 17, 19, 263–64; displeasure with, 46, 51–52, 54, 158, 305, 319; letter by, 98; and letters to Frederic, xiv, 120, 155, 177, 187, 193, 195, 199, 215, 247; loans from, 75, 233, 252, 253, 263–64, 294, 301, 322; and Agnes Jeannette (Hill) Lockley, 12, 371n43; and Margaret Mair, 302, 305, 312, 336; and millinery shop, 303, 308, 309, 321, 335; and millinery work in Albany, 86, 174; moodiness of, 16, 114, 145–46, 345; neuralgia of, 175–76, 181; and religion, 51–52; removes to Albany, xi, 6, 15–16, 34, 36; vaccination of, 175; and George Watson, 331–33, 338, 343–44, 345

Lockley, Emma Louise (Dollie), 4, 16, 350–51; characterized, 312, 328; and Lockley courtship, 14; on Emma's suitor, 338; and Elizabeth, 171, 335–36; father's letters to, xiv, 41–43, 206–9, 368n6; and name and nickname, 379n10; and name and nickname of, 176

Lockley, Fred, Jr., 352–53, 386n2, 407n14

Lockley, Frederic: and abolition, 23, 24–25, 100; and African-Americans, 23–25, 100–101, 325–26, 373n91; arrest of, 278–79; as apprentice, 9–10; and *Arthur Frankland*, 11, 163; and artillery, 77, 78, 95, 167; on Francis C. Barlow, 190–91; and Barlow's Skedaddle, 201–3; bible commentary of, 21–22, 144, 173; on Blacks, 41–42, 74, 157, 234–35, 325–26, 373n90; on card playing, 7, 73, 370n20; and childhood, 6–9; on children's education, 124, 299; and close calls, 194–95, 208–9, 245–46; on Confederate deserters, 22, 212, 248–49, 251, 273, 277, 279, 280, 281, 282, 373n82; on contrabands, xii, 23, 24, 41–42, 45, 99–101; as cook, 20–21, 31–32, 34, 36, 65; on Copperheads, 84, 102, 104; on Cousin Jack, 114, 116, 141, 166, 192, 371n42, 381nn19–20; and criticism of fellow soldiers, 39, 125, 141–42, 102–3, 166, 177; on desertion, xvi, 22, 94, 231, 282, 372n81, 373nn82–83; discharge of, 345–46, 347, 349–50, 373n86, 407n2; and Dollie, 70, 103, 142–43, 339, 368n6, 379n10; on drinking, 7, 70–71, 370n24; on Richard Duryea, 289, 372n80; on education, 7, 8–9, 10–11, 100, 124, 325–26, 324, 329, 330; and Elizabeth's letters, 74, 81, 379n9; on emancipation, 24, 53–54; emigration of, 11, 12; epitaph for, 407n19; and

Lockley, Frederic (*cont.*)

father's death, 12; financial concerns of, 53–54, 56, 69, 75–76, 80–81, 86, 158–59, 274; on fear of poverty, 54, 79–81, 158–59; on food, 20–21, 31–32, 48, 58–59, 94, 185–86, 198–99, 208, 232, 392n16, 392–93n27; and foraging, 10, 21, 54, 225–26, 228; and Gertrude, 209, 284, 323; on grammar, 7, 10, 117; on Homer, 74, 100; ill-health of, 283, 285; on instructing Blacks, 100–101, 325–26; and intimacy, 62, 70, 116, 119, 163, 166, 169, 288, 307, 346, 377n14; and intoxication, 70–71, 104, 164, 169, 370nn24–25; and Josephine, 66, 88, 182, 189, 238, 330, 337, 341; on Josephine's education, 124, 299; later children of, 407n14; letters to Dollie, 41–43, 206–9; on Lincoln's assassination, 315–18, 319–20; and Fred Lockley Jr., 352–53, 386n2; 407n14; on Lord Byron, 100, 177; on marching, 185, 186, 187, 189, 192, 198, 200–201, 214, 225, 291; on military discipline, 22, 90–91, 99–100, 104, 118, 121–22, 123, 145, 198, 372n80; on military life, 78–79, 89, 116–17, 135–36, 137, 143–44, 167, 329–30; and New York City, 11, 12, 13, 50; and nursing of others, 20–21, 46, 49, 164, 168, 171, 173–74, 372n77; and Ossian, 10, 67, 162; on parenting, 18, 158–59; and promotions, 62–63, 157–58, 126, 127, 141, 157–58, 254, 268, 274, 398–99n19; as proofreader, 13, 351; on rape, 144–45, 385–86n10; on rats, 136–37; on reading, 15, 21–22, 24, 26, 61, 77, 124, 299; rejects promotions, 92, 204, 372n81, 393n37; on religion, 53, 75, 175, 323; on Sanitary Commission, 122, 184–85, 186, 201, 202, 208, 232; on Shakespeare, xviii, 10–11, 21, 60, 125, 142, 144, 319, 333, 336, 356, 378n6; quotes Shakespeare, 70, 156, 296, 279, 320; on slavery, 24–25, 53, 324, 346; on soldiers' mail, 1–2, 115, 137–38; on soldier's funeral, 161–62; on temperance, 71, 378n16; on Union deserters, 22, 36, 46, 93, 94, 95, 164, 173, 187, 271, 276–77, 301, 303, 373n83, 402n37; on urban temptations, 135, 304–5, 306; on value of letters, 1, 115, 137–38; on visitors in camp, 312, 332–24, 330; and watch, 15, 116, 173, 282, 305, 326, 401n11; on William Shannon, 68, 82, 85, 89, 103, 124, 164, 213, 238

Lockley, Gertie, Tute, Tutie. *See* Lockley, Gertrude

Lockley, Gertrude, xxii, 4, 14; characterized, 145, 171, 332; and father's letters, 74, 110–11, 209, 284; ill-health of, 157, 162, 337, 338; letters to father, 260, 280; name and nicknames for, 16; and reading, 88, 128–29, 145; vexing to Elizabeth, 97, 247, 309

Lockley, John (cousin Jack), 13, 116, 166, 192; and Eleventh Maine Infantry Regiment, 324; identity of, 12, 96, 371n42, 381n19; worries about, 96–97, 114, 141, 324, 338

Lockley, Josey, Josie, Jossie. *See* Lockley, Josephine

Lockley, Josephine, xxii, 4, 14 16, 174–75; education of, 124, 299; and Elizabeth, 151; letters from her father, 182, 206, 209, 238, 341; letters to her father, 66, 88, 189, 256, 337; marriage of, 352; and name, xviii, 330; pictures of, xxii, 119; vaccination of, 176

Lockley, Mary (mother), 7–9, 12, 376n5

Lockley, Mary (sister), 9, 12, 192; secessionist sentiments of, 82, 84, 98

Lockley, Samuel (father), 7, 10–11, 12, 376n5

London, 6, 7; poverty in, 159

Macaulay, Thomas Babington, 10, 21

McCaulay, Daniel, 313

McClellan, George B., 33, 35, 82; and 1864 election, 254–55, 397n1, 398n10, 12, 399n27, 399n29; loyalty of, 103, 236, 248, 259, 382n9

Maher, John, 287

Mair, Maria H., 3, 14, 27, 94; and Dollie, 335, 344; on Emma's suitor, 335; and Frederic's letters, 296; incompatibility of, 162, 173, 177–78, 302, 305; and Lockley courtship, 45, 119, 120

Mark Tapley (fictional character), 47, 376n4

Mather, Frederick, 125, 130, 383n10; arrest of, 181, 389n4; and *Arthur Frankland*, 163; capture of, 191, 196, 392n12; and Elizabeth, 21, 116, 303–4, 342; parole of, 300, 392n12

Maximilian I, Ferdinand, 313

Meade, George Gordon, 20, 134; at Gettysburg, 109–10; and Joseph Hooker, 107, 383n16; at North Anna River, 185; and Petersburg assault, 189; and Reams Station, 227, 228

The Merchant of Venice (Shakespeare), 319, 320

Metcalf, E. H. (grandmother's son), 177, 235–36

Metcalf, Margaret (Elizabeth's mother), 3

Metcalf, Margaret (Elizabeth's grandmother), 3, 14, 198; financial assistance from, 159, 160, 294; and Frederic's letters, 74, 161, 281; and grandson, 177, 235–36, 242; health of, 321–22; indebtedness to, 245, 249, 252, 253, 260, 322; and Lockley courtship, 119, 120; and Schuylerville, 58, 114, 351

Voltaire (François-Marie Arouet), 21
voting fraud, 268, 399n27, 399n29; and Joseph
   M. Murphy, 266–68

Wadsworth, James S., 181
Warren, Gouverneur, 221, 223, 225, 260
Washington Chronicle, 192, 268
Washington DC, 181, 222, 266; and capitol
   dome, 143–44; defense of, xii, xiii, 37, 49,
   94–95, 106–7, 204, 219; departure from, 182,
   184, 187, 188, 195, 223; and deserters, 93,
   95; and fame of the Seventh New York, 142;
   and Grand Review, 337, 353; and regimental records, 268, 270; soldier riot in, 346,
   406n9; and vice, 78–79, 135, 164, 168–69;
   and wounded soldiers, 179
Waterman, Smith, 255

Watson, George, 331, 336, 338, 341, 344, 352
Weed, George W., 315
Weed, William G., 255
Weldon and Danville Railroad, 210
Weldon-Petersburg Railroad, 221, 224, 261,
   393n4; and Barlow's Skedaddle, 201–3;
   destruction of, 225–26; at Reams Station,
   227–30
Williams, William J., 95
Wilsey, Edgar H., 314, 328
Wood, Benjamin, 102, 382n7
Wood, Fernando, 102, 198, 382n7, 382n9
Wood, William G., 255, 286
Wooster, Mrs. Benjamin W., 96
Wright, Horatio, 204, 219, 224
Wright, Nathaniel, 230